The Stars Are My Friends

The Stars Are My Friends

Eric Holloway

SERENDIPITY

This book is dedicated to my wife Susan, without whose help this work would never have been completed

Copyright © Eric Holloway 2005
First published in 2005 by
Serendipity
First Floor
37/39 Victoria Road
Darlington

All rights reserved
Unauthorised duplication
contravenes existing laws
British Library Cataloguing-in-Publication data
A catalogue record for this book is available from the British Library
ISBN 1-84394-170-8

Printed and bound by Cromwell Press, Trowbridge, Wilts.

Foreword

While I was waiting to go before an Aircrew Selection Board in 1941, my brother-in-law who was already a much-decorated Fleet Air Arm pilot gave me this advice. "Don't be too intelligent. If they think you are clever, they will make you a navigator." I qualified as a pilot a year alter and was to spend much of the next thirty years flying with a navigator. Some were more clever than others!

Lakers Airways was lucky to have two who were exceptional, Dick Bradley, the chief, had a brilliant brain and Eric Holloway whom he took on as his deputy in 1969. Eric also has a very good brain but unlike Dick is usually on the same wavelength as the rest of us. The two together ran the most efficient department in the airline for twelve years.

After Eric joined he was often my navigator. He always wanted a high standard of flying from his pilots and was not slow to voice his displeasure if course or speed deviated from those required. His own standards were high and he expected it of others. I enjoyed my flights with him but flying with a navigator finished for me in 1971 with Lakers purchase of DC10 aircraft.

The crews on the first conversion course waited in California for Eric Holloway to come back from Gatwick to explain how we were to operate the triple INS Navigation System with which the aircraft were fitted. Some of us whose schooldays were in the distant past were finding it difficult. Obviously a great deal of hard work had gone on in the Navigation Department at Gatwick to produce procedures which were as practical and as near foolproof as possible. At the end of the course, with Lakers second brand new DC10 strapped to my backside, I was extremely grateful that Eric Holloway was with us on the Flight Deck, especially on the Atlantic sector. It was perhaps a little unkind of him to mention in his book the somewhat 'firm' arrival at Gatwick.

Ten years later Laker Airways folded and it could have been the end of the story. However, a small group of Ex-Laker people refused to be beaten. Determined to start another Trans Atlantic Airline they persevered and eventually succeeded. That story is the final chapter in Eric Holloway's book. I was indeed lucky to be at the right place and the right time at the start of Virgin Atlantic Airways. The achievement of the small team involved in launching a daily service to Newark in an incredibly short time was remarkable; that it kept operating with only one Boeing 747–200 aircraft is almost unbelievable. It was the beginning of a great airline and Eric Holloway was the essential man in that team. His experience and acceptance by the CAA was vital to the Operations Department and the Airline. Many of us feared that his worsening health, which he makes light of in his book, would deprive us of his services. With amazing courage he battled on and indeed it is good to know that he is still doing so can recall so much from his eventful life to put it in this book.

Captain Gordon Steer

Preface

This is the story of a quite ordinary person who became a professional aviator with a career covering fifty years, thirty-eight of which were spent flying around the world, amassing nearly twenty thousand hours of flying.

The idea of writing my flying memoirs came about through many people asking about my personal experiences during the war, and later in civil aviation. At first it was quite difficult to recall things that happened such a long time ago, but as I progressed many events came back, each triggering others, all of which became clearer until I could put them together in a fairly accurate and logical sequence. Discovery of diaries kept in 1944, '45, and '46, together with my four flying log books, helped to recall some wartime and post war events, but even so, it was extremely difficult to remember precisely what really happened. It's not just a matter of trying to recall events of the past; the detail needs to be reasonably correct as well. Not an easy task!

Any errors are unintentional and it is hoped that any person named will not be offended.

Reginald 'Eric' Holloway
March 2005

Contents

Dedication

Foreword

Preface

Chapter 1	The Beginning	1
Chapter 2	Service Life	7
Chapter 3	Aircrew Training	14
Chapter 4	Ferry Command	29
Chapter 5	36 Squadron	41
Chapter 6	Sunderlands	52
Chapter 7	230 Squadron	63
Chapter 8	Civilian Life	93
Chapter 9	Civil Aviation	96
Chapter 10	BOAC Flying Boats	99
Chapter 11	BOAC Hermes and York	124
Chapter 12	BOAC Argonaut	135
Chapter 13	A Career Change	144
Chapter 14	BOAC Stratocruiser	149
Chapter 15	BOAC Britannia 312	158
Chapter 16	Air Traffic Control	182
Chapter 17	Transglobe Airways	196
Chapter 18	Laker Airways	217
Chapter 19	Virgin Atlantic Airways	265

Chapter 1
The Beginning

My parents James and May Holloway lived in a small rented house at 20 Union Street in the centre of Northampton. I was born there on 22 October 1921 and my brother Ron on 12 March 1920. When I was born my father named me Reginald and my mother Eric. So I was christened Reginald Eric but mother had the final say and I was known throughout my life as Eric.

Opposite the house was a small sweetshop run by Mrs Pettit, an old lady whose husband was an undertaker, his business being located in premises next to the sweet shop. He had a quite beautiful black hearse drawn by two magnificent black horses who supplied us with plenty of droppings for our small garden. On funeral days the hearse, with the horses' heads decorated with black feather plumes, would emerge from the yard with Mr Pettit at the reins dressed in black wearing a top hat, preceded by another man, also wearing black clothes and top hat. There was always an air of dignity and solemnity as the procession went on its way to the funeral and unlike today, men would remove their hats as the hearse passed by.

My brother and I would spend our small amount of pocket money to buy sweets of our choice, which were stored in large glass jars on shelves behind the counter. The sweets were two ounces for a penny (two and a half pennies would be the equivalent of today's penny,) and would be carefully weighed by Mrs Pettit; but she was a generous soul and always added more to what she had weighed out. Usually we only had a half-penny's worth!

Union Street no longer exists having been swallowed up by a huge indoor shopping centre many years ago. Grandmother, on my mother's side, lived with her second husband, Jack Ferret, at a house and shop in Lady's Lane which was the next street up the hill a hundred yards from our house. Mother had two sisters Daisy and June but tragically, all three died within a year of each other before the war started.

Grandmother was a very lovely lady and I enjoyed going to see her. I clearly remember that she always had a pot of soup simmering on the hob of the oven, which was part of the fireplace, and on cold days she would sometimes give me a bowl of the soup. Grandfather was a barber and had his barber's saloon in the room in front of the living accommodation where my brother and I had our hair cut by him. The shop always seemed to be full of customers who appeared to be good friends and with whom he chatted constantly. He sold cigarettes, tobacco and various toilet items. To us children he was always our real grandfather because we did not know that grandmother had lost her first husband. Both grandmother and grandfather Jack Ferret died during the war.

My father was part of a large family with two brothers, Harry and Stanley, and four sisters, Nellie, Beatrice, Agatha, and Emily. His parents, (my paternal grandparents), died when he was very young so sadly I never knew them or ever saw photographs of them.

When I was about seven years of age my parents adopted a baby girl who was named Barbara. She slept in the same room as my parents and when it became necessary for her to have her own bedroom, it was decided that the house was too small for the five of us and we moved to Lindsay Avenue in the Abington area of Northampton. This was almost in the country and I remember having to walk along a path through two fields of wheat or some other crop, to reach my school at Weston Favell. A pleasant walk in warm dry weather, but in winter not quite so nice. Compared to Union Street the new house was much larger and had a very large garden at the rear and a smaller one at the front. When we moved in, the garden was much neglected and needed a great deal of work to get it into a decent state. Oddly, there was an old motorcycle that had been left behind by the previous occupants and, discovering that there was petrol in the tank, my brother and I soon got the engine started. We found how to engage gear and had great fun riding slowly around the garden. Mother disapproved of this, but father raised no objection until he started to dig over the ground. In the avenue there were grass areas between the pavement and the road where children used to meet to play. When the Silver Jubilee of King George V took place in 1935, to celebrate the occasion tables were set up on the grass areas for a large street party attended by all the immediate residents.

My mother died when I was sixteen after suffering dreadfully for many years from cancer. During the course of her short life she spent several long periods of time in hospital and had many surgical operations, including amputation of a leg. During her long illnesses I lived with my father's brother Harry and his wife Annie in Chesham, Buckinghamshire. Uncle and Auntie had two daughters Kath and Rita and I was treated as part of their family whenever I was there. In fact Uncle and Auntie treated me as if I was their own son. After the war I visited at short notice and on seeing me, Auntie said, 'My boy has come home,' and promptly burst into tears of joy. They both lived well into their nineties and I often visited them.

Sad to say, I lived at home in Northampton only during the periods when my mother's health was reasonably stable, which was not often. Mother had a wonderfully warm and loving personality and bore her long illnesses with great fortitude, seldom complaining about her poor health. The rented house we lived in at Abington was lit by gas and when my mother had her leg amputated, it became obvious that she could not light the gas herself. At his own expense father had mechanical switches installed that would automatically light the gas from a pilot light at each gas lighting point. I remember that all doors and woodwork in the house were painted dark brown which made the appearance of all the rooms quite dull and dreary. Transport was never a problem, as I cannot ever remember my father being without a car. This was somewhat essential due to the frequent occasions that my mother had to attend hospital, some of which were in emergency. Shortly after moving to Lindsay Avenue, father had a garage built on the back garden with a driveway from the front of the house. I remember that when the threat of war came, he had a pit dug in the floor of the garage that was concreted and damp proofed so that it could be used to service the underside of his car or used as a bomb shelter. When the war started and black out precautions had to be taken, I helped my father fix plywood shutters on hinges inside the windows of those rooms that were in use most of the time. The shutters also served as protection from blast if bombs dropped nearby, although none ever did.

When I was twelve, my parents bought me a bicycle with three speed Sturmey-Archer gears and I used this to travel wherever I needed to go. On one of the occasions that I had to go and live in Chesham, I rode the 50 odd miles there and had the use of it until I rode back home to Northampton some months later. I was only thirteen years old when I did that journey which, looking back, makes me realise how independent I was.

From about age nine I would look up at the stars and wonder how they came to be there. I did not possess binoculars or a telescope so could not observe them closely. The gas street lighting was not very bright and the stars and planets were easily visible. Wearing warm clothing, I would spend long periods of time trying to identify constellations from diagrams in books borrowed from the library, ultimately being able to identify individual stars by name, watching them nightly as they progressively changed their position with the advance of the seasons. I had no idea then that the stars would become so very important to me in the years that lay ahead.

Although I was not a Catholic, my education started in Northampton at a convent school where nuns were the teachers. Later it was split between schools in Northampton and a very good secondary school in Chesham which I enjoyed attending. The disruption to my schooling had little affect on me and I seemed to do well whether I was at home or in Chesham.

Father was a self-made businessman who worked extremely hard in the early days of his marriage to successfully establish his business. Sadly, he had little education and thought that because he had done so well in business, further education was unnecessary. In spite of good reports from school and winning of scholarships, he refused to allow me to use the scholarships to improve my education, compelling me to leave school at the earliest possible age! His business was connected with the large open market in Northampton where he employed several people to do manual work. He owned almost half of the market stalls, which he hired out to market traders on the market days of Wednesday and Saturday. These had to be erected and dismantled on each market day, work commencing about 2.30a.m. and finishing after 10p.m.. On winter days when it became dark very early, he would hire out pressured paraffin lamps to the traders.

As a result of the depression during the 1920s, large numbers of people were unemployed, including many with good education who took whatever work they could find, some working for my father. His rather bigoted view was that if those who were well educated could not find a decent job, then there was no point in extending education beyond the elementary stage. Accordingly he restricted the education of his children to the absolute minimum level.

Looking back to my early years, it seems that it was almost inevitable that I would take up a career in aviation, but it did take a war to make it happen. From an early age, perhaps because my father was a non-flying member of a flying club at Sywell near Northampton, aeroplanes fascinated me. My father and I had occasional flights and the first time I flew I was very young and could scarcely look over the edge of the open cockpit, but felt no fear at all. Ignorance certainly was bliss! My father and I both went up in an aircraft of Alan Cobham's air circus, again in an open cockpit, which I thought was a wonderful experience. My brother Ron, usually much more intrepid than I, refused to take advantage of the opportunity and it came as no surprise to me when he allowed himself to be conscripted into the army for war time service, rather than volunteer for the Navy or the RAF.

Perhaps the most marvellous sight in pre war aviation were the Air Pageants when vast numbers of RAF aircraft flew in formation, some performing aerobatics. There was a great deal of glamour in those pageants and doubtless many people, inspired by the demonstrated skills, joined the Royal Air Force Volunteer Reserve. Although suitably inspired, I was not old enough to join.

When the war broke out I was seventeen years of age, working as a printing apprentice with a firm in Northampton who specialised in producing the colour printing blocks for shoe company brochures. The printing department only employed one man named Herbert Shaw who had served in the army during the 1914/18 war. He was a pleasant enough chap and had many gory tales to tell of life in the trenches, which he constantly repeated to the point of tedium. Unfortunately he was gassed in the trenches and was discharged as medically unfit for further service. Afterwards his health was poor and he always had a nasty chesty cough. He was a very kind and loving family man with a nice wife and daughter, and his hobby was fishing and grafting roses on to rootstock, the success of which could be seen in his small but very colourful garden. We often went fishing together on the river Nene and with his guidance I became quite a proficient fisherman. I kept my fishing rods and other equipment for many years until my grandson expressed interest in them and they passed to him. The printing work was pleasant enough but I could not ever envisage doing it for the rest of my life. Fortunately future events in my life put me on an entirely different career path.

The war started in September 1939 and when I reached the age of eighteen in October of that year, I informed my father that I was going to volunteer to join the RAF as aircrew. His immediate response was to deny me his permission! He said that he would not allow me to volunteer until I was twenty-one when he thought that he could no longer legally prevent me from enlisting. This of course was totally incorrect, and in fact, from the outbreak of war almost everybody was eligible for call up, if required, at age 20. I can understand his feelings about the armed forces because he became an orphan at a very early age and, I believe, was forced to join the army as a boy entrant, hating every moment of service life. His attitude caused me great frustration and relations between us were often very strained.

In early summer of 1940 my patience ran out and I went to the RAF Recruiting Centre in town to enquire about joining as aircrew. After being given details, I made an application, attended for interview and was told that I was acceptable for training as air crew but would need to have a second interview to determine which category was suitable for me. At the second interview I was told that I could be trained as a Wireless Operator/Air Gunner, or if I brushed up my trigonometry, there was no reason why I could not be accepted as a Navigator or Pilot. There was nothing really wrong with my knowledge of trigonometry; I simply had a mental blockage (nerves I suppose) when answering some questions at the interview. It was then that I was told that due to the large number of volunteers, it would be some time before any training could commence. I was given the option of either deferring enlistment until a training course became available, or enlisting immediately to carry out ground duties whilst awaiting a flying training course. With the antagonism that existed between my father and myself, I opted to enlist immediately and take the first course that became available. There was a frightful row when I announced my intention and he did everything possible to make me change my mind. I was quite adamant and waited for joining instructions to arrive from the RAF. Our parting was with such acrimony that I vowed never to spend another night under his roof; I never did! In later years after he had re-married, we did reconcile our differences and I do believe that secretly, he was proud of my achievements. When back in Northampton on leave I stayed at my fiancé's home with her parents who always made me welcome. We had become engaged when I joined the RAF.

Chapter 2

Service Life

It all started for me on 24 September 1940 when I reported to RAF Station Cardington in Bedfordshire, a day that stands out in my memory. I was treated with some semblance of respect until I had signed the attestation documents after which my fellow recruits and I became 'Orrible little men' at the mercy of the drill instructors. I could not understand why recruits, regardless of their age or size, were always 'Orrible little men' in the eyes of drill instructors! It was then that I had a feeling of relief that I had only signed on for the period of the emergency that some thought would be of short duration! How wrong they were!

I was one of a mixed group of recruits with only a small number destined for aircrew training and it was not long before feelings of resentment against prospective aircrew became apparent. Accommodation was in sparsely furnished barrack blocks, each person being allocated a 'bed space' with a collapsible metal bed, a three-piece mattress (known as biscuits), and a steel cupboard (without a lock) for personal possessions. The communal washing and toilet facilities were extremely basic and totally lacking in privacy.

When not sleeping, the bed and its area had to be kept in 'apple pie' order with the blankets folded exactly in the prescribed manner. Woe betide anyone who thought that he could do otherwise! Floor cleaning was the responsibility of everybody in the dormitory and it had to be cleaned and polished until you could almost see your face reflected by it.

Recruits were expected to get quickly into the RAF routine, this starting with a medical examination, (cough please!), followed by inoculations and a talk by the Medical Officer who gave advice on personal hygiene and protection from anti social diseases! Having just left home where frequent bathing and changes of clothing was the norm, I thought that a lecture on personal hygiene somewhat superfluous, particularly as recruits were issued with only one change of shirt, socks and underwear, and had only a weekly laundry service!

I remember a very nasty chap in the squad was called 'Razor', not because he was that sharp or bright, but because he carried two cutthroat razors with which he threatened anyone who angered or upset him. (Never the drill instructors of course!) The intimidation continued until one of the recruits, a professional boxer, knocked him down, broke his razors and warned him that if he stepped out of line again, he would be dealt with more severely. He did not bully anyone again!

In the short period of time at Cardington, all were issued with uniforms and given some basic training before being sent off to Morecambe where, in the drill sergeant's words, 'Instead of looking like airmen, you will be turned into proper airmen!'

My arrival at Morecambe was coincident with many recruits coming from various other induction centres and we were quickly formed into squads with whom we stayed throughout the training. I was fortunate to meet someone who lived at Greens Norton, a small village near Northampton, and we became firm friends. His name was Sid Birchmore, a married man with a young son, who had evacuated his family from their home in Wimbledon, to get away from the Blitz. At 32 years of age, he must have been just on the age limit for acceptance as aircrew when he enlisted!

Trainees were accommodated in what pre-war had been bed and breakfast boarding houses near the sea front. When the folks at home heard of this, they got the impression that it was some sort of seaside holiday. Nothing could have been further from the truth! The boarding house owner packed recruits in rooms so tightly that there was little or no space to move between the camp beds that the RAF provided. There were no cupboards or drawers for personal possessions and these had to be kept in kit bags placed underneath the bed. The landlord of my accommodation made up a daily roster of jobs that had to be done, which included cleaning the place from top to bottom, washing up and other menial tasks. Obviously as servicemen we knew that we had to keep our rooms neat and tidy, but the duties he imposed were almost tyrannical, he giving the impression that he had authority to do so. It later emerged that he had 'an arrangement' with one of the senior drill instructors! He received rations from the RAF to feed us, but as the meals were so inadequate and tasteless, we all were convinced that some sort of fiddle was going on. It took many complaints to the CO and some plain speaking with the landlord before things improved. Needless to say, it was quickly established that we were not totally responsible for keeping his boarding house clean or doing the menial tasks of his choosing, and these largely ceased.

The Station HQ offices were in buildings that probably had been commandeered, and trainees often had to do 'dogsbody' duties there when they were not drilling. The Station Warrant Officer, who was very senior in his rank, treated everyone fairly and was popular with all ranks. During my posting he was commissioned and went unusually (to me) straight from Warrant Officer to Flying Officer bypassing Pilot Officer rank. On the day of his departure from Morecambe, a party was thrown in celebration of the occasion and he personally provided drinks for everyone present, including the 'dogsbodies,' which I thought to be a friendly and generous gesture.

During the training we were taken several times to a rifle range and given instruction on the Lee Enfield .303 rifle that included live firing at a target. Having owned an air gun prior to joining the service I thought that my skill with this would help. Not a bit of it. The first shot I fired was careless in that I only loosely shouldered the rifle and the recoil bruised my shoulder. However, once I got used to the recoil I did manage to hit the target in a reasonable fashion for some of the rounds that I fired. When firing had ceased we were shown how to clean the gun using oil and a 'pull through'. The gun was then ready for use by the next group of trainees.

In addition to rifle training we were instructed in the use of the hand grenade. The instructor demonstrated how the grenade was primed by inserting the fuse, explaining that the weapon was harmless until the pin had been removed and the clip released. Then to our horror he removed the pin, allowed the clip to be released and threw the grenade on the ground. Prior to this he had said that the grenade he had in his hand was a live one, but omitted to tell us that fuse was a dummy. We were then taken to an area where we were told that each of us would throw a live grenade over a heavily sandbagged wall. We had to remove the pin, release the clip and then throw the grenade over the wall, ducking below the wall after throwing it. I was less than happy about that and thought it was quite dangerous. When my turn came I was nervous but did as instructed and successfully threw the wretched thing over the wall. One chap scared us all by freezing and not throwing the grenade after releasing the clip. Fortunately the sergeant standing behind him was obviously aware that this could happen and grabbed the grenade from him and threw it, shouting 'everybody down' as he pulled the trainee down with him. He did not accuse the trainee of being careless or stupid, but did emphasise to everybody that in the light of what had occurred, it was essential to remember that the grenade was a very dangerous weapon and should be handled carefully and correctly.

During the time at Morecambe, several groups were trained to be a Guard of Honour for a Civic Function that was to take place. As the actual parade was to be on grass in the local park, it was necessary to learn how to march in step on grass. This sounds easy, but in practice proved to be an extremely difficult procedure to master, it being some time before the rear of the parade was in step with the front.

The PT instructors, mostly professional sportsmen, were very fit and expected everybody to be equally so. On the whole they were fair and provided that recruits did what was expected of them, it was a friendly relationship. At the end of the day's drilling and PT, theoretically the time was our own, but due the very high standards required of appearance, a lot of time in the evening was taken up with cleaning boots and polishing buttons. There were times when I wondered if all the 'Bull' was necessary in order to become aircrew but, of course, it was the means of instilling self discipline which is so very essential in flying.

A Corporal PT instructor with a rather aggressive manner had been a boxer in civilian life and constantly reminded us of this by saying that he would like to get some of us in the ring with him. One of our squad, a law student who had boxed for his university, asked the Corporal if they could have a friendly bout. The challenge was immediately taken up and we witnessed a very skilled display by both opponents with the honours going to the law student. The Corporal was a good sport and accepted his defeat with good grace but did not subsequently voice a wish to get any others into the ring.

The regular Air Force drill instructors showed recruits how to keep uniforms neat and tidy with tips about pressing trousers by laying them neatly folded underneath the mattress, having first put soap on the inside of the creases. Buttons and boots were cleaned the hard way with spit and polish until they were bright and shiny. Some resorted to getting boots and buttons buffed on machines at shops in the town, a practice that was forbidden. Anybody foolish enough to get caught was severely disciplined.

Drill took place wherever there was space, be it a back street or open area and regardless of the weather. At one stage, squads were taken to the Lake District to climb the rather steep hillsides surrounding one of the lakes. This was extremely difficult for those who had never done it before, but it was well worth the effort on reaching the summit where the views were magnificent.

Weekend passes were given during the course but most of us were a long way from home and found travel too expensive. Married men with homes not too far away usually went home, sometimes with surprising outcomes. One very mild mannered and pleasant fellow recounted that after the first meal at home, his wife became very cold and aloof. He had not the faintest idea why, but eventually she told him that he was getting into coarse ways, to which she was not accustomed. Apparently, as they started a meal he said 'Darling, please pass the ****ing salt' without realising exactly how he had phrased it. Strong and quite foul language seemed to be a habit in the RAF. One very coarse drill sergeant verbally abused the law student recruit (questioned his parentage), resulting in them almost coming blows. Although threatening to charge the man, other than a lot of blustering, he did nothing and allowed the matter to drop rather than have the CO learn what had really occurred.

Training continued until the required standard was reached, after which everybody was given posting instructions and issued with railway warrants before being sent off with two or three days leave prior to reporting for duty at the next RAF station. It was then that I realised that if I had not elected to enlist immediately, after basic training I would have been on my way for aircrew training.

My first active posting was for ground defence duties at RAF Station High Ercall near Wellington in Shropshire, which was reached by a very tediously long and slow rail journey. In wartime the trains were always full and I had to stand most of the way from Northampton. I left the train at a 'Request Stop', which I recall was Oaken Gates Halt. Its platform was only large enough to take about two carriages and needless to say, I was not in either of those. Together with others posted there, I had to throw my kit bag out of the door and clamber down after it! I seem to remember that High Ercall airfield was located some distance away from Oaken Gates Halt and RAF transport was sent to collect those who were reporting for duty.

When I arrived in winter 1940, RAF Station High Ercall was a small isolated airfield with very little flying activity and I never did discover what its role really was. Certainly there were no RAF aircraft based there and there did not seem to be many people stationed there. I never saw any aircrew other than those who flew Hampden bombers in on flying training details. Regular Air Force NCOs and prospective aircrew awaiting posting for flying training staffed the ground defence unit that was remotely located on the furthest side of the airfield away from the main HQ buildings.

I almost became a casualty when a Corporal Armourer gave instruction on the rather antiquated Lewis gun to the group with whom I had arrived. His practice was to dismantle and reassemble the gun with the class seated around a long wooden table. Lacking dummy ammunition, he used a live . 303 round to show how it passed from the drum to the breechblock. When the round had reached the point of entering the firing chamber, he removed the drum and tilted the gun so that all could see what was happening. Unfortunately, he tilted the gun too much, causing the round to enter the chamber and fire. There was a scream from a man sitting next to me and he fell to the floor with blood pouring from his leg. The corporal attempted to stem the flow of blood but the bullet had shattered the bone and virtually severed his leg that later had to be amputated. I was sitting with my legs crossed and the bullet must have passed between my two legs before hitting the victim. The Corporal, regular RAF, was a decent enough chap and an excellent instructor, but inevitably was charged with neglect. His defence was that in order to fully demonstrate the action of the gun; he was compelled to use a live . 303 round since no dummy ammunition was available. The subsequent enquiry resulted in him being reprimanded rather than being demoted, the mitigating circumstances of the dummy ammunition obviously going in his favour. No one could disagree with the verdict, but I think that everyone was more sorry for the victim who was a farmer, knowing that his future life would be greatly affected by such a severe injury. It certainly shook me up and made me aware how easily one could be injured without realising that there was any danger. Curiously, although we had that ground instruction on the Lewis gun, none of us actually fired the gun in practice and although I manned one of the defence sites, I never had occasion to fire the weapon.

There was excitement on two separate occasions when the station was 'visited' by a German bomber that dropped bombs and strafed the airfield. The bomber came in so fast no one really saw it sufficiently well to fire at it until it was out of range! Those who did open fire had no hope of hitting the aircraft and were later told that they should not fire indiscriminately and waste ammunition. It seemed farcical that ground defence units should not to *attempt* to shoot the aircraft down, but the unit commander obviously saw it differently. Fortunately, the bombing caused little damage and no one was hurt. It seemed to me that no one was really concerned that the enemy had paid a visit and I remember an officer saying that the bombers had probably become lost on their way to their target and seeing an RAF airfield, decided to bomb it.

The winter of 1940/41 was very cold and in one period there was heavy snow for several days, so severe that the airfield was cut off from the outside world preventing food supplies reaching the station. Food started to run out, bread in particular and several, myself included, volunteered to go to the village to replenish supplies. We walked in the bitterly cold weather through the snow with snowdrifts that were higher than the hedgerows. No one on the HQ side seemed bothered about the ground defence unit, but presumably the NCOs in charge of ground defence had regular contact with HQ.

During my time at High Ercall, I was interviewed again by a travelling aircrew board and told that I could commence training as a WOP/AG fairly quickly, but if I wished to wait for navigator or pilot training, for which I was then considered suitable, there would be a fairly lengthy delay. Not wishing to continue on ground duties, I opted for WOP/AG hoping for my stay there to be shortened. One of my friends opted for pilot training and ironically commenced his aircrew training before I did. We met again at the end of the war and he, like myself, was commissioned and had survived the war, finishing up on Pathfinder Mosquitos and awarded a DFC. In hindsight I suppose that I should have waited for pilot training but on the other hand, I may well have failed the course or killed myself during training.

In the spring of 1941 I was posted to Blackpool to be given a Morse training course, hoping to commence aircrew training immediately after completing the course. Being posted was always an absolute bore, as a departure could not be made from any RAF station until a fully signed clearance certificate had been handed in to the orderly room. This entailed visiting almost every section on the station to get the required signatures certifying that there was no outstanding debt, or equipment to be returned. On a large RAF station, this could take all day as no transport was ever provided for this requirement. Many people have missed trains due to delays with the clearance certificate and I personally almost missed my own wedding!

Chapter 3
Aircrew Training

It is difficult to remember in detail the events that took place at Blackpool in 1941, over 60 years ago, other than to say that I had no difficulty in learning the Morse code or reaching the required speed of, I believe, 18 words a minute. This I attributed to a superb civilian instructor who was a retired Merchant Navy Radio Officer. He was patient and tolerant with everyone, doing his utmost to help his students through the course, even to the point of giving individual coaching where needed. Not everyone passed the course but the failures certainly could not be attributed to his instruction. I do remember the very good advice he gave in the early stages of training. He told us to practise Morse in our head, or out loud if it helped, by converting road and street signs, bill boards, and even words in books, into Morse. Often trainees could be heard voicing Morse dots and dashes as they walked around.

The instruction and final test was in a very large hall over a Burton's tailor shop, and probably the term, 'Going for a Burton' originated there, referring to those who failed Morse tests in the Burton's hall. It was also a term used to describe someone who had failed to return from an operational flight, or died as the result of it. Either explanation could be correct but I have no idea which. The final test did produce some drama when one candidate, realising that he could not complete the test, threw his headset onto the floor and stormed out of the hall.

The accommodation was again in boarding houses but the conditions were far better than those experienced at Morecambe. I must say that I made many friends amongst the aircrew recruits but inevitably lost contact with them and today can only wonder how many survived the war or indeed, are still alive.

Having successfully completed Morse training, the next posting was to RAF Station Yatesbury, located in the lovely Wiltshire countryside close to the village of Calne. This was one of several RAF Signals Training Units for aircrew or ground personnel. It was a typical wartime RAF station with mostly wooden buildings for living quarters, classrooms, offices and messes. The living quarters were heated by a large solid fuel stove in the centre of the building, and was a menace to keep clean. If a bed was close to the stove, the occupant roasted – in cold weather away from it, he froze.

The grass airfield was of reasonable size and had Dominie and Proctor aircraft for in-flight signals training of aircrew. Some pilots who flew the aircraft were civilians, and together with NCO pilots, were commanded by a Flight Lieutenant.

The course was particularly enjoyable for me as I had always been very keen on radio prior to joining up and had successfully constructed several pieces of radio equipment. It was quite a long course lasting from early June to mid September 1941 during which time technical instruction was given together with Morse practice. Progress tests were given during the course and these had to be passed before continuing to the next phase of training. Inevitably some trainees failed during training and were posted off the station to take up other duties.

Discipline on this course was far more rigorous than any experienced before and it seemed that aircrew trainees were victimised for the slightest error or indiscretion. Usually no formal charge was made, instead those being punished were put on kitchen cleaning duties washing greasy baking tins in the 'tin room', as it was called. The kitchens were always understaffed and this was probably their way of getting temporary help. The dormitory had to be kept spotlessly clean with bedding folded exactly as required. Personal appearance also had to be perfect whatever the weather and this was checked daily on parade prior to being marched to classes. Even in our leisure time, it was compulsory to march from place to place and not walk or stroll. Failure to conform meant a stint in the dreaded 'tin room'. Doubtless the discipline was for our own good but it was not seen like that at the time.

The food served was plain and as nutritious as wartime rationing would permit but totally lacked variety and in consequence was very boring. The breakfasts always included the particularly unappetising greasy fried soya sausages and fried bread but one could always opt for lumpy porridge, the lesser of two evils! One particular dish, cheese and potato pie, appeared frequently as the evening meal and of all the foods on offer, I found this the most palatable. However pleasant or unpleasant the food was, it was ladled out by cookhouse staff with none too clean hands who literally threw it on to the plate!

The Station Warrant Officer, an impeccably turned out man, was very strict and seemed to delight in humiliating trainee aircrew. Feelings ran high amongst a small group of aircrew trainees and late one night they confronted and physically assaulted him. There was a thorough investigation into the incident that resulted in several trainees being suspended and posted away for punishment. Thankfully, I had no part in that and certainly did not condone it. Like many others, I had smarted under what I considered was unjust discipline and punishment, but later realised that only my pride had suffered, not my career. I thought that perhaps some time in the future I might meet up with that particular Warrant Officer and have the opportunity to voice my opinion on the way trainees were treated. I was commissioned when we did meet again very briefly just before I was demobilised. He was smartly dressed as always and I remember him asking if we had met before? The opportunity had come, but it would have been too petty to say other than, 'Yes, but it was a few years ago.' On reflection, with the standard of behaviour today being what it is, I cannot help wondering if the discipline to which we were subjected during training in the RAF was not the making and the strengthening of our character. I like to think so!

The course gave technical instruction on the use of the older type of radio equipment used by the RAF and there was constant Morse practice to increase our speed above the basic we had achieved at Blackpool. Towards the end of the technical course, which I thoroughly enjoyed, aircrew candidates were told that gunnery schools had long waiting lists that resulted in my course's in-flight signals training being cancelled. This was extremely frustrating for everybody concerned as we were all anxious to get on to operational flying. It made me personally wonder if it would not have been wiser if I had waited for another course when interviewed at High Ercall rather accept the one I took. However it is easy to be wise in hindsight and really there was nothing to be done then except wait.

On 6th November 1941 I completed the course, passed out with a very satisfactory assessment and was promoted to the next higher rank of Aircraftsman First Class. Officially I had become a qualified tradesman and perhaps more importantly, in the words of the disciplinary Sergeant who sarcastically informed me of my promotion, I was no longer the lowest form of animal life in the Royal Air Force. This promotion also gave me an increase of pay; always welcome! On the following day I was posted to RAF Station Oakington, an operational Bomber Command airfield in Cambridgeshire, to carry out ground radio duties.

I reported to Oakington with others and learned that I would be immediately detached to RAF Bourne in Cambridgeshire that was the satellite airfield of Oakington. There I would carry out radio duties with Aerodrome Control until a gunnery course became available. From memory I believe that Bourne had been in use for less than a year and had a squadron of Wellingtons. I seem to recall that it was 101 Squadron, but that might not be correct. This was an operational squadron and at last I felt that I was about to do something useful for the war effort whilst waiting (somewhat impatiently) for my aircrew training to continue. I tried to regard this posting as a continuation of aircrew training as I would be working closely with operational aircraft.

My task (with others) was to assist in positioning a mobile Watch Tower Caravan to the runway in use, connect its telephone to the Watch Office in the HQ building and carry out Watch Office or Watch Tower Duties. In the present day these would be Air Traffic Control duties. The telephone connection was achieved by unrolling telephone cable from a huge drum and physically dragging it across what seemed to be a sea of mud to the caravan that had been positioned by a tractor to the side of the active runway. An attempt was made to use the tractor to drag the cable but the strain was too great, causing it to break.

The duty pattern was shift work and I personally found that the most interesting shifts were those when the bombers were departing, or later when they returned. If the wind direction changed, the Watch Tower Caravan, Chance Light and telephone line all had to be repositioned. By the end of my stay at Bourne, I had muscles that I did not know existed and had learned a lot about controlling aircraft, general airfield control, and other airfield duties.

A pilot was always on duty in the Watch Tower Caravan for operational departures and arrivals but at other times my colleagues and I controlled movements under the guidance of the Duty Pilot at the other end of the telephone in the Watch Office. Operational departures and arrivals were normally controlled by visual signals with Radio Telephony used only in emergency or outside the periods of operational flying.

During my stay, there were a number of operational losses and some crashes, bringing home to me how serious and dangerous flying could be! Despite this, the morale of the squadron and the station seemed to be high. I watched a Wellington taking off on a night flying test in the morning prior to operations the same evening and as it passed me it seemed most unlikely that it would get airborne. Sure enough it remained on the ground crashing through a hedge at the end of the runway, careering across a road before coming to a stop in a field where it burst into flames, killing all on board except the rear gunner. He was seen to leave the aircraft by rolling out of his turret backwards, bouncing several times on the runway before coming to a stop. Although badly injured, he was very fortunate to have survived. Apparently the ground engineers had failed to secure the fuel tank access flaps on the wings and this disturbed the airflow over the wings enough to prevent the aircraft getting airborne.

Bourne was the main diversion for Oakington and on a brilliantly clear night with a full moon, two Stirlings returning from an operational flight to Brest were diverted to Bourne. Within minutes of receiving the diversion details Oakington advised us that there was an enemy fighter in the area. As a matter of urgency, contact was attempted with the Stirlings on R/T, but neither aircraft answered the calls. With an obvious misplaced sense of security both aircraft flew over the airfield close together with their navigation lights on and almost immediately were attacked by a JU 88 which shot one down in a field not too far away, where it caught fire and blew up. The other Stirling called on R/T but was told to stand off because the JU88 was strafing the airfield. I had left the caravan to take cover under the Chance Light and could hear bullets hitting the runway and the Chance Light above me. The JU88, having lost contact with the remaining Stirling, broke off the attack and left the area. We learned later that it was intercepted and shot down by a night fighter before it got to the English coast on its way back to its base.

The rather shaken pilot of the surviving Stirling was advised that the bandit had gone and given landing clearance. Unfortunately he came in much too fast and ran off the end of the runway, finally stopping on the grass beyond the end of the runway with the aircraft's nose projecting over a hedge. The aircraft was undamaged and when the crew left it to be debriefed by the intelligence officer, the ground staff towed it to the dispersal area. It is interesting to note that in a 1997 publication, *Cambridgeshire Airfields in the Second War*, the author Graham Smith relates that on the night of 3/4th October, a Stirling returning from Brest was attacked 6 times and shot down by a Junkers 88, killing all the crew except two who baled out. This information conflicts with what I remember of that night as I am certain that there were two Stirlings involved. Perhaps he thought it unnecessary to mention the second Stirling as it landed safely.

Another incident occurred with a Wellington that had a large bomb 'hang up'. In spite of everything the crew could do, it stayed on and as the aircraft touched down, we in the Watch Tower Caravan saw a mass of sparks under the aircraft as the bomb dropped off. The crew knew nothing of what had happened until they got off the aircraft, but fortunately the bomb did not explode. The bomb finished up on the grass beside the runway and was recovered by the armourers some time later. I believe the bomb was called a 'cookie' and was about 4000 pounds weight.

On return from night operations, Wellingtons and Stirlings would land routinely but frequently some had suffered damage with engines shut down, or had casualties on board. I saw a navigator get out of the nose hatch of a Wellington and was horrified to see him walk towards a propeller that was still turning. Fortunately he stopped just inches away from it! Obviously the stresses of the flight had dulled his senses, as he seemed to be in a trance.

The advantage of being stationed at Bourne was that it was within hitch hiking distance of Northampton enabling me to get home on 48 hour passes to spend time with my wife to be, having become engaged when I joined the RAF. On days off, it was permissible to go into Cambridge and it was there that I fell foul of RAF regulations that subsequently delayed my Commissioning. Whilst walking with a friend, we came across a very drunken (Australian) officer who was being violently sick at the side of the road. We decided to ignore him but were stopped by two Army military policemen and reported for failing to salute an officer. When answering to the charge, I told the CO that I thought it best to ignore him rather than draw attention to his condition. He was sympathetic but emphasised that it was the King's Commission being saluted and not the man. I was dismissed without punishment but to my cost, it went on my record.

There were occasional visits to Oakington to learn more about Group and aircraft operations within the Group. As most information was classified, there was very little to be learned other than how important a satellite airfield can be when bombers returning from operations have to be diverted away from their home base. Oakington was planned as a permanent RAF Station with large hangars and brick buildings and it contrasted sharply with Bourne that, although having runways, had only draughty Nissen huts heated by the dreaded primitive solid fuel stoves.

I was particularly envious of Oakington's Watch Tower where it was possible to change the runway in use without the great amount of physical effort needed at Bourne. Oakington was home to Number 7 squadron equipped with Stirling bombers and these seemed enormous compared to the Wellington. However, I learned later on during the war that its performance was not all that was desired of a heavy bomber.

There was an incident at Oakington that could have been disastrous. A Bomb Aimer from the Stirling Squadron was told to show a group of Air Training Corps cadets, (they were called something different in those days), around a 7 Squadron Stirling bomber. He took them on board the aircraft indicating each crew position and when he reached his 'office', the bomb aiming position, he was asked how the bombs were released. To demonstrate, he selected switches on the bomb distribution panel and pressed the bomb release to show them how the distribution controller released the bombs. When he and the cadets got off the aircraft no ground staff were to be seen anywhere, but bombs were lying underneath the aircraft which he had inadvertently released during his demonstration. He was completely unaware that the aircraft had been bombed up ready for operations that night!

Dropping bombs reminds me of an incident involving a Wellington bomber that had returned to Bourne after an abortive raid and still had its bombs on board. It was ordered to proceed to a nearby bombing range to drop its bomb load before landing at Bourne. The corporal in charge at the bombing range was informed what was going to happen and some time later in a very agitated state, he said that the 'Blankety Blank' idiot of a pilot had dropped the whole load live on the range, scaring him almost to death. Fortunately he was uninjured.

After what seemed to be a long time period of time at Bourne, aircrew training resumed for me in May 1942 when I was posted back to Yatesbury to be given an abbreviated refresher course lasting six weeks that included In-flight training. The discipline on the course was still rigid, but not quite as severe as my previous stay at Yatesbury. I sailed through the ground course with great enthusiasm and went straight on to In-flight signals training.

The flying training involving flight communication exercises was done on Dominie and Proctor aircraft, twenty short flights being carried out in 19 days clocking up 20 hours of flying. During these flights, the exercises were carried out using the RAF's older transmitting and receiving equipment, which involved changing from one frequency to another by selecting and installing different coils from a box of coils carried. In the Proctor this was quite difficult as it was a very small aircraft with little room to spare. Some exercises included taking bearings using the loop antenna and passing the information to the pilot. One was expected to carry out the exercise within a given time period, which if exceeded could result in failure. Fortunately I was not troubled by that limitation. It was only later that I learned that the radio equipment fitted on board those aircraft was not the same as that used operationally in Bomber Command. Looking back it seems ridiculous to have in-flight training on equipment that I probably would not use again.

It was early summer and the convection currents over the hills caused some sickening turbulence, which then I thought quite severe. It was not of course, but I had not flown a great number of times before and always in less turbulent conditions. I was never airsick flying with the RAF, but did feel queasy at times. The rule was that if you were sick in the aircraft, YOU cleaned it up. Some students did fail the course due to airsickness and although one could have sympathy for them, everyone knew that flying duties could not be efficiently performed if constantly airsick.

On 20 June 1942, I passed out with very good reports, was promoted to Leading Aircraftsman and posted to Number 8 Gunnery School at Evanton in Scotland. This was located close to Number 4 (Coastal) OTU at Alness where I would go nearly two years later. It was a very pleasant posting and I thoroughly enjoyed the time there. Flying was done on Botha aircraft, a very nice modern aircraft in appearance, but one that was in fact plagued by technical problems that gave pilots little confidence in it. I believe it was originally intended to be a torpedo bomber but failed to reach the required operational performance level.

There was a story circulating concerning a trainee in the Botha gun turret who was aiming at a drogue being towed by another aircraft. He was taking such a long time to open fire causing the impatient instructor to shout over the intercom 'Fire Fire', whereupon the pilot, believing the aircraft to be on fire, crash-landed it on the beach they were flying over at the time. I have no idea how factual that was, but perfectly true was an incident I did witness. I was standing with a group of trainees in front of a Botha outside the hangar being given a pep talk by the CO. One trainee standing closer to the aircraft was obviously bored by what was going on and constantly fiddled with the propeller. As he moved the propeller against the compression, the engine coughed, turned a couple of revs and severely injured his arm. It appeared that the mechanics working on this aircraft had run the engine immediately before we assembled and it was still hot. I was told later that hot engines could do strange and unpredictable things!

The course was most interesting and in spite of the poor reputation of the Botha, I really did enjoy the flying. The gunnery exercises were fun, perhaps because I managed to get more than the average number of hits on the target drogue and ground targets. It may well have been luck, but never having been put to the test in anger, I will never know. The rather haphazard way of assessing the hits was to count the coloured holes in the target drogue. To explain this, the ammunition fired by each student was tipped with different paint colours that stuck to the drogue as the bullets passed through.

The course, that lasted four weeks, included ground instruction on all the aircraft turrets likely to be encountered and the Browning .303 machine gun that was standard on most aircraft. Instruction was also given on Vickers Gas Operated Gun and the ancient Lewis Gun. We were taught how strip and re-assemble each gun and how to clear stoppages that might occur in action. Ground exercises were carried out sitting in a turret of a ground installation, learning how to operate it and the guns with hydraulic power or manually. There were seven flights of about an hour each, during which time all drills and exercises were carried out without incident.

The course also included instruction on the various types of bombs, including incendiary devices. We were taken to a bomb storage area and shown the various sizes of bombs, how they were fused and the safety precautions that were present on the bomb to prevent it exploding if accidentally dropped from the aircraft whilst on the ground. A Corporal instructor demonstrated how the fuse was put into the bomb and to show how harmless it was with the safety device, he hit the nose of the bomb with a large lump hammer. Nothing happened of course, other than putting the fear of God into all the trainees. It rather took me back to the hand grenade training at Blackpool.

On 24 July 1942, having passed out with an above average assessment, (I think everybody did) I was promoted to Sergeant and given seven days leave for my wedding, before reporting to Number 15 Wellington OTU at Harwell. After nearly two years of time and effort, I had at last become qualified, although more training lay ahead before becoming operationally qualified.

Departure from Evanton on Saturday July 25 was greatly delayed by the dreaded clearance certificate and there was some difficulty getting home to Northampton where I was due to get married on Sunday. The train services were chaotic and it looked as though I would not make it in time, but to the relief of all, I arrived home about midnight on Saturday.

We were to be married immediately after the Sunday morning service and in the words of the song, 'There was I waiting at the church, waiting at the church … etc.' with no sign of the bride. Canon Davies, who was to conduct the service, said rather impatiently that he would give her another five minutes after which we would either have to cancel the wedding or have a double wedding together with the next couple waiting to be married. Neither wedding party wanted this to happen, but happily my bride to be turned up in time for a normal wedding ceremony, having been delayed by car trouble! When my father-in-law complained to the driver, he was told it was one of those things and 'Didn't he know there was a war on!' This was the standard excuse for everything at that time.

We honeymooned in London for the rest of my leave, staying with the parents of my best man, Sid Birchmore whom I had first met at Morecambe. He was following the same training pattern as myself but did not qualify until six months later. He flew on Boston aircraft with Bomber Command, was commissioned and left the service as a Flying Officer, collecting a DFC on the way. Apart from several air raids, the honeymoon went well. Well it would, wouldn't it?

The short honeymoon over, I reported to RAF Station Harwell on 30

July 1942 where at last I seemed to be moving towards the day when I would take up an operational role in the war. Two days after arrival I did two short flights in a Wellington to demonstrate my gunnery proficiency from the rear and front turrets. Inevitably there was ground instruction to be undertaken before flying started in earnest, this taking three weeks to complete. On this course I was trained on the Marconi T1154/R1155 communication equipment that was used operationally. Pretty well everything one needed to know about operational flying was taught and on completion I felt very happy about my role on the Wellington. This was immediately followed by a detachment of two weeks duration to RAF Station Hampstead Norris, the satellite airfield of Harwell, where nine flights of about 3 hours duration were done on the dear old Avro Anson on various cross-country routes. Mostly flights were to the west or north-west and on one, a landing was made at Jurby on the Isle of Man. Some went north-eastwards to Cranwell and over RAF bomber airfields in Lincolnshire. During these flights I did normal In-flight radio duties screened by an instructor on rest from operations. Similarly, an instructor screened the student navigator. On one flight the student navigator became completely lost and got into a bit of a flap. The instructor, a Polish Flight sergeant, seemed quite unconcerned with his student's plight and made no attempt to help him. He waited until the student admitted he was lost and then took over and without any apparent calculation gave the pilot a course to steer. About 25 minutes later the airfield came in sight, leaving the student quite speechless. I certainly was very impressed. Doubtless the instructor had flown that route so many times he knew every landmark en route. I did not fly again with the instructor or the trainee so do not know if the trainee failed the course.

At the dispersal area one morning waiting to fly, an Anson from Harwell approached and as it came in to land, the instructor navigator remarked that the 'Annie' was perhaps the safest aircraft flying and he would willingly do another operational tour if it was in that aircraft. He should have kept quiet because as it touched down, the undercarriage folded up and it came to a grinding halt in a shower of sparks. Fortunately no one was hurt and the aircraft was soon repaired and put back into service.

The Anson did not have a hydraulic system to raise and lower the undercarriage, it being the duty of one of the other crew members, usually a student, to manually operate it by winding the undercarriage handle a great number of turns very rapidly when ordered by the pilot. The aircraft also had a primitive arrangement to enable crews to relieve themselves in flight. This consisted of a funnel attached to a tube which was routed to the outside the aircraft. It was quite common for the tube to become detached from the fitting at the side of the fuselage with somewhat 'soggy' results. As with airsickness, the same rule applied – if you created the mess, you cleaned it up after landing!

Once back at Harwell I flew a long Wellington day training flight in terrible weather, after which came the serious business of crewing up. Trainee aircrew assembled in a very large hall and were instructed to form themselves into crews. Those who knew each other soon crewed together, but for the life of me I cannot remember how my crew was formed. However, I can say that I was lucky to crew up with four very good chaps and never had reason to doubt the ability of any of them. It was quite obvious that we could not be five individuals trying to operate a bomber, but had to be a well co-ordinated team. We were very similar in age and background with a common aim of getting into action and hopefully surviving the war. The crew comprised pilot Sergeant Johnny Peck, navigator Sergeant Bob Verguson, bomb aimer and front gunner Sergeant Les Blick, rear gunner Sergeant Ray Wilson, and myself. Johnny probably thought he might be shot down over Germany because he studied German the whole time we were together. This prompted me to take up the same studies using a correspondence course.

In the Wellington the wireless operator's position faced forward immediately behind the pilot separated by a screen to stop light shining out. It was the warmest place on the aircraft and often I would feel very hot while rear gunner, bomb aimer and pilot complained of the cold. The communications equipment as stated earlier was Marconi T1154/R1155 that had become standard on most operational RAF aircraft. It was very easy to set up and operate and I rarely experienced any faults with it. After the war I would continue to operate it for several years on civil aircraft. There was an inter-com system to enable crew members to talk to each other, a radiotelephony unit used by the pilot or crew to talk to the ground and one other very important piece of equipment called IFF (Identification Friend or Foe) that gave our defence sites information to confirm that we were a friendly aircraft. A Lorenz SBA receiver was fitted for the pilot's use during poor weather conditions to enable him to make a blind instrument approach. More about that later.

I had to become acquainted with the coding and decoding of messages. I cannot remember exactly what the coding device looked like but I think that there was a card with codes of the day that had to be inserted. It had a pencil with lead at one end and a small metal spike at the other end, the spike being inserted in a slot for each individual letter and moving a slide down to the bottom of the device. One could then read the coded letter, which would be written on the message pad. This was repeated for every letter in the message and was quite a tedious procedure if the message was a long one. Once the message had been coded, it would be transmitted in Morse Code to the ground station. During flights I remember that I had to receive encoded messages and decode them. Being mostly practice messages they were of no operational significance but they had to be correctly received and decoded in order to pass that particular exercise. There could, of course, be occasions when the message instructed the pilot to abandon the exercise and return to base or perhaps another airfield, but this did not happen to me.

The Wellington had an underside hatch in the nose opening inwards through which crew members normally entered the aircraft. This would be the exit all crew members (excluding the rear gunner) would use if it became necessary to bale out. The rear gunner had the easiest way out as all he had to do was turn his turret athwartship, open the doors and roll out backwards. The hardest part for him was to clip on his parachute which was located in the fuselage forward of the turret. The astro hatch had a transparent Perspex dome that could be removed and had sufficient space to allow exit wearing full flying gear including a parachute. There was also a hatch above the pilot that opened outwards but could not be used by other crew members until the pilot had exited the aircraft. It is doubtful if this could have been used to bale out. At a point in mid fuselage, on each side were knock out panels in the geodetic frame through which escape might be possible. However, they were very small and it is doubtful if anyone wearing full flying gear could get through.

A cynic likened crewing up to Russian roulette saying that at that stage no one could possibly be aware of other crew members' capabilities, and therefore, it was impossible to find the perfect crew. Perhaps he had a point, but it was not one that I could share. A weak member could jeopardise the safety of the rest of the crew but the whole purpose of this phase of the training was to discover one's weaknesses and learn how to overcome them. If they could not be overcome, it meant leaving the crew.

The OTU was a very important part of crew training and had to be taken very seriously. Once crewed up we went through the course without too much trouble, apart from difficulty landing one night in absolutely filthy weather conditions after quite a long flight. Johnny was carrying out a Lorenz SBA approach by listening to radio signals that gave an indication if the aircraft was on, to the left, or to the right of the radio beam. The approach was quite normal until the aircraft got down to 400 feet when, still in cloud, all signals disappeared causing him to abandon his attempt to land. Several approaches were made without success and as the fuel was getting low, Johnny said that he would climb to 3000 feet and we would bale out! This went down like a lead balloon and perhaps in desperation, we persuaded him to have one final attempt. On this approach the Artificial Horizon instrument failed and the aircraft broke cloud at very low level in a very steep bank angle. I was standing in the astro dome looking for the runway's lights ahead, but saw them appear above my right shoulder rather than below and ahead where they should have been. Yes, we were almost upside down! Johnny saw them at the same time and hauled on the controls to get the aircraft level, the aircraft just scraping over the airfield water tower at about 50 feet before he managed to get full control and land. It was rather a close call and we were quite shaken by it. The Duty Officer, a non-flying type, was inspecting guards in the water tower at the time and saw the aircraft zoom over, subsequently reporting Johnny for dangerous low flying. Quite rightly, no action was taken when Johnny explained the circumstances. Fires could be seen on the ground as we landed and possibly could have been other Wellingtons that had crashed in their attempts to land. There were, to my knowledge, several crashes that night. It was discovered at the enquiry that nobody on our course had been told that in order to carry out a Lorenz SBA approach, it was *necessary* for the special aerial to be extended!

Of aerials – the Wellington had a long trailing aerial on a reel in the fuselage that had to be wound out beneath the aircraft to enable the radio to be operated. It was used on all flights if en route radio communication was needed, so care had to be taken before landing to ensure that it was reeled back in. It was quite common for wireless operators to forget this, particularly if they were returning from a hectic flight, which some were. Fortunately, whilst at Harwell I did not have any such problems. If flying in or near electrically charged clouds or rain, it could become necessary to reel in the aerial and earth it, this potentially being quite a hazardous operation. On one occasion whilst attempting to earth the aerial, I was thrown across the aircraft fuselage by an electrical discharge causing severe bruising despite wearing bulky flying clothing.

Although not operational, there were lengthy flights routed around UK when there was always the chance of being intercepted and attacked by German night fighters. For this reason, both gun turrets were always manned. The primary defence against low flying enemy aircraft was Barrage Balloons and on some occasions when the exercise required the aircraft to fly at lower levels, I can recall 'Squeakers' being heard. These were radio transmissions from transmitters carried by the balloons to warn aircrew of their presence. The log entry, 'Alter course Squeakers' seemed to appear quite frequently in Bob's navigation logs.

On bombing exercises a photographic flare, a rather sensitive device, had to be dropped from the aircraft through the flare chute located in the fuselage aft of the navigator's position. We had been warned that if it did not immediately clear the chute, it could ignite inside it with disastrous results. I believe that it was Bob who put one in the chute where it stuck for several moments before falling out. All I could hear was Bob cursing loudly until it cleared the aircraft. We had to drop many flares during our training flights but I was never happy doing that particular duty.

During the course we had some weekend passes and Bob's parents invited my wife and me to spend the weekend with them. Bob and I travelled from Harwell and my wife met us at Bob's home in Essex. It was a very welcome break considering that I had only a week with my new wife before leaving for Harwell. One Sunday when we were not flying, my father in law drove the family to Oxford where they all met up with Bob and me for a meal together. These short breaks certainly eased the tension that inevitably built up during the OTU course.

An essential flying exercise that had to be carried out was a maximum weight take-off carrying a full bomb load, dummies of course, which had to be dropped on a target at the bombing range. I seem to recall that the Wellington's maximum bomb load was about 4000lb and could be a mixture 250lb or 500lb bombs. It could carry the 'cookie' weighing 4000lb but I never got to carry one of those. In fact, I believe that it needed a modified bomb bay to carry that bomb and only the Wellingtons fitted with Merlin engines had the capability. It was quite astonishing to discover how the performance of the aircraft was degraded by the heavier weight being carried, the controls being very sluggish compared to lighter Wellingtons flown on previous details. The sobering thought was that the take-off weight on most operational flights would always be close to the maximum and we would have to get used to the quite marginal performance!

Nearing the end of the course, trainee crews were (quite unexpectedly) told to stand by for operations, and there was a mixture of excitement and apprehension in anticipation of this. A night flying test was carried out with a screen pilot who to our regret found the aircraft allocated to the crew was not serviceable for operations. Later we were told that it was for a 1000 bomber raid to Cologne but never discovered if we were to go to the main or diversionary target. On these flights, one member of the crew would always be an instructor 'on rest' between operational tours, flying in a supervisory capacity. We actually flew that night with an instructor navigator, flying eastwards on a very strange route until well over the sea before returning to Harwell. Nothing untoward happened during the flight and we returned to base safely. Harwell did lose some aircraft sent on operations to Cologne that night and I thought it was most unfortunate for the instructors who lost their lives, having survived their operational tour.

A week before the course ended, it was announced that the first three crews to finish the OTU course would be posted to Ferry Command to ferry Wellingtons overseas. Those crews nearing the end of their training were not happy with this news, feeling that having been trained for bomber operations, postings should be to Bomber Command. Inevitably it would seem, my crew finished in the first three. So after 27 flights, God only knows how many take-off and landings on 'circuits and bumps' and 100 hours flying, it was with regret that the crew set off for yet another Training Unit, this time to 1446 Flight, Ferry Command at RAF Station Moreton in Marsh.

Chapter 4
Ferry Command

The stay at Moreton in Marsh was very pleasant with the atmosphere being so much more relaxed than at Harwell. Theoretically we were a qualified Wellington bomber crew ready to take up an operational role as required, although doubtless there would have been further training had we been posted to a squadron in Bomber Command. The crew was given (I believe) a brand new Wellington Mark 1c with markings 'H' Harry, which was to be ferried to a destination overseas, as then unspecified. We were briefed on the items that needed to be checked before the aircraft could be dispatched overseas, together with the in-flight procedures of ferry flights. This involved doing some fairly lengthy flights to check that the aircraft's fuel consumption was within the limits laid down, and to give time to ensure that all of the systems on the aircraft were serviceable. I had no problems with the radio equipment but other equipment did cause concern.

The autopilot ('George') was one item that gave every crew, mine in particular, a great deal of trouble, and was directly responsible for delaying the crew's first ferry flight. It was a Heath Robinson affair compared to today's modern aircraft but with only one pilot on board, it was the only system that could give him a chance of relaxing on long sectors. The wretched 'George' also indirectly led to my first landing incident. On every flight in our allocated aircraft, Johnny experienced problems with 'George' and although we thought it had been finally rectified, en route to Portreath for the ferry flight it failed again, necessitating a return to Moreton in Marsh. A very irate Flight Commander, deciding that Johnny was incompetent, ordered an instructor pilot 'on rest' from operations to take over the aircraft and determine if it really was unserviceable. After a tour of thirty operations the screen pilot understandably was tired and perhaps twitchy, but he did find it unserviceable. Ironically, coming in to land he dropped the aircraft in very hard, almost ground looped it and burst a tyre on the port side! The crew was more than pleased to get Johnny back in the pilot's seat!

After each flight, the aircraft was serviced very thoroughly, giving plenty of time for leisure activities outside the camp whenever we felt like doing so. I was particularly friendly with Bob, having met his family during the OTU course. Bob's father was a fireman in London, a job that was hazardous enough in normal times but more so during the Blitz. Bob said that he was going to slip off (unofficially) to London to stay the night with his family in Dagenham and invited me to join him. On two occasions we took a train to Paddington and then went by underground tube train to his home. Although not confined to our RAF Station, we were not allowed to be more than a certain distance from it, a distance that was greatly exceeded. At Paddington it was necessary to get through the barrier past service policemen who were inspecting servicemen's passes. Having been told that aircrew members were seldom checked, we confidently walked through and fortunately were not stopped. Nevertheless it was a rather stupid thing to have done and had we been caught, the outcome could perhaps have been serious enough to affect future promotion. We could have been in very serious trouble on the second occasion because Johnny had been told to get his crew together and depart for Portreath and he knew that we had gone to London. He was on tenterhooks until we arrived back only just in time for the flight!

We got to know other ferry crews during the stay, all of whom were preparing for their first ferry flight but, oddly enough, did not meet anyone who was there to do a *second* ferry flight. That and the fact that we were issued with khaki uniforms and desert summer clothes, including topees, should have given a clue as to what might be lying ahead.

There was a very friendly atmosphere in the crew room and when crews got to know each other, there were enjoyable times to be had on and off the base, including some wild parties. My wife came to stay for several days towards the end of the time at Moreton in Marsh, and stayed in the same guesthouse as the wife of John Kennedy, the navigator of another crew. The wives became good friends and kept in touch for a long time. I had told my wife that if I did not turn up at the guesthouse after duty at the end of the day, I most likely would have been delayed by flying duty. Bob's father also came and spent a few days with us, which gave us all a lot of encouragement. For security reasons, crews were not given advance warning of their departure for overseas and on the departure day for Portreath I seem to remember that we were confined to base and banned from making any phone calls. When we eventually flew to Portreath for the overseas departure, my wife was not told until we were well on our way to Gibraltar. It would be over a year before we would see each other again.

The departure point from UK was usually RAF Station Portreath for destinations overseas but the destination airfield and routing was not revealed until the last moment. When 'George' had been changed for the 'umpteenth' time, the aircraft was declared serviceable and Johnny air tested it as we flew to Portreath on 28 November 1942, ready for a late evening departure on the next day.

Portreath was exceptionally well organised, perhaps more so than any airfield previously visited. Crews were given very precise instructions on the procedures to be observed leading up to take-off and it was emphasised that they had to be strictly adhered to. Our destination was Gibraltar but there were other destinations that night. Crews were given an exact time to start engines and told that as there was total radio silence, only visual signals would be given to start taxying, and again to commence take-off. We were warned that by the time the aircraft was three quarters down the runway, another aircraft *could* have commenced its take off run. If that occurred there was no way to avoid an accident if the take-off was aborted unless able to get rapidly off the runway well clear of the aircraft behind. A sobering thought!

Fortunately the departure was without incident, but the aircraft went into cloud soon after take-off and the weather continued to be foul right up to the cruising height of about 15000 feet where the aircraft was icing up badly. The only consolation was that it was unlikely that any German night fighters who might have been around could have seen us! Regardless of the weather conditions I was quite excited at the thought of seeing more of the world, never having ever been out of England.

There was an overload fuel tank fitted on the rest bed in the fuselage aft of the navigator's position to give the required extra range and two hours out when Johnny switched over to it, both engines stopped! Johnny's first thought was that the booster pump had failed and ordered me to manually pump the fuel to get the engines started again. I ripped my oxygen mask off to get to the overload tank but with the effort of pumping, quickly suffered from the effects of lack of oxygen. Fortunately Bob saw what had happened and got me back on oxygen. Meanwhile, the aircraft was descending like a brick and Johnny himself switched the engines back to the nacelle tanks, squirting de-icing fluid into the carburettors as fast as he could. After much popping and banging, at about 5000 feet both engines started running smoothly and we returned to Portreath.

On landing, as you might imagine with all that had happened, I forgot to reel in the trailing aerial and it was lost. On the ground Johnny discovered that the overload tank had *never* been filled, but as he had signed the Form 700 as having the tank full, he was reported as being negligent and responsible for endangering the aircraft. We heard nothing of any action being taken against the person whose duty it was to have filled the tank and thankfully, no action was taken against Johnny.

I seem to recall that the overload tank was not fitted with a contents gauge so how on earth could any pilot check if it was full!

The next night we operated a ten-hour flight to Gibraltar without incident, flying over the sea the whole time with our first sight of land being Cape Finisterre in the distance on the port side of the aircraft. Prior to landing Johnny did a circuit of the airfield keeping well clear of Spanish Airspace and ever mindful of the notorious turbulence that the 'Rock' created. I got some very good photographs as we circled despite the fact that photography from the air would have been prohibited, but at the time I did not give much thought to that. Although it was late autumn, we were much further south and the temperature was warmer than when we left UK; more importantly it was dry.

In 1942, Gibraltar had an extremely short east/west runway, (it is not much better today) with sea at each end. There was ample space for parking various types of aircraft that were in transit to the many destinations, all being parked in lines with only just enough room to taxi from any particular line to the take-off point. There were lines of aircraft on both sides of the runway so that if an aircraft developed a swing on take-off, it had to be corrected very rapidly to avoid colliding with those parked. In fact, John Kennedy whose wife stayed in the same guesthouse as my wife in Moreton in Marsh, was in his aircraft waiting to be given taxi clearance when a Wellington swung off the runway, collided with his aircraft and a propeller sliced one of his legs off. Fortunately he survived, but for him the war was over.

The only night spent in Gibraltar did not allow more than a brief visit to the town where Bob, the only smoker, took full advantage of duty free cigarettes and stocked up with them. I do remember that when water was drawn from a well near to the living quarters, small red worms could be seen in it, but apparently these were quite harmless and no ill effects were suffered.

Less than two days after arrival, we departed for El Adem en route for Cairo. At maximum take-off weight, the aircraft accelerated very slowly down the runway and as the red lights at the far end passed under the wheels it was only just airborne and virtually hanging on the props. At this critical stage the lower escape hatch blew open causing Johnny more than a little concern. It seemed ages before there was enough speed to safely retract the flaps and climb away. I suppose the RAF did observe weight limitations in those days but these would not have been to the same requirements as civil aircraft today. The aircraft's performance certainly gave the impression that it was a great deal heavier than we had been led to believe.

The intended route was over the Atlas Mountains into the Sahara

Desert flying from Algeria into Tunisia and thence into Libya. With the take-off performance being so poor, it seemed most unlikely that the aircraft would be able to clear the high ground of our intended route, so we flew clear of all high ground until we reached a safe altitude and could rejoin the intended route. The flight was in darkness for the first few hours and there was nothing of interest to be seen during the eleven and a half hour flight apart from seeing a light flashing the letter 'V' from the ground below. It was daylight when we landed at El Adem for fuel and there were clear signs of the military activity that had taken place only days before we arrived. Of the aircraft that left Gibraltar that night, only four got to El Adem and one of those crashed on landing, killing everybody on board. That particular aircraft was on final approach when its nose suddenly pitched up and stalled before crashing into the ground. Johnny thought it might have been due to inefficient flap control by its pilot. The Wellington had hydraulic flaps and if the controller was not operated carefully, the flaps could rapidly fully extend or fully retract with possible disastrous results. Apparently the flaps had to be "milked" in and out with the controller that was fitted on the aircraft we were flying. A later modification cured the problem but it had cost the lives of many crews, particularly at OTUs with inexperienced pilots.

We spoke to the other two crews, and they like us, had opted to route clear of the high ground after departure from Gibraltar. Another hazard was that with Gibraltar being so close to Spain, it was possible that observers on the Spanish side alerted the Germans when aircraft departed. Certainly we were warned to keep a careful watch for enemy night fighters throughout the flight.

Whilst the aircraft was being refuelled at El Adem, there was time for us to look around before continuing to Cairo. The airfield had taken a hammering during the desert campaign and crashed aircraft, wrecked vehicles, and tanks could be seen on and around the airfield. I took several photographs including one of a ME109 that had been shot down and another of a Hurricane that looked as though it had been destroyed by strafing aircraft. There was nothing in the way of food available, but we did manage to get a cup of tea before leaving. This was scrounged from ground staff by Ray Wilson who never failed to find a cup of tea wherever it was!

After refuelling, the ferry flight continued without incident to the Cairo area but to Bob's dismay, we could not find LG224 the destination airfield, having been given incorrect co-ordinates for the airfield. We combed the area flying over the Pyramids and the outskirts of Cairo looking for LG224 and I took several photographs. In the gathering gloom of dusk, the runway lights of an unknown airfield were spotted and Johnny decided to land there. It turned out to be a maintenance airfield with little or no facilities for transit aircraft, particularly as none were expected. A sergeant on a bicycle marshalled the aircraft to a dispersal point and told us to shut down the engines. Having no transport other than his bicycle, he led us to a tent nearby where he told us we could spend the night. He was able to provide mattress covers and blankets, and said that straw was available in a heap outside the tent that could be stuffed into the mattress covers to make a bed. It was a pitch-black night and there was no light to see what we were filling our mattresses with. At the time it was thought that the straw had a strange strong smell, but having been on duty for over twenty hours, all were too tired to bother and immediately fell asleep. The next morning we discovered that we had filled our mattresses from a manure heap close to a tethered donkey instead of clean straw from another heap nearby. This caused great amusement to the Sergeant when he came to collect us in a transport, but we were in no mood to appreciate the humour of it! Collecting our belongings and equipment, we were taken to the Sergeants Mess where we were able to clean up and have breakfast, the first meal since leaving Gibraltar. After this we were driven to the Operations office where instructions were given how to reach LG224, apparently only a short distance away. Needless to say, on arrival Johnny and Bob got a rocket for landing at the wrong airfield!

Having safely delivered the aircraft, the crew were taken to an Aircrew Transit Camp at 22 PTC Almaza and allocated a tent where we would be sleeping. Instructions were given how to find the Sergeants Mess, Station HQ and other station facilities. The living conditions were extremely harsh and to some extent quite primitive, although not nearly as bad as those the army had to endure! The lavatory facility was simply a large hole in the ground with many lavatory seats mounted above it, totally lacking privacy. It was not unusual to find people sitting together playing cards or a game of Draughts. Although it was the cool season of the Middle East, the daytime temperature got up towards 80 degrees and heated the tented accommodation up to a quite uncomfortable level. However once the sun had set, the temperature dropped very rapidly to a surprisingly low level.

Despite feeling very tired, the first thought was to get back to UK and civilisation as quickly as possible for either another ferry flight, or a posting to Bomber Command. On enquiring at HQ as to how we were going to get back to UK, we learned that the Transit Camp was completely full of aircrew in much the same situation as ourselves. The penny now dropped why there were no crews at Moreton in Marsh on their second ferry flight, and why we had been given desert uniforms. Each day there was an informal parade at which the very large number of crews would be asked to volunteer to do air tests, short ferry flights or other aircrew related duties. Crews could be posted to join Middle East bomber squadrons, but as the loss rate was low, or so we were told, this did not happen very frequently. Once the morning parade was over, everyone was free to do anything including visits to Cairo, transport permitting. Fortunately there were many lorries going to and from Cairo whose drivers would allow crews to ride with them. In our short stay we visited Cairo, Heliopolis, the Pyramids and several other places of interest. After the rationing in UK it was strange to go to a café and see eggs and chips on the menu. In a normal order of eggs and chips there would be six eggs, that may sound a lot, but three of those eggs would only be the equivalent of one egg at home.

We discussed the situation and it was mutually agreed that we did not join the RAF to get dumped in a pool of flying crew and decided to get out as soon as possible. When volunteers were required to ferry a Wellington to India, we opted to do it. There was no real competition amongst crews to take on voluntary tasks, most taking the 'old sweats' attitude of not volunteering for anything. Some thought us quite mad to be volunteering to go to India, that was even further away from home. Regardless of that, we thought it would be a change to get away from the nauseating combination of tents, sand, and flies. Anyone who served in the Middle East would doubtless agree that flies are one of the worst pests that have to be endured, particularly at meal times when a plate of food would be covered with the wretched things before one could start eating!

After being briefed on the route to be taken to India, five days after our arrival we were shown to the aircraft, HX 769 'F' Freddie, and carried out the pre-flight checks before departure. The Wellington was a bomber, but ironically was destined for a Coastal Squadron located in Southern India. It was the most clapped out aircraft that I had flown in up to that date, but little did I know that I would fly others in much worse condition in India. In the three days it took to reach Karachi Civil Airport, we flew over the almost featureless desert and over the River Jordan for the first night stop at Habbaniya in Iraq. Before leaving Cairo, we had been warned that the tribesmen at Habbaniya were hostile to the British and liked to take pot shots at aircraft landing and taking off. We did not see any tribesmen and if any did shoot at us, they must have missed because no bullet holes were found.

The second sector flown was with absolutely clear skies to Sharjah, flying over Bahrain en route. Having been to Sharjah many times since the war, an airfield with a magnificent terminal and long runway, it is interesting to note that there was no runway then, the landing being made on hard packed sand with the landing run centre line marked with an oil slick. Scheduled to stay overnight, the crew slept in the Fort using rooms normally used by BOAC passengers on overnight stops. Not palatial accommodation by any standard, but certainly better than a tent! The Wellington was parked on the sand outside the Fort guarded by two Indian soldiers.

Finally, on 13th December, again with clear skies, we continued on to Karachi Civil airport that was easily identified by the huge airship hangar that was built to house the R101 on its ill-fated journey to India in the 1930s. In the three sectors flown to reach Karachi many faults had accumulated on the aircraft and it needed urgent attention. In order to get the servicing done, we were ordered to ferry the aircraft to the nearby RAF Station Karachi Drigh Road where RAF servicing facilities were available, returning by road to the Civil Airport. There was sleeping accommodation available at Karachi airport where one of the large passenger lounges at the Civil Airport had been converted into a dormitory for the use of transit crews. Unfortunately that was fully occupied and we once again drew the short straw, finishing up in a tent. The washing, catering and toilet facilities were totally inadequate but just had to be accepted. We could only be thankful that it was winter in Karachi with the seasonal weather keeping the temperature within reasonable limits.

It took 12 days to get the aircraft serviceable and the crew was ordered to ferry it back to Karachi Civil Airport on Christmas Eve 1942. Christmas day was quite depressing as we were so far away from home and hardly knew a soul there. No Christmas celebrations took place and the day passed like any other.

On Boxing Day the aircraft departed Karachi for Santa Cruz airport in Bombay, flying over the vast and desolate Gulf of Kutch. Two days were spent at Santa Cruz before continuing the delivery flight to Tanjore. In the cool of the morning, we took off from Santa Cruz but had only reached Poona when engine trouble forced us to return. Johnny considered it necessary to land at the first aerodrome available, which was Juhu. With no spares readily available, it was to be early February before the aircraft became serviceable. Quite a deplorable situation really but in fairness to those in charge, it must have been extremely difficult to get aircraft spares at short notice with the war in Europe taking priority. I must say that the few senior officers I saw all seemed very relaxed and there seemed to be no real sense of urgency to get things done. The war seemed far away, but in reality, on the other side of the country, in Burma the Japanese were having things very much their own way.

Initially our accommodation in Bombay was the Hotel Delamar

located at the intersection of Marine Drive and Churchgate Street, very close to the central shopping area of Bombay. It was quite an ordinary hotel but at least it was clean and comfortable, unlike tented accommodation. Johnny signed the bills for our accommodation, which were then sent to the RAF Accounts section. Unfortunately, some days later the powers that be decided that we had to move to accommodation at Kooka Court in Worli that was not quite so pleasant. The RAF accounts office paid pay and allowances and there were no parades or duties, most of the time being spent at Breach Kandy swimming pool. It was pleasant to relax, sunning ourselves at the pool in the glorious Indian winter weather of almost cloudless skies and daytime temperatures about 80 degrees. There were other crews who had become stranded with their aircraft in similar fashion to us and the custom was to meet daily at the pool to exchange news. After a time, the inactivity became monotonously boring and we longed to get airborne again.

One day I had the good fortune to meet an English family named Crossley who invited me to be their guest for dinner that evening. This made a very pleasant change from the normal boring routine and over the weeks that followed, I got to know them well and was frequently their guest. Through them I met Mr Jarman who also worked in Bombay and he drove around Bombay showing me many places of interest including Hindu and Parsee temples, which I found to be very interesting.

The Crossleys and the Jarmans had lived in India for many years, Mr Crossley being the area manager for Singer Sewing Machines. He was close to retirement age but there was little chance of he and his family being able to get a passage home until the war ended. His wife was considerably younger and they had a son of about six or seven. They were perhaps more homesick for England than I was, having missed their home leave due to the war. I telephoned them each time I went through Bombay and did write from time to time but inevitably, contact was lost.

Eventually the aircraft became serviceable and when we had air tested it, we were told that its destination had been changed and were ordered to fly it to Allahabad. For some inexplicable reason, this involved returning to Karachi for two days before proceeding to Allahabad. On arrival back at Karachi Airport we found the tarmac quite congested with many types of RAF aircraft all waiting to be ferried. Fortunately, this time there was room for us in the large dormitory for the two days we had to stay there. We were quite relieved because the thought of going back into a tent after the comfort of Bombay was not very appealing. Even though the aircraft had been perfectly serviceable when we landed, we were ordered to do yet another test flight prior to leaving for Allahabad.

On 12th February we departed for Allahabad and flew 6 hours 30 minutes in absolutely perfect flying conditions without incident to our destination. Apart from heat haze, the weather was clear but there was turbulence due to hot air rising from the sun-baked ground that was light brown in colour and almost featureless. Immediately on arrival at Allahabad we were told that we had been posted to 36 Squadron at Tanjore near Trichinopoly, which we knew to be a Coastal Squadron. The squadron had been based in Singapore flying Wapiti aircraft and was wiped out by the Japanese in the battle for Singapore. Despite protests that we were a bomber crew, the orders remained unchanged and to our dismay, we were issued with travel warrants and told to proceed immediately by train across the hottest part of India to Tanjore in Southern India. We stayed in Allahabad long enough to see some local places of interest and did a boat trip on the River Ganges. The Rivers Ganges and Jumna join at Allahabad at what is considered to be a holy place with people travelling for many miles just to bathe in the waters. With sewage flowing into the rivers, they are not particularly clean and it was quite nauseating to see Indians drinking from the rivers!

The journey to Southern India did not start well as a very comfortable reserved carriage that we thought was ours, was in fact reserved for a small group of officers. Despite protest from Johnny, we were evicted and put in a less comfortable compartment and told that it was reserved from Itarsi by others and that we would have to get off there. It was an express train from Allahabad to Itarsi and we hoped that we would be able to get on another express from there to Madras. Alas, this was not to be and after 24 hours in Itarsi, we boarded another train for Nagpur located on the Central Plains where we would again change trains. On reaching Nagpur, to our horror we found that we were completely stranded because no one had bothered to arrange transportation on to Madras and Tanjore. An army RTO said that he knew nothing about us and added that we were not his responsibility. Express trains did run from Nagpur to Madras where we would change trains for Tanjore but there was never space available on them, or so we were told. The RTO's advice was to requisition a third class compartment on the first local train going south towards Madras and keep going. We had no authorisation to do this, our only documentation being travel warrants and the posting notice to 36 Squadron given to us at Allahabad. Realising that all the grumbling in the world was not going to help, we decided to get going without further delay. When the next local train came in, we requisitioned a third class compartment large enough to let us stretch out sufficiently to sleep, and went on our way.

In all it took eight days to reach Tanjore and in hindsight, was an experience none of us would like to have missed. I remember stops at Wardi, Kezpati, Bezwada and many other places whose names I cannot recall, before finally arriving at Madras. At some of the stops there was no platform and passengers had to descend to ground level from the train on flimsy wooden steps provided by station staff. There were no fences around the stations at the remote locations and the railway line sometimes went through the centre of the villages. Children played dangerously close to the railway lines but they immediately cleared away from the line if a train approached. A lot of the journey was on a single rail track and sometimes it became necessary to wait at stations where a dual track was available to allow trains travelling in the opposite direction to pass or non-stop expresses to overtake.

At each stop we had to lock the door to prevent Indian travellers invading the compartment, and throughout the journeys, there were many that rode on the outside of the carriages clinging on for dear life. The toilet facilities were primitive to say the least, (a hole in the floor!) but at least there was water available for washing provided that the tank was topped up at each stop. This water was not suitable for drinking and we had to quench our thirst at the many stopping places en route. On reflection, although it was uncomfortable, we saw more of India than many present day tourists would, and some of the scenery en route was quite splendid.

I believe that the train stopped at every station en route, staying long enough at some to enable the driver, fireman and guard to have a meal. Also travelling on the train were two Indian Army Subalterns who were experiencing the same conditions on the journey as us. Being Indians, they were able to select food from the station vendors suitable for their needs. The Crossleys had warned me against eating anything that could not be identified, or was not protected from flies, and this ruled out most things. We existed on oranges that were cheap and plentiful, and drank water. Care had to taken where drinking water was obtained but fortunately none of us suffered from drinking what we were able to get.

After a couple of days on the fruit diet, we became very hungry and could not face the prospect of going without proper food for much longer. We asked the Indian Subalterns if there was any way we could get some cooked food that was safe for us to eat. They were very co-operative and conveyed to the guard that we were very hungry and would like to buy some hot food. Between them they organised a curried meal at the next lunch stop in the central plains, but for the life of me, I cannot remember where it was, or how it was organised!

We were taken into a small village where we were given a wonderful curry meal, mutton or goat I think, by an Indian family who lived in what seemed to be a mud hut. They had covered their table with clean white cloth and had boiled oddments of cutlery to ensure that it was clean before we used it. We were treated royally with what seemed to be the whole village trying to peer into the hut to watch us eat. They wanted no money in payment and when we left to get back on the train, (we were assured earlier that it would not leave without us); many people waved to us until the train was out of sight. We did, of course, leave some money for them. It was a pleasant experience but it was also to be the only proper meal we had until we arrived in Madras. The Indian Army Officers left the train at one of the stops during the next day and we then had to stay on our oranges and water diet for the remainder of the journey.

Eventually we got to Madras and stayed at a Salvation Army Hostel until we were able to continue our journey to Tanjore. In Madras we met a Missionary, Deaconess Collett, who showed us around the area. It was a welcome break from travelling but after a good night's sleep we continued our journey to Tanjore where on arrival, a transport arrived to take us to RAF Station Tanjore. The welcome to the squadron was somewhat subdued when it was learned that we were yet another bomber crew and nobody really wanted to know us. I believe that Wing Commander Mellor was the Commanding Officer, but learned some years later that on 22 October 1942 (my birthday), F/Lt Ted Hawkins DFC took temporary charge of the squadron when it was being reformed after having been wiped out in Singapore by the Japanese. I had no idea then that Ted Hawkins would become a Wing Commander and Command 230 Squadron (Sunderlands) that I would later join. He retired as an Air Vice Marshall with CB, CBE, and DFC and I had the pleasure of meeting him in the 1980s at a 230 Squadron re-union. It really is quite a small world isn't it?

Chapter 5

36 Squadron

Tanjore airfield had a laterite runway and was located in a very rocky and dusty area with very little vegetation to be seen. I was told that when F/Lt Ted Hawkins DFC took over the squadron, the only accommodation available for anybody regardless of rank was a tent with a charpoy bed, but with the apparent luxury of having sheets and pillows and somewhere to get food! We arrived to find that we were to be accommodated at Vellum where more suitable accommodation was provided in the form of 'Bashas' that were wooden framed huts roofed and sided with palm leaves. The bed provided was a Charpoy that had a frame made of hard wood with rope interlaced from side to side on which a thin mattress was placed. The Medical Officer told us that the ropes were a breeding place for fleas, but provided that immediate and suitable action was taken, they could be eliminated. We soon learned that it was essential to stand the legs of the Charpoy in tins filled with paraffin in order to stop ants and other crawling insects invading the bed. The Malaria carrying mosquito plagued most of India and it was compulsory to sleep inside a mosquito net securely tucked under the mattress and to take anti malaria pills. Also, due to the high temperatures it was recommended that salt tablets were taken daily and as a reminder of this, dishes of these were put on the dining tables. Southern India does not enjoy a winter climate, except at the hill stations, and the weather remains hot throughout the year with extremely high humidity and heavy rain in the monsoon season.

The Sergeants Mess was a decent sized Basha that was reasonably furnished with a few comfortable armchairs. The food provided, cooked by RAF cooks and served by Indian waiters, was typically English and initially was quite enjoyable. However, I soon discovered that the diet was quite restricted with frequent servings of tinned Soya sausages and with very few fresh green vegetables available. Salads and other cold foods were not usually served as they could cause attacks of sickness and severe diarrhoea. The Officers Mess was a Colonial style building away from the airfield and was probably commandeered soon after the airfield was built.

One advantage of being in India was that with labour being so cheap, even the lowest paid airman could afford to have a 'bearer' (servant).

The bearer would clean the quarters, do the dhobi (laundry), clean footwear and do any other jobs required. He would provide, (at our own expense), early morning tea which he got from the 'Char Wallah' who was always around. The tea he provided was strong and stewed but was most welcome with the water supplies being rather unreliable. The bearer would probably work for several airmen, perhaps, two NCOs or one officer. They were allowed to sleep close to the living quarters in order to be always available whenever required. Bob and I shared a bearer, a young lad of about 15, who was very efficient in his work. He was a Christian having been converted by a local Roman Catholic priest, and he never ceased telling people of his new faith. When we left for North India later on, he made his way alone to reach our new RAF Station so that he could continue to work for us. Unfortunately he fell seriously ill with tuberculosis and at the Station Medical Officer's insistence, we had to pay his railway fare and send him back to Vellum. The MO told us that his condition made it unlikely that he would live very long.

In the month after our arrival at Tanjore we did no flying whatsoever and there were no duties for us to perform – it seemed a strange way of running a war! The crew managed to travel together around the area quite a lot, visiting the famous temples of Tanjore and Vellum. In Tanjore there was an arch over the main road called 'Coronation Arch' but I have no idea which coronation it was.

The Group HQ was in the Nilgiri Hills at Bangalore where in 1944 on my second posting to India I would be interviewed by a commissioning board. It came as no surprise to me when my application for a commission was deferred at that first interview, the saluting indiscretion at Cambridge going against me. However, I was told that I could re-apply six months later.

The town of Ootacommund nestling in the Nilgiri Hills was quite English in appearance and it was there that I met Cynthia, a very lovely young lady known as 'The Ooty Beauty'. She had a great number of men vying with each other to date her, but those who were successful complained that she always had her young sister Patricia with her. Coincidently, after the war Patricia married a BOAC colleague of mine, and they lived close to me in Southampton.

The squadron, which was wiped out by the Japanese in Singapore, was originally equipped with Wapiti aircraft that, I believe, carried a torpedo. However, the only time I saw a torpedo was when the navy brought one along to show the crews what it looked like and give instruction and information on its use. About a month after our arrival in Tanjore, the squadron was ordered to relocate to Dhubalia, an airfield in Bengal, north of Calcutta. Needless to say, most of the bomber crews went by rail, but I was one of the exceptions, flying with a Flight Commander, Squadron Leader Sloan. After take-off from Tanjore we flew around the many temples in the area and I managed to take a decent photograph of them. We transited Vizagapatam and Cuttack en route to check out what Wellington aircraft facilities were available at those airfields. The further north we flew the greener the countryside became and as we approached Dhubalia I could see that there was a fairly large river close by but did not discover its name. In the monsoon months it burst its banks to the discomfort of all who lived close by, including all living at the airfield!

The squadron quickly established itself at Dhubalia but was so overstaffed with crews that there were probably more than two crews for each aircraft. Given this and the constant problems that plagued the Pegasus XVIII engines, crews were not detailed to fly very frequently. When we did fly operationally, the operational brief was to patrol the Burma coast looking to attack any target that appeared worthwhile. Someone at Group HQ with a sense of humour, coded the operational routes FIRPO with a colour suffix such as red, scarlet, blue etc. Firpo was the name of a very nice and fashionable restaurant in Calcutta that served the most delicious ice cream.

Usually operations were carried out from Argatala, an advanced base on the border of India, it being the most suitable airfield for operations along the Burma Coast. Aircraft were flown from Dhubalia to Argatala fully bombed up, crews staying overnight before departing in the cool of the early morning. Depending on the mission, bombs or depth charges could be carried, the bombs having delayed action fuses fitted since all targets would usually be attacked at low level. The targets could be submarines, coastal shipping or land targets, whatever the pilot thought worthwhile. There seemed to be some trouble with the delayed action bomb fuses and I can remember that one crew landed at Argatala and were walking away from the aircraft when it blew up, fortunately without injuring anyone. It was generally thought that the delayed action bombs were the cause but it was never confirmed and the practice of carrying a full bomb load on the ferry flights to Argatala continued.

One morning as the crew I had been rostered to fly with was about to depart from Argatala on an operational coastal patrol, several USAF Mitchell bombers came in to refuel. As their target was more or less on our 'Firpo' track, my pilot for that operational flight, Sergeant 'Butch' Burnett, decided to delay so that we did not arrive in their target area with Japanese fighters around. The USAF crews thought that we were very timid until we told them that we were a single aircraft and only had four .303 guns in two turrets for defence. They saw the point and agreed that it was prudent to delay our departure! Argatala was quite close to Japanese airfields and often experienced hit and run bombing and strafing raids, although I was never there when it was attacked.

With the mix of bomber and coastal crews on the squadron, I think someone said that if bombs were dropped, it counted as a bomber mission, but if Depth Charges were dropped, the hours counted towards a Coastal tour. I may be wrong about that, but given the number of crews and the shortage of serviceable aircraft, it seemed most unlikely that anyone would *ever* finish an operational tour! The aircraft were in poor condition and some only just air-worthy. My original crew ferried a Mark VIII "Stickleback" Wellington back to the squadron from Assansole and found that it would not cruise at an indicated airspeed greater than 99 mph. I seem to remember, (rightly or wrongly), that the airspeed indicator was not calibrated in knots. On another occasion, the fabric around the fuselage had not been doped properly and started to peel off in flight. It was not funny having fabric streaming behind the tail with daylight showing through the geodetic fuselage, but we survived.

On a delivery/collection flight to Assansole with Johnny and Bob, we had to stay overnight, as the aircraft to be flown back was not ready. The monthly beer ration had arrived and a party was scheduled for that evening in the Sergeants Mess. I cannot remember what the beer ration was, but I think it was about six bottles a month, providing that the ship carrying it had not been sunk on its way to India. Beer was not produced in India and what did arrive, came from Australia. I was not a beer drinker; in fact, I hardly drank at all. Johnny was a non-drinker and non-smoker, but Bob had a liking for both. The beer soon ran out but the party continued with Indian produced Lighthouse Gin, a particularly potent and vile concoction that was the only alcoholic drink available. Someone must have spiked my drink because my recollection of that night was very hazy. Apparently, between the mess and the sleeping quarters were slit trenches and, according to Johnny who was trying to get us to our beds, one of us fell into a slit trench! By the time Johnny got him out, the other had fallen in! Eventually, Johnny got me back to my bed and then went back for Bob. The morning dawned and I could hear the birds singing and I was at peace with the world – well that is until I sat up and my head almost exploded! Bob and I felt very fragile and it was a sorry pair who later that day flew the aircraft back to Dhubalia. I vowed that I would never drink again and do not think that I did until I was on the ship going back to England.

The Pegasus XVIII engines were totally unsuitable for tropical flying and there were constant problems with sticking exhaust valves that caused them to backfire and lose power. I well remember one operational flight when we were down to about 100 feet with power loss on both engines, expecting to ditch at any time. We ditched our bomb load and headed for Coxes Bazaar only to be told that they were under attack by Japanese Zeros who were strafing and bombing the airfield. In the distance we could see the Zeros quite plainly but they either did not see us or if they did, were out of ammunition and left us alone. We managed to reach Chittagong with both engines sounding awful where a safe landing was made. When we took off next day for Dhubalia in the cool morning air and with the engines at normal temperature, they sounded normal and behaved perfectly. I personally enjoyed the night spent in Chittagong, as I was able to attend a classical music concert given on gramophone records by a group of airmen who were professional musicians. It seemed quite strange to have such an event at a place as remote as Chittagong.

Life on the squadron was reasonably comfortable apart from the heat, ever-increasing humidity, flies and mosquitoes, but the worst thing was the lack of flying that was terribly frustrating for all aircrew. The sleeping quarters were the usual 'Bashas' but were of a decent size with room for comfortable chairs and space for hanging clothes. Naturally everybody had bearers to take care of their cleaning and polishing requirements.

There were many snakes around and I did see a very large cobra close to the sleeping quarters. I had been previously advised to keep perfectly still if I found myself close to a snake. This I did and it soon glided away into the undergrowth. Another day, but some distance away from the living accommodation, I saw a fairly large python that had swallowed a small animal, the shape of which could be clearly seen inside it. In such a condition it would have been very easy to kill it, but pythons are not really dangerous to humans and were best left alone. The experts told us that snakes probably had the same amount of fear for humans as we did for them, but I am not entirely convinced of that. Certainly one got used to seeing them around and it was normal practice in the morning to bang one's shoes on the ground before putting them on as some small snakes seemed to like sleeping in shoes. One night while I was reading in bed, I saw a snake on the roof rafters above my mosquito net and to my horror it dropped onto the net and then to the floor where it then slithered away out of the Basha. I certainly had no intention of attempting to kill it!

There was an occasion when a tiger was reported to be in our area and it had killed a local villager. An Englishman, who apparently used to hunt tigers, was called in to shoot it. His view was that it was almost certainly a very old animal that was too slow to catch its natural food. The tiger was probably stalking cattle when disturbed by the villager, thus provoking the attack. We were told that even though old, it was still quite dangerous and should always be vigilant. Aircrew carried Smith and Wesson .38 revolvers, but the hunter said that even if we were lucky enough to hit it, the chances of killing it with a .38 were very slim and if wounded, it could become enraged and almost certainly attack with possible fatal results. Most other ranks carried rifles in the trucks ready for use in the event of an attack, but again, it was most unlikely that a .303 rifle bullet would stop a charging tiger unless it was hit in a vital spot. The CO had given his permission for ground staff to carry rifles, but soon rescinded that when he heard bullets whistling around his quarters as people blazed away indiscriminately. I thought I saw the tiger cross the road in front of the lorry in which I was riding on my way back from the aircraft one evening. Airmen in the back of the open lorry immediately opened fire into the bush without having anything to aim at, and certainly without success. I must say that it is no fun having someone firing away only inches above your head! The Englishman set up a hide and spent several nights in it without seeing anything and the scare died down.

The area around the airfield was not heavily populated, having only small villages set in clearings amidst dense jungle like vegetation. Someone told me that the population of India then was nearly five hundred million people, mostly living in villages. Sixty years on, that population has 'exploded' to almost a billion.

Entertainment was whatever one cared to make for oneself. I think that there was a station cinema but cannot be too certain about that. My evenings usually were taken up with playing Bridge whilst some preferred poker or other gambling games despite gambling being prohibited. There was little to drink in the mess other than locally produced spirits that had almost lethal after effects and, as I knew to my cost, were to be avoided. If and when the monthly beer ration arrived, it was usually drunk the same evening. With the onset of the monsoon season, enormous thunderstorms built up in the late afternoon and the electrical storms gave the most magnificent displays.

Crews were allowed to go into Calcutta but the hotels in my price range were not very good and I was so sickened by the abject poverty that I soon stopped going. It was terrible to see starving people living on the pavements of the streets. Quite often people died where they lay after suffering from all sorts of diseases and afflictions. Perhaps the only pleasure of Calcutta was to visit Firpos restaurant on Chowringee for tea, pastries and a dish of their delicious ice cream. We were told that Firpos ice cream was about the only safe ice cream that was available in India. I would see much more of Calcutta in the post war years when flying for BOAC, but discovered that it had not improved very much from the time of my first visit.

Being bomber trained, I did very few flights, and rarely with my own crew. In fact, during the three months at Dhubalia, I only had 14 flights, and some had less than that. On the 1st June 1943 I did my last flights with 36 Squadron, flying to Jessore and returning on the same day. Shortly after that, the squadron was ordered to relocate to North Africa to reinforce the Desert Air Force. This news delighted everyone, as it would get us a little closer to home. However, my hopes were quickly dashed when it was announced that bomber crew members, excluding rear gunners, would remain at Dhubalia. Ray Wilson became Sgt Saunders' rear gunner and went to North Africa with the squadron, he being the first to leave the crew formed at Harwell. I heard that he was commissioned in 1944 but have no idea if he survived the war as no one had any direct contact with him. Bob, fed up with the inactivity, volunteered to join 31 Squadron flying Dakotas over 'The Hump' in Burma and after a stint doing that, got back to UK early in 1944. We met again in May 1944 when I was on leave and remained in contact until after the war, but eventually lost touch. Les Blick was posted to 215 Liberator Squadron based at an airfield quite close to Dhubalia, but I was saddened to learn that he was killed in a flying training accident.

The day came when all the serviceable aircraft had been flown out and only bomber crews were left in a ghost airfield with abandoned unserviceable Wellingtons being the only aircraft remaining. The monsoon with its oppressive humidity started and very soon most of the area was under water, a feature of that part of India in the rainy season. Very quickly everything became damp and it was depressing to think that this would last for the two or three months of the rainy season. There were plenty of transport vehicles available and crews were given authorisation to use them around the airfield but not outside the perimeter. Often the roads were so flooded that it was impossible to see where the edge of the road was, making it unsafe to drive. With the floods came the snakes that could be seen swimming in the ditches. Many were venomous and were to be avoided, but happily I did not hear of anyone sustaining a fatal bite. Conditions were so wet and miserable that all were relieved when a signal came through posting the bomber crews to the Aircrew Transit Pool at Poona. All remaining flying crew, including Johnny and me, left Dhubalia on 20 June 1943 travelling from Calcutta by train for four days arriving in Poona on 25th June. That journey was not without incident when it was discovered that all the NCO crew members were to travel in third-class carriages with wooden seats and no acceptable toilet facilities. We refused to travel unless we were given second-class carriages and it delayed the departure for 24 hours until suitable carriages were found. The monsoon rains with its associated high humidity was affecting Poona, but generally was not as uncomfortable as Bengal.

Poona, situated in the Nilgiri hills, was a pleasant place with beautiful scenery in the dry season but with the monsoon season having started I did not see it at its best. There was, of course, the famous Poona Club, but as I was not an officer, that was not available for me. The Aircrew Transit Pool, where I was to spend nearly eight weeks, was a dreadful place which daily lowered morale. Every morning there was a routine parade but there seemed little chance of getting posted to an operational squadron in India. There were some very minor non-flying duties that were allocated to aircrew and one of my colleagues worked in the orderly room. This proved to be most fortuitous as a signal came through requiring that all Coastal Command crews be sent back to UK without delay. In theory this did not apply to the bomber crews from Dhubalia but our colleague in the orderly room was persuaded to change our records to designate us as Coastal Command crews. It obviously worked because quite rapidly we were all posted to Worli Transit Camp in Bombay to await transport back to UK.

Once again back in Bombay I was able to contact my friends the Crossleys and the Jarmans and frequently enjoyed the hospitality of both families. Although completely demoralised by my experiences of squadron life and India in general, at least it seemed that I would soon be back home with my wife. We wrote to each other very frequently and numbered each letter so that we knew if any were not delivered. Strangely enough only a very small number from her were not delivered but some took a very long time to reach me.

After waiting over a month for a ship, we were told that we would be embarked on the MV *Britannic* for the journey back to UK. The ship sailed from Bombay on 23rd September and I took a photograph that is now in my photograph album with the caption, 'The only view of Bombay worth seeing – that from the stern of a boat heading for England.' There is an Indian saying that if you visit India without visiting the Taj Mahal at Agra, you will surely return! I personally was destined to return many times in the future and even today have not visited Agra, although I have flown over it several times. Perhaps that counts as a visit!

The first part of the voyage was quiet and pleasant and on arrival in Aden on the 28th September 1943, in oppressive heat the ship anchored in the harbour at Aden. None of the transit passengers was allowed to disembark, but from what I could see of the colony from the ship, it looked a God forsaken place with a daytime temperature well over 100 degrees Fahrenheit. In later years with BOAC I would visit again and discover what a truly horrible place it is. After a short stay the journey continued through the Red Sea to then enter the Gulf of Suez and on to Port Tewfick at the Southern end of the Suez Canal, arriving on 3rd October. There was a good view of Mount Sinai as the ship went through the Gulf of Suez.

Aboard the MV *Britannic* the accommodation below deck was very cramped and extremely hot with little air circulating so we were looking forward to reaching Port Tewfick where we were told that we would disembark for a few days. Little did we know that would not be as pleasant as we envisaged! The ship duly reached Port Tewfick and on disembarkation NCOs and other ranks were sent to tented accommodation in a sandy area on the outskirts of the town. Life there was extremely primitive and the food and toilet facilities once again defied description. There was hot running water for washing but it had not been planned that way – it was hot because the cold water pipes ran above the ground for a very long distance exposed to the sun. The first persons to use the showers could almost be scalded. The only advantage of being ashore was that visits to the nearby town were permissible. The ship remained at Port Tewfick for nearly two weeks, presumably provisioning for the rest of the voyage and waiting for its turn to go through the canal. It was rumoured that there had to be a sufficient number of ships assembled to make up a convoy, but I have no idea if that is correct. Rumours constantly circulated throughout the entire voyage.

Once passengers were re-embarked, the ship went through the canal and had a brief anchor stop at Port Said before continuing the journey westwards in convoy. One could not help marvelling at the size of the Suez Canal knowing that when it was constructed, there was none of the equipment that is available today to help the engineers. Once in the Mediterranean Sea there were the usual anti-submarine tactics of frequent changes of course as the ship made its way westward toward Augusta in Sicily, a place I would frequently visit after the war when flying with BOAC. After the stop in Augusta the convoy continued to Algiers where it arrived on 25th October. There I managed to get ashore and look around the Arab Souk market places, but without any local currency, I could not buy any souvenirs.

The voyage from Bombay to Algiers had been pleasant and uneventful, however after leaving Algiers things became very hectic when a ship close to ours was torpedoed and sank. The *Britannic* made a very sharp turn that caused the ship take on a very pronounced list, which rumour said was caused by fuel oil and cargo shifting. It took well over a day to correct the problem.

Once through the Straits of Gibraltar submarine alerts were more frequent, but I did not hear of another ship being torpedoed. As the ship got closer to England, the weather became more unsettled and the transit of the Bay of Biscay was in fairly stormy conditions. I spent most of the time away from my accommodation in the bowels of the ship, preferring to be near the open decks against the possibility of the ship being torpedoed. I did spend a lot of time in the Radio Room chatting with the Radio Officer and sipping some of his Duty Free 'Scottish Water', the first alcoholic drink since my dreadful experience with Indian gin some months before. He was pleased to see the stormy weather, saying that it was more difficult for U-Boats to find and attack shipping in rough seas. The ship docked safely in Liverpool on 5th November, but my colleagues and I had to remain on board until 7th November. On disembarkation, RAF personnel issued travel warrants and gave instructions where to report after leave. After a year away from home I was about to be re-united with my wife.

In the year abroad, I had flown a total of 250 hours of which I had logged only 75 hours of operational flying. I considered this to be a pitiful contribution to the war effort, but through no fault of mine. Once back in England, Johnny and I went on leave to await our postings, hoping that it would be to Bomber Command. During the voyage we had agreed to apply to be posted to Bomber Command and request to be crewed together again. The application for Bomber Command was successful for Johnny who was posted almost immediately to a heavy conversion unit and then on to Lancasters. He survived the war, reaching F/Lt rank and winning a DFC. I was not so lucky, being first posted to Haverford West in December 1943 to join a Coastal Command Leigh Light Wellington squadron, but sent on leave when the CO found I was not Coastal trained. Next was a posting to Silloth, again with Coastal Command Wellingtons, where I hung about doing nothing until I was advised that I would not be sent to Bomber Command and again sent on leave. At the end of 14 days leave I was recalled to Silloth and told that I had been posted to a Beaufighter squadron, but pending posting instructions, was again sent home for a further 14 days leave. When I reported back to Silloth I thought that at last I would settle down on a squadron and do something useful, but this was not to be. I was told that the Beaufighter posting had been cancelled and that I would be given a firm posting within two or three days. My last and final posting late in February 1944 was to Number 4 Sunderland OTU where, being operationally qualified, I was welcomed. Since arriving back from India in November 1943, apart from travelling to Haverford West and Silloth, most of the time was spent on leave which, although very satisfying for me, did little for the war effort. Even today, I wonder how on earth we ever won the war!

Chapter 6

Sunderlands

I made the long train journey from Silloth to Alness and en route met WOP/AG Sergeant Bob Stagg who, like myself, had been shuffled from place to place looking for a permanent posting. We would crew up together and remain on the same crew until his tragic death by drowning in 1945. On reaching Perth, there was no connecting train and we had to find a place to stay the night, as there was no onward connection until the following morning. An uncomfortable night was spent in a rather seedy and run down bed and breakfast house close to the station that seemed to be the home of the local prostitutes. On the following morning we thankfully left Perth for Inverness where we changed trains and proceeded to Dingwall. We were met by RAF transport that took us on to RAF Station Alness located on the western side of Cromarty Firth and only a few miles from RAF Evanton where I did my gunnery course. Although it was the depth of winter I remember thinking what a very pleasant place it would be in warmer months.

I believe that in everybody's life there comes a point when looking back one can say that was when the future was determined. In my case I know that it was the posting to Sunderlands that ultimately put me on course for a long career in Civil Aviation.

I was once again fortunate to crew up with a fine bunch of fellows, most of whom I stayed with for the rest of the war. The Captain was an Australian instructor named Ross Bohm who was 'invited' to take over the crew when the notional Captain he was training failed the course. Ross was a Regular RAF officer and an excellent pilot who had done a good amount of operational flying. Unfortunately he had a rather brusque and somewhat aggressive manner, which did not endear him to the crew and made him a difficult person to get to know and understand. He was, perhaps unkindly, given the nickname of 'The Feuhrer' due to the manner in which he initially treated the crew, including those holding commissioned rank. Along the way, as his F/Lt rank suggested, he had fallen foul of someone senior and that had affected his promotion prospects. Later I learned that it was the Wing Commander commanding 230 Squadron that we were destined to join. As it was essential that there should be no clash of personality amongst a newly formed crew, we were consulted before he actually did take over. Some very frank words were exchanged before the crew agreed to accept him as our Captain.

Ross could not be faulted for his flying ability although once, when flying over the sea out of sight of land north of Aberdeen, without warning he declared an emergency and landed in the open sea. He let the aircraft drift and interrogated each of us as to what we would have done had it been a real emergency. Rather a dramatic way of assessing a crew's capabilities, but as everyone did precisely what was expected, it gave him confidence in the crew and we in him. The sea conditions were reasonable and he said that landing and taking off again was no different from doing it at base. I could not help thinking that at base there would be marine tenders to assist if we got into trouble, but out at sea there was nothing!

The rear gunner, George Hodgson, had done a part tour on Lancasters and was returning from a bombing mission over Germany when his aircraft got off track and flew into a hill killing everybody on board except him. He was found later with a severely injured back, still seated in the gun turret that had separated from the aircraft. Fortunately he recovered from his injuries and wishing to continue on flying duties, was posted to Sunderlands, which would not compel him to remain in his turret for the long periods of time that was necessary on a Lancaster. The rest of the crew, with the exception of the second Pilot, were new to flying and had no operational experience. Eventually the crew was made up of two pilots, a navigator, two wireless operator/air gunners, a wireless operator/mechanic/air gunner, two engineer/air gunners, and two air gunners. As the more experienced of the wireless operators I was nominated as the Number 1, which later proved to have its advantages. After some changes and/or substitutions, the final crew became F/Lt Bohm, F/O Holstein-Rathlou, F/O Madely, Sgts Holloway, Stagg, Bevan, Jarrett, Ambrose, Hodgeson and Barnard. Once we settled down as a crew there was little or no formality and all were known and addressed by their Christian names when together as a crew and away from other people. Not surprisingly, Ross Bohm as the aircraft commander insisted on being addressed as 'Skipper'.

F/O Holstein Rathlou had the nickname of 'Baron' and we were curious how he came to be called that. It seemed that he was the youngest son of a deceased Danish Count who had moved to Canada with his family when Hitler first came to power. I later learned that by moving to Canada the family virtually surrendered their Danish estate to the Nazis when they invaded Denmark. He had a brother named Rudolph and a sister whose name I did not know, but neither of these joined the Canadian Armed Forces. Baron's real names were Emil Frederick von

Holstein-Rathlou that quite clearly indicated why he was known as 'The Baron'! He was married to a French Canadian before joining the RCAF and had flown as a Civil Aviation pilot for Canadian Railways, the forerunner of Canadian Pacific Airways. When Baron joined the RCAF he had already logged a large number of Civil Aviation flying hours operating in the difficult and inhospitable area of the Canadian North West Territories where great skill and careful flying was needed. His flying experience was a great asset to the crew.

The OTU lasted three months during which there was ground instruction followed by ten flights of varying duration totalling about 45 hours in all. The ground instruction was first class and I enjoyed it immensely. It was not an intensely concentrated course and there was plenty of leisure time to explore the area and enjoy the beauty of that rather cold and snowy part of northern Scotland. My wife took her annual leave and joined me to spend a most enjoyable two weeks together, during which time she got to know the rest of the crew. We stayed as paying guests at the home of a widow who was pleased to have the income. The first night we spent together was hilarious because as we got into bed, it collapsed. A very anxious widow called to ask what had happened but we were laughing too much to give sensible reply! Once reassembled, the bed was found to be very comfortable and I enjoyed my wife's leave to the full. Our son was born nine months later so it became a memorable two weeks! Having been separated for nearly a year just after we were married, the large amount of leave I had between arriving back from India and going to Alness almost, (but not quite), compensated for the inconvenience of the time spent away in India.

As the end of the course approached, the crew eagerly awaited posting instructions to a squadron, hoping that it would be to Pembroke Dock or elsewhere in UK. I personally was quite shattered to learn that it would be overseas again, this time to Dar es Salaam in East Africa. This news was particularly hard to accept as my wife was expecting our first child. I did attempt to get out of the posting on compassionate grounds but was told that as childbirth was a natural occurrence, my request would not be considered.

When the posting was announced it became necessary to remove a Singhalese member of the crew who had been training with us right from initial crewing up. The powers that be obviously thought it unwise to have an Asian member of crew when we reached East Africa. This was not racial discrimination or a criticism of that person's ability as he was both very popular, and good at his job. Although sorry to be taken off the crew, he realised the problems that he was likely to encounter in Africa.

On 12 May 1944, the entire crew went on leave prior to reporting to 302 Ferry Training Unit Oban where we were to be trained on Ferry Command procedures. I had done a similar course at Moreton in Marsh nearly two years before, so I knew what to expect. We travelled by rail from Alness to Edinburgh, changing at Inverness and Perth and on arrival at Edinburgh, we were inoculated against about every possible sort of tropical disease and then dispersed to our leave destinations, albeit with very sore arms!

During that leave, my wife and I spent a few days in London where we met up with Bob Verguson from my Wellington days. Johnny Peck was to have joined us but due to operational requirements, did not make it. At the end of leave, I said goodbye to my wife little knowing that it would be nearly two years before we would see each other again.

I travelled through the night, arriving in Oban at 5.15 in the morning having met up with George Hodgeson for the latter part of the journey. Later that day, the crew were allocated Sunderland ML868 that was to be ferried out to 230 Squadron in East Africa. After the mandatory ground school was completed, ML868 was collected from Wigg Bay and over the next seven days, 20 hours was flown to check its performance prior to departure for Dar es Salaam.

Sergeant aircrew could be eligible for promotion to Flight Sergeant after one year in the rank, but promotion of wireless operator/air gunners was contingent upon being tested and re-graded as a Grade 1 WOP/AIR. Due to my travels around India, there had been no opportunity to take the re-grading test and I was almost a year overdue for promotion. Ross Bohm, to his credit, immediately made arrangements for my re-grading to be done in Oban on 1st June 1944. After successfully taking the required tests, I was re-graded and promoted immediately to Flight Sergeant, unfortunately without it being backdated to my year in the sergeant rank thus losing a year's seniority and back pay.

On 10th June 1944, without being given the opportunity of saying goodbye to our families, we took off from Oban in the sparkling new Mark III Sunderland ML868, and set off on a long twelve-hour flight to Gibraltar. This was not long after D-Day but as we flew through the night and were routed well clear of that area, no activity whatsoever was seen during the flight and we arrived at Gibraltar at 8.30 a.m. on Sunday 11th June. Three very pleasant days were spent in Gibraltar with only a short air test to perform in that period. The stop in Gibraltar gave plenty of time to look around the Rock and the town in delightful weather conditions, quite different from the previous visit in 1942. The view from the top of the Rock was quite breathtaking with clear sight of Spain and North Africa, and we met the apes that live on the Rock. A take-off was attempted on 13th June but problems were experienced with the starboard inner engine that caused a delay of 24 hours. The following day the aircraft got airborne at 6a.m. and we flew 13 hour 40 minutes to Bathurst in West Africa, arriving at last light.

An amusing incident occurred during the flight to Bathurst. The route taken kept the aircraft over the sea but always in sight of land, passing some countries we were not allowed to fly over. Because it was a day flight, only sun shots were possible making map reading desirable. Vic Madely gave the pilots the topographical charts for the route chosen and in error Ross and Baron selected a chart for an entirely different piece of coastline. They pored over the charts for nearly 40 minutes until Vic decided it was time to put a pinpoint against his air-plot. He called for a latitude and longitude from the pilots which when plotted, was a good distance away from where we really were. You can imagine the ribbing the pilots took when Vic said that they had been using the wrong chart, a fact that he was aware of when they started map reading. In fairness, we were some distance from the coastline and the odd thing about map reading is that when something on the ground looks like a feature on the map, it is very easy to accept, incorrectly, that they are the same. It is always best to start map reading at a known position and have continuity throughout the whole time map reading is being carried out.

A week was spent in Bathurst, an established RAF Flying Boat base, enjoying the sights at what was probably the last civilised place in Africa until our final destination was reached. The first night was very uncomfortable, the climate being very hot and sticky, something not experienced before by most of the crew. Little did we know then that it would become very much worse as we progressed further south towards the Equator.

On landing it was discovered that the port inner oil tank had split and six gallons of oil had been lost. The oil tank had to be replaced, together with a rocker box on the starboard outer engine. These faults took two days to be rectified and gave us ample opportunities in the leisure time to visit local places of interest and enjoy some very pleasant swimming at the beach.

The aircraft was fully serviced and air tested before continuing the journey to Abijan on 21st June, flying for 9 hours in reasonably good flying weather and arriving at 4.30p.m. for a two night stop-over. There was a pleasant restaurant in town where we enjoyed an excellent meal served with wine. Quite a luxury after the austerity of England!

The further south the journey progressed down the West African coast, the more uncomfortable it became with the ever-increasing humidity. It was easy to understand why that area of Africa is called 'The White Man's Grave.' The temperature varied very little by day or night and as it was the rainy season, the humidity was almost unbearable. The only relief came when we got airborne and got a good circulation of air through the aircraft. It was quite a short flight to Lagos Apapa, but on this sector a line squall was encountered which almost caused the aircraft to crash! It was penetrated at about 3000 feet and the most frightful turbulence and torrential rain was encountered. At one stage the aircraft was down to about 100 feet with both pilots struggling to maintain control. Afterwards, Ross Bohm said that he had never experienced anything like it before! I would encounter many similar line squalls in the Kano/Lagos area of Nigeria some years later when flying for BOAC.

At Lagos we stayed in an extremely comfortable guesthouse owned by Joe Harold who I was to meet many times later when staying in Lagos with BOAC. Victoria Beach at Apapa was superb for surfing and Ross in typical Australian fashion, showed us how it should be done. Bob Stagg was a non-swimmer and Baron gave him a great deal of instruction in an attempt to teach him how to survive if he found himself out of his depth in the water. Unfortunately Bob never mastered it.

The leisurely progress towards Dar es Salaam seemed most odd and inexplicable. At the time the crew wondered if Ross was unhappy about going back to a squadron, but he made no reference to it and obviously nobody felt like asking him. We did discover his misgivings when we arrived at the squadron some weeks later.

On 25th June, two days after the arrival in Lagos, the aircraft left on a 5 hour 20 minute flight to Libreville, located just north of the equator. On the following day the equator was crossed without any ceremony on a 4 hour 20 minute flight to Banane at the mouth of the Congo. The weather in that area was even more oppressive and uncomfortable and unfortunately there was no relief from this except when airborne. The very limited accommodation in Banane, a BOAC flying boat station, was a quite small hotel with very poor catering facilities. The whole crew went to a restaurant in town where we could at least get a decent meal. After the meal we walked around the area but saw nothing of great interest.

We had been carrying freight from Lagos destined for Banane and this was off-loaded on arrival, together with a civilian passenger who had also joined us in Lagos. It seemed at one stage as if it might be necessary for the aircraft to have a maintenance inspection before continuing, but much to our relief this was cancelled at the last minute.

With such a horrid climate, it was a pleasure to leave on a 4 hour 25 minute flight following the River Congo north-eastwards towards to the next port of call, Coquilhatville located almost on the equator. The stay there, as guests of BOAC, was very comfortably and the crew was well looked after by their staff. The war seemed an awfully long way off! On reflection, today one would have to pay a lot of money to do this trip, but that certainly was not in our thoughts at the time.

After what seemed to be the mandatory two days off, we were airborne again on a 3 hour 45 minute flight flying eastwards to Stanleyville where we emerged from the gloom of the worst side of Africa and entered a more civilised area. This was quite definitely one of the more pleasant stops and it was enjoyed to the full, staying in the Sabena Airlines hotel. A visit was made to the Stanley Falls named after Stanley, the American journalist who searched for, and found Dr Livingstone. The crew visited a Missionary House and the Belgian Nuns showed us around their small museum. Baron particularly enjoyed meeting the French Nuns as it gave him, a French Canadian, an opportunity to converse in French.

Unfortunately I ate something that disagreed with me and spent 24 hours in absolute misery. I was lucky to find a photographic shop that had film suitable for my camera and I bought its entire stock of 17 rolls of film. Prior to this I had experienced great difficulty in buying even a single roll of film at any place where we stopped. Two days later on 1st July we took off for a 4 hour 50 minute flight to Kisumu that we mistakenly thought would be our last stop before Dar es Salaam. The best laid schemes of mice and men!

Immediately on arrival at Kisumu, Ross was told that 230 Squadron had left Dar es Salaam and had relocated to its new base at Koggala Lake in Ceylon. This news was extremely depressing, as it now appeared that there was still a very long way to go before reaching the squadron. We had been in transit for such a long time that the novelty of visiting new places had worn off and all anyone wanted to do was to get to a fixed base and stop living out of suitcases! Strange to say, the squadron had moved to Ceylon long before we arrived at Kisumu and we could not understand why we had not been told of the move and, perhaps, routed more expeditiously to the new base.

Two weeks were spent in Kisumu, which was quite a reasonable place but seemed to be plagued with all sorts of flying insects. Its saving grace was that it was a fully equipped flying boat base with a slipway for getting flying boats out of the water. ML868 was beached and given a thorough servicing ready for the onward journey to join the squadron at its new base. During the stay when the flying boat was in the water, the crew did mandatory night boat guard duties, which were often disturbed by the most horrendous thunderstorms that could be imagined, a nasty feature of that part of Africa in the rainy season. At the last minute, the departure was delayed and the aircraft was ordered back to Stanleyville where some trouble had broken out. After an air test to check the aircraft's serviceability, we returned to Stanleyville to do what was necessary. Three days later we made our way back to Kisumu, hoping to move a little faster towards the squadron. This was not to be as there was yet another three days stop over before setting off for Ceylon.

Aside from the frustration that all were now feeling, the Kisumu stops did allow the crew to participate in some of the activities at the base. One sport was fishing from the flying boat, having been told that there were many different species of fish to be caught, some extremely large. Stan sharpened an ordinary wire nail, bent it into a hook, baited it with stale bread and threw it into the water. Despite the hook not having a barb, almost immediately he had a catch and hauled in a very large catfish followed quite rapidly by another, equally as large. The primus stoves were immediately lit and within minutes of the fish, having been cleaned and gutted, were sizzling away in the frying pan. It was the first fresh fish we had eaten since leaving UK and it seemed like a feast!

Both engineers normally went swimming from the flying boat until the day that they heard that a crocodile had taken an African from the slipway during the previous evening. They stopped that activity immediately! No crocodiles were seen from the flying boat and it may well be that the flying boat was moored too far away from the shore, but doubtless they were around. In fact, there was a great deal to be seen in the shape of game and wild life in the area. We did not see any hippos, but after the war when I went through Lake Victoria on BOAC flying boats, the take-off/landing area was always thoroughly checked by the marine tender to ensure that none were there. Hitting one of those on take-off or landing could have destroyed the flying boat.

Lake Victoria is about 5000 feet elevation and almost on the equator so although the days are hot, the nights can be pleasantly cool if there is a breeze. Spending a night on the Sunderland could be very comfortable unless swarms of the very nasty lake flies were active; in which case it was sheer hell! With the facilities available on board, it was often preferable to being ashore. Certainly the menu could be quite varied, cooking food on board as and when required.

Remarkably, in Kisumu I came across Bernard Pearce, the son of a shoe manufacturer who employed my father in law in Northampton where I lived. He was one of the team of engineers who worked on the aircraft. We obviously had much to talk about particularly as he knew my wife! The next time we met was after the war in Northampton.

The aircraft had been in transit since 10 June and it was 20 July before it departed Kisumu for Kasfareit located in the Suez Canal area. Some tremendous thunderstorms were encountered soon after leaving Kisumu, but the weather cleared as the flight progressed steadily northward to the next night-stop in Khartoum. It was then the height of summer with day temperatures reaching nearly 120 degrees in the shade, certainly not the nicest place to visit at any time! Two days later we continued to Luxor where again it was extremely hot, but with much lower humidity. That two-day stop over gave an opportunity of visiting the Valley of the Kings, an experience I am pleased that I did not miss.

We arrived at Kasfareit on 24th July, having flown 16 hours 20 minutes in three sectors and I was back in exactly the same area reached in 1942 when I had ferried the Wellington bomber to the Middle East. The Wellington ferry took nearly 26 hours flying time in three sectors, whereas in the Sunderland we had flown nearly 78 hours in 17 sectors. The observation from my diary reads that Kasfareit seemed a very nice place and had lots of amenities available to the crew. On the debit side, it seemed that the aircraft would be there for some considerable time!

I could not help wondering why on earth we had taken the circuitous route via Kasfareit instead of going more expeditiously via Dar es Salaam, Seychelles and The Maldives to Ceylon. There were probably good reasons for this, but they certainly were not obvious at the time. A month was spent at Kasfareit, part of which was having THREE engines changed. Although the Sunderland was fitted with the same Pegasus XVIII engines as the Wellington 1c, it did not suffer anything like the troubles I had experienced on 36 Squadron. Possibly the fact that we had our own engineers on board who, before each flight, packed graphite grease around the exhaust valve guides, accounted for this. Nevertheless, three engine changes in the flying time we had done seemed a bit over the top. Long after the war I read a book *Sun On My Wings* written by Wing Commander Dundas Bednall in which he stated that in his opinion, the Pegasus XVIII engines were totally unsuited for tropical flying. He apparently constantly asked those in charge to consider equipping 230 Squadron with the more efficient Mark V Sunderland that had Pratt and Whitney engines.

Kasfareit was a very busy base and most probably the aircraft had to wait its turn to get the necessary work done. Communication was extremely poor and very little information was given to the crew. I constantly wondered if we really were at war?

From a leisure point of view, Kasfareit was enjoyable as we were allowed frequent periods of absence from the base. This gave the opportunity of visits to Cairo, Alexandria and other places. I went to the

Pyramids at Giza and then on to Alexandria, which I found to be totally different from Cairo. I remember the latter visit vividly with pain and discomfort. With others, I had got a lift back on an open army lorry and fell asleep in the 100 degrees heat, getting so sunburned that my face blistered very badly. This was considered to be self-inflicted wound in the Middle East and I could have been in serious trouble if I had been needed for duty.

There were plenty of small cheap hotels in Cairo and some of us stayed at one that was in every sense, a 'flea pit'. Bob Stagg woke up in the morning to find himself covered in flea bites, some so severe that his eyes were almost closed by the swelling. Inspection of his mattress revealed that it was alive with fleas, as was mine. I must have been thick skinned then, as I did not get bitten. We *very* rapidly changed hotels!

Amongst the amenities at Kasfareit were some very pleasant swimming pools, a cinema and decent mess facilities. It certainly was one of the more organised and civilised places that had been visited, provided of course that one did not have much work to do. Several of the crew, myself included, hitchhiked with George to an army camp near Suez to meet his brother who he had not seen since the war began. That outing made us realise just how much better the RAF was treated than the army. The soldiers lived in tents, but no beds were provided and they used any flat pieces of wood they could find and propped them on stones. Then, wrapping themselves in a blanket, they lay down on the wood to sleep. Needless to say, they had no sheets or pillows. If wood could not be found, they slept on the sand. Not a pleasant thought considering the large number of crawling insects including poisonous scorpions that could be around. Apart from a breakfast of the dreaded tinned Soya Link sausages, the food was quite good considering how primitive everything else was. We stayed the night as the whole area was under a curfew and there was no means of getting back before the curfew started. As guests we were given the honour of sleeping on boards instead of the sand, but I had a very rough and uncomfortable night! The RAF types had no stamina!

Eventually the aircraft was considered serviceable and we air tested it on 25th August 1944, a flight that turned out to be a decidedly 'dicey' experience. During the air test the Air Speed Indicator malfunctioned causing the aircraft to almost stall. Only the superb flying skills of Ross and Baron saved us from a nasty accident.

Someone at the squadron must have discovered how long the aircraft had been in transit and ordered it to get to Ceylon without further delay. On the following day, we departed for Koggala, flying almost every day until base was reached. Stan Ambrose was compelled to stay behind because he had fallen ill with a mysterious fever that prevented him from flying. (He was not able to rejoin the crew in Koggala until early October.) En route stops were made at Habbaniya, Bahrain, Karachi (where BOAC handled us), and Bombay (Trombay Harbour), flying 29 hours 30 minutes in the period to 31st August, the day of our arrival at Koggala. In Bombay I managed to telephone Mrs Crossley who I had met in India in 1943, but there was insufficient time for me to pay them a visit.

It had taken an almost unbelievable 82 days and 120 hours flying hours to reach the squadron, where much to our surprise, Ross Bohm was relieved of his command of the aircraft, promoted to Squadron Leader and posted away from the squadron. I know that he survived the war but believe that he went missing on a private flight over or near Vietnam. During the transit period we had got to know Ross pretty well and despite our earlier misgivings, were sorry to see him leave.

Chapter 7

230 Squadron

Immediately after Ross Bohm departed from the squadron, Wing Commander Bednall asked the crew if we would accept Baron as our Captain. It was quite unusual for a second pilot to be made up as a Captain on the squadron, but with Baron's experience, clearly it was the best choice. Baron was an excellent pilot with a lively and likeable personality and it was unanimously agreed to have him as our Captain. Harry Ling became second pilot and when a third pilot was needed, one was assigned from the squadron's reserve of pilots.

We were delighted to learn that each crew had its own aircraft and we would keep ML868. Photographs of this particular aircraft have been printed in many aeronautical publications since the war and 'She' became quite a star. Having your own aircraft is much like owning a car in that it is a matter of pride to ensure that it is always clean and serviceable. Some crews painted the wardroom to give it a more homely appearance and in fact, Wing Commander Bednall had the exterior of his aircraft, 'P' Peter, painted dark grey. This was not for cosmetic reasons but because he considered that a dark grey aircraft would make it more difficult to be spotted by the enemy. Unfortunately that aircraft was lost on operations when being flown by Squadron Leader Ingham and his very experienced crew. Wing Commander Bednall had left the squadron before this loss occurred, having been replaced by Wing Commander Lionel Powell, a most pleasant man who I kept contact with after the war until his death.

Ceylon, now Sri Lanka is a very beautiful country that has mountain resorts with tea plantations, golden sandy beaches and a climate some think is better than India. It has its rainy (monsoon) seasons that can be most unpleasant, but these were certainly not as bad as Bombay and other places to the north. The base at Koggala was a large fresh water lake with adequate space for Flying Boats but it did require a steeper than normal final approach on landing which some pilots found difficult, and the full take-off run had a bend in it.

There was a landing strip mainly used by the Royal Navy aircraft that were flown off Aircraft Carriers prior to them entering harbour at the Naval base at Trincomalee on the east side of Ceylon. The navy used the strip for training and treated us to all sorts of aerobatics until on 7

November 1944, one of their Corsairs stalled and crashed into the sea whilst doing a very tight turn immediately after take-off. At that time there was a great deal of rivalry between Naval and Sunderland pilots, each attempting to show that their aircraft was the more manoeuvrable after take-off. Following that accident the Station Commander quickly put a stop to that type of flying.

The lake had more than its fair share of crocodiles and I can remember that in July 1945, a new Flight Commander, Squadron Leader Monson, fell into the lake whilst attempting to transfer from the launch to the aircraft while it was taxying on a training detail. Only his crocodile mutilated remains were ever found and he was buried with full military honours at Liveramentu Cemetery in Colombo. Even today his grave and those of others who lost their lives in Ceylon are well tended by the local authorities. Fred Coppard, a squadron ground engineer with whom I am still in touch, visited the grave in 1997 and took photographs, which he showed me.

Catalina aircraft of QANTAS Airways used Koggala for the very long distance non-stop flights to Perth in Western Australia. The Great Circle distance between Koggala and Perth is 3095 nautical miles and this track passes close to Cocas Keeling Island, which was not occupied by the Japanese but was, nevertheless, quite often bombed by Japanese aircraft. With this in mind doubtless the islands would have been avoided unless refuelling was necessary. I have an Australian friend who was working for QANTAS and he told me that the island was only used as an emergency fuel stop and on one occasion while his Catalina was being refuelled, the Japanese tried to sink the aircraft with bombs, albeit without success. Non stop flights to/from Koggala usually took about 30 hours in each direction and my friend told me that he did one of 36 hours which left them desperately short of fuel on arrival at the destination. At Koggala with calm or light wind conditions, at their very heavy take-off weight there were occasions when they could not get airborne at the first attempt and needed the tender to go across the lake at a fast speed to disturb the flat calm of the water. I believe one Catalina took off, had an engine failure en route before Critical Point and returned to Koggala, flying for about 24 hours without getting anywhere! Cocas Keeling Island did have a runway that was suitable for Liberator and Lancastrian aircraft, which QANTAS also operated.

I seem to remember that there was a Canadian Catalina Flying Boat squadron based at Koggala whose operations were classified and never discussed. I learned after the war had ended that they carried out long distance flights well inside Japanese held territory where they landed and dropped off people engaged on secret missions.

The crew soon settled down to squadron life and attended lectures on squadron operational procedures before operations could commence. The new CO, Wing Commander Powell, required that in addition to his own role on the aircraft, each member of the crew should be taught enough to enable him to take over another's in an emergency. I volunteered to do navigation and spent many hours being taught the wonders of compasses, astro, sextant, plotting etc. Whenever the opportunity arose I would navigate under the watchful eye of the navigator and this allowed me to 'shoot' some of the same stars that I had observed before I joined the service. This navigation experience helped me in Civil Aviation after the war.

Baron turned out to be a fine captain and always kept the crew well informed of everything that was going on. He required all members of the crew to be proficient in their job and would not tolerate sloppiness. He jokingly told us that the only decoration to which he aspired was the Victoria Cross but as this award was mostly posthumous, he would happily forgo the honour. Our feelings were much the same as his! He was very keen that we should learn to use our revolvers properly in case we were shot down and had to defend ourselves. He requisitioned extra .38 ammunition and we went to the beach for target practice. It was quite astonishing to discover how difficult it was to hit anything unless very close to what was being aimed at. I personally did not fancy our chances against the Japanese if we were shot down.

In leisure time it was permissible to swim from the beach at Koggala but due to heavy surf and a strong undercurrent, it was certainly not recommended to other than strong swimmers. Often we swam at Willigama where crews carried out live dinghy drills, but the best beach by far was located at Closenburg where the surf was sufficient to give those with surfing skills an opportunity to practice. More importantly, it was the safest place to swim.

As part of the crew's air/sea rescue training, we were flown to a point out of sight of land where the Sunderland taking us alighted on the sea and deplaned the crew into a dinghy. The aircraft then took off and flew out of sight, leaving us to carry out emergency signalling procedures to enable the Sunderland to home back to the dinghy using radio signals transmitted from the dinghy radio. The weather was really quite nice with very little swell, but the lack of wind did make it difficult to launch the kite carrying the aerial. After many attempts it was managed and the Sunderland came back to retrieve us from the dinghy. There was a marine tender close by should difficulties have arisen, but it remained out of sight, only coming to the site to collect the dinghy after the exercise. We had been briefed that we would only be picked up when the

Sunderland had homed back to the dinghy. Rather a dramatic exercise but one that gave us confidence against the possibility of having to do it in anger.

The nearby town of Galle, built inside the walls of a fort, had shops, restaurants and quite a decent hotel, which in the early days of RAF Koggala was used as the Officers Mess. There was a reasonable cricket pitch and often matches were played between different groups from the base. Colombo was a good 70 mile drive and normally only visited when on leave or 48 hour breaks. The round trip could be done in a day but the only road was very narrow and winding, passing through many villages congested with pedestrians and rickshaws, making the journey tediously long. Colombo was a very pleasant place with cinemas and many places of interest including an Aircrew Club where NCOs could stay whilst on leave, its greatest asset being that a decent English meal could be obtained there.

When not required for flying duties, the day started very early with a visit to the aircraft to carry out the daily inspection and ensure that it was fully serviceable for operation at short notice. With the high temperature and unpleasant level of humidity that was always present, aircrew duties usually finished by about 1p.m. allowing a period of relaxation at the hottest time of the day. That could be in our quarters for an afternoon siesta, or at the beach. As normal in the tropics, it was a punishable offence to become unfit for duty due to sunburn but we soon became acclimatised and this never became a problem. It was compulsory to take anti-malaria pills and salt tablets were recommended.

In the early part of the war with the Japanese, there was a real threat of an invasion of Ceylon by the Japanese and many engagements took place between the enemy and Royal Navy ships, Naval aircraft, and aircraft of Coastal Command. By the time I operated on the squadron, aircraft were mainly looking for submarines in the Indian Ocean and the Bay of Bengal. This was a very boring job, but nevertheless a very necessary task that had to be done efficiently. My crew never saw a submarine and I have no idea if any other crews did during my time on the squadron. The long flights gave me plenty of opportunity for practical navigation under supervision and I derived a great deal of satisfaction to see the success of my efforts.

As stated earlier, the squadron had the misfortune to lose Sunderland 'P' Peter without trace. Several Sunderlands, including ours, searched the area for three days but no trace was ever found. This loss was a complete mystery and naturally there was speculation as to what might have happened. This was narrowed down to either being forced down by a cyclone that was known to be in their area of patrol, or (very unlikely), shot down by a submarine. Sadly the truth will never be known.

Some squadron pilots, notably Ted Garside, Gerry Toller and Syd Lane, were all captains and destined to join BOAC after the war when I would fly with them. Ted Garside was awarded a DFC for operations flown from a lake inside Burma. The squadron had one all Australian crew whilst other crews had individual Australian, Canadian or New Zealand crew members. Baron of course was a Canadian.

Routinely we flew anti-submarine patrols of up to 13 hours, combining these patrols with supply trips to Addu Attol in the Maldives, and Diego Garcia that today is a USAF B52 Base in the Indian Ocean. Addu Attol and Diego Garcia were given numbers for security reasons so if we went to Addu Attol it was to number 28, or Diego Garcia number 29. I don't think for one moment that the Japanese would have been fooled, but it must have kept someone happy.

The Sunderland carried eight depth charges on bomb racks that could be winched out electrically or manually from the bomb room to the operating position under each wing when attacking a target. There was also plenty of space in the bomb room for extra depth charges or bombs to be carried that could be reloaded on to the bomb racks in flight if and when the first lot had been dropped. The depth charges and bombs carried weighed about 250 pounds and their weight and shape made them very difficult to handle, particularly if flying conditions were turbulent.

Addu Attol had some very nasty coral reefs and one Sunderland taking off tore a great hole in its hull. It managed to get airborne and reach Koggala and as it flew over the lake, the extensive damage could be quite clearly seen from the ground. The pilot, F/Lt Tommy Moonlight, did a magnificent job landing the aircraft and heading it towards the slipway where it grounded. Beaching it was a simple task from where it stopped.

On 15 November 1944, Lord Louis Mountbatten (The 'Supremo'), made one of his morale boosting trips to Addu Attol in the Maldive Islands. The Station Commander, Group Captain Geoffrey Francis DSO DFC, took over our crew with Baron as his co-pilot. Our role was to carry out an Anti Submarine patrol and provide Air/Sea Rescue cover in case Lord Louis's converted Mitchell bomber went down. Geoffrey, now deceased, was a former CO of 230 Squadron when it was operating in the Mediterranean.

The Sunderland and the Mitchell both arrived in the Maldives safely and after lunch we departed ahead of the Mitchell in order to be about mid point when it overtook us. Unfortunately, about 2 hours after departure we were recalled as Lord Louis's aircraft had blown an engine and he needed the Sunderland to transport him back to Ceylon. On landing back at Addu Attol, Lord Louis embarked and we returned to Koggala, landing after sunset. Lord Louis was highly qualified in radio and communications and I believe, was responsible for the re-writing of the Admiralty Manual of Wireless Telegraphy. He spent some time chatting with the crew and asked me quite a lot about the Sunderland radio equipment. Whilst on the flight deck, he told me to use R/T to call a destroyer that was on patrol in the area. Using a prearranged call sign and frequency, the destroyer came in loud and clear, enabling Lord Louis to chat with the ship's Captain whom he knew personally.

The gunners served him a hot meal in the Ward Room of the Sunderland consisting of tinned McConachy Irish stew, tinned potatoes and tinned peas. When he remarked that he had enjoyed it very much, Barney our second gunner muttered something to the effect that if he had to eat it as often as us, he probably would not have thought it so nice. After the flight, Lord Louis sent a letter of thanks to Geoffrey Francis with a copy to each member of the crew. I still have my copy.

Diego Garcia was the furthest base away from Koggala and in those days did not have a long runway. In fact, I cannot remember it having a runway at all in 1944/45. I do recall that it was a desolate place and at the highest tides the island was very close to being under water. Swimming was allowed off the jetty in absolutely crystal clear water, but it was always necessary to have a lookout on duty for sharks that occasionally came into the shallower water. While I was there the lookout shouted 'shark' at the top of his voice and the swimmers came out of the water so fast, one would have thought that they were walking on water!

Amongst the ground staff based on the island were several keen anglers one of whom I noticed regularly caught large fish. I watched him reel one in, chop its head off and throw it back into the sea. When I asked why he killed the fish rather than throw it back into the water, he said that it was a Barracuda and in his opinion was the most vicious and hated fish in those waters. I could not help wondering if by throwing it back into the water with its head cut off, would it not attract the sharks?

The highlight of the New Year 1945 was on 11 January when I received a telegram from my father in law informing me that on the 5th of January my wife had given birth to our son, Terence Michael Holloway. Wing Commander Powell personally gave me the telegram and I celebrated the event with the crew in the mess that night! Little did I know then that my son would make his career with the RAF and retire as a Group Captain.

Early in 1945 it was learned that the squadron was to be equipped with the Mark V Sunderland fitted with the more powerful, and certainly more reliable, Pratt and Whitney engines. It also had the very efficient H2S Radar fitted, which was somewhat similar to that used with great success by Bomber Command. Wing Commander Bednall the former CO had constantly requested Pratt & Whitney engines, complaining that the Pegasus XVIII engines were unsuitable for tropical flying. A team of experts came out from UK to teach crews how to operate the H2S and we soon found it to be a wonderful piece of equipment. Having been used to ASV that would only show the target as a blip. I found its display to be very useful in that the detail of the terrain could be seen making it ideal for map reading if flying over or near land. It had scanners located under each wingtip since a single scanner could not be located on the hull. This gave 360-degree coverage around the aircraft. Its disadvantage was that it radiated a signal that could be used by the enemy to find us! Crews were instructed that if the aircraft was forced down, the equipment should be destroyed by any means possible to prevent it falling into the hands of the Japanese. I cannot imagine how we were supposed to do that, but it did seem to me that the Germans must have recovered H2S equipment from shot down RAF bombers and surely passed the information to their Japanese allies?

We were quite sad at the thought of losing our faithful ML868. She had done us proud and only on one occasion gave any cause for anxiety. On that occasion we were escorting a convoy that had the Duke of Gloucester, the Governor designate of Australia, on board one of its ships. Our orders were to remain with the convoy whatever the circumstances, until relieved by another aircraft. Towards the end of the patrol just before the relief aircraft was due, the number 4 engine lost oil pressure, overheated and almost caught fire. The appropriate emergency drills were carried out but as the propeller was the type that could not be feathered, it continued to rotate with smoke pouring from the engine. The SNO of the convoy flashed us a message to ask us if we knew that we had an engine on fire! Our main worry was that the engine would seize and possibly cause the propeller to break away, but this did not happen. We signalled Koggala immediately and as the convoy was within sight of Ceylon, the relief aircraft arrived fairly quickly, allowing us to return to base where the engine was changed. On that particular patrol, as we joined the convoy, one of the escort vessels opened fire on us for reasons we never did discover, but ceased firing when we *repeated* the colours of the day. Obviously a lack of communication somewhere, but the Navy was known to be 'Trigger Happy!'

On 19th February 1945, Baron and I had our first flight on a Mark V Sunderland; PP146 captained by F/Lt Comrie, a New Zealander. We were very impressed with the H2S radar but initially neither of us were impressed by the aircraft, as it seemed to vibrate a great deal. The engineer was not particularly good at his job and Baron thought that the vibration was due to the propellers being out of synchronisation.

On 26/27th February 1945, ML868 was flown to Korangi Creek where we collected ML800, a Mark V Sunderland that was to become our personal aircraft. I had flown every minute of the nearly 400 hours that ML868 had accrued since leaving Oban and, apart from the Airspeed Indicator incident at Kasfareit, she had done all that was expected of her. Many years later I learned that she was stripped of everything useful, taken out to deep water and sunk together with many other scrapped Sunderlands! Those aircraft would probably be worth a fortune today!

Compared to Ceylon, which is always hot and humid, Karachi in its wintertime can be very much cooler and we found the stay there extremely pleasant. It was a welcome change not to be saturated by perspiration immediately any physical activity took place.

During the night-stop in Trombay, I telephoned Mrs Crossley who told me that she and her son were just about to leave for two months at the Hill town of Ootacommund. It was good to know that they were well.

In addition to being faster than the Mark III, the Sunderland Mark V carried more defensive armament. It had two .303 Browning guns in the forward turret, four fixed ones controlled by the Captain firing forward, two .303 Vickers guns firing out and down from each side of the galley, two .50 waist guns, one each side and four .303 Brownings in the rear turret. There was an optional mid upper turret fitted with two .303 Brownings, but this created quite a lot of drag and some aircraft had them removed in order to extend its range.

On the navigation side, it was fitted with an Air Position Indicator (API) and a more efficient Direct Reading Gyro Compass (DRC) system that was to be a great help to navigation on long flights. The API took information from the DRC together with True Air Speed data and converted it to latitude and longitude, a significant help if the aircraft was rapidly changing its heading when in action. Obviously the accuracy was only as good as its compass input but it did prove to be useful within its limitations. Eventually the mid upper turret was removed from our aircraft and we were quite astonished by the reduction in cruise power needed to maintain the optimum patrol speed.

Sunderland ML800 was ferried back to Koggala via Trombay and Redhills Lake Madras, to commence its operational role. Two attempts were made to take-off off from Madras and on each occasion, the number 4 engine cut dead. After each attempt, the aircraft was taxied back, the engine run up and both magnetos checked and found to be quite serviceable. As the aircraft was very light, Baron said that if it happened a third time, he would keep the aircraft going and get to Koggala where it could be more closely inspected. We got airborne despite the engine cutting and continued to base. Once in the air the engine ran normally and Baron, who had a great deal of experience with Pratt & Whitney engines, knew what the problem was likely to be. Apparently in the fuel system of the engine there is a rubber diaphragm that had perished, starving the engine of fuel at full take-off boost, but allowing sufficient flow at lower boost settings.

In March we carried out several fighter affiliation exercises with a Spitfire who attacked us from all quarters. After each exercise flown, the Spitfire pilot came to the debriefing and remarked that he found it extremely difficult to get a killing shot at us. The speed, at which we were flying, gave maximum manoeuvrability and at times Baron was turning with almost a ninety-degree bank angle. The Spitfire pilot's opinion was that he was always too fast and could only get a brief glimpse of us, whereas he thought that our gunners might have nailed him. It certainly gave the crew a great deal of confidence. I must say that apart from Baron and myself, everyone on board was airsick, and I felt uncomfortably queasy.

Early in 1945 the army retook Akyab in Burma and the squadron were ordered to proceed there as soon as possible to commence operations. There was nothing on shore in the way of accommodation and a supply ship, the SS *Manela*, was sent to provide accommodation, fuel, bombs, depth charges, ammunition, communications and general support. I believe that the SS *Manela* had been a flying boat support ship for many years. Moorings had to be laid for the flying boats, and the very essential fuelling tenders and marine craft provided. The logistics of this operation must have been very complex and it amazed me how smoothly things went. In the meantime, it was learned that once based in Burma, the operational task would be extended to attack small surface craft using bombs fitted with 11 seconds delay fuses and/or depth charges. Thus in its new role, aircraft were likely to encounter opposition from surface craft, something that never happened on the anti submarine patrols unless a submarine was attacked, which we never did.

There were all sorts of theories how a heavily armed coastal ship should be attacked. One was that three Sunderlands would fly in a circle around the target at 120 degree intervals and on being given a signal from the designated bombing aircraft, the two strafing aircraft would turn towards the target to strafe and attract the ground fire. The bombing aircraft would commence its bombing run a few seconds after the strafing aircraft and hopefully bomb without encountering ground fire. Well that sort of thing is all right in theory, but in practice it did not quite work out as planned. We constantly practised until on one practice with us as the designated bombing aircraft, another Sunderland who in error thought *he* was the bombing aircraft, met ours almost over the target ship. He seemed to hold his course and Baron realising that we were about to collide, threw the aircraft into a 90-degree banked turn, passing so close to the other aircraft that bottom of our hull filled their windscreen. This we learned from the other crew when we landed! After that incident, there were second thoughts and that particular procedure was discontinued. I personally wondered how on earth we would ever get *three* Sunderlands in the *same* area at the *same* time! Wisely, I kept my own counsel.

On 17th April we departed Koggala in ML800 for Cocanada where we night-stopped, continuing on to Akyab on the following day. Although Akyab had been cleared of Japanese, they were never too far away and crews had to be in a complete state of readiness to evacuate aircraft should it become necessary. Japanese aircraft did raid Akyab from time to time, but mostly at night. While the squadron was at Akyab, at night there was usually a flare path laid out on the water in the landing area and often it was bombed. The squadron intelligence officer was of the opinion that the Japanese probably thought that it was an airfield but I was not convinced, my own view being that they were speculatively bombing the flare path hoping to damage or destroy any aircraft about to take-off or land. Once operations started, it was normal procedure to re-arm and refuel the aircraft immediately it landed from its operational sortie in order to be ready for the next one. This policy caused my crew severe problems a little later on.

Accommodation on board the SS *Manela* was reasonable for Officers and NCO aircrew apart from sleeping space being very limited. On the credit side, the food was better than normal for aircrew but unfortunately this was not so for ground staff. Ground staff was accommodated in the bowels of the ship where it was most uncomfortably hot in the airless conditions.

Operations commenced about a week after arrival, initially looking for two Japanese cruisers that had escaped the Royal Navy's attention. The operational area was close to the Anderman Islands and the squadron had aircraft continuously in the air searching for the cruisers. On one sortie a homebound aircraft passed very close to us as we went out on patrol. Aircraft were flown at the most economical speed to fully cover the patrol area, normally taking 16 hours or more. One aircraft took nearly 20 hours and was not particularly flush with fuel when it landed. To get to the patrol area, the aircraft had to be flown down the coast of the Anderman Islands at almost sea level in order to be below the Japanese radar. The aircraft was fitted with a radio altimeter which could be set to the required height, having green, amber and red lights which illuminated to indicate when the aircraft was at, above or below the required height. Baron preferred to fly between 50 and 100 feet, that meant that the aircraft had to be flown very carefully. Despite Baron's skill, occasionally the hull would gently touch the sea, a quite startling experience.

The patrols were planned so that there was always an aircraft in the patrol area and this meant that there had to be variable departure and arrival times. On one patrol in the search area at night, I was operating the H2S when at maximum range, I got just a hint of a target dead ahead, which I knew could not possibly be land. As we continued towards the single target it became two and Baron ordered everyone to be on full alert against possible interception by Japanese aircraft that the cruisers might have carried. It was a pitch-black night with the aircraft flying in rain at about 800 feet just below cloud with virtually no forward visibility. Baron decided to close in and try for a visual sighting and continued heading towards the targets. As the aircraft closed on the targets, they became multiple targets, but Baron held his heading until we flew right over the unknown targets without any visual sighting. At the time the multiple targets appeared Baron ordered the IFF to be switched on, reasoning that it was most unlikely that the Japanese had a large number of ships available. The IFF equipment sent out an identification signal indicating to our own forces that we were friendly. This probably saved our lives because what we flew over was a British naval task force heading for Burma. We learned later that the navy had picked the aircraft up on their radar and plotted it all the way in, preparing to open fire when within range. Our orders had been not to break radio silence unless there was a positive visual sighting of the enemy cruiser(s). Although the radar had indicated targets, nothing could be seen so radio silence was maintained and the patrol was resumed. At debriefing after landing it was confirmed that it was a Royal Navy task force that we had found, and it was explained that we were not told of its whereabouts beforehand in case we were forced down and captured by the Japanese. No trace of the cruisers was ever found by Sunderlands of 230 Squadron but later on during a patrol in the Gulf of Siam, we did sight destroyers and a cruiser! After the war I read that Royal Navy aircraft from an aircraft carrier did intercept and sink one of the cruisers in the area that we had been searching, but did suffer casualties themselves.

With the army and navy advancing rapidly against the Japanese, Rangoon was about to fall. My crew, captained by Flight Commander Squadron Leader Sheardown, was briefed to take sixteen VIP passengers including General Oliver Leese, General 'Boy' Browning, Air Marshall Sir Keith Parks, General Truscott, and Group Captains Pollard, Mills and Cummings into Rangoon as soon as it was safe to do so. With the aircraft re-armed and re-fuelled after its last patrol, it was very much overweight to carry out the task. Whilst it is easy to get the bombs and depth charges off, reducing the large fuel load did present a problem. Once the refuelling tender fuelled an aircraft, it usually went back to the supply ship to refill its tanks, leaving it with no space to take fuel back from aircraft. Regardless of that, it takes a much longer time to de-fuel, and in any event, the fuel coming off may have become contaminated! The easiest way to get rid of the unwanted 900 gallons of petrol was to get airborne and jettison it.

For most operating systems on an aircraft, there is usually a procedure for checking it before flight. In the case of fuel jettison, there were two tubes in the galley area that could be passed down through the hull so that when the engineer opened the fuel jettison valves, the fuel flowed down through these tubes, leaving the aircraft well clear of the engines. The particular pre-flight drill was to deploy the tubes down through the hull and then retract them back again. In Akyab there was such a fierce current flowing in the mooring area so that when the tubes were deployed, the current bent them backwards, partially sealing them. The engineer had deployed them easily enough, but it took a lot of effort to seemingly retract them. Without any knowledge of what was happening, he separated the retraction lever from the tubes causing damage to the jettison tubes sufficient to prevent fuel completely leaving the aircraft.

The take-off was normal and the fuel jettisoning procedure commenced with the senior engineer at the engineer panel controlling the flow. He noticed that the rate of jettisoned fuel was very much less than it should have been and almost immediately there was a panic call from the galley saying that there was an overpowering smell of petrol below deck. The second engineer lifted the bilge boards and was horrified to discover that the bilge was filling with petrol! Jettisoning was immediately halted, all electrical equipment switched off and the engineer started to bale out the bilge with assistance from everyone available. This was not easy as there were very few bowls suitable for the task and it could only be got out it out in very small quantities. The fumes were overpowering and no one could spend more than a few minutes baling out without being overcome. Due to the danger of creating sparks that would have blown the aircraft to pieces, Baron decided that it would be prudent to land the aircraft without delay. He briefed everyone to put on lifejackets and take up a position near the doors and said that he would land, cutting all four engines just after touch down. A safe landing was made without further incident and the aircraft drifted with all doors open allowing the fumes to escape. The fire pinnace came alongside, secured the aircraft, and flushed the bilges until no fuel or fumes remained. The excess fuel on the aircraft was drained into the sea and the aircraft made ready for the VIP flight on the following day. The broken jettison tubes could not be replaced until the aircraft was next beached.

At 9a.m. on 10th May 1945 the aircraft took off with the VIPs on board en route to Rangoon with an escort of several Thunderbolt fighters. The flight took 3 hours 45 minutes and with the exception of General Browning, all the VIPs were happy to remain in the wardroom or other seating areas, apart from the usual visits to the flight deck. General Browning took a great deal of interest in the aircraft and in particular the guns. He did his best to persuade the waist gunners to let him fire the .50 calibre guns but was told that as there was radio silence we had no way of telling the Thunderbolt pilots what we were doing and they might think that we were being attacked. He accepted this explanation without comment. As we approached Rangoon, the golden dome of the Shwe Dagon Pagoda came into view, a quite beautiful sight.

A landing was made in the Rangoon River where a small naval craft with Admiral Martin on board, directed the aircraft to moor up to a very large metal battleship buoy. Several unsuccessful attempts were made, Baron being somewhat dubious about the wisdom of trying moor the aircraft with its very flimsy aluminium hull to a very large metal buoy. Eventually, the inner engines were stopped and as the aircraft approached the buoy against the current, Barney jumped on to the buoy holding a rope hoping he could attach it to the buoy. Unfortunately he slipped, dropped the rope and only just managed to avoid falling into the river. On the next approach, Stan in the bow compartment threw the rope to Barney who caught it and secured it to the buoy. Once the aircraft was secure, the engines were stopped and Barney was taken off the buoy.

The VIPs disembarked to the naval craft where Admiral Martin was waiting to meet the group and take them ashore. Later we were told that it would be necessary to spend the night on board the aircraft, but to be ready to take off at short notice if it became necessary. Baron did not like being moored to the huge metal battleship buoy, particularly as there was an extremely strong current flowing in the river, and asked the Navy find a more suitable one. Once a smaller buoy had been found, the moorings were changed. We did go ashore in the docks hoping to get into the town but were intercepted by a Captain in the Military Police who informed us that although Rangoon had theoretically fallen, Japanese snipers still occupied some of the large buildings. He said that it would be safe to go a short distance outside the docks and gave us an escort of two Gurkha soldiers, comforting us with the statement that snipers would probably not fire at us if we had a Gurkha escort. We were not particularly inspired by that statement and after a brief look around the dock area, returned to the Sunderland for the night. It seemed pointless to risk getting shot by snipers just to look around the city.

At 9a.m. on the following morning, the aircraft flew back to Akyab without the VIPs who had obviously decided that it was safe to stay. We took back with us two nuns who had been prisoners of the Japanese for nearly two years. The nuns were quite amazing, showing no sign of fear or indeed, any emotion. They would not discuss their treatment by the Japanese but doubtless they would once they got back to India.

Two days later, on 13th May, the aircraft was flown to Redhills Lake Madras that had become our main base for servicing of the aircraft, it being closer to Burma than Koggala. Daily inspections and minor servicing could be carried out with the aircraft at its moorings in Burma, but no facilities were available to beach the aircraft if that was needed. The return to India was coincident with the return of all other squadron aircraft, to allow for the transfer of the operational base from Akyab to Rangoon. This involved moving the supply ship SS *Manela*, to Rangoon and creating another flying boat base in the Rangoon River at Syriam, a move that would put us very much closer to the Japanese supply routes.

About this time, our navigator Vic Madely left the crew to go back to UK for a Staff Navigation course, after which he was to return to the squadron as Navigation Leader. Flying Officer Arthur Gillow, an Australian from Launceston in Tasmania, took over from Vic and remained a permanent member of the crew. Arthur had already completed his first operational tour on Blenheims in the Middle East.

Madras had a great deal more to offer than Koggala but as I had noticed when I was at Tanjore in 1943, it always seemed to be very much hotter. Swimming was permitted in the fresh water of Redhills Lake that was the reservoir for Madras, and it was quite normal and pleasantly cooling for good swimmers to jump off the aircraft when it became too hot on board. With the exception of Bob Stagg, the crew were good swimmers. Baron was an extremely powerful swimmer and had done his utmost to teach Bob how to swim, but he lacked confidence and apart from a dog paddle action, could never master swimming. On 18th May 1945, engineers Stan and John were on board with Bob carrying out the daily inspection and as it was a stifling hot day, they decided to get into the water to cool off. Bob always used a lilo mattress on which he would lie and paddle himself around. On that particular day, it was very windy and he quickly drifted away from the aircraft. In his attempt to get back, he overturned the lilo and instead of dog paddling towards it as he had been told to do, he panicked and grabbed at it, missing each time he tried. Stan and John heard his cries for help but could not reach him before he sank and drowned. It was terrible to think that he lost his life in such a fashion and Baron felt responsible for not being able to teach Bob to swim. The body was recovered two days later and it fell to me to make the formal identification. All that I could think of at that time was of our first meeting en route to Alness early in 1944. He was buried with full military honours in Redhills cemetery where six of the crew were pallbearers. It seemed so sad to lose his life in such a manner.

Hostilities in Europe having ceased, we flew the aircraft to Koggala to join in the somewhat belated VE Day celebrations being held there. Engine problems occurred prior to take-off from Redhills and it needed three attempts to get airborne. With the fanaticism of the Japanese still very much in evidence, it was difficult for us to see an early end to 'our' conflict and how we envied our colleagues back home in England. The only thing that spoiled the VE Day celebration was that one of the crew spiked Baron's drink. Usually a mild mannered man, he became so angry it was almost frightening. When he joined us at Alness in 1944 he declared that he was a teetotaller and a non-smoker, and I could see no reason why anyone would want to change that. Years later I learned that he did drink, but when he joined the RCAF he made a promise to his wife Cecile, that he would not drink again until he returned home, a promise he kept! As a professional aviator he considered that wartime flying was dangerous enough without adding to that danger with drink.

In the first week of June the squadron flew back into Rangoon to continue operations against the Japanese. There must have been fighting going on very close to the base because we were ordered to circle well away from the landing area for over an hour before being given permission to land. The squadron was briefed that operational flights would be carried out in daylight and would be shorter than previous patrols. The aircraft took off with less fuel but was able to carry extra depth charges and bombs to use against small coastal shipping, reloading the racks after each attack. Not an easy task as I said previously.

There was tented accommodation on the east shore of the Rangoon River at Syriam and some ground staff was moved there from the ship. This proved to be very unpopular, it being so miserably hot and uncomfortable under canvas. The Japanese troops were only a few miles away and the front line wavered frequently, often bringing the enemy very close. This necessitated having the aircraft ready for take-off at extremely short notice! There was devastation all around the area and Japanese bodies could often be seen floating up and down the tidal river. A Japanese soldier's body drifted up and down the river with the tide but nobody did anything about it until it became entangled in the ship's mooring lines when it became necessary for a working party to remove it. Not a particularly nice task considering how long the body had been in the water!

Within three days of arriving, the crew flew a daylight sortie, proceeding south down the Burma coast to cross overland near Mergui, then flying eastwards into the Gulf of Siam. Targets were soon sighted and according to my logbook, we made 7 attacks on a group of ships and barges dropping bombs and depth charges. Attacking barges with depth charges was not too successful since the barges usually kept to shallow water where the depth charges would not explode. Time delay bombs were much more effective when dropped accurately. However, given the awesome firepower of the Sunderland, severe damage could be inflicted on the smaller ships and barges by strafing, even though it may not have been enough to sink them.

Flying overland was not without danger from ground fire, and crews were briefed that if shot down, they should get into the inland high ground as quickly as possible and stay under cover. Apparently there were highly organised resistance groups and army personnel who would soon find any survivors and get them out. Quite a comforting thought, but I am glad that their help was not needed!

Four days later we went again into the Gulf of Siam where naval ships thought to be two destroyers and a cruiser were sighted. The Japanese sent up two biplane fighters that attempted an attack on our starboard beam. The waist gunner on that side opened up at about 800 yards range and one broke off its attack whilst the other dived away steeply with smoke pouring from it. The first repositioned for another attack but Baron went on to emergency power and climbed into a thin layer of cloud, which prevented them from finding us. Later we returned and took photographs of the warships and some airstrips that had been previously sighted. We then sighted groups of small ships and barges, making several attacks without any return fire being seen. The attacks were quite successful and we sank or damaged several of the craft attacked.

On the overland route to the Gulf on this and the previous operation, a train was seen proceeding along a single-track railway that doubtless had been constructed by prisoners of war. Baron said that if we ever had any bombs left, we would attack it. Fortunately we had used up everything on that patrol but reported its presence at the intelligence debriefing.

Two days later we were sent out to specifically look for a 10,000 ton

Japanese tanker close to Chumphon. It was the only large tanker the Japanese had in the area and its destruction could seriously disrupt their fuel supplies. The estimated position given to us by Intelligence was quite accurate and it was easily found but much to our surprise, it had a Japanese Navy Destroyer as its escort. There was no possibility of us being able to make a successful attack on the tanker but a flash report was transmitted to base giving its position. We had been told before departure that a force of Liberators would be sent out to bomb it when its position became known. Whilst shadowing some distance away from the tanker, a Japanese Zero fighter came very close, almost formating with us. We can only assume that he mistook us for a Japanese 'Emily' flying boat that was very similar in appearance to the Sunderland. It was close enough for us to have fired at it, but Baron told the gunners to hold their fire unless it attacked. He quite rightly assumed that had we opened fire, it would know we were hostile and doubtless would have brought other Zeros. It was quite startling to see the fighter so close and reminded me of my near encounter close to Coxes Bazaar in 1943. Once the position of the tanker had been confirmed and its position reported to base, we were ordered to resume patrol.

Fairly quickly a coastal vessel was sighted and attacked with bombs and machine guns at low level. Return fire was seen coming from the ship but it did not deter Baron who completed his bombing run, passing right over the ship at about 100 feet. George in the rear turret opened fire as soon as it came into his sights but about 10 seconds after passing over the ship, it blew up leaving a huge smoke pyre and only small pieces of debris in the water. Probably the ship was carrying explosives and either the strafing or a lucky bomb hit caused it to blow up. Later an attack was made on two ships; one of which sank and the other beached itself. We continued to strafe the beached vessel and severely damaged it causing casualties amongst the many people who appeared on deck. Doubtless it would soon have been put back into service, but its schedule would have been seriously disrupted.

The first wave of Liberators sent to bomb the tanker left it blazing furiously before it sank, but at least one Liberator was shot down and others suffered damage from enemy fire. The second wave of Liberators attacked the train that we had previously reported and were able to destroy it. It was an armoured train and gave a good account of itself before being destroyed, causing casualties to the Liberators. When we heard this, we were thankful that we had not tried to attack it since at our speed we would have been a sitting duck! In six days we had flown over 30 hours on three operational flights and were stood down prior to doing another VIP flight.

This time we were sent to Calcutta to pick up His Excellency the Governor of Burma, Sir Reginald Dorman-Smith, and fly him and his aides to Rangoon. On June 18 the aircraft was ferried to Calcutta, landing on the river at Bally, the BOAC flying boat base. The monsoon rains had started and the weather forecast was absolutely appalling with severe thunderstorms and heavy rain all along the route which gave Baron grave doubts as to the wisdom of flying on the following day. Early in the morning, the engineers had checked the aircraft and found that the starboard float and the bilges needed to be pumped out, but thought nothing more about it. The route weather forecast had improved and the flight took-off at its scheduled time, landing safely at Rangoon with our VIPs after another very turbulent flight through almost continuous thunderstorms and torrential rain. Two days later we returned the VIPs to Calcutta, again encountering thunderstorms and severe turbulence en route. The aircraft stood by in Calcutta for two days before we were told that we were no longer needed and were ordered back to Rangoon.

Before each take-off, the bilges and the starboard float needed to be pumped out but the engineers still did not seem to think anything was amiss. On 27 June, we flew an 11 hours 10 minutes patrol finishing up at Koggala where the aircraft was beached and inspected. It was then discovered that we had bullet holes through the starboard float, the hull, and one that went through the number 4 engine, fortunately without hitting a vital spot. This had obviously happened when we attacked the ship that blew up!

After the aircraft had been declared serviceable and had been air tested, patrols were flown to Rangoon and back to Koggala where we were told that the whole crew was to be sent on 14 days leave. This was not popular, as we preferred to carry on with operational flying while our luck was holding out. Nevertheless, Harry Ling, Arthur Gillow and I decided that we would go into the hills at Newara Eliya to have a break and promptly made arrangements for departure. I was particularly friendly with Harry and Arthur as we all had similar interests and preferred to lead a quieter life than the rest of the crew, some of whom, Baron excluded, had some rather hectic parties. Colombo to Newara Eliya was a tedious journey of bus and train, normally taking about eight hours. The hotels were always quite full and we had to spend one night at St Andrew's Hotel and another at the Priory Hotel before we could get into the Grand Hotel, our first choice. The cool climate in the hills made a welcome change from the terribly sticky heat of Burma. I remember walking up a steep footpath to the summit of perhaps the highest mountain in Ceylon, but by the time I got there the cloud thickened and I could hardly see a hand in front of my face. It was really quite chilly and I was pleased when the sun broke through again to give a magnificent view of the terrain around and below. It was an enjoyable break despite our misgivings when we were sent on leave.

On return to Koggala after leave, it was announced that the squadron would cease operations for a short time and would commence intensive training for 'Operation Zipper', the invasion of Malaya. The aircraft was flown to Madras on 2nd August where, to our bitter disappointment, we learned that Baron was to leave us. Apparently Canada was not officially at war with Japan and once the war with Germany was over, arrangements were put into effect to repatriate the Canadians. It had taken the authorities some time for them to reach Baron, but off he went rejoicing that for him, the war was over! He and I were destined to meet many times in the future when I flew to Canada with BOAC and other airlines. I could never quite understand why Canadians were posted for duties against the Japanese if they were not at war with them! It was a double disappointment as Arthur Gillow also left the squadron to return home to Australia. A flight sergeant navigator, 'Doc' Watson, who had seen action in Europe and the Middle East prior to joining the squadron replaced Arthur.

One good piece of news awaiting me was that I had been promoted to Warrant Officer rank and had a good amount of back pay due to me. However, I was still awaiting the result of my latest interview for a commission.

Two days after Baron departed, the crew was introduced to Flying Officer Tony Ellwood, a son of Air Marshall Sir Aubrey Ellwood, who it was proposed should take over the crew. The squadron had been withdrawn from Burma to prepare for operation 'Zipper' that would be the invasion and recapture of Malaya. Rumour was that it was intended that the squadron aircraft and those of other flying boat squadrons would land in the open sea in the Straits of Malaya where they would drift between sorties, being supported as before by the SS *Manela*. The same source (rumour) put the estimate of casualties to the squadron of about 60%. Fortunately the war ended before the invasion started.

In the meantime, we were training with Tony Ellwood as our captain, but not without some misgivings. He was an excellent pilot having been trained on fighter aircraft, but had very little experience on Sunderlands. Every member of the crew considered that his flying was somewhat irresponsible, to the point of being downright dangerous. He persisted in very low flying, hopping over palm trees with just inches to spare causing the crew sufficient concern to request another captain. As might be imagined, this caused quite an upheaval, particularly as he was the son of a very senior officer. It took some very plain speaking to convince Tony that we had survived the war so far, and at this late stage, had no intention of becoming casualties of irresponsible flying. Once an understanding was reached, things took a turn for the better and Tony and I became firm friends.

The squadron continued to train for the task that lay ahead when the news came that the Americans had dropped a devastating new bomb on two targets in Japan. Shortly after this we learned that the war was over, the Japanese having unconditionally surrendered. The news was almost unbelievable but almost immediately everyone's thoughts turned towards getting back home. This was to prove to be more difficult than anyone thought possible and it was some time before repatriation actually commenced!

On Wednesday 15th August, Squadron Leader Alan Deller took command of our aircraft and crew, flying south to Koggala. It was intended that a return would be made to Redhills on the same day but on arrival the aircraft was unserviceable and as preparations were well in hand for an end of war celebration, Alan delayed the return. There was a bonfire party with plenty of beer available but my thoughts were with my wife and son several thousand miles away and I did not feel like celebrating. I remember sitting alone on the beach looking up at an almost cloudless sky filled with stars.

The aircraft became serviceable on 18th August and we returned to Redhills where for the next three weeks, training flights continued with Tony. Orders were given to remove armament equipment from the aircraft to reduce its weight and give a greater load carrying capability. Tony decided that he would like to paint the wardroom of the aircraft sky blue and asked for volunteers. Everyone pitched in and the result was a very pleasant wardroom, which was the envy of other crews.

It was about this time that Harry Ling, who was very experienced, was transferred to a crew that had just joined the squadron captained by F/O Syd Lane. In his place we were given F/O Davies who had just joined the squadron. This did not go down very well with the crew who thought that Harry, having been with us throughout our operational flying, should have stayed until we were demobilised.

Wing Commander Ted Hawkins DFC, who had replaced Wing Commander Powell as the Commanding Officer some weeks previously, took command of our crew with Tony Ellwood newly promoted to F/Lt as his second pilot for a special relief flight. On 13 September we flew a

12-hour flight from Madras to Singapore taking six nurses and a large amount of medical supplies. En route the aircraft flew over the northern tip of Sumatra and we were perhaps a little wary because there had been no confirmation that the defences in that area were aware that hostilities had ceased. There were some areas where the Japanese had carried on fighting for some time after the war ended! As we flew over the land, I was map reading using the H2S radar wondering if someone was going to start firing but fortunately nothing happened. On arrival in Singapore the nurses and supplies were taken off and transported to a military hospital, but with little or no accommodation available ashore, the crew, apart from Wing Commander Hawkins and Tony Ellwood, was compelled to live on board until the return flight to Madras. This did not worry anyone unduly as we could usually live and eat far more comfortably on board.

When we did get ashore we could see fully armed Japanese soldiers roaming around the base with apparently no one to take charge of them. They tried to give us their weapons, that at least giving us the comfort of knowing that they were not hostile. There were stories that when British forces first arrived, they discovered the bodies of Japanese who had committed Hari-Kari. Those who knew Seletar from before the war said that the base had been totally neglected. The sports field had knee high grass and the swimming pool was full of rubbish and had snakes swimming around. The hangars and stores were all open with everything strewn about on the floors, looking as though thieves and vandals had been around. Doubtless they had! In accordance with the terms of the surrender, most aircraft had their propellers removed but quite a few were still in an air-worthy condition. It amazed me to see the very large number of aircraft that the Japanese had, it being far in excess of the numbers the intelligence reports had indicated. There were several aircraft, including Zeros and Petes, in a fully serviceable condition that could have flown. There was also a Kamikazi aircraft on the airfield that looked in a serviceable condition, which forcibly brought home to us what a bloody battle it would have been if the invasion had been necessary.

The squadron's immediate task was to fly the seriously ill ex prisoners of war to India where they could receive urgent medical treatment. Five days after arrival, with Wing Commander Ted Hawkins in command, we flew back to Madras carrying 13 ex POWs on stretchers who were in a pitiful state. During the flight the CO informed us that eventually the squadron would be moved to its permanent base at Seletar in Singapore. From that moment in time, there was a constant stream of aircraft of all types flying medical supplies in and ex POWs out. Most crews were carrying out three or four round trips to Singapore each month, doing between 85 and 100 hours flying. Some flew direct to Singapore whilst others were compelled to land at Penang for fuel.

When the squadron's move to Singapore had been confirmed, every aircraft carried a large amount of squadron freight, this necessitating most flights landing at Penang for fuel. On one flight we transported the squadron's sailing dinghy to Singapore and could only load it in the bomb room. Unfortunately it was too long to get it completely in and a part of the bow protruded from the bomb room and the port bomb room door could not be closed. It must have caused a great deal of drag but it was transported safely to Seletar, albeit with a fuel stop in Penang.

Sadly, one of 230's Sunderlands took off from Singapore in appalling weather and disappeared. The captain was F/Lt Levy-Haarsher, a very experienced Sunderland pilot whom I first met at Alness in 1944. No contact was made with the aircraft after its departure and it was thought that it might have come down in the sea en route to Redhills. My crew (and others) flew air-sea rescue patrols until it was discovered that it had crashed into a hill just inside Malaya where it had burst into flames, killing all on board. I was part of a burial party that unsuccessfully attempted to reach the crash site travelling by army lorry. The road up the mountain through a rain forest was just a slippery mud track and in trying to negotiate a bend, the lorry overturned, fortunately without injury to anyone. The efforts to reach the site had to be abandoned and it was left to the army and RAF ground staff to do what was necessary. It was a dreadful thing to have happened to an experienced crew, but more so for the ex prisoners of war who had survived the war despite terrible treatment at the hands of the Japanese! I believe that other aircraft were lost during the airlift and sometimes the squadron was called upon to fly air-sea rescue patrols looking for aircraft that had disappeared. Nothing was found on the patrols that I flew.

If Harry Ling had not been transferred to our crew when we joined the squadron, and had remained with Levy Haarsher, he would undoubtedly have been killed in the crash! Perhaps fate took a hand and saved him.

News came that people in the Kuantan area of Malaya were starving and the squadron was ordered to mount a food airlift. The landing/take-off area there was not really suitable, as it was located in a narrow river that was not a straight stretch of water. The airlift proceeded well until aircraft 'T' Tommy sank on landing, probably due to hitting something in the water that penetrated the hull. Alternatively it may have been due to its 10,000 pounds of rice not being correctly spread throughout the aircraft, so that when the aircraft made an extremely heavy landing, the rice probably caused the floor to collapse under its weight, opening up the hull causing the aircraft to sink. We landed there with great difficulty and when our load of rice was off-loaded, a gang of engineer fitters who had come with us stripped the sunken aircraft of everything moveable and the aircraft was then abandoned. The take-off was extremely hazardous due to the abandoned aircraft obstructing the area. The navigator of 'T' had a good sense of humour as his navigation log showed. No navigation was required for the simple coast crawl to Kuantan and his navigation log simply read 'Slipped Moorings, Airborne, Landed, Submerged!' The river was not very deep and when it sank, the flight deck was above water so the flight crew did not even get their feet wet.

I was re-called to Madras fairly urgently on 25th October with no reason given, flying on a 209 Squadron aircraft captained by its CO, Wing Commander Robinson. On the flight I imagined all sorts of things had happened back home but to my delight, on arrival I was told that I had been commissioned and was now a Pilot Officer. Accordingly, I was sent off the station as a Warrant Officer to kit myself out and return as a commissioned officer. Unfortunately the NCOs on my crew took my commissioning very badly, not because of jealousy, but because they thought things would never be the same. Harry Ling was more philosophical about it himself, preferring to remain as a Warrant Officer where, he said, he was a 'King' amongst the lower ranks.

Almost immediately, I was appointed Acting Signals Leader in place of the officer who had been posted away. Months later, I was relieved of this post by F/Lt Don Brawn who oddly enough, also came from Northampton.

Sometimes the aircraft would remain in Redhills for several days before returning to Singapore and often the mess received invitations to parties and functions in Madras. One invitation was for a ball given by the Governor of Madras, an occasion that the Station Commander considered was important enough to require representatives from all squadrons. These invitations were not popular because everyone was afraid of drinking too much and putting up 'A black!' As there were no volunteers, I was detailed to attend together with another equally junior officer. I did not habitually drink but had a wonderful time enjoying the excellent buffet and the company of one of the Governor's daughters who seemed determined to teach me how to dance. She was not too successful, accepting that I appeared to have two left feet!

The flights to/from Singapore continued and eventually the squadron became permanently based at Singapore. When that happened Tony Ellwood and I shared a room in the officers' quarters. We both enjoyed classical music and Tony had a wonderful collection of record albums and a record player. His collection was very comprehensive and included two sets of Elgar's Violin Concerto played by Yehudi Menhuin, (old 78s of course), one set of which he gave me when I left the squadron to return home.

I continued to practise navigation whenever possible and did quite a lot of the more simple sectors. Additionally Tony required me to have pilot instruction so that on the long sector from/to Singapore, I could do a two or three hour stint at the controls hand flying the aircraft. Like the Wellington, the Sunderland autopilot was mostly unserviceable, but it was a beautiful aircraft to handle. Once trimmed, in smooth flying conditions it could almost be flown hands off with just a touch of rudder if a wing dropped. I would normally take my turn at the controls on long sectors. I was also given training in the Squadron Link Trainer.

As Singapore started to get back to normal, social activities increased and life became much more pleasant with various clubs in town opening up again. I played a decent game of Bridge and found that I could always get a game either in town at the Tanglin Club or in the Officers Mess. Activities on the station were quite varied and most people found interests to occupy them after peace had been restored. I was appointed the Squadron Welfare Officer which I certainly found unusual and in an odd way, interesting. It did however, have its sad and less pleasant side. Airmen who had been away from home for up to four years were finding it difficult to accept that they could not just leave the service and go home. Some discovered that all was not right at home and asked me to write to their wives or girl friends in an attempt to sort out their problems. In the short term, listening and sympathising with the situation could help, but I soon discovered that it was never advisable to intervene and become involved. Inevitably some became extremely depressed and desperate and had to be referred to the station padre who was more qualified to deal with problems of that nature.

As the weeks dragged on with no apparent hope of early demobilisation, morale reached a very low level, leading to dissension within the ranks and ultimately to mutiny. That, however, has no part in my memoirs, it having been dealt with far more effectively elsewhere.

There was a great deal of celebrating in the mess each evening and parties started in the mess often continued at clubs and bars in town, sometimes quite exuberantly. One evening, a large group of officers from the squadron, myself included, went into town and removed a huge concrete tiger from outside the Tiger Brewery and took it back to the squadron HQ. The squadron's coat of arms bears a tiger and I suppose it seemed appropriate at the time to take it. The Station Commander, Group Captain Geoffrey Francis, was not amused and ordered that it be returned from whence it came. A lorry, block and tackle and many people were required to get it back to the brewery, yet it appeared that it was transported to the squadron on a jeep. I cannot imagine how on earth we ever accomplished that feat and confess to having no recollection whatsoever!

One of the of the first dining in nights in the Officers Mess was attended by Lord Louis Mountbatten as the guest of honour and it fell to me that evening to propose the loyal toast. All were on their best behaviour and no unseemly activities took place while Lord Louis was around. Immediately after his departure, a very loud and boisterous party commenced and these always alarmed me. At each end of the bar were two very large glass containers that somewhat bizarrely had a small live cobra in each of them. I was afraid that someone in his cups would smash a container and release the snake, putting people at risk. Thankfully this did not happen and eventually common sense prevailed and the snakes and the containers were removed!

As Christmas 1945 approached, repatriation to England was the main topic of conversation but there seemed little news or urgency about this. From time to time information was circulated about the release groups that were about to be demobilised. I cannot remember precisely how a person's release group was calculated and allocated but believe that it was a combination of date of enlistment, length of service and age. There seemed to be no one who knew the rules sufficiently well enough to explain it properly. Everyone knew his own release group and waited for it to be announced. When it was announced, they knew that it was only a matter of time before being told which ship would take them home. It seemed unfair that when a release group was announced, those in UK would have most likely have been fairly quickly sent to the release centre and demobilised. Being overseas was quite different in that one still had to journey home to UK, thus delaying the actual date of demobilisation. Furthermore, key personnel on the squadron, be they officers, NCOs, or airmen, could not be sent home until a replacement arrived to take their place. As the delays built up, I soon realised that the best civilian jobs could have already gone to those who were released first. Quite an intolerable situation!

Group Captain Geoffrey Francis called me to his office and asked me if I had considered staying in the service. He explained that his next appointment was to be the President of a Permanent Commissioning Board and at that time, he was of the opinion that the service was going to lose most of its experienced aircrew and ground staff officers. This concerned him greatly and was the reason he asked several officers to consider making The Royal Air Force a career. Initially it was only a casual interview and he told me not to decide one way or the other until further information became available, and after I had given it a great deal of thought.

Christmas 1945 was really a 'non event', although in all fairness, the CO did his best to ensure that the normal Christmas parties were held. It is a tradition at Christmas for officers to serve the other ranks with their Christmas dinner and I found it to be quite an enjoyable experience. There was a lot of friendly comment and an atmosphere of good humour prevailed with the problems of release dates being forgotten. However, shortly after Boxing Day the squadron was brought up to readiness for urgent operations to Java where there was civil unrest. On 31st December we departed for Batavia to evacuate people caught up in fighting that had broken out between rebels and Government forces. The aircraft was compelled to land in the open sea off shore from the harbour where naval vessels ferried passengers to the waiting Sunderlands. We were warned not to get within rifle shot range of the shore as the rebels were firing at anything they could see. On take-off from Singapore, there was sufficient fuel on board to enable the round trip to be completed without refuelling. The flights were just under four hours in each direction and the Sunderland could easily carry round trip fuel. The sea was extremely rough in stormy weather making the landing quite bumpy and somewhat hazardous. It took 2 hours 30 minutes to load the passengers and we had no idea exactly how many people were on board. As we started the take-off run, the waves were breaking over the wings and it took several attempts before Tony was able to get the aircraft on the step and accelerate to take-off speed. Once airborne the aircraft was checked for damage and during this inspection, passengers were found in all compartments of the aircraft. There was even a woman and her two children looking very frightened, huddled together in the very small toilet in the bow of the aircraft. It was a very turbulent flight back to Singapore where a safe landing was made and the passengers disembarked. Nearly fifty years later, I learned that the flight carried out on that day qualified me for a medal that was sent to me by post!

On New Years Day the crew were detailed to fly the aircraft to Ceylon as soon as it was serviceable. This took two days and on 3rd January the aircraft was flown to Koggala where all of the crew, except Tony and I, proceeded on leave to Diyatalawa. On the following day, Tony and I flew to Redhills where we departed for Kingscliffe, Ootacommund. It was a tedious journey by train and bus, leaving at 3p.m., travelling all night and arriving just after midday on the next day. The two weeks leave passed very pleasantly and after a similar overnight journey, we arrived back in Redhills. Almost immediately we were ordered to fly to

Negombo by a TATA Airlines DC3 and then by train and bus to Koggala where the rest of the crew were waiting. Needless to say, the aircraft we were scheduled to take over was unserviceable and over a period of four days it took a taxi test, an air test and three attempts to take-off before leaving for Redhills.

The standard of servicing of the aircraft had seriously deteriorated to a much lower level than it was during the war. Doubtless this was due to losing experienced ground engineers when their release groups were called.

Early in February the aircraft left Redhills en route for Singapore, but extremely bad weather en route caused a diversion to Penang for a night stop, continuing to Seletar on the following morning. Penang was a popular place as there were buyers for almost anything that crews had for sale! I had some Chinese banknotes that were of no value because the necessary signature had not been overprinted on them. I, together with others, had found the banknotes on the beach at Koggala where they had been washed up from the wreckage of the ship that was carrying them when the Japanese sank it. Apparently the banknotes were to be the new currency of China when the next issue took place. The notes that I had were high denomination and a Malayan who saw them in my wallet, immediately urged me to sell them to him. I told him that they were quite worthless but later learned that other crews had sold their 'souvenirs' for a very high price!

There followed a period of inactivity from flying duties that I found very boring and the only cheerful thing that happened was to receive a copy of the *London Gazette* sent to me by my wife in which my promotion to Flying Officer was promulgated. The CO accepted this as authorisation and I was officially promoted and had quite a bit of back pay due to me.

In this slack period, it became the custom of all officers with station duties to meet in the squadron Medical Officer's office for coffee after sick parade had finished. In the last week of February while having coffee, 'Doc' noticed that I looked seedy and promptly gave me a check over. Discovering that I had a raging temperature, he sent me off to hospital by ambulance where I spent seven grim days until the fever broke. It was never discovered what was wrong with me and the diagnosis was put down as P. U. O. (Fever of unknown origin).

I left hospital on Monday 4 March 1946, and on return to Seletar was informed that my release group had been called and that I should make preparations for departure. This involved packing my heavy baggage to be put into the hold, and packing a suitcase with items I would need on the 21 day voyage home. It seemed unbelievable that after such a long time, my service life was coming to an end. Group Captain Francis called me to his office and offered me an extended service commission to stay in the service, with the likelihood of it becoming a permanent commission at a later date. I was quite tempted by this and asked if I would still be repatriated if I accepted. Unfortunately he could offer no such assurance as he was effectively gathering officers for the Far East Command stations. This left me with no option but to decline the offer, mainly because at home I had son I had not seen.

I was sorry to be leaving but promised the remainder of my crew that I would keep in touch with them somehow or other. George Hodgeson and 'Bev' Bevan, being somewhat older then most of the crew, had left about a month previously. During the run up to boarding the ship, officers were asked to volunteer as troop deck officers. The duties associated with this were not particularly arduous and the incentive was that troop deck officers would be allocated a cabin. Never ever volunteer is the service maxim!!! I did, and as had been promised, was allocated a cabin. They omitted to tell me that my cabin was the first class lounge of the *Capetown Castle* that had been converted into an officer's dormitory that I would share with 300 other officers, mostly army. I should have known better!

There was a riotous party in the mess the evening before I embarked and I confess that I cannot remember very much of the events that took place. During the celebrations that evening, an Engineering Officer who had just arrived on posting to the squadron, told me that he had travelled out with a Squadron Leader Padre who was known as 'Bish' and was to become the Station Padre. It turned out that the padre in question was Len Ashton who was a very close friend when I lived in Chesham before the war. Shortly after I joined the RAF, Len who was at Bristol studying for the Ministry, went on holiday to his home in Chesham that was the next house to my Aunt and Uncle. My future wife and I were staying with Aunt and Uncle on my leave and Len conducted a mock wedding ceremony, which was great fun. Len went on to become an Air Vice Marshall Padre and Chaplain to the Queen. It was a great disappointment that I did not get to meet him before my ship sailed away from Singapore. I did meet him many years later when he was the Chaplain at St Clement Danes Church in London, and again at his home in Chesham shortly before he died.

The day before the ship sailed, Ted Hawkins came on board to say goodbye to the squadron members who were leaving and told me that the squadron had been ordered back to UK. He added that doubtless it would arrive back in England before I did. Had I known about that, it might well have been just enough to make me decide to stay in the service.

The journey home was very pleasant and being a troop deck officer did not affect my social activities on board. I joined three other people to make up a four for Bridge every afternoon during the voyage. We cut for partners and remained partners for the rest of the voyage. My partner was a very pleasant army Major, and the opposition was an army Lieutenant and an elderly lady who before the war taught Bridge at the Tanglin Club in Singapore. She was a captive of the Japanese but would not at any time discuss her treatment by them. We had small stakes to avoid overbidding and at the end of the voyage I think that my partner and I had won about two shillings and sixpence each. I remember that the ship was quite overcrowded and that meals had to be taken in shifts precisely at the time allocated, but other than that, the fact that I was going home put everything else out of my mind.

As the ship sailed into the Solent, it passed most of 230 squadron's aircraft, including mine, moored at buoys in the river at RAF Calshot. It was quite a wonderful sight and it gave me great pleasure to know that I had been an active member of that squadron. Once the ship had docked, disembarkation started almost immediately, but in a very disciplined manner. Groups were led through the Customs shed where Customs Officers selected people at random and asked what they had to declare. It was all very painless and we were soon through to the Southampton Docks Station where a train took us to our destination. On the train I was chatting with a couple of officers in the compartment and I learned that one of them was a jeweller in civilian life. Apparently he had used his expertise to purchase some nice and quite valuable pieces of jewellery in Singapore. I asked him if he had declared what he had with him and he assured me that he had been quite honest with the Customs Officer and was allowed through without anything being inspected. Apparently when asked what he had to declare, he said that he had about £5000 worth of jewellery! The customs officer's sarcastic reply was 'I suppose you have the crown jewels as well? To which he replied, 'No just £5000 of jewellery!' The customs officer just laughed and waved him through! He assured me that the value was £5000, which in those days was a great deal of money. I could only envy him his good fortune!

Officers spent the night at RAF Shawbury prior to being taken to RAF Hednesford that was being used as a demobilisation centre. At Shawbury I was given a signal from Group Captain Francis saying that now that I was back in UK, perhaps I would think again about remaining in the service. As far as I was concerned, my decision had been made in Singapore and there was no turning back. Accordingly I requested that this be conveyed to Geoffrey Francis.

After a good nights sleep, I was awakened by a very attractive blonde WAAF batwoman who brought me a cup of tea and took away my uniform to be pressed. Shortly after breakfast, officers due for release were transported to RAF Hednesford where demobilisation formalities were carried out. The issue of civilian clothes was quite farcical with insufficient time being given to make proper selections from a quite limited display on offer. I certainly ended up with clothes that I would not normally have chosen and a hat that I never ever wore. I suppose that everyone's thought was to get through as quickly as possible and get home. On 20th April 1946, I was given six weeks overseas leave due to me and told that after that had expired, I would be discharged from the Royal Air Force, but would be subject to recall if required. After nearly six years of RAF service, I set off for home, arriving late evening. During that journey my thoughts went back to RAF Cardington, remembering the enthusiasm with which my colleagues and I had joined the service to fly. I could not help wondering how many were still living, probably not many, but I was one of the lucky ones. People have often asked if I was ever frightened, to which the answer is yes, but not to the extent of being unable to carry out my duties.

Two years after last seeing my wife, I was back with her and my fifteen months old son Terry, whom I had only seen in photographs that she had sent to me. My first sight of him was as he lay asleep in his cot with golden curly hair showing on the pillow. The next morning I awoke to see him standing in his cot looking at me, ducking down when I looked at him. His mother said, 'This is your Daddy,' whereupon he smiled, said 'Daddy' and held out his arms to be picked up. The reunion was complete!

After a period of my life when I never had to worry about where the next meal would come from and had no particular financial worries, I was now one of a huge number of unemployed ex-servicemen looking for suitable work. My service gratuity of just over £100 seemed a lot of money but if I did not quickly find a job, it would soon disappear! I knew that I was lucky to have survived the war without injury and although I did not know it at the time, luck would remain with me in the years that lay ahead.

Chapter 8

Civilian Life

Before leaving Singapore Tony had asked me to go and see his father, Air Marshall Sir Aubrey Ellwood, at the Air Ministry when I eventually got back home. I thought that the Air Marshall would be much too busy to bother with me, but Tony assured me that would not be so as his father would be pleased to get first hand information of him and the squadron. When Tony made that request I did not know that the squadron and he would be back in UK before me.

It must have been about a week after I had been demobilised that I went to The Air Ministry in London, and asked if Sir Aubrey would see me. It was obvious that he was expecting me to call as I was taken almost immediately to his office. He showed great interest in what I had to tell him about Tony and the squadron but then asked what I intended to do now that I was about to leave the RAF. He was aghast when I told him that I intended to take all the leave due to me before making any plans. Quite forcibly he said that there were now good jobs to be had, but it was no good expecting them to still be there when I had finished my leave. He wrote a brief note to the Squadron Leader in charge of the Officer's Appointments Section and told me to go to see him immediately. The Squadron Leader read the note and then asked me what I would like to do. I had not given any thought to this and therefore had not the faintest idea what I would do other than being determined not to return to printing. After some discussion, he asked if I would be interested in Civil Aviation, as he knew that BOAC and BEA were recruiting ex RAF aircrew. I had never considered making aviation my career but it was certainly an attractive option and it made sense. I asked for further details and was told that he would make some enquiries on my behalf and, since there was no telephone at home, he would write when he had further information to give me.

About ten days later, he wrote and asked me to telephone him as soon as possible. When I spoke to him he told me that there were vacancies for Navigators with British Overseas Airways (BOAC) and vacancies for Radio Officers with BOAC, British European Airways (BEA) and British South American Airways (BSAA). He went on to say that he did not think that I had sufficient navigation experience to satisfy BOAC and perhaps I should consider becoming a Radio Officer. It was then left that he would make specific enquiries with the various airlines and write to me.

Some days later I received another letter, once again asking me to telephone him as soon as possible. When I did so, he asked me which company I would like to fly with as a Radio Officer. In consideration that BOAC operated flying boats of which I had considerable experience, I chose BOAC. He then sent me application forms for employment with BOAC that had to be completed and returned to him for his action. Shortly afterwards, I was quite astonished to receive a letter from BOAC asking me to attend for an interview at their offices in Stratton Street, just off Piccadilly in London. The interview and subsequent medical examination went well and I was invited to join as a trainee Radio Officer on a course commencing in July. Quite naturally I accepted with the thought that a new career opportunity could be there for me.

About six weeks before the training course was due to start, BOAC wrote explaining that unforeseen circumstances compelled them to defer the July course until December. This came as quite a shock and caused me to re-evaluate the situation. There was nothing to indicate that they would not employ me in December, but my leave had almost run out and when it did, my income would be reduced to zero. This was not a nice situation to be in for a married man with a wife and child to support, so I decided to look for interim or alternative employment. Prior to this I had been in touch with the firm with whom I had been apprenticed who said that because Herbert Shaw had died, they had closed their printing department, but offered me an opportunity to join another firm to complete the apprenticeship. This was totally unacceptable and by mutual agreement, my apprenticeship was terminated.

Through an uncle of my wife, I was told of a job opportunity with The British Thompson Houston Company as a trainee manager in their lamp factory. I applied and after the usual interviews, was offered a job at their factory in Rugby, some 20 miles away from my home in Northampton. It was a great relief to receive this job offer and I commenced work immediately, feeling that perhaps it was better to forget about flying. The work was quite interesting and I found the company and my colleagues very pleasant to work with. I soon realised that the trainee manager offer was something my wife's uncle had thought up and I would need many years of experience in the lamp factory before I could hope for promotion to a higher level.

I had to purchase some form of motorised transport to get to and from Rugby and managed at very high cost to buy a very old OK Supreme 250 cc motorcycle. It was not in particularly good condition but served my purpose perfectly, although a car would have been more comfortable.

It had a drip feed oil lubrication control that had to be varied with speed and I can recall that if I went too fast, the oil controller was unable to provide enough lubrication and at times the engine was close to 'seizing up'. During the war there were plenty of second hand cars available, mainly because petrol rationing prevented their use, but with peace all the bargains were snapped up very quickly. During the war my father bought several second hand cars just for the tyres, which were then very difficult to obtain. He gave me one of his cars to use while I was on leave from India and said that he would keep it for me until the war was over. Unfortunately, as I was out of the country for such a long time after the war ended, he completely forgot about his promise and got rid of all except his own car, leaving nothing for me to use.

Having heard nothing further from BOAC, it seemed that I would have to make a career with BTH, although in all honesty I loved flying and missed it a great deal. With the very real possibility of remaining with BTH, my wife and I decided to move to Rugby so that I would not have the long journey each day to and from work. My wife's uncle had been widowed just before the end of the war and having a three-bedroom house to himself, he invited us to move in with him. This was a good arrangement for everyone, particularly him, as he no longer needed to cook and clean the house himself.

The months went by and then out of the blue a letter arrived from BOAC inviting me to join them in December. After a great deal of thought, I resigned from BTH and accepted the BOAC offer. BTH were extremely complimentary in the reference they gave me, saying that they were sorry to lose me but fully understood that I was returning to a flying job for which I had been previously trained. I discovered many years later that my decision to go back into aviation caused my wife a great deal of distress!

Chapter 9

Civil Aviation

On 6th December 1946, I reported to BOAC's training school at Aldermaston Airfield, which was located close to Harwell where I did my Wellington Bomber OTU in 1942. There were many students at the BOAC Radio and Navigation school, all studying for Civil Aviation Licences. Most were ex RAF and many had flown together or had served on the same squadron during the war. On the first day of my course, Radio Officer students were introduced to the Chief Radio Instructor, Percy Neve, who generally outlined the course and gave details of what was expected of students. Bearing in mind that all were qualified RAF aircrew with operational experience, it was generally thought that it was just a course to brush up one's knowledge prior to taking the licence examinations. Nothing could have been further from the truth! The course went in stages from basic radio, covering everything advanced theory. Furthermore, the Morse speeds reached in the RAF were considered to be the absolute minimum acceptable for Civil Aviation. Effectively this meant that everything taught during RAF service had to be learned again, but in much greater depth.

Accommodation was provided in the same Nissen huts used by the RAF and although very basic, it was quite adequate. The course was very demanding, but the standard of instruction and the instructors could not have been better. During the course, I developed a friendship with a senior radio instructor named Fred Herzog and for many years until his death in the 70s, we met quite regularly. He was very small in stature and for some unknown reason, was called 'The General'. Fred enjoyed the hobby of amateur radio and he encouraged me to take it up, enabling us to have radio contacts from time to time.

The winter of 1946/47 was very severe and prior to starting the course, I decided to replace the somewhat unreliable OK Supreme motorcycle with something more up to date. There was plenty of surplus military equipment available and I was fortunate to obtain a brand new ex WD Norton 500cc 16H motorcycle, which was painted in army Olive Green and had never been used. It was covered in protective grease that took ages to clean off, but it was a superb machine and its engine never gave the slightest trouble. However, the ice on the roads in that horrid winter of 1946/47 caused me to come off three times on one journey from

Northampton to Aldermaston and I decided that two wheels were not safe enough for me. New cars were impossible to buy and second hand ones prohibitively expensive, so I bought a sidecar thus making the Norton safer and allowing me to transport my wife and son around.

At the end of the course, which lasted until early May 1947, the licence examinations were sat at Harwell with approved Civil Aviation examiners conducting the proceedings. Some candidates failed completely, some partially and others, myself included, passed at the first attempt. Those unsuccessful, were put back for further instruction, which meant that they were left behind when those who had passed commenced flying. I became the holder of Provisional Licence Number 1417, which was converted to First Class Radio Operators Licence number 372 at a later date. If my memory serves me correctly, only Provisional licences were being issued at that time, possibly due to the large number of candidates being examined. At a later date a further examination had to be passed to secure the First Class licence. I was well aware that the career I was starting may not have been possible without the help Air Marshall Sir Aubrey Ellwood gave me, for which I would always be grateful. I tried to keep in touch with Tony Ellwood and on one occasion visited him at a garage in London where he was working as a car mechanic. His boss was an impatient and rather abusive person who constantly harangued Tony for no good reason and it came as no great surprise for me to learn that he left the garage and re-joined the RAF. He became a member of perhaps the first RAF flying display team, flying Meteors. I was saddened to learn that he lost his life when the Meteor he was flying, inexplicably flew into the ground at great speed from a very high altitude.

Navigator and Radio Officers who had passed the licence examinations were posted to the BOAC Flying Unit, also based at Aldermaston, to carry out flying duties on training flights on Dakota aircraft with an occasional flight in a Viking. The Dakota was a flying classroom with a trainee navigators and (I think) only me as a trainee Radio Officer, supervised by an instructor. All overseas training flights positioned to Heathrow for customs formalities and landed back there on the return to UK, followed by the return flight to Aldermaston. The facilities at Heathrow at that time were very primitive with pre-fabricated buildings used as offices and very limited airfield navigation facilities, quite unlike the huge airport complex that exists today. Thirteen sectors were flown to places in Europe, including Gibraltar where I had been before during the war on RAF Wellington and Sunderland aircraft. Stops were made at several places for fuel including Copenhagen, Stockholm and Gothenburg, doing a total of about 45 hours flying. The Captains on those training flights were all ex Imperial Airways and had a great deal of experience. I got the impression, perhaps erroneously, that those of us who had joined with only RAF experience were not considered to be really qualified airmen. Certainly there was no attempt to put us at ease or engage in any social activity away from the aircraft.

Once the required stage of proficiency was reached, students were posted away for Line flying duties. My posting was to Number 4 line at Hythe near Southampton, to operate on Flying Boats. Before being given my posting instructions, I was asked if I had any fleet preference and naturally opted for the Flying Boats that I knew so well. I did discover later that I would have been equally acceptable for North Atlantic routes where it would have been financially more rewarding, but it made no difference to my career.

Realising that I would be working 100 miles away from home, I decided that I must have a car and with great difficulty managed to buy a 1931 Austin 7 Saloon for £100 that had to be paid for in cash, seriously depleting my meagre savings. With the average wage in 1946 being about £4 a week, the purchase was equal to nearly 6 months salary. The car had a great number of miles on its speedometer, but had been well maintained. Although not particularly comfortable, it proved to be very reliable, only letting me down once in the whole time I owned it.

It was about this time that my brother died. He was badly injured during the fighting in Italy and received further injuries when the Germans bombed the hospital where he was being treated. Transferred to another hospital, he was injured yet again when that hospital was bombed. Those dreadful experiences were enough to break anyone's spirit but he recovered sufficiently to allow him to be sent home and demobilised. He received constant medical treatment after demobilisation but his war experiences had obviously taken their toll and his marriage broke up, causing him to take his own life. Unfortunately his death affected my father so much, that he never got over losing his eldest son in such a manner.

Chapter 10

BOAC Flying Boats

My first visit to Hythe, located on the south-western side of the Solent opposite Southampton, was on 1st July 1947 when I reported to Number 4 Line to meet the Chief Radio Officer, Len Cheeseman, and his deputy Bernard Pettman. Both were ex Imperial Airways but unlike the Training Captains I had encountered at Aldermaston, they were very friendly and helpful. Bernard was a Radio Amateur and we became good friends, remaining so for many years until his death in the 1990's.

I had driven from Northampton to lodgings in Southampton on the previous day and on the following morning took the Ferry from the pier in Southampton to Hythe. It was a clear sunny day and many flying boats were gently moving on the water at their moorings in the Solent close to Hythe. It was as though I was returning to 230 Squadron again to see so many aircraft, but this time they all had civil aviation markings. As the Ferry approached Hythe pier I could see several flying boats beached on the hard standing close to the slipway, being worked on by engineers in much the same manner as they would have been on the squadron. This put me totally at ease and it was like being on the squadron again.

Number 4 Line operated a variety of Flying Boats fully fitted out as luxury civil aircraft, operating routes to South Africa, Australia and Hong Kong. In March of 1948, the Hong Kong route was extended to Iwakuni in Japan. BOAC crews operated the routes throughout with the exception of the sectors from Singapore to Australia and back, which were operated by QANTAS crews. No one bothered to tell me how long some of the trips were and it came as quite a shock to learn that those to Japan could be up to 42 days and to Hong Kong, up to 37 days. Not exactly conducive to maintaining a good marital relationship! I had already found temporary lodgings in Southampton for the periods of time when I needed to be available for duty, but it soon became apparent that travelling the 100 miles each way whenever I was needed for flying or other duties was just not convenient. With insufficient savings to consider buying a house, the only alternative was to find unfurnished rooms. This I managed fairly easily with a widowed lady and her two small daughters at their house in the Shirley area of Southampton, but at a fairly high rent, which strained my budget to its limits. When my wife and son moved in, the restrictions imposed on us by the widow were so harsh that eventually we found better rooms with a couple with whom my wife had become friendly in the next house along the road. At that time all I wanted to do was settle down with my wife and son until we could find a house of our own. Looking back to those days, I realise how difficult it must have been for my wife who not only would be separated from me for the lengthy periods I would be away on flying duties, but also, she would be a long way from her own family and friends in Northampton.

Inevitably there was ground training before Line flying commenced, this being carried out by two ex Imperial Airways Senior Radio Officers, 'Paddy' Cussans and Jimmy Armitage, both of whom were Base and Line Training Radio Officers. Once again I found both very helpful and thoroughly professional in every aspect of their work. Although fully conversant with Sunderland flying boats, it was necessary for me to know each civil variant that BOAC operated. The 'Hythe', 'Plymouth', and 'Sandringham' were all Sunderland civil types, but each had differences that had to be learned, together with the appropriate emergency procedures. The 'Hythe' was the least sophisticated of the fleet, being a fairly simple conversion of the military Sunderland for civil use. The Sandringham was a basic Sunderland airframe specifically modified and furnished for civil use. Both of these types had a later version of the somewhat unreliable Pegasus XVIII engines used by the RAF, but I soon found that the BOAC engines did not give anywhere near the amount of trouble, doubtless due to the higher standard of maintenance. Furthermore, fully feathering propellers were fitted, unlike the RAF Mark 3 Sunderlands. Plymouth aircraft were by far the more efficient aircraft, being fitted with the same very reliable and more powerful Pratt & Whitney engines that were on Mark 5 Sunderlands. Fortunately the radio equipment on all three types was identical so I only had to learn one installation, which was much the same as it was on RAF Wellingtons and Sunderlands.

Before Line Training commenced I had to be fitted out with additional uniform for use in the tropics so that as well as my navy blue uniform, I was issued with a rather smart khaki gabardine uniform with rank markings on shoulder boards, and washable Bush shirt and shorts. The captain, at his discretion, decided which uniform would be worn on any particular day and I can remember arriving in Johannesburg on a cold evening with the temperature only in the low 50s wearing bush shirt and shorts. BOAC also provided shirts appropriate to the uniform being worn and arranged laundry services at some stations en route. The net result of this was that one's suitcase was bulging by the time all the uniforms and civilian clothes had been packed.

One task undertaken by the Radio Officer that I had not done before was slipping moorings on departures, and mooring up on arrival. Nothing difficult about it really, provided fingers were kept clear of drogue ropes and mooring lines. BUT – try it on a windy day, with temperature just above freezing, the wind blowing a gale, waves breaking over the bows and driving rain drenching you. Believe me, it was no fun! Radio Officers were provided with white overalls and wet weather clothing to protect their uniform. This protective clothing had to be removed and stowed before returning to the flight deck. The mooring duty meant that a Radio Officer was needed for every flight even though he would not necessarily carry out any radio communication duties. The Captain gave slipping and mooring instructions in Morse code using a whistle, which in windy conditions and with engines running could scarcely be heard. He would whistle 'S' to slip moorings. 'P' if he wanted the port drogue deployed or 'S' for the starboard. Drogues were used to slow the aircraft and to hold a particular line of approach to the buoy. There were often heated exchanges between the Captain and the Radio Officer when the instruction was wrongly interpreted.

Resplendent in my dark blue uniform with its two wavy gold rank stripes signifying a Second Radio Officer, I did 14 training flights under supervision totalling about 35 hours flying, including a round trip to Augusta in Scicily, before being sent down the route. Augusta was a delightful place to visit with its large and virtually unrestricted harbour for take-off and landing and usually with good weather conditions. The weather could get rather stormy at times during the winter months but seldom prevented scheduled arrivals and departures. There were many places of interest, including decent bars where a few ales were imbibed in off duty periods. The accommodation was good and the food, compared to what was available in UK, was excellent.

On departure from UK on overseas flights, crews were normally collected from their homes and taken to the Harbour Heights hotel in Poole for the night. The exception was the Radio Officer who usually had to operate when the aircraft was positioned to Poole during the afternoon prior to its departure on the following morning. He was also required to operate back to Hythe after customs clearance on return to UK. First Officers who had held Flying Boat commands in the RAF commanded some of these positioning flights. The departure was from Poole Harbour, which was the International Departure point for flying boats. However, early in 1948 a Flying Boat Berth would be established at Berth 50 in Southampton Docks and the overnight stop discontinued. At most bases a marine tender would take passengers and crew to/from the aircraft, which in rough weather could be very uncomfortable. At Berth 50 the flying boat was moored to a buoy close to a floating pontoon and then towed back into the pontoon enabling easy and convenient access to the aircraft. However, when that change was implemented, very early pick up times were needed as the departure time was usually soon after dawn. The entire crew would be collected by BOAC bus with the last person to be collected being the captain, no matter how far away he lived! On return to UK, crews were driven back to their homes by BOAC transport.

On 8th September 1947, I left Poole, operating on a Plymouth Flying Boat 'Portsea' GAHZE en route to Hong Kong with 'Paddy' Cussans accompanying me to give supervision on the round trip, and carry out my flight check on the final sector. The crew stayed with the aircraft and flew every day for 7 days until it reached Hong Kong, flying about 50 hours. After a 40-hour stay in Hong Kong while the aircraft was being serviced, the return journey was flown in 5 days taking about another 50 hours flying time, landing at Poole on 21st September. In 14 days the crew flew about 100 hours, which by any standard is very hard work.

From Poole we flew to Marseilles for a fuel stop, continuing on to Augusta in Sicily for the first night stop. Being summer the weather over France and the Mediterranean was delightful with scarcely a cloud to be seen. The flying boats were not pressurised and rarely flew above eight to ten thousand feet, which meant frequent heading changes to avoid any cloud likely to give turbulence. From time to time frontal systems had to be flown through, resulting in rough flying conditions much disliked by passengers and crew. In those days there was no organised airways system and the route chosen by the Captain and navigator was usually in consideration of the en route weather and upper winds. The flight over France had to avoid the high ground and usually routed through what was loosely referred to as 'The Toulouse Gap' to Marseilles, landing on a lake at Marignane. The water of the lake could often become very choppy if the Mistral wind was blowing strongly down the Rhone valley. From Marignane the route took us through the Bonifacio Straits between Corsica and Sardinia with very high ground on each side of track, then directly out over the sea towards Palermo in Scicily. I believe it then tracked along the north coast until able to turn south over the sea towards Augusta. Navigation aids were not plentiful and we relied on the skill of the navigator to keep us on track and away from the mountains or high ground. The first sight of Mount Etna, the semi active Sicilian volcano, was very impressive. I would see this on many occasions in the future and occasionally with a smoke plume at its peak.

The first night stop allowed the opportunity to get to know our passengers who were accommodated in the same large hotel styled building that housed the crew. Some would be staying with the aircraft until Hong Kong was reached, whilst others would disembark at places en route where other passengers might join. Unlike today, flying was not the normal means of travelling abroad and it was only the fairly wealthy who could afford the fare. Some travellers and their families were based overseas and used BOAC to get them to/from their overseas base, their fares being paid by the companies who employed them. Often unaccompanied children of families based abroad travelled from/to boarding schools in UK for the longer school holidays.

After landing one could not relax too much as the next departure was going to be about 6.30a.m., which meant a wake up call about 4a.m. The company doctor recommended that a full English breakfast should always be eaten prior to every departure and on most occasions the crew did, hangover permitting! There is nothing worse than flying on an empty stomach with the sort of flying conditions that could be experienced on flights to/from the Far East. The catering on board was really quite superb for passengers and crew, but if turbulence occurred, some would soon regret eating it.

The flight to Cairo was completely over the sea until the Egyptian coast was crossed at Mersah Matruh from whence it tracked into Cairo for the second night stop. Again the weather was clear with only small amounts of white cumulus cloud to be seen. The landing area was on the River Nile at Rod El Farag and I never ceased to be amazed how quickly the BOAC Marine Craft marshalled the felucca river craft clear of the area. The river craft were not the only hazards as there was a very large steel bridge on the approach path that had to be avoided. Normally landing or take-off was in daylight but if the aircraft ran late, at night the landing run would be indicated by a line of not very bright floating lights – all good fun if you are not of a nervous disposition! Passengers and crew were accommodated on a rather ancient and not particularly comfortable houseboat moored closed to the jetty. The temperature on landing was in the high 80s and as the small bedrooms on board had only rather noisy fans for cooling, most people had a somewhat restless night.

We were now two hours ahead of UK time so that the next departure time of 7a.m. was really 5a.m. at home. With the flight first going to Basra and then on to Bahrain, there would be a very tiring days work by the time Bahrain was reached. It was reasonably cool at take-off but very quickly the ground became heated by the sun and this produced the most awful turbulence, to the discomfort of all on board. Due to high ground we could not take the direct track to Basra and had to initially fly northeastwards from Cairo to cross over the lower ground of Jordan before it was safe to turn east into the desert. Navigation aids were few and far between and I did not envy the navigator his job in the slightest. The desert looked most inhospitable with its scrub and sand dunes, but the colours to be seen particularly fascinated me, ranging from dirty brown to quite reddish shades. If rain ever fell on the desert, which it occasionally does, within hours flowers and greenery would appear and transform the desolation to give it a rare sort of beauty. I must say that on a later flight in winter, I saw snow lying on the higher ground of Jordan. Over the desert, depending on the route chosen, oil pipe-lines and small landing strips might possibly be seen, visibility permitting.

Position reporting communication to the appropriate ground stations throughout the entire round trip was on high frequency radio, using Morse. I remember that Cairo's call sign was SUO, and its powerful signal was usually easily readable with even the poorest atmospheric conditions. Further east it was a different story and often it became necessary to pass messages through any ground stations that could be heard, who hopefully would pass them on to the appropriate station. Sometimes other BOAC flying boats in the air heading in the opposite direction could be contacted and asked to relay messages. Radio Officers would, whenever possible, assist the navigator by getting bearings from radio beacons located on or close to the track, using the Direction Finding (D/F) equipment fitted on board.

Of prime importance was the reception of actual weather information for the destination and alternative stations. Sandstorms often reduce visibility to almost zero in the Persian Gulf and further east severe monsoon conditions could temporarily prevent aircraft landing. For this reason, and because forecasting was not to the same standard as today, it was essential that all weather broadcasts for the sector being flown were copied and given to the Captain. Another task of the Radio Officer was to listen to BBC overseas news broadcasts and write out a summary for the passengers. This was a task that I thoroughly disliked because it was almost impossible to write fast enough and get all that the newsreader said. BOAC also had Passenger Information Bulletins that gave information about the flight together with a map showing the track and the estimated times at various points along the track. This was normally the navigator's task.

Passengers could send cables from the aircraft, at quite a high cost to them, but few took advantage of the facility. It was not a job that I particularly cared for as the method of calculating the charge to passengers was rather complicated and I seem to remember that Radio Officers were held responsible if messages were undercharged. To send a cable, contact was made with Portishead Radio that operated 24 hours a day on several radio frequencies. Portishead used powerful transmitters and provided that the right frequency was selected, communication was possible almost anywhere on BOAC's route structure. Fortunately not many passengers took advantage of the facility and I cannot remember sending more than half a dozen in the years that I was a Radio Officer. One would never have thought then that in the future people would be able to telephone to home or office from the aircraft in flight as they do today.

The arrival and transit of Basra was in a stifling 110-degree heat with high relative humidity and it was extremely unlikely that it would be much cooler at Bahrain. The flying boat base was located at Shatt al Arab where the rivers Tigris and Euphrates meet and even if sandstorms or rising dust were not present, the haze caused by the fierce heat always dramatically reduced the visibility. After re-fuelling at Basra, the flight continued over the Persian Gulf to Bahrain for the next scheduled night stop. Flying over the water at least gave a respite from the sickening turbulence of the desert.

Bahrain is situated on the island of Muharraq that is joined to the main island of Manamah by a causeway. I had flown over its airfield during the war in a Wellington bomber en route to Sharjah. The arrival was on schedule with a temperature 100+ degrees, and with the same energy sapping high relative humidity, it was not a pleasant place to be. Passengers and crew were taken by a BOAC bus to its rest house to spend the night. The Captain and passengers had their own rooms but the rest of the crew, (all male), spent the night in a large dormitory that was cooled only by two large and very noisy ceiling fans. This was the most uncomfortable night of the whole flight and I slept very little.

On the following morning, with only one sector to Karachi to be flown, the take-off was at the seemingly reasonable local time of 8.30a.m., (5a.m. UK time). With the temperature only a little below 90 degrees, the aircraft struggled to reach flying speed and even when airborne its climb was very sluggish and it took a long time to reach the cruising altitude of about 7000 feet, despite having the more efficient Pratt & Whitney engines. Fortunately there was no limit to space in the take-off area and the flying boat could keep going straight ahead until either it left the water or the take-off was abandoned due to overheating of the engines.

The route taken initially was over the sea towards the Strait of Hormuz to avoid some nasty high ground over the Oman Peninsula.

Once clear of the peninsula, the route ran parallel to the coast of Iran through the Gulf of Oman until India (now Pakistan) was reached. Little or no cloud was encountered until the flight approached the India border when high and medium cloud started to form. En route were the small airfields of Jask, and Jiwani, both previously used by Imperial Airways flights as staging posts. Any radio aids they possessed were of very low power and of little help, but fortunately the ground was clearly visible and the navigator could fairly easily check the aircraft's position. On the final stage of the flight there was a very powerful radio beacon located close to Karachi airport that could be used for homing. If the visibility was good approaching that beacon, it was easy to proceed visually to the flying boat base at Korangi Creek. It was a very pleasant six and three quarter hour flight and as it was mainly over the sea, any turbulence encountered was quite light.

After disembarking from the aircraft, passengers and crew were taken by a BOAC bus to the city to spend the night in the Carlton hotel, a quite pleasant air-conditioned hotel in the centre of Karachi, run by an English family. Despite the fact that the temperature was in the low 80s, the relative humidity was far less than that at Bahrain and it felt reasonably comfortable. I stayed in that hotel several times and was usually impressed by the standard of food provided. There was always a cold buffet with various meats on offer and I particularly enjoyed that until on one occasion when selecting a slice of meat, I discovered a large dead cockroach under it. I rather lost my appetite for food at that hotel! Eventually BOAC built an air-conditioned rest house at Korangi Creek with plenty of leisure facilities available for BOAC crews and those of QANTAS, who also stayed there.

It was a more comfortable night than that experienced in Bahrain, and after the usual full English breakfast, the aircraft departed at 7a.m. on an eight-hour flight to Calcutta. This seemingly reasonable hour was in fact 1.30a.m. in England and although we were on our fifth day away from England, our bodies certainly had not become accustomed to the five and a half-hour time change! The heavily laden Flying Boat again struggled into the air and climbed en route for Calcutta, and as it was the monsoon season, there would be a lot of bad weather to circumnavigate. Fortunate or not, I had been well blooded by the Indian monsoon weather during my service with the RAF and I knew what to expect. On this occasion we flew mostly between layers of cloud at about 8000 feet but often passed around or through rain showers with little sight of the ground. Occasionally it was necessary to deviate well away from track to avoid towering cumulus or cumulo-nimbus clouds with their particularly nasty turbulence. This sector could be quite limiting and dependant on the winds, some aircraft had to land en route on a lake at Raj Samand to refuel. If this was necessary the navigator had the horrible task of finding the lake. Fortunately for me, that and future flights I operated on in this sector never had cause to land there. Navigation was difficult as the ground could not be seen and any radio aids were badly affected by rain or lightning static. Occasionally the aircraft would emerge from the cloud into a clear piece of sky, enabling the navigator to take a quick sun shot. Approaching Calcutta the weather was not particularly good with low cloud and rain, but as usual the very experienced ex Imperial Airways Captain made light of it and smoothly set the aircraft down on the Hooghly River. It is a filthy muddy river that is usually littered with all sorts of debris, garbage and the occasional animal carcase. Despite that, there were always Indians to be seen bathing from the banks.

Once ashore, passengers and crew were taken by BOAC bus to the Great Eastern Hotel where the fifth night would be spent. The roads were always congested with trishaws, cars, lorries and milling masses of humanity, making the journey tediously slow. The traffic noise was deafening with the Indians driving with their hand almost continually on the horn. I was no stranger to the poverty of India but I could never get used to seeing people living (and sometimes dying) in squalor on the streets, begging for anything that would make their life a little easier. After any transit of Calcutta, the aircraft journey log would list the number deaths reported due to smallpox, typhoid and any other tropical diseases. This information was entered by the local health authorities and would always conclude with a statement, 'The health of the city is considered satisfactory'!

Passengers and crew stayed at the Great Eastern hotel that had a Raj style look about it. It possessed a magnificent dining room that was not only enormous in size, but had at least two waiters for each of the many tables who vied with each other for privilege of serving guests, almost as if they were only paid if they served guests. Unfortunately the magnificence of the dining room was not present in the very ordinary bedrooms and bathrooms that were quite sparsely furnished and the occupancy shared with quite enormous sized cockroaches!

I was not looking forward to the last three sectors over the next two days, as I knew that almost certainly we would have to penetrate the Inter Tropical Front (ITF). This is a broad band of intense tropical storms that more or less girdle the earth. The ITF has now been renamed the Inter Tropical Convergence Zone (ITCZ). This front follows behind the sun as its declination moves seasonally north and south over the equator. If the ITCZ is particularly active, thunderstorms within the front can be enormous with cloud tops in excess of 60,000 feet and accompanied by torrential rain, frightful turbulence and perhaps some of the most vivid electrical storms to be seen anywhere in the world. Such storms were always avoided if possible. It is not unusual to find cyclones at certain seasons in the Bay of Bengal, these always causing devastation in their path on the ground and almost heart failure for airmen seeking a way through or around it.

The aircraft departed at midnight English time on a short four and a half-hour flight to Rangoon carrying its load of jaded passengers and perhaps even more jaded crew. The weather was surprisingly good until south of Akyab when it got very stormy with the aircraft bouncing all over the sky. This was where I had done a great deal of operational flying in the RAF so nothing really surprised me as we groped our way through the filthy weather for a landing on the Rangoon River. That brought back a few memories, especially when the golden dome of the Shwe Dagon Pagoda that I had seen so many times before, came into sight! It was a very sad and sick looking lot of passengers, (and some crew), who disembarked before re-fuelling took place. I would think that anyone with Rangoon as their destination thanked God for their safe deliverance there.

Refuelling over, it was back on board again to battle with the elements during the short two and a half-hour flight to Bangkok where we would have the final night stop. It was quite rough for the first hour before crossing from Burma into Thailand, routing over the lowest part of the high ground separating the two countries. Approaching the low plains of Thailand, the weather cleared up and soon we were able to see Bangkok in the distance. The approach and landing was uneventful and a smooth touch down was made on the very muddy and quite winding river. The worst was now behind us and we could scarcely wait for the scheduled day off on arrival in Hong Kong.

After disembarkation the crew was taken to the Trocadera hotel that was used for the final night stop. It was a beautifully clean hotel but had extremely thin mattresses on the wooden slatted beds, which whilst possibly being beneficial to those with back trouble, were extremely hard and uncomfortable. There was not a proper bathroom, a large vat of water being provided in the room's courtyard from which water could be ladled over the body to bathe. Given the sixteen hours break before the next departure, I took time to look around the shopping area and have a couple of beers with other members of the crew before dinner.

The departure for Hong Kong was at 7a.m. (midnight in England) and it was a most enjoyable seven-hour flight with no really bad weather en route. True it was necessary to divert around towering Cumulus and the occasional Cumulo Nimbus cloud, but we were in sight of the ground most of the time over Thailand, Laos and Vietnam. I clearly remember how green everything looked, such a contrast to the desert sectors over which we had flown. With no political problems in those days, the track taken was almost direct to Hue where there was a radio beacon to home onto. From there we flew to the south of Hainan Island before turning on track direct to Hong Kong. Paddy Cussans had briefed me that Hong Kong often experiences very poor weather and he was at pains to see that I got weather reports at very frequent intervals.

Operational procedures in flight on the flying boats were much the same as land planes, except that on arrival at a flying boat destination, the let down procedures could be quite different. A blind approach system called BABS could be used at bases that were so equipped, enabling the Radio Officer to determine the distance the aircraft was from the ground facility and if to the left or right of the required track. It enabled the Captain to descend to a safe height when it was hoped to be below cloud and able to execute a visual approach. Hong Kong was equipped with BABS and in fact, we did a BABS approach for practice, probably for my benefit, even though the weather was reasonably clear.

Another approach aid at some flying boat stations was the QDM system whereby the Captain was given headings to steer by a ground station or by the Radio Officer using the aircraft's loop aerial in conjunction with a radio beacon. When the indications were that the aircraft had passed over the radio beacon, the Captain would carry out a timed procedure turn over a safe area and descend back towards the beacon hoping to become visual and land. Once below cloud, Flying Boats always had to perform a visual approach and landing since there were no instrument guidance systems available to take the flying boat down to a precise landing point.

The first sight of Hong Kong before landing in the harbour was quite spectacular with seemingly hundreds of small craft in the water. The approach, dependant on the wind and water conditions, could be from the south-west via Cheung Chau Island, or through the south-east gap via Waglan Island. On this occasion the approach was via Cheung Chau. The operational area was controlled by BOAC marine craft that kept the small boats away whenever aircraft were landing or taking off. Poor visibility and low cloud often present could sometimes make it necessary to break cloud over the sea close to Waglan Island using the radio beacon sited there, and then creep through the gap to land in the harbour. Such an approach was quite impressive with the land rising steeply on each side of the inbound track. This approach was only permissible if the cloud conditions and visibility in the harbour were adequate. If all efforts failed, and ONLY as an absolute emergency and with sea conditions permitting, the aircraft could land in the sea and taxi through the gap to the harbour. A slow, tedious and uncomfortable procedure that was not to be recommended! Fortunately I never experienced that particular procedure. Flying boats were sufficiently manoeuvrable to be able to safely circle over the water between the island and the mainland provided that the visibility was adequate.

A smooth landing was made, and with a great deal of relief that the outbound journey was over, we disembarked and were taken by company bus to the hotel where two nights would be spent at what perhaps was the most comfortable hotel on the entire route. This was the Peninsular Hotel where BOAC had the air-conditioned sixth floor reserved for its crews. In those days the hotel had a magnificent view overlooking the harbour but when I visited Hong Kong in 1997, a skyscraper had been built that completely dwarfed it and obscured its view of the harbour.

The Colony, now part of China of course, consisted of Hong Kong Island (and many other islands) together with Kowloon City that was located in the onshore territory that stretched to the border with China. It was quite strange to stand at the border fence and look out over 'No Man's Land' into China. Over the years I took every opportunity to see as much of the Colony as was possible in the off duty time available and made many friends amongst the residents and had many happy experiences. It has changed very dramatically since my first visit over fifty years ago, becoming a colony of skyscrapers. I believe that is called progress!

Throughout the entire round trip, although not qualified to navigate, I took a great deal of interest in what was going on and gave what assistance I could, such as it was. I certainly could commiserate with the navigator who at most had only, but not always, sun, moon, map reading, and the odd radio aid position line for navigation assistance on the flights that were mostly in daylight. On future flights some navigators allowed me to take practice sun shots that gave me pleasure when the position line was plotted.

Perhaps one of the nicest times to be in Hong Kong is at New Year when, on the stroke of midnight, all ships in the harbour sound their hooters to usher in the New Year. The Chinese New Year ceremonies in February are also great fun to watch, having their own charm and spectacle.

With rationing in force at home, it was strange to see shops in Hong Kong filled with food and clothing that was not readily available in England. Paddy told me that most aircrew purchased an extra suitcase in Hong Kong, and filled it with tinned food and sweets to take back home. Quite naturally I took advantage of that 'perk' which was welcomed by the family on my return. It was possible to have a suit made overnight at a nearby tailors shop and many people, including myself on a later trip, took advantage of the opportunity. Food was not subject to customs duty but clothing was, although customs officers were very fair and I never paid duty on any clothing that I bought.

Currency restrictions were in force in 1947 and crews were only allowed to take a limited amount of Sterling out of the country. Accommodation and food was provided by BOAC but other expenses such as drink, cigarettes, etc, had to be paid for out of one's own pocket. Before departure from UK, BOAC Currency Coupons could be purchased, £2 of which could be exchanged for local currency at each night-stop on route. Salaries were not particularly high in those early days and most people had little money to spare for luxuries. I soon learned that, for instance, in Bangkok one could use the allowed £2 of currency coupons to buy a new leather brief case, and still have enough left over to buy a few beers. On return to UK, the brief case could be sold for at least twice the amount paid for it in Bangkok. This was just one of the 'perks' used to supplement one's income, albeit perhaps not quite legal.

A food allowance was paid to crews stopping in Hong Kong, which allowed the opportunity of eating out away from the hotel. For a long time this was the only BOAC station on the eastern routes where allowances were paid, elsewhere the hotel provided food to BOAC's account. One could not fault the food provided but it did mean that there was little incentive to get away from the hotel on a night stop.

I took full advantage of exploring the shopping areas of Nathan Road and the Central shopping area of Hong Kong Island. One could cross from Kowloon to Victoria on the north side of Hong Island on the Star Ferry in about ten minutes for a fare of a few pence, and once there one could take the Peak Tram to get a magnificent view from almost the top of the mountain. On later trips there would be opportunities to visit Repulse Bay and Aberdeen, both of which are located on the south side of the island. Aberdeen was noted for its two floating restaurants that served a most delicious selection of fish. In recent years one restaurant was destroyed by fire and I cannot say if it has been replaced.

With only one day off in Hong Kong, the aircraft returned to Poole, flying every day for five days logging another 50 hours for a total of 100 hours in 20 sectors during the 14 days. Homebound, with the exception of Marignane, the aircraft stopped at the same places as the outbound journey but did not night stop in Bangkok or Calcutta. The first day was Hong Kong/Bangkok/Rangoon, second day Rangoon/Calcutta/Karachi, third day Karachi/Bahrain/Basra/Cairo, fourth day Cairo/Augusta and the fifth day back to Poole. The third day was particularly long, a duty period of 19 hours of which 14 and three-quarter hours were spent in the air. However, travelling westbound the time changes are in one's favour giving progressively later morning departure times. The schedules operated gave little time for sightseeing at night-stops, but I usually preferred to get a good night's rest and be fresh for the next early morning start. Some with more robust constitutions than I possessed, would burn the midnight oil at local bars or places of interest.

The flying and long duty days, together with the time changes each day was extremely tiring and it took several days to get back to normal on return to base. (It is called Jet Lag these days). Flying Regulations then in force permitted crews to fly a maximum of 100 hours in any 28 day period, but that total could be exceeded provided that an approved Ministry of Aviation doctor authorised an individual fit to continue flying. Normally no one was rostered by BOAC to exceed the maximum monthly hours, but if operational circumstances dictated, crews were expected to comply. I did hear that one navigator operated from UK to Tokyo and was returning homebound only to find that at Karachi, the outbound navigator had been taken ill, necessitating him to return to Hong Kong. The same regulations authorised the Captain to extend the crew's duty day to whatever he thought fit, but in the light of accidents that occurred, the regulation was reviewed and amended to a more sensible level

The Captain throughout my first flight, who I shall not name, was a very senior ex Imperial Airways pilot. He was an absolute martinet and the discipline he imposed on board and on the ground was extreme and (perhaps) unfair, so much so that I almost regretted joining BOAC. During my RAF time, flying crews were expected to be self-disciplined but could always get on with the job without being constantly badgered. Not so on my first flight with BOAC when the Captain did not think he was God, he knew he was where the crew were concerned. In fairness however, he was a superb pilot!

I can remember a later trip when for the first four days of the trip, the Flight Deck Officers and the First Officer in particular who was being checked out for a command, had been constantly shouted at by the Captain in flight. He seemed incapable of giving orders in a normal tone of voice and I think most of us resented the way he addressed us. During the evening, the crew were enjoying a drink in the bar when the Captain came in and offered to buy a round of drinks. There was an absolute stony silence until the First Officer quietly said, 'I have to fly with you, I do not have to drink with you'. There was an embarrassing silence! Strangely enough the Captain made no reference to that during the remainder of the trip, but still continued to be just as aggressive. I am happy to say that despite what occurred, the First Officer was promoted to Captain rank. My wife met that Captain some time later and could not understand why crews found him so difficult as she thought him to be a very polite and charming person.

I realised that the veteran ex Imperial Airways Captains had been flying since the early 1930s, pioneering many routes and I could almost accept their quite strong feelings about the seemingly inexperienced youngsters who joined BOAC from the RAF. The first time I experienced this was when flying with ex Imperial Airways Senior Training Captains on Dakota and Viking aircraft at Aldermaston but did not think too much about it. Paddy was quite a laid back character and his advice was to concentrate on doing the job properly and avoid personality clashes if they occurred. Being ex Imperial Airways himself, he said that most of the senior Captains were very reasonable once they knew that they could rely on you to do the job properly. Paddy's advice proved to be correct as my later flights became more relaxed and pleasant.

The veteran flying boat Captains possessed a wealth of experience and were capable of handling almost every situation that arose, mostly in an unflappable manner and one could learn a great deal from them. I certainly benefited from listening to their advice when it was offered and enjoyed some of the hair-raising stories they told of their early days in aviation. In all fairness, only a small number were difficult to get on with, whereas flying with the others was enjoyable and more than made up for the difficult ones. BOAC Captains had a seniority list that enabled them to 'Bid' for vacancies that could arise on other fleets. The most prestigious and financially rewarding route was the North Atlantic and in consequence the most senior of the Captains on the list operated that route.

An amusing story concerned a rather gruff Senior Captain named Burt who, due to the 'Bark' in his tone of voice, was called 'Barker' Burt by crews. A young steward was told to go to the flight deck and ask 'Barker' what he would like to drink. He hesitantly said 'Excuse me, Captain Barker, would you like coffee or tea?' Barker glared at him and rather forcibly said 'The name is Burt'. The young steward said 'Alright Bert, my name is George, so what would you like to drink?' I believe that there was a stony silence until the Captain exploded, and not with mirth!

At the end of the round trip Paddy, satisfied with my operating performance, checked me out for operations on the Middle East and Far East routes. Being checked out was important financially as, from the date of the successful final flight check, one became eligible for flying pay of £150 a year, which then was quite a substantial increase in salary.

The nice thing about accumulating the 100 hours flying rapidly meant that a good period of time off could be expected on return to UK. This was most agreeable after being away for 14 days, or more. However, it was not unusual for BOAC to roster training flights at Hythe in order to utilise the unused hours permissible in the 28-day period. On return from a trip it was normal to be given the roster for the next period of duty, which helped to plan social activities. After a break of two weeks, I was sent off to Hong Kong again, but this time it was a trip of 28 days duration that followed a similar pattern as before to Hong Kong. This time however, BOAC had implemented a 'Slip Crew Pattern' at some stations. On arrival at a slip station, the operating crew got off and another took over, thus allowing the aircraft to continue its journey. This shortened the time that it took to get passengers to their final destination, and gave better utilisation of the aircraft. Ultimately nearly all BOAC aircraft would be scheduled with slip crews.

Karachi was one of the first slip stations with crew slipping in both directions and with similar departure times problems could arise. I heard that two flying boats transited there at the same time, one eastbound and the other westbound and when route information was circulated soon after getting airborne, passengers discovered that they were on the wrong aircraft. Both aircraft returned to Karachi to change the passengers, and were about to depart again when one Captain decided to check that the baggage was on the right aircraft. Sure enough it was not and had to be switched over!

On arrival in Hong Kong on my second trip, there were three shuttles to be operated to Singapore and back, two going via Bangkok and the third a direct flight. That roster gave some days off in Hong Kong and the aircraft night-stopped at each station en route to Singapore and back. These shuttles were not popular with crews as they greatly extended the time away from UK. More importantly, although the salary being paid was higher than some other professional jobs, it was totally inadequate and did not allow for leisure activity at stopovers en route. I can recall sharing a large bottle of beer with two other people on the final stages of a long trip away from home since none of us had sufficient money for each of us to have a bottle. My wife and I had a very serious discussion about this when I returned from my first trip, but it was blatantly obvious that I had committed myself to this somewhat nomadic career and had little option other than to continue.

In the early days of my civil flying career, probably the nicest place to night stop was Marseilles. After landing, the passengers and crew were accommodated at the Hotel Roy Rene in Aix en Provence. I believe that Winston Churchill stayed here on his painting holidays when he would have an entire floor of the hotel allocated to him. Located in a very beautiful and picturesque area, its only drawback was the long drive from Marseilles. With food rationing in England it was strange to see the abundance and variety of food available. The Maitre D'Hotel of the Roy Rene always urged crews to select egg items from the menu, knowing that eggs were strictly rationed at home.

Flying boat Captains were very skilled at identifying reference points in landing areas and even in poor visibility, they appeared to be quite adept in finding the correct landing point. There was a general misconception that flying boats always had plenty of water available for take-off and landing, and although mostly true, one never knew if there might be a small boat in the area ahead if the landing was executed very long, or a longer than normal take-off run occurred. At Bangkok, the base was in a winding muddy river and the approach after cloud break needed to be very accurate. Fortunately, the landing area and initial take-off run was straight and on take off, the river did not start to bend until the aircraft was on the 'step' when adequate rudder control would be available.

Flying boat accidents did occur, one of the most serious being at Bahrain where in extremely poor visibility with blowing sand, the aircraft descended perhaps too rapidly, hitting the sea in the wrong attitude causing it to crash and sink with some loss of life.

At base, a flying boat on a test flight attempting to land unusually *across* the Solent at Hythe in a gale force wind hit the water in the wrong attitude and sank immediately. No one was killed but Radio Officer Jimmy Armitage was trapped underwater on the flight deck in zero visibility and only escaped by guiding himself via the pilot's 'Horizon Wire' to the First Officer's window where he was able to swim out.

Another, ferrying from Poole to Southampton, flew into high ground on the Isle of Wight, killing all on board. There were many incidents involving damage to the hull and/or floats when landing in rough water, but on the whole, flying boats were very safe in the very experienced hands of their Captains. Perhaps more importantly for passengers, they were extremely comfortable. There was a saying that on a flying boat, a passenger could be sick in absolute comfort!

During my first year on flying boats, BOAC recruited six Air Stewardesses to fly as cabin crew. This was an experiment to see if they could operate efficiently with male cabin crew, given the long duty hours they were expected to operate. There were some critics who thought the idea quite ridiculous but the outcome was a complete success and it became normal to have one female rostered as cabin crew. I believe that a similar trial was made on another Fleet that proved equally successful.

After a time, I found the flights to Hong Kong and Singapore quite boring and looked forward to the opportunity to visit other places. On one flight I was rostered to continue to Sydney, but when the aircraft reached Singapore it was all changed and a QANTAS crew took over. It would be many years before I would visit Sydney.

Some flights had to make a transit stop at Kuwait, which then had no proper airfield for land planes. The flying boat alighted on the sea in quite an exposed area that always seemed to have very strong winds and rough water. Take-off and landing were very bumpy but the worst problem was seasickness. During the quite long transit with the passengers remaining on board, the aircraft was moored in rough water and many passengers did actually become seasick, some quite severely. Although never seasick myself, I must say that it was a relief to get airborne on the next sector to Bahrain.

My first year on 4 Line was pretty well uneventful and about 850 hours were flown. Some engine failures were experienced from time to time but none that caused undue concern. It was frustrating not being able to navigate as I did on the RAF Sunderlands, but as I did not hold a civil licence to navigate, I was not qualified, or indeed employed to do so.

The terrain over which we flew varied sector by sector as did the weather conditions by season. The most inhospitable were the sectors from Cairo to Karachi where for the most part it was almost featureless desert, although mountains were visible at some points on the route. The tracks taken had to avoid high ground due to the limiting altitude that could be flown without oxygen. India in the dry season is very dry and dusty but as soon as the monsoon rains commence the, countryside turns green almost overnight. Bengal is greener than most other parts of India and thunderstorms can be encountered throughout the year giving very turbulent transits of that area. I remember one old Captain being asked how best to fly through a thunderstorm and his terse one word answer was 'Don't!' However, often there was no option other than to strap in tight and go through it. From my RAF days in India and Burma I recall that the most vicious thunderstorms were those when the cloud was a dirty muddy brown colour and these gave turbulence that was so severe that could only marvel at the strength of the aircraft. These were referred to as 'Brown Squalls' when I flew with 230 Squadron during my RAF days but I never heard a civilian meteorological officer use that term.

Probably the most beautiful scenery to be seen is over Thailand where the vegetation is a vivid brilliant green that extends over the hills. It is similar over the lower ground of Laos and Vietnam into the Gulf of Tonkin. At the altitudes we flew, it was possible to clearly see many features such as lakes, villages and roads that could not possibly be identified on the topographical charts that we carried.

Early in 1948 the Solent Flying Boat came into service. It was developed from a Sunderland Mark IV, which I believe was called the Seaford. This had many modifications from the Hythe/Sandringham/Plymouth flying boats including a redesigned fin and rudder, different floats and was fitted with the more powerful Hercules sleeve valve engines. Its performance in terms of range and payload was much improved over Pratt & Whitney and Pegasus powered aircraft, and after a series of proving and training flights, it was put on the South African route to Johannesburg. I did several training flights and found it to be a very nice aircraft to operate. On one training session, the Training Captain supervised several three-engine take-off and landings that I found to be most impressive. Obviously a three-engine take-off would never be done with passengers on board but it could enable an aircraft to be positioned from one base to another if an engine had failed and a spare was not available. I read somewhere that a BOAC flying boat at a station overseas could not start one of its engines, which was serviceable other than a faulty starter motor. Even though there were passengers on board, the Captain attempted to start it, albeit unsuccessfully, by wind milling it on a three engine take-off. A three-engine landing is always a possibility on any commercial flight, be it a land plane or flying boat.

Late in November 1948, I did my first flight to Johannesburg on the Solent with Captain Dick Reid in command. Dick, Imperial Airways vintage 1932, was a really splendid pilot and we became close friends and remain so to this day. He started in 1932 as Radio/Second Pilot, flying on Argosy, Hannibal, or Atalanta aircraft, whichever they cared to roster him to fly on. His hobby was amateur radio and we had much in common to discuss during flight. Dick, very active and fit at 93+ years of age, lives in Jersey, and we talk to each other almost every day on amateur radio HF R/T. When the Hong Kong route was extended to Japan in 1948, Dick was based in Hong for three months checking out each Captain into Japan. Dick had a rigid no smoking rule for crew, which some smokers found unreasonable, particularly as he was sometimes seen puffing his pipe in the bow compartment during flight. Doubtless he considered that to be the Captain's 'perk'.

On our flight together, all went well until just after take off from Lake Marieut, the reservoir of Alexandria, when number 4 engine failed, compelling a landing back at Alexandria. Overnight another Solent was flown from Southampton to Alexandria and after we had air tested it, the flight continued on its way south, running 24 hours behind schedule until we reached Victoria Falls where we quickly refuelled and continued to Vaaldam, arriving only 5 hours behind schedule.

Lake Marieut was home to large numbers of ducks that could be quite a hazard on take-off or landing, rising in great flocks in front of the aircraft. I was on board during a landing when the windscreen was completely obscured by blood from the ducks, fortunately without mishap to the aircraft, although the Captain did have to land the aircraft by looking out of side window rather than the windscreen. The locals were always grateful for such incidents and rapidly collected the dead and dying ducks from the water for their next meal. The Station Engineer had the horrid task of cleaning blood from the wings and windscreen and sometimes removing mutilated remains from the engine intakes.

As with the Eastern Routes, the flying was in daylight with scheduled night stops. The African route from Southampton was via Augusta Sicily (night stop), Alexandria, Luxor (night stop), Khartoum, Port Bell Uganda (night stop), Victoria Falls (night stop), and finally, Vaal Dam near to Johannesburg. The return route was identical, the round trip taking about 65 hours over 12 or 13 days depending on the day of departure from UK. Some months later, an additional stop was made en route from Victoria Falls to Port Bell landing on Lake Nyassa at Cape McClear. The water in that lake was very clear and the BOAC Station Engineer often drank straight from it. Not something to be recommended, I thought!

Apart from the transit of Khartoum in the hot season, this route was considered to be very civilised compared to the Far East and was much requested by crews. The only drawback with the route was that the Inter Tropical Front (ITF) had to be flown through in both directions which involved having to fly around, or sometimes through, massive and often quite violent thunderstorms. Approaching Johannesburg on one occasion, a violent thunderstorm was encountered with severe turbulence, torrential rain and large hailstones. The next morning it was reported in the newspaper that hailstones larger in size than golf balls had caused tremendous damage to houses with corrugated iron roofs in the Pretoria area. On that particular trip there was a lovely 80-year-old lady travelling to South Africa to see her grandchildren for the first time, and she seemed quite unaffected by the violent turbulence. While every other passenger was airsick and refusing food, that fearless lady ate everything in sight, including a very large portion of peaches and thick rich cream. Even the chief steward went pale when he saw her tucking into that!

The scenery over Central and South Africa can only be described as breathtaking, with large herds of wild animals frequently being visible in those days. With the terrain in Central Africa being between 4000 to 5000 feet, it was a simple matter to descend 2000 feet or so from the cruising altitude to a fairly low level, giving the passengers a closer look at zebras, elephants and other wild animals. After take-off from Port Bell, the route northwards passed close to Murchison Falls where large numbers of crocodiles, hippos and other animals could be seen as the aircraft climbed out en route. These sights were of great interest and certainly added to the enjoyment of passengers. Hippos were a potential hazard at Port Bell and the area needed a thorough inspection by the marine craft before take-off or landing could take place. The most impressive sight on the African route was Victoria Falls. Captains always circled several times at low level to give passengers a good view of perhaps one of the most spectacular waterfalls in the world. It almost defies description and is well worthy of a visit.

The sector back into Southampton from Augusta with Dick was quite unforgettable due to the route weather encountered. It was absolutely atrocious from the southern French coast northwards over France, with the aircraft icing up very badly. As the aircraft was flying over high ground, it was impossible to descend without putting the aircraft in danger. Dick climbed to 15000 feet and got over the worst of the weather and I can remember seeing frost on his flying boots, an indication of how cold it was on the flight deck. The heating on flying boats was quite primitive and incapable of coping with very low temperatures, particularly on the flight deck. There was no pressurisation and the windows on the flight deck were not airtight resulting in cold air constantly circulating, to the discomfort of the flight crew. When it was very cold, we wore greatcoats and wrapped blankets around our legs in an attempt to keep warm. For those who would say that 15000 feet is far too high for passengers without oxygen, I would agree, but the steward kept a watchful eye on them. It was far safer to climb as we did, than risk descending into unknown high ground.

Early in February 1949 I left Southampton on a Solent to South Africa with two Captains on board, one checking the other out on the route. It started badly with engine trouble shortly after take-off, necessitating a return to Southampton. The trouble was not serious and two hours later a departure was again made for Augusta. The flight then went well until shortly after departure from Victoria Falls number 3 engine failed, compelling a return to Victoria Falls. Three hours later when the engine fault seemingly had been rectified, the aircraft took off again for Vaal Dam. However, just before arrival the number 3 engine had to be shut down again and the approach made on three engines. At about 100 feet the aircraft encountered a vicious dust devil causing a wing to drop, resulting in a very heavy landing and rapid deceleration. Water entered the aircraft up to about waist level on the lower passenger deck, the flight deck remaining dry. Although there was damage to the aircraft, fortunately there was no injury to the passengers beyond getting wet, and they and the crew disembarked safely. As is normal with accidents, the crew was immediately suspended pending an enquiry that was held on the following day. The enquiry absolved the check Captain of responsibility and he and the rest of the crew were reinstated and cleared to operate. The Captain under supervision remained suspended and returned home as a passenger. Repairs to the damaged aircraft were lengthy and my crew flew the next aircraft to arrive in Vaal Dam back to UK without further problems.

There were often difficulties slipping moorings on departure and it was essential that the Radio Officer did not release the mooring line until the Captain gave the command to do so. It was equally important to ensure that the rope around the bollard did not jam, so it had to be wound in such a way that, as the engines caused the aircraft to move, rope could be smoothly fed out until the order to slip was given. Mooring up also had its problems. The approach to the buoy, normally with the two inboard engines shut down, had to be straight and slow enabling the strop on the buoy to be picked up with a boat hook and placed over the bollard. I recall mooring at Alexandria on one occasion when the approach to the buoy was straight enough but far too fast even with both drogues deployed. The Captain saw this and immediately shut down the remaining two engines, hoping to drift towards the buoy. Unfortunately one engine continued to rotate after the other had stopped, causing the aircraft to swing out of line with the buoy and outside my reach with the boat hook. The buoy was fairly close to the concrete side of the lake, which would have caused damage if the aircraft had hit it. I threw the boat hook like harpoon and by sheer luck it went through the loop of the strop and engaged with it. We drifted to the extent of the boat hook's rope when I was able to gradually pull it back in and moor up safely. The Captain treated me to a very large whisky in the hotel that evening!

The future of the flying boats seemed to be somewhat uncertain as BOAC continued to order new land planes, the main hope for flying boats resting with the huge 'Princess' flying boat. Meanwhile a new route was opened up to Nairobi, landing at Lake Naivasha, well north of the township. This route did not have the normal night stop schedule, the aircraft continuing on its way with a 'slip' crew being used at Alexandria.

In mid May, I departed at 9a.m. from Southampton and after refuelling at Augusta, continued to Alexandria where another crew took over. Twenty-four hours later we took off from Alexandria on the next aircraft to arrive, refuelled at Khartoum six hours later and finally landed on Lake Naivasha at 10a.m., having flown through the night. On the following day we flew the same aircraft back to Alexandria via Khartoum, departing Naivasha at 10a.m., arriving at Alexandria just after midnight. After the crew had rested for twelve hours, the aircraft was flown to Augusta for a night stop, and then continued to Southampton. In the period of six days, a total of 49 hours had been flown which was quite exhausting. This flight was made during a period of civil unrest in Egypt and the crew was virtually imprisoned in the Cecil Hotel at Alexandria with armed guards keeping the mobs away from the doors. An armed guard escorted the crew to and from the aircraft at Lake Marieut.

On 8th September 1949, I flew to the Farnborough Air Show in a Solent commanded by Captain Upton, a very senior ex Imperial Airways Training Captain. A fast and low fly past was made which was not particularly impressive compared to the high performance aircraft flying there. However, when we did a *very slow* fly past with flaps down into a stiff head wind about 25 feet above the runway at about 20 knots above stalling speed, this really impressed the crowd below and spectators could be clearly seen waving as we went slowly past. I would dearly loved to have been on the ground to see what, in those days, was a huge aircraft effectively just drifting past

About this time I saw an advertisement in the local paper about a semi detached house that was to be built in the Bitterne area of Southampton. I duly applied to the builder who told me that he had received many letters from prospective buyers and that he would put me on his list. He took me to the building plot that he owned and I could see that the foundations were already laid. Apparently these had been laid in 1939 but the building could not be completed when the war broke out. I progressed to his short list and shortly after he offered me the opportunity to have him build the house. However, there was a catch! He wanted a deposit of 10% of the £1500 purchase price and would need me to apply for a building licence from the local council. Fortunately I could afford the deposit, and enquiries with a building society indicated that I would have no trouble getting a mortgage. When I applied for the building licence I was horrified to learn that the council had allocated licences for the next two years and I would have to wait until others could be allocated. I complained to the builder who was completely unfazed by what I had learned and said that I should write to my MP, my local councillor and the Town Clerk, and as an ex wartime aircrew officer, complain at the treatment I was receiving. All of this was done with great speed and very quickly I was invited to see my local councillor. At the meeting he started the conversation by saying that he wanted to explain why I could not be granted a licence for at least two years. I was infuriated by this and asked why, as an ex serviceman who had served his country throughout the war, myself wife and child could not be allowed to build a decent place to live. All of my arguments fell on deaf ears and perhaps in anger, I reminded him that the local elections were about to be held and that he would not receive my vote, and perhaps not those of many of my friends. Strange to say, several weeks later I received a letter granting me a licence to build; the snag was that the applicant to build the other half of the semi-detached property did NOT.

Once again the builder was not unduly concerned and simply told me to go to the council offices and ask to be put in touch with people who had building licences but had no land available. At first they were totally uncooperative and refused to release any information, but after a period of negotiation they put me in touch with another ex-serviceman who was acceptable to the builder. During the waiting period I had received letters from the Town Clerk accusing me of trying to jump the queue ahead of more deserving cases, but these I ignored. It took just over a year from the time I first contacted the builder to moving into our new home. Before the house had been completed, I asked the builder if he could build a garage at the top of the driveway. He agreed to do this for only an extra £132, but subject to planning approval. I hesitated, wondering if I would have to go through the same tedious process with the planning authorities. Not a bit of it! The builder submitted the plans and approval was given within a week. My troubles were not over, for when I tried to have the garage wired for electricity, the very stringent conditions imposed by the electricity company delayed the wiring for almost six months before it was carried out. It was ironic that the flying boat base would be closed within the next year and I would be compelled to operate out of Heathrow airport with the necessary 60-mile drive each way. At least I had a house to call my own!

The plot was very large and had been used as a dumping ground from 1939 to 1949. Many lorry loads of rubbish had to be removed before I could clear the ground of brambles and weeds of all descriptions, which took several days to burn on a bonfire. When clearing the ground I came across what looked to be an unexploded incendiary bomb and took it to the police station. The policeman told me that I was stupid to have handled it and should have called for the bomb disposal squad. I learned later that it was a live German explosive incendiary bomb and had it gone off in my car, it could have killed me and destroyed the car!

The months went by without incident but then news came that the 'Princess' flying boat would not be taken up by BOAC and that flying boat operations would cease late in 1950. The reason given was that flying boats were not economical, but it may well have been due to the fact that the Turbo-prop engines for the 'Princess' were not ready and were not likely to be so in the near future. I did see it flying over Southampton Water with Centaurus engines installed, which unfortunately did not produce enough power for its proposed operational role. It certainly was a most impressive sight!

In May I did another trip to Johannesburg with Dick Reid in command, which went absolutely on schedule and without incident and included a transit of Cape Maclear. Very appropriately, on 8th November 1950, my last Flying Boat flight was with Dick when we air tested Solent Southampton G-AHIN. That was the end of a flying era that I will always remember with great pleasure. In the three years with BOAC Flying Boats of Number 4 line, I had flown nearly 2,500 hours, made a great number of friends and emerged without a serious accident. It was time to move on yet again.

Chapter 11

BOAC Hermes and York

My next posting was to Number 2 Line based at Hurn near Bournemouth. This line operated Hermes and York aircraft out of London Heathrow with training carried out at its base at Hurn. The Hermes, a British built aircraft of post war design, unfortunately did not perform as well as its American competitors, but the York was a well tried and reliable aircraft developed from the wartime Lancaster bomber. Navigators and Radio Officers could be rostered to fly on both types with most flying being done on the Hermes. The Hermes radio equipment AD107/108/7092 made by Marconi was the most up to date British equipment then available. It performed well and apart from minor faults, gave little or no trouble. I wish I could say the same for the aircraft! The York, of course, had the familiar and reliable wartime Marconi T1154/R1155 that only lacked the sophistication of the more modern equipment of the Hermes.

After a three week ground course that gave me Christmas at home, flying duties commenced on the Hermes on 28th December 1950, operating familiarisation and training flights from Hurn airport. Powered by the latest mark of Hercules engines, these were more powerful than those of the Solent flying boat, but engine problems seemed to occur rather frequently. It had a tricycle undercarriage but rather strangely the Hastings, its RAF counterpart, had the more conventional undercarriage of main gear and tail wheel. The aircraft had what seemed to me to a nose up attitude in flight, but perhaps that was its design. To me, its only apparent advantage was that it was pressurised, enabling it to fly at higher altitudes than the flying boat where it sometimes *might* clear cloud and adverse weather in temperate climates, but seldom in the tropics. Bad weather can be experienced almost anywhere along a route and it is the pilot's task to ensure that the passengers have the smoothest, (and safest), journey to their destination. In tropical areas dangerous flying conditions could sometimes prevent flying direct between points on track and deviations around the worst of the weather often become necessary.

When I joined the Fleet, it served Africa and the route structure was from London Heathrow to Johannesburg via Castel Benito (Tripoli/Libya), Kano (Nigeria), Brazzaville (Belgian Congo), and

Livingstone (Northern Rhodesia), with crew changes taking place at all stops with the exception of Brazzaville. Other routes were to Entebbe (Uganda) via Rome, Cairo, Khartoum and Nairobi, with crew changes at all stations except Khartoum and Nairobi. It also served Lagos and/or Accra via Tripoli and Kano, with crew changes at Tripoli and Accra or Lagos. Crews were positioned along the route in a slip pattern to enable the aircraft to fly through to its final destination and back to London, with only fuel stops en route. The days of flying mostly by daylight had virtually come to an end, with the exception of York aircraft, whose schedules operated without slip crews, flying mostly by day.

Operating on a slip crew pattern had disadvantages in that the take-off or landing could be at any time, day or night, giving rise to the problem of trying to sleep during the day prior to a night flight. The only advantage was that crews normally never had less than 24 hours at any slip station enabling the crew to have adequate rest and the opportunity of sightseeing. However, it did extend the overall length of the round trip. Use of the houseboat at Cairo was discontinued; crews being accommodated at Osborne House, a rather dreary and depressing BOAC operated hotel located in a very noisy area near the centre of Cairo. York aircraft were mainly freighters, operating comparatively leisurely schedules to various eastern destinations, the furthest of which were Hong Kong, Manila or Singapore. I always found it made a pleasant change to be rostered to fly on a York despite its lack of pressurisation.

Operating out of Heathrow involved me in a two hour drive from/to Southampton, making the first and last days of each trip very tiring, but as I had a house built in Southampton, I had no intention of moving. Another reason for not moving was that I had joined the RAFVR and commanded a small signals group covering quite a large area in the south of England. At that time BOAC objected to its crews joining the RAFVR but after a lot of pressure, they allowed me to do so, provided that I did not fly. The reason for this was that any hours flown would count in the 100 hours allowable in any 28 day period and would deprive BOAC of utilising those hours.

BOAC had its own hotel at Sunningdale, adjacent to the golf course where crews were accommodated for stand by duties or delayed flights. During stays, crews were allowed to use the golf club, much to the chagrin of club members! Standby could be anything from 24 hours to 7 days, dependent on which line one was with. Some lines only required crews to standby for a flight 24 hours ahead of the one to be operated. Other lines rostered standby duties for a whole week making it necessary to cover more than one flight a day. This meant that flying staff always had to be ready to move at short notice to the airport when called out. Some flights were less popular than others with crews and it was not unknown for certain 'rogues' to call in sick just before reporting for those flights, causing the standby to be called out to operate. Miraculously, of course, they recovered within 24 hours when they could operate a more agreeable flight!

Tripoli was quite a popular stopover as it was the only place overseas where fresh meat could be bought and taken back to UK. Quite an advantage in ration controlled UK! The meat had a blue stamp to show that it had been inspected and passed by the military health authorities. The area was under Military Administration who issued a local currency that was legal tender only in Libya and had no value outside the country. Crews with surplus currency would use it to buy souvenirs and meat from the local shops in the Souk or spend it in bars. The town boasted a casino that was also a hotel and one could gamble and/or get a decent meal there. One chap had a small amount of currency left and with it being useless outside Libya, put it all on a number on the roulette wheel. Murphy's law prevailed of course, and he finished with a greater amount than he had bargained for.

The hotel used by BOAC for its crews was the Del Mahari on the outskirts of Tripoli, a pleasant enough place but had only a tiny bathroom situated and shared between two bedrooms. The occupant of the other adjoining room wishing to use the bathing or toilet facilities could often surprise anyone failing to lock the adjoining door. Burglaries often took place, particularly if an adjoining room was not occupied. The hotel roof was not fully waterproofed and when heavy thunderstorms were experienced it was not unusual to find one's room flooded. Fortunately rain was not a frequent occurrence in Libya.

Perhaps the most civilised crew slip station was Johannesburg which had plenty to offer in entertainment and sight seeing. The least popular, hardly surprising, was West Africa, the 'White Man's Grave', with its wretched high temperature and relative humidity that made life a misery. Apart from a beach at Accra, there was very little else to occupy crews during stopovers. That particular beach had very dangerous surf and one or two people got into difficulties swimming there.

At Lagos airport it was possible to buy stems of green bananas very cheaply to take back home to ripen. The Nigerian lady who sold the bananas was very popular with crews and enjoyed haggling over the price. I bought a stem from her and put it in the airing cupboard to ripen when I got home. My wife cut off a hand of bananas that had ripened only to discover a very large Tarantula spider with scores of little spiders in a nest between the bananas. Her scream could have been heard across the road without difficulty. Fortunately she suffered no harm and

I disposed of the nest immediately. At Kano in northern Nigeria, one could buy cheap Rattan baskets of various sizes decorated with coloured Nigerian patterns. These we filled with very small chicken eggs, a hundred of which could be bought for less than £1. The eggs were always welcome at home with rationing still in force, and the baskets could be sold on to neighbours or friends. In wintertime the eggs were mostly edible but one usually avoided buying them in the very hot weather since most would have gone bad by the time they reached home.

My stay on Number 2 Line lasted eleven months during which time I was transferred to fly on the York permanently. I had experienced some quite severe stomach problems for several months and the Ministry of Aviation Doctor who gave me my annual medical examination, thought that this might be due to my dislike of the Hermes! This was a complete surprise to me as I had not at any time voiced any opinion about the aircraft. The transfer did not worry me in the slightest, it being easier to accept what had been decided and go along with it.

I must say that I did experience a lot of engine and technical problems during my time with Number 2 Line, as did many other crew members. I was on board a Hermes that had a very serious incident with its undercarriage. On the flight from Heathrow to Rome, everything was normal until the undercarriage was selected down for landing at Rome when one main gear showed a red light. The gear was re-cycled several times with no success and other procedures were then tried, all of which took quite a long time. Fuel was getting rather low but fortunately, after another re-cycle of the gear, all three green lights illuminated. The landing was very smooth, but as the aircraft decelerated, the same red unsafe gear warning light illuminated and the warning horn sounded continuously. The aircraft was taxied very cautiously to the parking area where the engines were stopped. The ground engineer came on board and rather dramatically told the Captain that he did not know how we had managed to get three greens as the main undercarriage leg on one side had completely fractured at its pivot point. The aircraft was delayed until a new main leg had been flown from London to replace the damaged one.

I had heard that one of the earlier Hermes delivered to BOAC was on a training flight when the nose gear became jammed. All attempts to lower it failed, but the Flight Engineer poked a section of rod stripped from an overhead luggage rack through an inspection hole in the floor of the flight deck and manually forced the nose wheel down into the locked position. I believe that he was highly commended for his ingenuity, which saved the aircraft from serious damage.

Due (it was rumoured) to the sleeve valve clearance being reduced on the Hercules engines, there were many in-flight failures resulting in engine changes. I was on board a flight into Johannesburg at night when one engine had to be shut down due to loss of oil contents and pressure. Shortly afterwards, a fire warning came up on another engine, and as the aircraft was flying in almost continuous thunderstorms with severe turbulence, the Captain was reluctant to shut it down. The engine instruments gave no adverse indications whatsoever, so I was ordered to sit by the window adjacent to that engine and report if I saw any signs of fire. Fortunately, it was a false warning and a safe landing was made at Johannesburg on three engines without further difficulty. After landing the engine that had been shut down was found to have failed and was subsequently changed. The other engine was perfectly serviceable, having only a faulty fire wire in the warning system that was easily rectified. False fire warnings do occur on most aircraft from time to time and the appropriate shut down procedures have to be carried out, unless circumstances dictate otherwise.

The Hermes engines suffered from an oil problem known as 'coring', a situation when the oil contents gauge drops back to show zero contents in the oil tank. On one occasion about two hours out of Brazzaville en route from Livingstone, this occurred with the aircraft I was on. The Flight Engineer had experienced this particular fault before and was not unduly concerned as the oil temperature and pressure remained normal. The engine was kept running while the Flight Engineer, who had access to the back of his instrument panel, inter-changed oil contents gauges to prove that the gauge was serviceable. After landing, the oil tank was checked and found to be empty, the oil having passed into the sump. This was drained off, the tank refilled with clean oil and the engine started. Inexplicably the oil contents again went to zero. This was most perplexing and Engineering Department at Heathrow was consulted to get their advice. Their reply was, 'Check the filters – If clean, change the engine.' Rather confusing really, because if the filters were NOT clean, the engine would still have to be changed! After the engine had been changed, the flight continued to Kano where another crew took over. I learned later that the same aircraft had a second engine change at Tripoli, following yet another in-flight shut down.

It was very pleasant to be permanently on the York with flying being mostly by day with night stops, operating a very similar schedule to the flying boats. This suited me perfectly, particularly as it flew hard on both the outbound and return sectors. It was always on the eastern route, mainly to Singapore, and the 100 hours maximum flying time was done in 12 to 14 days, giving the remainder of the 28-day period off. The disadvantage of flying freighters was that they often carried monkeys and birds back from Manila or Singapore and the catering was not to the same standard as passenger aircraft. In the heat of the tropics the smell from monkeys was absolutely vile and almost unbearable, improving only when the aircraft got airborne and clean air circulated through the flight deck. After five days with the monkeys, the crew got used to the smell, but if travelling home on public transport there could be some very odd looks from other passengers. A special 'dirty uniform allowance' was paid for uniform cleaning if flights involved the carriage of monkeys. In the early days of animal flights, it was quite common to have several monkeys and many birds die due to the very cramped conditions of their carriage, and the fact that there was nobody other than the crew to feed and water them. Ultimately a cargo supervisor was carried and it was his job to look after the animals, and perhaps more importantly, prepare and serve the crew with food and drink. Today, carriage of livestock on aircraft is very strictly controlled to avoid suffering during flight.

The cargo supervisor on one flight had a very small baby bear that he had to feed and water at frequent intervals and as it looked to be so playful and innocuous, he took it out of its cage to give it freedom to move around. That turned out to be very unwise because although quite small, it gave him a very severe bite that required medical attention at the next stop.

Wild and quite dangerous animals were sometimes carried and crews quite naturally were concerned with the possibility of these escaping in flight. A leopard did escape from its cage while the aircraft was parked at Castel Benito airport during a night stop. When the crew arrived at the aircraft on the following morning, the animal was sitting on the Captain's seat looking out of the side window that fortunately was closed. It was recaptured after it had been shot with a tranquilliser dart, but from then on more care was taken with the security of the cages.

On one trip to Singapore, all went very well with a supervisory Captain checking out another Captain on the route. As the aircraft turned on to the final approach for landing at Singapore (Kallang), the supervisory Captain pointed out that the spire of the white painted Cathedral and the dome of the Town Hall were directly in line with the runway. He went on to say that in very poor visibility, the runway might not be visible, but by flying in a straight line over both buildings, the runway should come into sight shortly after passing over the last building. Very useful information indeed!

A departure was made two days later, taking off just after dawn with a full load of freight. In the tropical heat, the aircraft staggered up to 8000 feet when number 2 engine backfired very badly. The engine was shut down and the propeller feathered. Almost immediately number 3 engine did exactly the same thing, requiring that it also be shut down and its propeller feathered. An emergency was declared, as there was no means of dumping fuel on the York and at its very heavy weight, it was obvious that it would be extremely difficult to maintain a sensible height before landing. The tower reported poor visibility in thick mist/fog whereupon the supervisory Captain reminded the other Captain of his advice concerning poor visibility. The approach had to be absolutely right as there was no hope whatsoever of being able to go round again on a missed approach with two engines inoperative. The church spire and town hall dome could both be seen poking up through the mist, and these were lined up and flown over as the aircraft descended towards the runway. Shortly after passing the last building, very dimly the runway lights appeared and a safe touch down was made. The cathedral and the Town Hall today are totally obscured by the skyscrapers that have been built and of course, Kallang airfield no longer exists. Having landed, it was extremely difficult to taxi back to the parking area as every fire engine and emergency vehicle that Kallang airport could muster had turned out, obstructing the taxiway. This can be explained by the loss of a BOAC Constellation some time before, which crashed and eventually burst into flames on the runway, killing many people trapped on board whose lives should have been saved. The loss of life was blamed on the fire department that apparently did not take the correct and immediate action. They were obviously not going to let it happen again! The problem with both engines that had been shut down on the York turned out to be faulty magnetos and both ran perfectly when new ones had been fitted.

I did a very pleasant trip in January 1952 that involved flying five small elephants from Bangkok to Heathrow. This was going to be done in a blaze of publicity involving a *Daily Express* reporter named Bernard Wicksteed, (now deceased), who wrote a column entitled 'It's fun finding out!' BOAC had its own reporter 'Tip' Pyle on board for company publicity purposes, and there was also a representative from the circus that had bought the elephants. His name was Harry but for the life of me, I cannot remember his last name. Harry was said to be an expert on elephants but we subsequently learned that he was nothing of the sort. His job was simply to keep an eye on things and telephone the circus each evening with a progress report.

It was a normal freight flight to Singapore that did not start too well as shortly after take-off, the aircraft had to return to Heathrow with technical problems. Three hours later when the defect had been cleared, the aircraft flew leisurely to Singapore with night stops at Rome, Beirut,

Bahrain, Karachi, Calcutta and Bangkok. The aircraft was then ferried empty back to Bangkok where the elephants were to be boarded. Stalls made of hardwood were installed inside the aircraft with one elephant assigned to each stall, the idea being that the elephants would be simply led up a ramp to the aircraft and in to the stalls. Once on board they would be chained by one leg to the aircraft floor. No one had told the elephants of the arrangements and they obviously disliked the idea because they refused to go on board. All morning and part of the afternoon was spent trying to get them loaded, without success. Eventually the Captain announced that if they could not be loaded within the next hour, the crew would run out of duty hours and the fight would be delayed until the next day. Bernard Wicksteed was most upset about that statement – apparently he had already written his article, pure fiction of course, describing the first day's activities *and* the arrival at Calcutta, wiring it to the *Daily Express* where doubtless it was on the presses being printed.

There were many spectators observing the efforts to board the elephants, one being a small Thai teenager. He spoke to the Thai BOAC station manager who conveyed to the Captain that the boy thought that he could get them on board. The offer was taken up and sure enough all five were led fairly docilely, into their stalls. The Captain's first instinct, totally impractical of course, was to ask if the boy would be willing to fly back to England with the elephants. Not surprisingly the young lad did not like that idea and would not agree. He did say something to the effect that he could usually get a baby elephant to do most things if he fed it with sweet potatoes, which is precisely what he had done to get them on board. Making sure that we had a plentiful supply of sweet potatoes, the engines were started but almost immediately all five started to go crazy, pulling down the overhead roof panels. Bernard, Harry and Tip who were in single seats alongside the elephants, rushed on to the flight deck asking where they could get out of the aircraft. Before things got out of hand, sweet potatoes were fed to the elephants with the desired calming effect. The aircraft taxied out to the runway and took off with the animals eating away to their hearts content. The aircraft trim was not quite correct and it leaped into the air so sharply that two of the elephants went down on to their knees. The climb and cruise en route to Calcutta went without a problem, other than the crew noticing that the aircraft seemed to lurch from time to time. When loaded at Bangkok, all elephants were facing forward with one foot tethered by a chain to the floor. When we landed at Calcutta they had all turned round and were facing aft, hence the lurching effect. It was the intention to off-load them each night, but as the aircraft was running so late they were left on board.

The following morning, the departure for Karachi went smoothly with Harry, 'Tip' and Bernard feeding the animals on take-off, and after a perfectly smooth flight, the aircraft landed at Karachi where the elephants were then off-loaded. The fun started the next morning when the Indians tried to get them back on the aircraft without feeding them. The five ran in all directions across the airfield but were eventually rounded up and boarded. The Captain said that was the last time that they would get off until they reached London.

Before leaving Karachi, some very green Lucerne was taken on board to feed the elephants and this could have caused a disaster. It was put in a large heap at the back of the aircraft behind the fifth stall to feed the elephants during flight. En route to Bahrain, one elephant that had become something of a 'rogue' became very unsettled and as the supply of sweet potatoes was getting low, Harry fed it some Lucerne. He plunged his hands into the Lucerne heap and almost burned himself from the heat generated by fermentation within the pile. Fortunately the aircraft was not far away from Bahrain where the then *very* hot Lucerne was quickly taken off and replaced with more suitable fodder.

The rogue elephant gave the Captain a great deal of concern, so much so that he sought advice from a veterinary surgeon living in Bahrain who offered to lend the Captain a humane killer to use on the animal if it got out of control. The offer had to be refused for the simple reason that if the animal was out of control, trying to use the gun might result in injury to anyone on board, or even endanger the aircraft. Instead, the vet provided some extremely powerful drugs in pill form that could be put inside a sweet potato and fed to any elephant giving trouble. During the flight to Cairo on the next day, the fractious one played up again and Harry gave it a very heavy dose of drugs. He said that when the drugs took effect the result was quite dramatic with it falling down on its knees with its eyes glazed. Harry thought that it was dead because it did not move for quite a long time. It certainly did the trick because we had no further trouble with it on the remainder of the trip to Heathrow. The following morning on departure from Cairo, it was still very drowsy, looking as though it had a hangover! It probably had!

The other four elephants were totally different from the rogue, and the crew made quite a fuss of them during the six days of the trip. We kept sweet potatoes in our pockets to distract them if they were irritable as we passed by them on our way to the toilet at the rear of the aircraft. They must have known we had potatoes as they gently curled their trunks around our arms in a somewhat caressing manner as if asking for a potato.

On arrival at Heathrow the press were well and truly in attendance and a J. Arthur Rank film starlet, Joan Rice, christened them 'Eeney', 'Meeney', 'Miney', 'Mo' and 'Half a mo'! Whilst that was going on, one of them ambled over to the crew who were watching nearby, obviously looking for potatoes! The professional elephant handlers soon manhandled all five into a special transport and I never saw them again. I sincerely hope that they are still alive and well. Captain Jackson, who commanded the aircraft on that flight, sadly died in a Britannia crash some years later. The other two members of the crew were Tony Cornford and Dave, 'The Dude', Kerr. I believe that Dave also died some years ago.

I soon got to know most of the pilots on the York and most flights were extremely pleasant and very relaxed. The atmosphere on the flight deck, monkey smells apart of course, was always very enjoyable. Without interfering with the navigation of the aircraft, I would take the odd sun shot and plot a position line on a chart to compare it with the Navigator's position.

The main problem with the York was its antiquated electrical system. At the end of one round trip to Singapore, the aircraft was making an approach to land at Heathrow when the entire electrical system went completely dead and left us with no radio communication. Fortunately the weather was clear and the pilots had the runway in sight with apparently no other aircraft on the runway, so they continued ahead and landed. I never did discover what caused the electrical system to fail completely, but I do know that it spent the next day in the hangar.

I only did one passenger flight on the York. That was to take a ship's crew of Chinamen from Rome to Hong Kong with night stops at Beirut, Bahrain, Karachi, Calcutta and Bangkok. The passengers had the ship's bosun in charge of them and he insisted that there would be no mess or rubbish left on board the aircraft. At each night stop the aircraft was in such a clean and tidy state that the ground handling personnel had little to do. There were two stewards on board and they told us that the Chinese put every piece of rubbish in their pockets to avoid making a mess. The Captain delayed the flight in Bangkok for 24 hours due to the weather forecast for the arrival time being well below limits. When the aircraft did get to Hong Kong the weather was not particularly good but a safe landing was made. The Captain was asked why he had cancelled the previous day and he replied that the forecast of overcast skies at 200 feet was well below company limits. He was then told that the weather forecast was overcast at 2000 feet and at the time we would have been arriving, it was broken cloud at 8000 feet. Someone at the Bangkok Meteorological Office had left a nought off the cloud base forecast! However, one could not take chances at Hong Kong with the landing facilities then available, and the only alternate airfield a great distance away at Manila in the Philippines.

There was no load from Hong Kong to Bangkok and as the Captain had been screening another Captain into Hong Kong, they decide to simulate an engine failure on take-off. The take-off on the runway to the south-east required a fairly immediate right turn to avoid a promontory straight ahead on the flight path. They had agreed to throttle back number one engine at about 100 feet altitude but when this was done the aircraft yawed to port so dramatically that full power had to be restored rather rapidly. I don't think that either of the pilots expected the simulated engine failure to produce the almost uncontrollable yaw and we were all pleased that it had not been a real engine failure!

I operated a York flight to Kuwait that then had no paved runway, the landing being made on hard packed sand with the centre line being marked with an oil streak. Its surface was very uneven and uncomfortably bumpy on both landing and take off. It brought back memories of the landing at Sharjah in a Wellington Bomber late in 1942. Today, Kuwait is a magnificent airfield with very long runways and very up to date facilities.

Chapter 12

BOAC Argonaut

In September 1952, I was posted yet again, this time to the Argonaut Fleet. The Hermes Fleet, previously known as Number 2 line, was to be progressively phased out of service with its York aircraft being taken over by Argonaut Fleet. As I had been flying permanently on the Yorks, I was one of the first people to be posted. The only disadvantage of being posted to another Line/Fleet was that a ground course was necessary to familiarise oneself with the aircraft and learn its safety and emergency procedures. By this time all Fleets had moved to a very large new headquarters building at Heathrow referred to by the crews as the 'Kremlin' and therefore, did not involve travelling to another area.

The Argonaut was a splendid aircraft and I enjoyed flying on it immensely. On one occasion it had demonstrated its performance when it landed successfully after it had become necessary to shut down two engines. It was categorised as a Canadair DC4M aircraft, having the American Douglas Aircraft Corporation DC4 airframe and powered by Rolls Royce engines. Another change from the basic DC4 was that it was fully pressurised, unlike the normal production line DC4s. It eventually flew most of BOAC's African, Middle East, Far East and South American routes, becoming a very efficient and successful workhorse. The great variety of routes enabled me to visit radio amateurs I had spoken to from my home in Southampton, many of whom were in Hong Kong. One particular friend came from Southampton and with his son at boarding school in Bournemouth, I was able to establish lines of communication between them by both radio and personal visits whilst in Hong Kong.

The Argonaut radio equipment was the same as that fitted on the Hermes and again I experienced little or no trouble with it. It had the normal dual installation of HF transmitting and receiving equipment, together with up to date landing aids and VHF communication equipment. The original Douglas flight deck was designed to allow operation by two pilots with provision for a third pilot. BOAC modified it by installing a Radio Officer's position on the port side in place of the third pilot's position and a Navigator's position on the starboard side by the emergency door. The navigator's position was simply a folding table that could only be erected after the aircraft was airborne. This was of great inconvenience to the Navigator who often had to be prepared to start navigating immediately after take-off and before the table was in place. There was never any provision for a Flight Engineer.

As with most aircraft built at that time, weather radar was not fitted, although it was really needed on the tropical routes operated. Penetration of intense thunderstorm cells always present in the tropics could be very uncomfortable and often dangerous. Structural failure resulting in the loss of the aircraft has sometimes been recorded when intense storms have been penetrated. As with the Hermes Fleet, all Navigators and Radio Officers could be detailed to fly on York aircraft, but as it was being progressively withdrawn from service, flights were few and far between.

Since joining BOAC I had become accustomed to operating to many different places and very much enjoyed my work and the variety of destinations. There were of course, drawbacks with this nomadic existence and I suppose that it was my wife and son who suffered most. It was nice to have a fairly reasonable length of time at home between flights, but it seemed that many things needing my attention occurred while away on a flight and it was left to my wife to do what was necessary. Neighbours thought I had a wonderful life visiting many places that in those days they would never be able to afford to visit and quite naturally envied me. They did not understand that flying was very tiring and on occasions fraught with problems and sometimes, danger. Believe me it's no fun flying on three engines in filthy weather at night wondering if another engine might fail, or if the weather at the destination might not be good enough for a landing to be made. This did not happen often but when it did, we all thought that we were not paid enough money for the job!

About this time there were rumours that BOAC intended to operate in the future with an all pilot crew who would perform the radio and navigation duties in addition to their own. I believe that this was the brainchild of Sir Basil Smallpiece who was not particularly popular with the non-pilot crew members, although in all fairness it did make sense to crew the aircraft that way. There was an immediate outcry from Navigators, Radio Officers and Flight Engineers and lengthy discussions took place between BOAC and The Merchant Navy and Aircraft Officers Association. The Flight Engineers stood firm and threatened to strike unless the plans affecting them were dropped, and in fact, they won their battle. Although the Argonaut did not carry Flight Engineers and would have been unaffected by the strike, BOAC could ill afford to have its lucrative Atlantic and Australian routes paralysed, quickly agreeing to continue using Flight Engineers. Flight Engineers still fly on some older types of aircraft but today's modern aircraft have no provision for one to be carried.

It was a losing battle for Radio Officers and after a long period of negotiation, a redundancy agreement was reached whereby they would train the pilots to operate radio equipment in exchange for a severance agreement. With communication by Morse being progressively replaced by High Frequency Radiotelephony (HF R/T), the plan was that by the time HF R/T was completely implemented world wide, all pilots would be capable of using it.

A true and quite amusing story circulated concerning a Captain who was being trained by an Australian Radio Officer. The Captain, a really nice chap, suffered very badly from a stutter and it took him a long time to stutter his way through a lengthy position report. After completing his transmission to the ground station, there was an absolute stony silence causing the Captain to ask the Radio Officer if the ground station had received it. The Australian Radio Officer's flippant reply was ' Christ, mate, he had enough time to chip it out in stone!' Even the Captain saw the funny side of that remark.

I was instructing the pilots of my crew one night as we flew from Calcutta to Rangoon and they were trying to make contact with Calcutta on H/F R/T. No contact was made with Calcutta but after many calls, London came up and asked if we would like him to pass our message. Freak range contacts such as that can often be experienced.

BOAC progressively went ahead with their plans for Radio Officer redundancy but after such a sticky time with the Flight Engineers, they were at pains to keep the peace with the Navigators and all went very quiet for a few years.

The Argonaut Fleet was very large and its huge route structure gave aircrew a variety of destinations. I personally was never rostered for a South American flight but would go there in later years with another company. Certain airfields with difficult terrain and approach procedures were put in a category that necessitated special clearance and/or training for Captains. Only those pilots cleared could operate into those airfields and this often presented the crewing department with a problem if a cleared Captain was not available to fly.

Some accidents did occur and two aircraft were lost at Kano in very similar conditions. On separate occasions, each took off with thunderstorms in the vicinity of the airfield and encountered a wind sheer soon after take-off. This resulted in the aircraft being unable to climb or maintain height causing it to crash with loss of life. On one of those accidents, the navigator opened the flight deck emergency door next to his position and jumped out of the aircraft. Unfortunately the fuel tanks had ruptured and the fuel ignited as he jumped into it, and he died from the burns he sustained. The Pilots and Radio Officer left by the forward passenger door on the port side of the aircraft where there was no fire and all survived.

During the summer months Kano was not a particularly pleasant place with its extremely high daytime temperatures of more than 100 degrees and often affected by extremely severe thunderstorms associated with Line Squalls. After dusk the surface temperature would gradually fall to about 80 degrees but an inversion layer would be encountered around 1000 feet which dramatically degraded the climb performance of the aircraft. On the credit side, in winter the climate was extremely pleasant except for those occasions when strong winds caused rising dust and sand, resulting in very poor visibility.

An Argonaut crashed whilst attempting to land at Idris airport in Libya where extremely strong winds caused very poor visibility in rising dust and sand. The cross wind on the main runway was well outside company limits necessitating an approach on the very short runway that had no direct landing aid. After two abortive approaches the aircraft crashed short of the runway threshold causing the aircraft to be destroyed and many to lose their lives.

Fortunately crashes did not occur very often and if the cause of the incident was self evident, crews could accept it as a hazard of their occupation and carry on as normal. I was convinced that it would never happen to me and of course, it did not! Mysterious crashes like those of the Comet aircraft raised a great deal of concern amongst crews until the cause had been established.

Many considered the liquid cooled Rolls Royce engines to be unsuitable for flying in the tropics and certainly the coolant temperatures were always higher than normal prior to, and just after take off in the tropics. Very high coolant temperatures could result in venting of the coolant that could exacerbate the situation.

Engine failures inevitably did occur, but seldom of such severity to cause crews serious concern. Aircraft engines had an 'On Wing' life quoted in hours that normally could not be exceeded. BOAC seldom went to that limit, preferring to remove and overhaul before a failure did occur. A piston engine nearing the end of its 'on wing' life invariably showed its age with lower than normal oil pressure together with higher oil temperature. One could be sure that the pilots would closely monitor the performance of any engine that was nearing the end of its permitted cycle. The technical log always showed the hours accrued on each engine and the number remaining.

The propeller's Constant Speed Unit (CSU) could give trouble, causing the propeller to 'overspeed'. The CSU keeps propeller revolutions constant at the selected setting, regardless of the engine's power. If the unit failed, the propeller revolutions could reach unacceptably high limits and the noise created would be quite disturbing. The only way to reduce the revolutions would be to reduce the airspeed of the aircraft but, of course, there is a limit to how much the airspeed can be reduced. The main danger with an over-speeding propeller is that it can separate from the engine giving risk of hitting the other propeller on the same side, or perhaps the fuselage or tail plane, which could cause serious structural damage.

I was on board an Argonaut flying from Livingstone to Johannesburg when we experienced an over-speed with the propeller on number 4 engine. Fortunately the propeller stayed on but the scream emitted from it was quite loud and there was a most uncomfortable 45 minutes flying before landing. The over-speed occurred when a piston connecting rod broke and penetrated the side of the engine, causing all the engine oil to be lost and preventing the propeller from being feathered. After landing the ground engineer came on board and cheerfully told the Captain that it was almost certainly a constant speed unit that had failed and could be quickly remedied. The ex Imperial Airways Captain, a very dour South African, told him to keep his feet clear when the cowling was removed as something might fall out on his feet. When the cowling was completely removed, a large hole on both sides of the engine was clearly visible.

I experienced another over-speeding propeller whilst taking of from Ciampino airport at Rome. Fortunately it was spotted in plenty of time, enabling the take-off to be abandoned. Once the CSU had been changed there was no further trouble.

Flying on the Far East routes to Singapore, Hong Kong and Tokyo could never be done without experiencing some filthy weather en route. The Argonaut had a far superior performance to previous aircraft I had operated on this route but needless to say, it was not sufficient to avoid the severe tropical weather. From June to September, the Monsoon season affects India and flights could be quite appallingly bumpy and uncomfortable. The weather was usually quite unpredictable and in those days it was almost impossible for the meteorologists to accurately forecast what might be expected. Comet aircraft were also flying across India, but with their ability to climb much higher than piston engine aircraft, they could often get over the weather or have sufficient warning to get around the worst of it.

A Comet left Karachi for Calcutta about 30 minutes before I was due to leave in an Argonaut flying the same route. The forecast was so bad that my Captain was in two minds about departing, but he asked the Comet Captain to get his Radio Officer to send back weather reports every twenty minutes. We departed and soon received the first report that gave broken cloud and smooth flying conditions and certainly no severe weather. Subsequent reports were exactly the same until the Comet landed at Calcutta. Similarly we experienced no severe weather en route and the Met Officer in Calcutta was quite amazed when we gave our report to him, particularly as he was still forecasting severe thunderstorms.

In the summer months, typhoons frequently occur on the Hong Kong/Tokyo route and these could cause diversions from either place if the eye of the storm was nearby. Furthermore, extremely vicious thunderstorms in the area of the Inter Tropical Convergence Zone could be quite active between Bangkok and Singapore depending on the season, giving perhaps the most spectacular electrical storms to be seen anywhere in the world.

Operating to Tokyo from Hong Kong at the time of the Korean War was fraught with problems due to the large number of military aircraft operating from bases in Japan and Okinawa. The Argonaut could usually fly direct to Tokyo from Hong Kong but invariably had to land in Okinawa for fuel on the return trip if excessive headwinds were experienced. The strength of the upper winds during winter in the area embracing Korea, Japan and Formosa are possibly higher than any other areas flown by BOAC. On one occasion, a BOAC Comet aircraft en route from Tokyo to Okinawa experienced headwinds in excess of 300 knots at its cruising level and had to return to Tokyo. During the Korean War when American Air Force bombers were returning to airfields in Japan or Okinawa, civil aircraft would be held to the limit of their endurance with priority being given to the landing military aircraft, some of which had suffered damage over the target.

Civil airliners were given special permission to land for fuel at United States military bases in Okinawa on a 'Hold Harmless Agreement' and passengers did not normally disembark. The primary airfield used in Okinawa was Kadena with Naha becoming available if Kadena was closed. The GCA approach at both airfields was superb and a great morale booster for the pilots when the weather was bad. Those US Military bases were not places to be if the aircraft became immobile on the runway, since the United States Air Force would not hesitate to remove it by any means at their disposal if it became necessary! On one occasion, a Comet landed at Kadena with hydraulic problems and could not clear the runway under its own power. With an America bomber stream approaching, the BOAC Station Engineer was told to either get the aircraft clear of the runway or they would move it off. Fortunately it was towed off with only minutes to spare.

At the time the Argonauts were operating, Kai Tak airfield in Hong Kong had two runways, the longer being 13/31 and the shorter, I think, was 09/27. Due to the terrain, landing was only possible on runways 09 and 31, whilst take-off could only be made on 13 and 27. The operation became tricky when the tailwind component exceeded the regulatory maximum permissible for take-off or landing. Take-off on runway 27 was extremely restrictive and for Tokyo and Singapore destinations, an en route fuel stop was almost certainly needed. On one flight to Singapore from Hong Kong using runway 27 for take-off, we had to land for fuel in French Indo China at Tan Son Knut airfield serving Saigon. When Kai Tak airfield was upgraded runway 09/27 ceased to exist, and what was then runway 13/31 became the parking and terminal area, and a new and very long runway was built on reclaimed land that extended 8000 feet out over the sea. Take-off or landing then became possible in either direction although some aircraft suffered a take-off weight restriction when using runway 31. Nowadays the virtually obstacle free new airport on Lantau Island is operational and is reached by travelling over a magnificent bridge connecting it to the mainland.

Kai Tak is no longer available to civil aircraft but many airmen, myself included, can hardly forget the spectacular approach to land on runway 13. That particular approach was quite safe when flown correctly, although it did not seem so on those occasions when I was a member of the crew! When I visited Hong Kong on holiday in 1998, the QANTAS Captain of the Boeing 767 my wife and I were flying on from Cairns, invited me to the flight deck for the landing. It was most impressive!

Hong Kong had its fair share of notable people visitors and I was there whilst Clark Gable was being filmed in the motion picture 'Soldier of Fortune'. I did have a glimpse of him in the Peninsular Hotel and he looked quite ordinary without his entourage of film colleagues. William Holden arrived at Kai Tak on a Pan American DC6 as I was sitting on the flight deck of an Argonaut waiting to start engines for departure for Tokyo. He was in Hong Kong to film 'Love is a Many Splendoured Thing' and received a very warm welcome from his film colleagues and the many film fans. His arrival caused us to have a late departure

I always enjoyed visiting Tokyo but with a stopover of only about 30 hours it was difficult to get out and see much of the area. The weather in summertime can be very hot with temperatures in the 80s or higher on some days. Winter can be quite cold and on one occasion I woke up to find a thick blanket of snow covering the Tokyo area. We experienced a long delay to our departure due to the snow.

One of the duties of the Radio Officer, who sat immediately behind the Captain, was to engage the control surfaces gust lock when ordered by the Captain. To do this one had to lean forward into an almost doubled up position to grasp the lever and engage it. After landing in Hong Kong in June 1956, as I engaged the gust lock I felt something click in my lower back but thought nothing more about it. At the hotel I woke up in the middle of the night with a most excruciating pain in my back. This caused me to lie sleepless until dawn when I struggled to the telephone to ask for a doctor. He appeared some time later and treated my discomfort as a joke, saying that I had slipped a disc in my back and would admit me to hospital. The Orthopaedic Consultant at the hospital wanted to operate but the BOAC Chief Medical Officer would not allow this to be done and instructed that I was to be returned home as soon as I was able to travel.

I spent a week in hospital before being taken by ambulance directly from the hospital to the airport where I was put in a fully reclining first class seat on a BOAC Constellation aircraft and flown home. Whilst in hospital, a typhoon passed very close to the Colony giving storm force winds and torrential rain. The windows of my room were wide open as there was no air conditioning and the rain blew in, soaking the bed as I lay there. I could not reach the call bell to summon assistance and it was about two hours before someone came to my assistance.

On arrival at Heathrow, Doctor Alan Sibbald, BOAC's aircrew Medical Officer met the aircraft and instructed the Nursing Sister to take me home by ambulance. I insisted that I could drive myself home but to the delight of the nurse, my old trustworthy Austin 7 would not start and she accompanied me home by ambulance. It was seven weeks before I could resume flying duties.

In 1955/56 BOAC announced that the services of Radio Officers would progressively be withdrawn but offered pilot or navigation training to those who were considered to be suitable. About the same time, Navigators were offered pilot training and many took up the offer. A few qualified as pilots, some going on to become Senior Captains. Late in 1956 I was interviewed and accepted for Navigator training starting in 1957. At the interview I was asked if I wished to be considered for pilot training but I had no ambitions in that direction and declined the opportunity. I was delighted to be accepted for navigator training by BOAC, my only regret being that it had taken so long for the change to be made. On 25th January 1957 I departed on my last trip as a Radio Officer, a trip of 22 days duration that stopped at almost every airport en route to Tokyo and back, logging exactly 100 hours. That last flight operated completely on schedule without any technical problems being experienced.

Looking back on my time with the Argonaut Fleet, the place that stands out in my mind is Beirut, which in those days was a beautiful city with many places of interest. I recall that annually the World Water Ski championships were held in the harbour and it was normal practice for crews to hire a rowing boat, stock it with beer and sandwiches and row to a good viewing point to watch the proceedings.

Sometimes the roster called for crews to operate into Beirut with possibly two days off and then operate out of Damascus. This involved a hair-raising taxi drive through the mountains over roads that were scarcely usable, particularly in winter where at the higher levels they were covered with snow. Amazingly I was not involved in an accident during those journeys but there were many wrecked cars en route as evidence of the danger.

In Damascus the crews used a 'watering hole' called Tommy's Bar located in a street called Straight that was said to be the original street mentioned in the Bible. (I have no idea if that assumption is correct.) Damascus, located on the edge of the desert had none of the sophistication of Beirut, but for me it possessed a somewhat mystical charm. It is many years since I was last in Beirut or Damascus but sadly political problems and the associated violence has devastated Beirut and reduced many areas to rubble.

The least pleasant stop on the Far East route in summer months was Bahrain where temperatures always exceeded 100 degrees Fahrenheit, which together with the extremely high humidity, made life particularly uncomfortable. Of course, during the winter months it can be a very pleasant place to stay despite its lack of places of interest. BOAC built a very nice fully air-conditioned building with individual rooms and en suite facilities to accommodate crews during slip stopovers, which was a vast improvement over the previous hot dormitory accommodation.

Chapter 13

A Career Change

Early in March 1957 I was nominated to attend a six months navigation course at The College of Air Training in Hamble, commencing on 11th March. I had no illusions about the course and the eventual examinations, knowing that it was going to be hard work but nevertheless, considered myself quite equal to the challenge. The Chief Instructor Squadron Leader Nick Hoy had a very formidable team of instructors that included his Deputy Roy Underdown who taught Meteorology, Tony Palmer (Navigation and Maths), and Max Johnson (Instruments).

On the first day Nick went briefly through the course schedule emphasising that successful completion of the course would only be achieved if each day's instruction had been totally absorbed, consolidating the same evening if necessary. He stressed that unless this was done, it would become impossible to keep up with the instruction schedule. The instructors were so skilled that they made it all seem very easy. Whatever was taught in a particular session, the instructor would indicate precisely what was needed to pass the examination, but equally important, how it would be applied in practical navigation. I remember Nick explaining that his job was to teach enough to pass the licence examinations, but added that some instruction was purely theoretical and would be of little use in practical navigation.

I developed my own method of study to ensure that I kept up with what had been taught each day. Usually I got home from Hamble by 5.30p.m. and would relax until the evening meal had been prepared and served. Afterwards I retired to my study and wrote up all the day's notes, ensuring that everything had been understood and absorbed. If there was anything hazy in my mind, I made a note to bring it up the next morning before the day's instruction commenced. The weekends were kept free of study in order to relax with my wife and son, but there were times when it was necessary to use that time for revision.

As the course progressed, my confidence grew and I was quite sure of the outcome but only shared this confidence with my wife. In August when the course instruction was completed, Nick gave out past examination papers to work through. I felt a little uneasy about answering those papers, thinking that if I did badly it could unsettle me for the real tests to come. On the Friday before the week of the examinations, Nick stressed again the advice he had constantly given on how to pass the examinations. Quite simply it was to read the question paper twice, deciding on the second reading which questions could EASILY be answered. Those questions were to be completed first before progressing through to those more difficult. This ensured that a good number of marks could be accumulated before tackling the questions which would be more time consuming.

On Monday 9th September 1957, I attended at the Ministry of Transport And Civil Aviation's Examination Centre at Berkeley Square House, London W1 where I sat the first of four examinations that day. On Tuesday, Wednesday and Thursday, two examinations were sat each day. Friday was taken up with oral examinations and practical tests. The week over, I returned home fairly confident of the outcome.

After a week off, the course gathered back at Hamble to discuss the examinations and await the results. Nick asked me how I thought the exams had gone and I said that although they were more difficult than I had anticipated, I was confident about the results. He also thought them quite stiff and even remarked that the wording of some questions was ambiguous. When he said that my spirits flagged somewhat but nevertheless, remained confident. Nick phoned to get the results and quite naturally everyone was quite tense. He came back into the classroom with the news that only two, myself included, had passed completely. The rest of the group had partial passes but happily no one failed completely. When the official results arrived, I saw that I had passed easily with an average of 87% over all subjects, the highest being 98% for Astro. Indeed, it seemed that the stars were my friends! With the course successfully behind me, I was immediately posted to the Navigation Training Unit of BOAC's Central Training Unit (CTU) at Heathrow, ready to start my new career.

At CTU I was told that there would be ground instruction on Company Navigation Procedures followed by in-flight navigation exercises on Dove aircraft. In twelve days I flew to Shannon and back six times and to Jersey twice, accruing nearly 47 hours flying of the 200 hours of navigation time required for the issue of my Flight Navigators licence. With the Dove flying completed, the next stage would be done on the Stratocruiser Fleet, flying to West Africa under supervision until sufficient hours had been accrued for the issue of my Navigation Licence.

Inevitably there was another course of instruction for the Stratocruiser covering Flight Planning, Instruments, Fleet Emergency Procedures, and an introduction to the Hughes Periscopic sextant. This sextant was a great improvement over the Mark IX and IXA sextants used on the RAF

Sunderlands, BOAC Flying Boats and Yorks. As the Stratocruiser was pressurised, there was no astro dome for taking sights, the Hughes sextant being inserted into a sextant mount, which allowed it to pass through the aircraft skin into the air above. This avoided dome refraction errors previously experienced with astro domes and allowed easier observation of very high altitude bodies. The sextant mount also had a moveable compass ring enabling heading checks to be made when astro sights were taken.

Astro navigation always gave me a great sense of satisfaction. To observe the altitude of three stars, plot their position lines on the chart and see all three lines more or less intersect is almost magic. The subject of astro navigation is very complex but practical application with modern tables is simplicity itself. For the time of the required astro fix, an assumed position is calculated. Longitude as close as possible to the assumed position is applied to the Greenwich Hour Angle (GHA) of the first point of Aries to produce a *whole* degree of LOCAL HOUR ANGLE (LHA). Tables of stars are then entered with a *whole* degree of both latitude and LHA to extract the calculated altitude (Hc) and azimuth (Zn) of stars for that assumed position. Three stars are normally used with azimuths ideally 120 degrees apart. The sextant altitude observed (Ho) is compared to the calculated Hc. If Ho is *greater*, the observer is on a position line at right angles to the azimuth *towards* the star. Conversely, if Ho were less, it would be *away*. If the azimuths of the stars chosen are 120 degrees apart, the optimum cut of the three position lines can be obtained. The Ho is measured above the *true horizon*, but in an aircraft, this horizon cannot be seen. To overcome this, the sextant has in effect a spirit level, the bubble of which is the horizon. The bubble can be illuminated and varied in size for accuracy since the tiny pinprick of light from the star can more easily be positioned in the centre of a small bubble. Using the sextant controls, the body is moved to the centre of the bubble which itself is centred in the eyepiece by the observer. As the azimuth of the body is known, when the body is in the centre of the bubble the variable ring on the compass mount can be moved so that the sextant is pointing to the azimuth. The aircraft's true heading can then be read against an index mark on the sextant mount. Very high altitude bodies do not give the accuracy needed for heading checks and for that reason lower altitude bodies are preferred. Assuming that the aircraft maintains its heading and the first star is positively identified, the second and third stars will be correctly seen using the Hc and Zn extracted from the tables. Due to pitch and roll of the aircraft that may be experienced, a single shot is not good enough. The mechanism of the sextant allows a shot to be taken continuously every second for up to two minutes. At the end of the two minute run, or sooner if required, the average is calculated by the mechanism of the sextant. Astro shots are normally taken at intervals of four minutes, each shot commencing one minute before the time of each position line, and finishing one minute after. The first position line has to be transferred by eight minutes along the track at the aircraft's ground speed, and the second one by four minutes. There are some corrections that have to be applied, but these are usually tabulated on the astro work sheet so that they are not forgotten.

The main disadvantage of astro fixing is that it takes over ten minutes to establish the position of the aircraft. However, if in good practice, a navigator can 'shoot' a star and plot its position line in the two minutes between the end of one shot and the start of the next. Once the first and second position lines are plotted, he has a good idea if an alteration of heading is required and can mentally calculate the new heading and pass it to the pilots immediately the third shot is finished. Given smooth flying conditions, clear skies, and the scale of the plotting charts used, it is possible for the three position lines to intersect exactly. Unfortunately there is usually some movement of the aircraft which can result in the three position lines giving a 'cocked hat', the centre of which *was* the aircraft's position. *Was*, because it takes at least two minutes to get the fix on the chart, by which time the aircraft would have moved along the track. It is not quite as simple as I have described, but it gives the general idea. The older sextants such as the Mark IX and Mark IXA had no facilities for heading checks and had a much wider field of vision making star identification essential. Another 'Post War' plus is obviously the tables of stars giving altitudes and azimuths for each whole degree of latitude, north or south, against the Local Hour Angle in whole degrees.

The identification of the first star is of paramount importance since it gives the true heading of the aircraft. Identifying stars is a matter of experience although some have positive means of identification with the position of adjacent stars. For instance, three major stars have two less brilliant stars in line with them, these being Altair, Antares and Alnilam. Capella is identified by an elongated triangle of stars alongside it. Rigel is close to the belt of Orion of which Alnilam is the centre star of the belt. Betelgeuse is bright yellow/orange also close to Orion's Belt. Aldebran has a yellowish light and is near to a group of seven stars (The Seven Sisters). Vega is a very bright star with two others less bright forming a triangle. Sirius, the brightest star in the sky, and Canopus can be identified by their sheer brilliance. Knowing constellations can provide pointers to other stars that are less well defined. The field of vision of the Periscope Sextant is not very wide, but a small movement can usually bring other stars into view to provide the necessary identification.

Stars were my hobby but now they had become very important to me in my work.

All that now remained was to accrue the necessary number of navigation hours to enable my Navigation Licence to be issued.

Chapter 14

BOAC Stratocruiser

Flying training on the Stratocruiser commenced on 5th November 1957 on the West African route that had been taken over from the Argonaut fleet. This was an excellent route for navigation, the weather normally being quite clear over the desert, allowing good Astro position fixing. However, in the summer months often violent thunderstorms could be encountered approaching Kano and on to Lagos or Accra. The BOAC Navigation Superintendent, 'Robby' Robinson, an old friend from Number 4 Line Flying Boat days, supervised the first flight and subsequently carried out my final flight check. I was told that subject to my navigating ability, it was likely that I would remain on Stratocruisers and would ultimately be cleared for North Atlantic flying.

Some years before, a Hermes went off track on the West African route due to an incorrect Compass Magnetic Variation Setting being used. The result of this was that the aircraft flew a true heading greatly different from that indicated by the compass and eventually ran out of fuel and crashed in the desert. A pilot was navigating the aircraft and it was apparent that he failed to identify the first star of his first astro fix resulting in shooting three different stars from those he had calculated. The position lines obtained were useless but probably gave a cocked hat of some sort on or about the required track. Having been fooled on the first astro fix, it was easy to repeat the error on subsequent fixes.

Robby stressed that when shooting stars for an astro fix, one should ALWAYS choose a positively identifiable star for the first shot from which the aircraft's true heading could be checked. With the aircraft's heading then accurately established, the second and third stars would then be correctly observed using their calculated altitude and relative bearing to the aircraft's heading. Nick Hoy taught the same procedures on the navigation course at Hamble.

After the third round trip, 'Robby' was completely satisfied with my navigating ability leaving only the Ministry of Aviation requirements preventing me from navigating unsupervised. From then on I was generally left alone to navigate with only an occasional visit to the flight deck by the supervising navigator to ensure all was well. When the necessary 200 hours of navigation had been accrued, my licence was issued and I was given clearance to operate unsupervised and told that I would remain on Stratocruiser Fleet. This was very good news because it meant that I would quite soon progress to navigating the North Atlantic.

'Robby' carried out my flight check on 16th March 1958, flying to Lagos and back in an aircraft commanded by Captain Nigel Pelly, a very senior ex Imperial Airways Captain. I knew that if I could satisfactorily demonstrate my ability to him, the battle for acceptance would be effectively won. The round trip was uneventful with Captain Pelly giving me a great deal of encouragement and advice.

On one West African flight I flew with Captain 'Buddy' Messenger, the Stratocruiser Fleet Flight Manager whom I found to be most pleasant and helpful. He was a very skilled and accomplished pilot and an excellent airman with many thousands of hours flying to his credit. We were at Lagos about to depart for Kano, having been briefed by the Meteorological Officer about a very active line squall lying across the track. Many Captains would have delayed until the bad weather had cleared but 'Buddy' decided that he would go and see what it looked like. On approaching the squall line, there were massive thunderstorms to be seen but he seemed quite unperturbed and headed the aircraft towards the blackest part of the clouds and penetrated the squall line. The rain was absolutely torrential but surprisingly the turbulence was quite light and after ten or fifteen minutes the aircraft broke out into clear skies, allowing the flight to continue to Kano. When Buddy and I were relaxing in the bar of the hotel in Rome, I asked him about his storm cloud penetration technique. He said that from his experience, the blackest part of the cloud is where the heaviest rain is to be found, but more importantly, the lightest turbulence. The brightest cloud gives more likelihood of severe turbulence. It was certainly true that day! Buddy died not many years later but by then, his son Peter had become a BOAC Captain on Comets.

The Stratocruiser was an extremely comfortable aircraft, having a spacious flight deck, although the Navigator was tucked into a corner out of sight on the starboard side. It was a very stable aircraft for astro and the results I obtained were very good. The retractable sextant platform was positioned in the centre of the flight deck and it seemed that whenever I started to take an astro sight, someone would nudge me as they tried to get past. It never ceased to amaze me that when shooting a star, the light of the star I was observing had probably taken several years to reach me. In daylight when the stars were not visible, only the sun and moon would be available unless the brighter Planets, Venus and Jupiter could be seen. Nick Hoy said that it was possible to see Venus in daylight on the ground when at its brightest by looking through a long hollow tube pointed in the right direction. I never managed that but often in the air I would pre-compute both Venus and Jupiter in daylight and use their position lines if they were visible, which with cloudless skies, was quite often.

I developed my own method of seeing planets by day. A minute or so before it was needed, the calculated altitude was set on the sextant and the sextant positioned to the required relative bearing. Then looking almost straight ahead without moving my eyes, the sextant altitude or the relative bearing, the planet would suddenly appear as a tiny pinprick of light that would become brighter as the eye became focused. The trick was not to take the eye off it for a second, but start the sextant running immediately. Once the run was completed, the time was observed at the END of the shot and the position line plotted accordingly.

Strange things can often be seen through a sextant, possibly the most fascinating being the Northern Lights when flying in high latitudes. The almost eerie flickering fingers of light constantly moving and weaving together have an almost hypnotic effect. The Americans at one time had a large balloon in space called 'Echo' that was only visible for a short period of time after sunset. I was taking a sight over the Sahara when the 'Echo' went through the field of vision of the sextant, momentarily distracting me. I saw it again for a short time after sunset from the beach at Honolulu when on holiday.

The Stratocruiser performed well on the West African route and I was very impressed by its performance. The shorter West African sector lengths presented no problems and even the high summer temperatures at Kano did not cause too much concern. Having said that, I was told that some Captains switched off the Automatic Feathering system when taking off from that airfield. I knew little of how that worked other than that if the engine power or torque dropped by a certain amount, the propeller would feather itself. Presumably, there must have been occasions when the system operated incorrectly, but fortunately it never happened on any of my flights.

The flight deck was usually quiet with the engines just murmuring at the low operating weights of that route, giving an atmosphere of peace and serenity. One clear moonlit night without any cloud in the sky, the First Officer remarked what a nice job we had. The Captain warned him against saying things like that as 'Murphy's Law' could give rise to the ringing of warning bells and the flight deck being lit up like a Christmas tree by red warning lights. Oddly enough, about an hour later as the aircraft was approaching Rome, an engine fire warning occurred with the strident ringing of the fire warning bell and the red light illuminating as if to prove the point. Fortunately it was a false warning.

En route to London from Rome on one flight, almost all of UK was blanketed by fog with only Prestwick remaining open. We diverted to Prestwick and waited around for several hours before the Captain decided that having been on duty for nearly 20 hours, we would not be able to return to Heathrow even if the fog cleared. With the forecast showing little improvement for two days, we were ordered by BOAC operations to get on the first available train to London. No sleeper berths were available but we travelled first class to London where we were collected and taken to Heathrow. I still had a two hours drive back to Southampton before I was able to get to bed, some 36 hours after commencing duty in Kano. Needless to say, the weather cleared up soon after getting on the train and we could have flown back!

Early in June 1958, I was given a short North Atlantic course that included a very comprehensive briefing on the route facilities and the airfields available en route. It was considered essential that newcomers to the Atlantic route should understand how greatly the upper winds could vary over the Atlantic. It was also emphasised that the actual weather at places like Goose, Gander, Stephenville, Sydney and Halifax could dramatically change from being absolutely clear to having the airfield close down with fog, low cloud, rain and even snow in the space of minutes. One of the Stratocruisers had a radio telex system fitted so that the actual weather at airfields on or close to the route could be monitored. It was an experimental installation and seldom worked sufficiently well enough to provide the necessary information.

On the 9th of June 1958, I navigated my first Atlantic flight to New York supervised by a training navigator named 'Bob' Tanner. Due to headwinds, the flight landed at Keflavik in Iceland to take on more fuel and I can recall Bob telling me that although the 'Monarch' service was scheduled to be non-stop, it rarely managed to do so. The total flying time for the two sectors to New York was 16 hours 25 minutes and left me quite exhausted having left home some 20 hours earlier. On completion of the round trip, having navigated to the required standard, 'Bob' cleared me for Atlantic operations.

At that time, Stratocruiser crews always had four days off in New York and Bob said that he would show me around the city, arranging to meet at 6p.m. that evening after a sleep. I woke up at what I thought was 5.30p.m. and looked out of the window to see the streets deserted and wondered why. It came to me when I switched on the television that it was 5.30*a.m.* on the following day and I had apparently slept through from 11.30a.m. on the previous morning! Atlantic flights were always quite exhausting and it took me some time to become accustomed to them, particularly with the five hours time change.

On one of the free days, Bob and I walked from the hotel on Lexington

Avenue at 47th Street down to Battery Point, passing through the Bowery, Washington Square, Greenwich Village, Little Italy and many others places of interest. It was a hot day and we made frequent stops at bars en route to Battery Point where we then took the ferry to Staten Island to have lunch at yet another bar. We returned to the hotel on a slightly different route along Broadway to Times Square and then down the famous 42nd Street to Lexington Avenue and then back to the hotel. It was nice to be able to visit New York for the first time but it was quite different from what I had imagined it to be and in some respects was an anti climax.

At all North American and Canadian stopover cities, crews were paid an allowance to cover food and it was nice to be able to eat at different places away from the hotel. This gave the opportunity to sample various different types of food, solid and liquid! There was rivalry amongst the crews to see who could find the cheapest breakfast within close walking distance of the hotel. The cheapest I managed was at a café close to 42nd street where for 99 cents I got a small glass of juice, bacon or ham and two eggs, toast and coffee (the bottomless cup). One could get very good and reasonably priced food at bars but perhaps the best buys were the Steak Houses, notably Tads and Flame, where a large steak, jacket Idaho potato and salad only cost about 3 dollars. It's all more expensive now, of course!

Inevitably I was shown the large department stores such as Macey's, Bloomingdales and others whose names I have forgotten. There was a vast selection of goods that were not available or were too expensive to be bought in England. I soon discovered the best things to buy and in the first two or three months on the Atlantic route I managed to replace most of our bed linen at prices that were unbelievably low!

The navigation procedures on the Atlantic were quite different from those of the West African route with a much greater emphasis on track keeping and regaining track if blown off by unexpected winds. At a Defence Line in the Atlantic running along the coast of Canada and the United States, were reporting points known as 'Fish' points, so called because all were given the names of fish. The aircraft had to be within very small tolerances of distance and time passing 'Fish' points and failure to observe those limits resulted in the aircraft being reported as having violated the Defence Line procedures. Fortunately the Stratocruiser was fitted with LORAN equipment, an excellent long-range radio aid that in good reception conditions enabled the aircraft's position to be determined very accurately in the space of about a minute. The Loran signals in the area of the fish points was usually very good, allowing perfect fixing as the aircraft approached them.

Each Loran chain comprised a Master and Slave ground station transmitting radio pulse signals that were received by the aircraft on a special receiver and indicated on a small Cathode Ray Tube. A pulse transmitted by the Master station was received by the Slave station which then, after a few microseconds delay, triggered off a pulse from the Slave station. Both pulses were received by Loran equipment in the aircraft that measured the *time difference* between the receptions of both signals. Special Loran charts were provided, these having time difference lines (Hyperbolae) from each pair of stations overprinted on them. Given two chains suitably located, position lines could be obtained from each chain enabling a 'fix' to be obtained from the point of intersection of the two position lines. The line directly between Master and Slave stations was the base line and was where the most accurate position line could be obtained. The *extended* base line away from both Master and Slave was unusable. The received signals were visually displayed on the small Cathode Ray Tube and it was very important that cross matching of signals did not occur. Normally a ground wave signal received from the Master would be matched with a ground wave from the Slave. However, during the hours of darkness sometimes only the sky wave of one station would be received, this resulting in 'Cross Matching'. If 'Cross Matching' was known to have occurred, correction values that needed to be applied were printed on the chart. Due to the ease of fixing with this aid, many navigators seemed unwilling to use astro unless it was absolutely necessary. The Company requirement was to check the compasses using the sextant at the commencement of navigation, and to fix at given intervals throughout the flight. I particularly enjoyed astro navigation and made a point of fixing the aircraft's position by astro at least once an hour to keep in practice. Fleet requirements were to establish the aircraft's position at least every 20 minutes, making no demands as to how this was done. In later years when more modern navigation aids became available, the Loran stations were withdrawn from service.

When I first started flying on the Atlantic, Loran did not provide fixing cover completely across the Atlantic by day and there was a 'Hole' of about 400 miles in the middle. At night, Loran sky wave signals could be received and used at greater distances and on some occasions the 'Hole' could be covered. In daylight the 'Hole' had to be navigated by astro using any bodies that were available. I was quite happy to use Sun together with Moon, Venus and Jupiter if they were visible.

The Stratocruiser carried a Radio Altimeter that I considered to be a really useful aid for the navigator. It was not easy to read accurately, but if readings were taken at every fix, a reasonable indication of drift could be obtained when flying over the sea. The aircraft flew with its altimeter sub scale set to the standard setting of 1013.2 millibars, so unless the atmospheric pressure remained constant, which it seldom did, when flying towards a depression the true height would decrease, or when flying away, would increase. From tabulated data, the drift over the period of time between observations could be calculated. By constantly observing the indicated true height from the radio altimeter, drift changes could be detected almost as soon as they occurred. When fixing was not possible, the required track could be roughly maintained by using the calculated drift.

In the early days of my Atlantic flying, weather ships were positioned at several places in the Atlantic and these could provide a bearing and distance of the aircraft from the ship's position. The ship also transmitted radio beacon signals at certain times that could be used by the aircraft's direction finding equipment to obtain position lines. The weather ships were normally within two or three miles of the assigned station and would provide the aircraft with the ship's actual position on request. In stormy conditions they could be well off station with no aids available to establish their position. On one crossing, I contacted a weather ship that gave me a bearing and distance but asked me if I could tell him what his latitude and longitude was. Apparently he had not been able to fix his position for three days due to extremely stormy weather conditions! Fortunately my fixing conditions were excellent at the time and I was able to respond to his somewhat unusual request.

The New York flights operated by the Stratocruiser were BOAC's prestigious Monarch Service, a luxury flight across the Atlantic having a number of bunk beds fitted for passengers to use in flight. Although scheduled as a 16-hour non-stop flight this was seldom possible and in fact, I only managed it once. That particular flight was with Captain John Kemp who seemed to achieve it more frequently than other Captains. His technique was to cruise over the Atlantic at a very low level of 4000 or 6000 feet where the head wind would be lighter than at the normal 8 to 10,000 feet. The disadvantage was that the flight could go through almost any cloud en route and experience the turbulence associated with it.

At the planning stage, options were always open to the Captain if the direct flight was not possible. Such options would be to make a fuel stop at Shannon, Keflavik, Goose Bay or Gander. In the winter months the weather at maritime airfields is always uncertain and can change from being wide open to being unusable in a very short period of time. If the direct flight was only just marginal, a fuel stop at Shannon was the best option, being cheaper than landings elsewhere.

One Captain I flew with opted to go via Shannon although it was extremely doubtful if the direct flight from there to New York was possible. As the aircraft passed Gander, it was obvious that there was insufficient fuel to reach New York and the Captain was informed. He then decided to make Boston his destination with New York as the alternate and re-clear from there, this being quite legal. Had he landed at Boston, the company would most certainly have asked him why he had chosen to land at Shannon instead of Gander and this was obviously in his mind because at Boston, he continued to New York, landing with far less fuel than he should have done. After passing Boston I entered into my log the fuel remaining, which was certainly much less than that required to justify continuance to New York. Fortunately we landed safely at New York albeit with little fuel, certainly not sufficient to divert elsewhere!

Navigating the Atlantic route gave me a great deal of pleasure and satisfaction, mainly I suppose because it was a long sector over water with nothing in between. No two flights were ever identical in respect of route winds and weather, and the tracks varied. Westbound crossings were usually flown at the lower levels of 8 to 10,000 feet into the normal westerly winds. Eastbound flights often reached levels of 21,000 feet with routing to take advantage of tailwinds that could be present. The engines fitted to the Stratocruiser were the large Pratt & Whitney R4630 with 28 air-cooled cylinders in four rows and I recall someone saying that the third row did not get sufficient cooling. I believe that they were also prone to ignition problems associated with fouling of the plugs, this resulting in backfiring. At higher altitudes when the supercharger was engaged this could be quite serious, giving risk of damage to the engine. If backfiring did occur at higher altitudes, invariably the Captain would request an immediate descent to a lower level where the supercharger was not needed. The flight engineer had an engine analyser with which he could inspect the ignition on each engine. I read somewhere that one BOAC Stratocruiser Captain reckoned that he spent as much time on three engines as he did on four. Fortunately that was not my experience.

In addition to the Monarch service, the Stratocruiser Fleet operated flights to Montego Bay in Jamaica flying via Bermuda and Nassau. On one flight from Bermuda to Nassau, the Astronaut Lieutenant Colonel Gus Grissholm was one of the passengers. He was a very pleasant chap and spent some time on the flight deck chatting to the crew. Shortly after this flight, he and his colleagues lost their lives when their Spacecraft caught fire on the launch pad.

As there is no airfield close enough to Bermuda for use as an alternate airfield, the Civil Aviation Regulations required that the aircraft arrive overhead Bermuda with far more reserve fuel than for other destinations. This higher than normal reserve requirement, called 'Island Reserve', meant that a direct flight from London was not possible and was always scheduled to have a refuelling stop. I did one very exhausting flight, landing at Keflavik and Goose Bay, taking 16 hours 30 minutes flying time to reach Bermuda. On the sector Goose to Bermuda, a headwind of 100 knots was experienced for a short time that reduced the ground speed to about 120 knots. Had the headwind continued to Bermuda, there would have been insufficient fuel to continue and we would have been compelled to divert. Taking that route meant that I was on duty for almost 21 hours with no relief. Three pilots and two Flight Engineers were always carried, two bunks being provided on the flight deck for their use. There seemed to be a constant procession of pilots and engineers to and from the bunks whilst I continued working!

One particular hazard at destinations in the Maritimes and perhaps as far west as Montreal was freezing rain. If this was forecast for a particular airport, it was prudent to choose another place to land. When flying in freezing rain, immediately a raindrop hits the aircraft it freezes and ice rapidly accumulates. In a short space of time the weight of ice accumulated can be enormous and ice can affect the control surfaces making control of the aircraft difficult. Approaching Montreal on one flight, the Captain was advised of freezing rain and on final approach the aircraft iced up so badly that it was necessary to use maximum engine power to keep the aircraft flying until the runway was reached. After landing it took the ground engineers a considerable time to remove the ice that had accumulated.

The Britannia 300 was gradually replacing the Stratocruiser on the Atlantic and this meant that the Stratocruiser was frequently used for charter flights. As pilots became trained as navigators they were utilised on the Stratocruiser, releasing navigators for Britannia and DC7 Fleets. I was told that I would be posted to the Britannia 300 Fleet and it was a certain degree of sadness that I went to my new Fleet. However I was not completely finished with the great lumbering, but lovely Stratocruiser.

Chapter 15
BOAC Britannia 312

In November 1958 I transferred to the Britannia 312 Series Fleet to navigate the 'Whispering Giant' turboprop aircraft, which together with the new Boeing 707 would progressively replace the Stratocruiser and the DC7C on the Atlantic. This aircraft was categorised as a Performance 'A' aircraft and before crews could be cleared to operate, they were given a performance course and required to pass a written examination. The course notes were based on a turboprop aircraft that was probably the Britannia 100. Aircraft in Category 'A' must demonstrate that it can take-off, land and fly en route in certain given conditions with far greater safety than hitherto. All piston engine aircraft were outside Category 'A' requirement with the exception of the DC7C that was given a special Category 'X'. The performance requirements of the DC7C was more stringent than other piston engine aircraft, but less so than Turbo Props and Jets.

Although the Britannia 312 was regarded as a long-range aircraft, with a full load it still could not always fly direct to New York, many flights requiring a fuel stop en route. Depending on the load carried and the winds, some westbound flights to New York, Toronto and Montreal could be flown direct in under 12 hours, with the return always direct in about 9 hours, cutting nearly eight hours off the round trip of the Stratocruiser. The Britannia 312 was a superb aircraft that cruised at 300 knots and if carrying a full payload, could operate at altitudes between 19000 and 27000 feet. It was well liked by its crews for its wonderful all round performance. The aircraft had a weather radar system fitted that made avoiding all but the very worst weather quite easy. Again the crew complement was three pilots, two flight engineers and one navigator with the usual procession of all, except the navigator, to the two bunks that were fitted. Its only real problem was that in certain temperature ranges, the engines accumulated ice in the inlet system and from time to time pieces broke off and went through the engine causing a partially flame out, known as a 'bump'. On tropical routes, the ice accumulation could be severe enough to cause engines to 'flame out' completely. Normally they could be re-lighted by an automatic system of 'glow plugs', but in extreme cases it would be necessary for the Flight Engineer and/or Pilots to perform manual re-lighting of the engine(s). With severe engine icing present it was possible to have all four engines 'bumping', not a particularly pleasant experience. Apart from this particular icing phenomenon, engine problems were few and far between and most Britannia delays were due to electrical problems that seemed to plague it.

Astro navigation was not quite as good as the Stratocruiser as the aircraft had a quite pronounced roll motion. Best sights were taken towards the front or rear of the aircraft where the relative movement was less. Beam shots were subject to the maximum error and were avoided whenever it was possible to do so.

The cruising levels were much higher than piston engine aircraft and with a light load the aircraft could get well above 30,000 feet. The Britannia was only fuel-efficient when flown at its optimum altitude, but due to the density of traffic on the route, this was not always possible. Depending on the outside air temperature, a Britannia 312 at maximum take-off weight would commence its cruise at about 18/19,000 feet. As fuel was consumed, the decreasing aircraft weight would allow further step climbs to be made, subject to Air Traffic Control, towards the destination. Ideally the aircraft should 'Cruise Climb' as Concorde did, but separation from other aircraft prevented this. Concorde could 'cruise climb' because apart from military aircraft, there would be no other traffic at its altitude. Cruise climb is achieved by (I believe) keeping the engine power and airspeed constant, which causes the aircraft to progressively increase its altitude as fuel is consumed and the aircraft's weight decreases. The strength of the upper winds generally increases with height, a favourable situation with tail winds, but not so good with head winds. Selection of the aircraft's track on Atlantic routes became very important with more or less track distance being traded against less head wind or more tail wind. Instead of the fairly narrow band of tracks that were used with piston engine aircraft, an analysis was made to find the 'best time track' for a particular flight. With the winds constantly changing in direction and strength, the best time track analysis was an ongoing procedure with the track possibly being quite different two or three hours later. An aircraft could have become airborne and cleared on its filed track, only to be told en route that a variation of track was needed. The BOAC Flight Planning and Operations Department at Heathrow did Atlantic flight planning for westbound flights and local planners at overseas stations liased with Heathrow to agree the final route eastbound. It was a good system that worked well, but as with many other things, would eventually be done by a computer.

Before the Britannia 300 series came into service, the 100 series commenced operations on eastern and southern routes. The Britannia 100 was a smaller aircraft with less range than its 'big brother', but was ideal for the routes it operated. It also suffered from the same engine icing problems, these being more prevalent on its tropical route structure than the 300 series on the Atlantic.

The North Atlantic route structure had the Britannia 300 series operating to New York, Montreal, Toronto, Detroit, Boston, Bermuda, and onwards to Barbados, Trinidad, Caracas, Bogata, or Nassau, Montego Bay, and Kingston. This variation of destinations certainly made life more interesting than just flying between the same two places on each side of the Atlantic. On my first trip to Montreal I had the very great pleasure of meeting up with my RAF Sunderland pilot Emil 'Baron' Holstein, who took me to his home at Pointe Claire where I met his wife Cecile and his son and two daughters. This was the first of many meetings with Emil and his family but sadly, early in 1999 he died of cancer.

New LORAN stations were brought into service, providing more reliable navigation fixing coverage on most of the North Atlantic route by day and night and the 400-mile 'Hole' in mid Atlantic then disappeared. The Loran coverage on the direct track from London to Bermuda was still not fully covered and astro was needed where Loran coverage ran out. The higher altitudes achieved by the Britannia certainly improved the reception of Loran signals, which in turn gave greater route coverage over aircraft flying at lower levels. More importantly, it put the aircraft above all except the very high cloud, giving good conditions for Astro fixing.

Not long after being posted to Britannias I was made a supervisory navigator and subsequently became an Instructor. On about every other flight, I had a pilot navigating under my supervision or being trained, giving me a financial benefit by way of a training allowance. BOAC had decided to go ahead with its plans to have a crew consisting of three pilots and one/two Flight Engineers, with one of the pilots designated to navigate the aircraft. No firm target date had been set for this plan to be implemented due to the large number of pilots to be trained. I found very few pilots really wanted to do navigation, their real ambition being to reach Captain rank and command the aircraft. Consequently some showed little interest in navigation, treating it as if it was a penance. Most were eventually checked out although some took far longer to reach the required standard than others. There were, of course, some who did not reach the required standard even though they might have been quite happy to navigate.

BOAC had problems with their pilots in respect of their advancement to Captain rank, there simply not being enough vacancies for those qualified for promotion. This was overcome by creating a Captain X rank.

Suitably qualified First Officers were promoted to the new Captain rank and were able to command an aircraft when rostered to do so, but would fly as a First Officer at other times. The details of conditions of service and pay were of no concern to me and I cannot say what they were. The system seemed to work well and it soon became quite normal to have two Captains on board, one commanding the outbound flight with (perhaps) the other commanding inbound.

Seven months after joining Britannia Fleet I was asked to go back to Stratocruisers to assist training pilots on five flights. This temporary posting was quite agreeable as I enjoyed flying on the Stratocruiser, although I much preferred to navigate rather than instruct or supervise. By this time the Stratocruisers were mostly flying charters across the Atlantic with high density seating which dramatically reduced the fuel available, necessitating more fuel stops. The first three flights went without incident but the fourth really went wrong.

The fourth flight, a charter to Boston, was to be the last commercial flight of GANUA, as on arrival at Boston it was to be ferried to the Boeing Aircraft Company in Seattle. There it would be taken in part payment for Boeing 707–200 aircraft that BOAC had contracted to buy. There should have been a trainee navigator for me to supervise but when I checked into Operations for the flight, I learned that no one had been rostered.

In the early hours of the morning of 29th July 1959 the aircraft took off from Heathrow heading for the first refuelling stop at Shannon. After it was refuelled, it departed for the second refuelling stop at Gander. Not long after take-off whilst climbing out on track, number four engine failed quite passively and the propeller was feathered. The excess fuel was jettisoned and the aircraft returned to Heathrow for an engine change. Thirteen hours later, and with a replacement engine installed, we set off once again for Shannon. We thought at the time that the replacement engine was either new or re-conditioned. This unfortunately was not correct, the replacement being an almost time expired engine that was put on just to see the aircraft through to Seattle! There was a delay at Shannon waiting for the Gander weather forecast to improve and it was shortly after midnight before we were able to depart for Gander. The weather conditions were extremely good, flying through a high-pressure system with little or no cloud and only very light upper winds at the cruising altitude of 8000 feet.

All was normal until position 53.00N: 27.39W, co-ordinates quite indelibly printed in my mind, when number four engine violently back-fired followed by a very loud bang. The Flight Engineer reported that the oil pressure was rapidly dropping and he was shutting the engine down. Almost immediately the aircraft vibrated severely and the starboard wing dropped abruptly causing the Flight Engineer to ask me to look out of my side window to check that the propeller was feathered. Although it was completely dark, with the wing floodlights on I could see that the propeller was feathered, but could also see that there was a large piece of cowling from the engine or its nacelle, standing up almost vertically on the wing. This tremendous drag was obviously the cause of the vibration and as I reported this, the Captain declared a full emergency saying that he could not control the aircraft and ordered a distress message to be sent. The aircraft had a very steep bank angle and was descending rapidly towards the sea. I quickly passed the aircraft's position to the third pilot who commenced sending it to London on HF R/T. Meanwhile the Captain and First Officer were both at the controls using all their strength to get the aircraft in a level attitude. This was managed as the altitude reached 1800 feet but by this time the aircraft was heading east having turned through 180 degrees and with the remaining three engines at maximum power. The reason that the Captain regained some semblance of control was because the metal panel standing vertically was bent back thus reducing some of the drag. The Captain asked for a course to steer to the nearest airfield, which of course was Shannon. As there had been no significant wind experienced outbound, I was able to quickly give him a heading to steer. Remarkably, the aircraft had become stabilised only a few degrees off the required compass heading, which for the pilots with their control problems was a godsend.

Having got the aircraft level and on course for Shannon, the Captain asked me to calculate how much fuel could be dumped to lighten the aircraft. With the remaining three engines still at maximum power with no indication when it could be reduced to a sensible level, it was impossible to give a precise answer. In actual fact, had any fuel been dumped it is doubtful if the aircraft could have reached Shannon, the fuel consumption remained so high.

Once the initial danger had passed, the Captain evaluated the situation and asked the purser to give his cabin report. Although the passengers must have been quite alarmed, there was no panic and all were seated fairly calmly with lifejackets on. The aircraft was a long way from Shannon and if another engine failed, it certainly would have resulted in ditching in the Atlantic. A very sobering thought! This was obviously in the Captain's mind because he did discuss with the other pilots the option of ditching in the sea where it was relatively calm and with a long swell, rather than possibly have to ditch later, perhaps in far less favourable sea conditions. The consensus of opinion was to carry on and try to reach Shannon. Almost every aircraft in the area had a radio set tuned to our VHF frequency and many heartening messages were received as they passed by, providing moral support.

Just prior to the engine failure, the Loran equipment had become unserviceable thus depriving me of my very useful and rapid position fixing aid. In fact at the time of the engine failure, with the assistance of the third pilot, David Nichols, I was attempting to repair the Loran set that I had removed from its rack, changing valves in a vain attempt to cure the fault. The violent movement of the aircraft caused me to cut my forehead on the equipment as I was bending over it. I pre-computed stars for an astro fix but on looking in the sextant eyepiece, instead of seeing a well defined illuminated bubble, the vibration was so severe that all I could see was a red blur! The only navigation aid available to me was a radio aid called Consul located in Ireland that gave me some semblance of track guidance. A BOAC DC7C en route to Heathrow from New York was almost at Shannon when its Captain heard the distress call and decided to return to the Atlantic to intercept and provide an escort to Shannon. When in radio range, I spoke to his navigator and it was estimated that we would meet just south of weather ship 'Juliet' at 20.00W. Approaching 'Juliet', the DC7C's red anti collision light could be clearly seen as it circled the weather ship awaiting our arrival. It formated slightly above and abeam of the Stratocruiser, giving our passengers a good view and doubtless a great deal of reassurance.

The sky was just showing the first light of dawn when the fire warning alarm of the number three engine became activated intermittently. With no adverse indications on the engine instruments it was unlikely that it was a genuine fire but there was nothing to be done except ignore it as the aircraft could not have continued flying if it was shut down. The DC7C viewed the Stratocruiser from all angles looking for signs of fire, but nothing could be seen and the alarm was silenced.

Shortly after the engine failure, the RAF Rescue unit at St Mawgan scrambled a Shackleton Air Sea Rescue aircraft to intercept and escort. When airborne, its Captain sent a message giving an estimated time of intercept that unbelievably was almost an hour different to that which I had calculated. When queried, they recalculated and passed the correct intercept time. It was comforting to know that they were coming as their aircraft carried ocean survival equipment, should it have been needed. Although on three engines and with the dreadful drag being experienced, the Stratocruiser was still flying faster than the RAF Shackleton's normal cruising speed. The RAF pilot had to increase engine power to maintain station when interception did take place.

The aircraft track was north of the Great Circle track used by Transatlantic Liners and I was given a constant stream of ship's positions, the idea being that if ditching became necessary, the aircraft could head for the nearest one. Quite pointless really because if another engine had failed, ditching would have occurred within two or three minutes! The main crumb of comfort throughout the emergency was that the Stratocruiser was a very good aircraft to ditch, Pan American having had two of theirs ditch in the Pacific. On one, the Captain virtually stepped from the aircraft into a rescue boat without getting his feet wet.

The pilots continued to have great difficulty keeping the aircraft straight and level, using pretty well maximum inputs of rudder and aileron to achieve it. To compound matters, the oil contents on number three engine became dangerously low, giving a rise in oil temperature and a drop in pressure. The Stratocruiser carried an auxiliary oil tank from which the Flight Engineer could keep the individual engine oil tanks topped up. Unfortunately, due to the high power needed to keep the aircraft flying, the oil consumption on the remaining engines was so high that the auxiliary tank became exhausted. It was then anyone's guess if another engine would fail! The Captain had tried to climb the aircraft but as soon as he raised the nose, the vibration increased and the airspeed decreased.

Approaching Shannon, the Captain briefed the crew about the landing and the possible complications. He had no idea how the aircraft would handle when the flaps and undercarriage were extended and stated that he would maintain his speed until on short final approach when he would lower the undercarriage and extend the flaps. He warned that if the undercarriage did not operate, he would land the aircraft with its wheels up, as there would be insufficient power available for an overshoot to be carried out. There was an anxious moment when the gear and flaps were extended but the aircraft handled well and a perfect landing was made. A fine example of flying by the pilots!

The piece of metal, the cover of stowage compartment on the engine nacelle, was over six feet long and did not fall off on landing. It had to be forcibly removed from its jammed position by the ground engineers. It had taken 4 hours 15 minutes to return to Shannon from the position where the engine failed, but it seemed far longer. After landing, the crew were kept clear of the public areas whilst Captain Don Bellingham, went to meet the press who had assembled. The Captain of the BOAC DC7C who escorted us was Lou Carey, and by a remarkable coincidence, his navigator, 'Taffy' Baldwin, was a good friend and a near neighbour of mine in Southampton. Oddly enough my wife had listened to the early news on the radio and heard that a BOAC Stratocruiser on a charter flight to Boston was in trouble over the Atlantic. She knew it was the charter I was flying and was quite concerned until BOAC phoned to tell her that the aircraft had landed safely!

Following a night stop in a hotel at Shannon, Captain Bellingham with both pilots and Flight Engineers, took the aircraft off on three engines and flew it to Heathrow where two engines were changed before the aircraft was ferried to Seattle. It was learned later that the cause of the failure was due to the engine's master connecting rod fracturing, resulting in massive damage within the engine. It was certainly unusual to have two engines fail in two days, both needing to be changed. Obviously the excessive power necessary to maintain flight caused the ailing number three engine to be also changed at Heathrow before the aircraft could be ferried to Seattle. A relief aircraft was sent to Shannon to take the passengers on safely to Boston without further incident. With the remainder of the crew, I flew back to Heathrow on a Pan American DC7C where all were stood down. Ironically, when the Pan American aircraft landed, engineers had to work on *its* number four engine before it could depart.

My fifth and final flight on the Stratocruiser took place ten days later, flying to Montreal via Keflavik on the outbound flight and via Gander on the return. With the events of the previous flight still in my mind, I was perhaps a little wary. However it turned out to be the most perfect flight one could ever ask for. I supervised First Officer John D'arcy and found his navigation to be first class. I believe that he had started a career in the legal profession but gave it up for flying. He retired as a Senior Captain many years later, having reached Senior Management level.

My annual leave had been arranged and the family left for New York, Philadelphia and Detroit, visiting friends at each place during the two weeks holiday. Having been returned to Britannia 312 Fleet prior to leaving on holiday, I was asked to navigate a 'Whispering Giant' back from Detroit at the end of the holiday when the navigator rostered to operate had become ill. After the traumatic experience on the Stratocruiser, I was quite pleased to be back on the Britannia.

Changes in the route structure constantly took place and it was always a pleasant surprise to receive the next roster and find yet another new destination. One could depart UK for New York and then with appropriate days off, perhaps fly to Bermuda and back in a day. Sometimes it was a flight to Bermuda for a night stop, returning to New York on the next day. BOAC had also implemented its round the world service with 312 Series Britannias operating Westbound to Hong Kong via New York, San Francisco, Honolulu and Tokyo, where it met up with 100 Series Britannias operating Eastbound and return.

Some crew schedules operated from New York to Jamaica via Nassau or Miami for a night stop, then on to Montreal for another night stop, after which it could then route from Montreal to Bermuda, and back to UK. The only drawback was that if an aircraft became delayed, BOAC operations would switch the crews around which could result in getting back home up to a week late. This was most unpopular but had to be accepted as an operational necessity.

This happened to me in early March 1960 when, having flown my roster almost to its end, I departed Kingston for New York via Montego Bay only to find on arrival overhead New York that heavy snow had closed the airport, causing us to divert to Montreal. A rapid return to New York was attempted but after departure from Montreal, we only got as far as Albany where the aircraft was put into a holding pattern. The landing delays at New York were in excess of three hours, putting the crew well outside their flight time limitations and the aircraft returned to Montreal for a crew rest period. This put me into a totally different crew pattern and I got home a week late.

Whilst in Kingston on that particular flight, the flight deck crew were accommodated as normal at Morgan's Harbour Country Club Hotel. During the 36-hour stopover we were able to watch the filming of the first James Bond movie 'Doctor No' that was using our hotel for its location. We watched a short scene with Sean Connery (James Bond) going to the bar and asking for a Red Stripe beer. It must have been shot at least six or seven times before Director Terence Young was satisfied. Sean Connery was dressed in a suit and a tie that must have been extremely uncomfortable in the 90-degree heat and high humidity because immediately the director was happy with the shot, Sean peeled off his clothes down to brief swimming trunks and dived into the pool to cool off.

That evening we were prevented from dining outside because the dining area had been converted into a Night Club for a scene they were going to shoot. We were watching from the bar area having a pre dinner drink when we were rudely told to remove ourselves by the assistant director. This did not go down very well with the crew and as we were guests in the hotel, he was sharply told what to do with himself. I think Terence Young came over and apologised for his assistant's rudeness, explaining that we were in the camera line of sight and asked us if we would mind standing in a different place. We told him that if his assistant had been polite with us rather than objectionable, we would have moved without any fuss at all.

My wife accompanied me on one of the multiple sector flights starting with New York. Two days later I went to Bermuda and back on the same day, taking my wife on the flight so that she could stay in Bermuda with friends. The intention was that she would rejoin me when I went four days later for a night stop. Unfortunately on my night stop flight a hurricane threatened Bermuda and the aircraft had to rapidly turn around and return to New York without my wife being able to join the flight. Fortunately she got back to New York to join up with me on the following day.

Direct flights to Bermuda from Heathrow could not usually be achieved due to the extra amount of reserve fuel that had to be carried. I was rostered for a Bermuda flight leaving at mid evening but a technical fault caused the departure to be delayed until the following morning. By then a large number of the passengers had been put on other airlines and this gave additional fuel making the direct flight possible. A navigator is never quite happy on the Atlantic sector to Bermuda if the flight is in daylight as the Loran coverage is quickly lost and then the only aid is the sun, moon or perhaps planets. When out of range of Loran, I computed Venus, which I thought was far enough away from the sun to be seen. To my absolute delight, it was clearly visible and for the next eight hours I was able fix the aircraft's position using Sun and Venus every half hour until the USA East Coast Loran signals were received sufficiently well for Loran fixing. It was most fortunate that any cloud en route was below the aircraft and I had no trouble seeing Venus. It only needs the faintest trace of cloud to obscure a planet in daylight! That particular flight gave me a great deal of satisfaction as the aircraft's position was fixed regularly and with no significant deviation from track.

The newly implemented twice weekly round the world route exceeded the agreed trip time away from home and BOAC decided to base crews at overseas stations for periods of three months or so. I cannot say where the Britannia 100 crews were based but the Britannia 312 crews were in Honolulu and Tokyo. Those in Honolulu flew to San Francisco and Tokyo, whilst those in Tokyo flew to Hong Kong and back with a night stop in Hong Kong. There was great rivalry amongst the crews to be based overseas and although my seniority was not particularly high as a navigator, I was told that I would be based in Tokyo for several months from early May 1960. Financially this was quite beneficial and there was the added bonus that families were allowed to accompany crews. The plum posting was Honolulu but with my low seniority, there was no chance of that. My son was in an important phase of his education and although he would have been perfectly happy to be away from school, my wife decided that they would not come out until mid July when the school term had ended.

The departure for my posting was on 9th May 1960 when I navigated to New York and then remained on board the aircraft as supernumerary crew to San Francisco where I had five days off before the next aircraft arrived. In 1960 San Francisco was my idea of the perfect place to visit with so many attractions to be seen. I took a Gray Line coach tour through the Muir Woods and Napa Valley to Calistoga National Park where 'Old Faithful', a hot geyser dutifully performed. Napa valley has beautiful countryside, being the grape growing area where many companies produce wine. The tour included a visit to The Christian Brothers Vineyard where samples of every still wine produced was available for tasting. One could easily get tipsy from just tasting!

The Muir Woods has a special beauty of its own with its huge and magnificent Redwood trees. The guide pointed out petrified Redwood trees that had been felled by a massive volcanic eruption and over a great period of time had turned into stone. Our life span was put in its correct perspective when the guide said that the eruption had occurred *two million years ago!*

In the local area there are many sights to be seen, including the very impressive San Francisco Bridge, The Powell Street trams, Alcatraz Island, Fisherman's Wharf and the beautiful Golden Gate Park with its many colourful plants and flowers. I particularly enjoyed the Japanese garden, a preview of what I would see in Tokyo.

The five days passed too quickly and late afternoon on 15th May, the flight departed for a 7 hours 30 minutes flight to Honolulu. This was a totally new area for me and I was pleased to be flying over the Pacific Ocean for the first time. Initially navigation was very easy with excellent Loran coverage, but as it got dark I found it more convenient to navigate by Astro. The flight was uneventful and a landing was made on schedule at 9.30p.m. Honolulu time. The two days spent there were taken up with sightseeing around the beautiful island of Oahu and attempting to ride the enormous surf breaking on the beach at Waikiki. I managed fairly well lying on the surf board but seeing the locals standing up on their boards made me realise that more skill was needed than I possessed.

On a conducted tour of The International Market, a rather amusing guide pointed out that long ago before the missionaries arrived, the islanders owned all the land. Then the missionaries came, bringing with them huge stocks of bibles and as the islanders became converted to Christianity, they accepted bibles in exchange for their land. Very soon the missionaries owned all the land, with the islanders having all the bibles! I wonder how factual that is!

The next flight was to Wake Island and on to Tokyo flying over Marcus Island, two sectors of nearly seven hours each. When I plotted the track on the chart, Wake Island was just a tiny dot with no other island or land nearby. It was an easy flight to navigate using Loran and Astro in reasonably clear skies at cruising altitude. There was no alternate airfield available for Wake Island and the 'Island Reserve' fuel requirement applied. It was a sobering thought that if the tiny island were to be missed, the aircraft would run out of fuel before any land could be reached. This of course happened to Amelia Earhart when she and her navigator Fred Noonan failed to find Howland Island on their flight from Lae in New Guinea during their round the world flight in June 1937. They did not have the advantage of Loran and their aircraft probably could not fly above the clouds to allow them to use Astro. It is strange how these thoughts came to me between Honolulu and Wake Island.

About an hour out of Wake Island, almost every crew member asked me how we were doing and how much longer we had to go. Someone even asked at what distance we were likely to see the airfield lights! The weather was perfect and the airfield's rotating beacon was seen some distance out. Being an American Military Airfield, everyone remained on board during refuelling, after which the flight continued to Tokyo. That flight of 6 hours 50 minutes was uneventful but seemingly took two days, having crossed the date line.

On arrival Rex Tapley, the Captain in charge of the crew detachment met me and took me to the hotel that was to become my home for the next three and a half months.

My posting to Japan was in the period when the country was struggling to establish its financial credibility and produce goods that equalled the standards of those manufactured in Europe. Neither had been achieved in 1960 but it was not too far ahead. It seemed to me that almost every Japanese male smoked very heavily and many were inveterate gamblers. In the city were arcades lined with pinball machines that always seemed to be in use. As one player left a machine, his place was immediately taken by someone else waiting to play. There appeared to be no prizes to be won and it seemed that the only attraction was just the pleasure of playing.

Japan produced a very passable whiskey called Suntory that compared well with some brands of Scotch whisky and one that I found quite palatable. Japanese produced beer was similar to those available in the USA that I also liked. Saki was always available but it was not to my taste.

The choice of accommodation in Tokyo was up to the individual but most took advice from the crews who were there, or had been there. I stayed at the San Bancho Hotel in Koji Machi, the grounds of which backed on to the moat surrounding the Imperial Palace. Whilst not a luxury hotel, it had all the facilities normally required, including air conditioning and a good size swimming pool. The British Embassy was located a short distance from the hotel and I was told that UK citizens were asked to register there. Registering was mainly for security reasons, but it was also a means of getting an invitation to some parties held at the Embassy.

Only the flight deck crew was based in Tokyo, the cabin crew operating to a crew slip pattern that kept them away from home for a very long period. They were accommodated in the centre of the city at a hotel located fairly close to the BOAC office. All flight deck crew on my posting had opted for the same hotel and we got on very well with each other. There were two Captains, three First Officers, three Flight Engineers and two Navigators to carry out the two flights each week to Hong Kong. My weekly schedule was a departure at 11a.m. on each Tuesday, arriving in Hong Kong at 5p.m. for a night stop. The departure from Hong Kong was at 11a.m. on Wednesday morning arriving back in Tokyo by 5p.m. in the afternoon. The other navigator, who was on stand by for my flight, flew to a similar schedule as myself, but departed Tokyo on Thursdays. On Fridays I was available for duty if required, but this never became necessary. This schedule allowed everybody three consecutive days off on Saturday, Sunday and Monday, during which time there were no restrictions on movements around Japan.

Early May is the cherry blossom season and a wonderful time to be in Japan with beautiful weather and pleasant temperatures. As the months went by, the weather became much hotter with temperatures up to 100 degrees and quite a lot of rain. Sometimes typhoons came close to Japan but never posed any great threat to Tokyo whilst I was there. Typhoons would often be quite close to the aircraft's track and there were some very bumpy rides going to and from Hong Kong. On one flight into Hong Kong the aircraft flew close to a typhoon heading for the colony and the many storm cells seen on the weather radar with its yellow display gave the impression that mud had been thrown at the screen! On landing we were told that the typhoon was going to hit the colony and were ordered to immediately evacuate the aircraft to Manila, the capital city of the Philippines. The typhoon did hit Hong Kong and the gale force winds closed the airport causing a great deal of damage. We flew the aircraft back to Tokyo direct from Manila on the following morning so that it arrived back in Tokyo on schedule, albeit with no passengers.

It was always hot and humid in Hong Kong but the schedule was very leisurely and gave plenty of time off for shopping. I had an

Australian radio amateur friend living in Hong Kong who was a pilot with Cathay Pacific Airways. When his days off coincided with my visits, we would meet for dinner and then go back to his flat high up on the Peak. It is interesting to note that he was a Radio Officer with QANTAS in 1939 and operated C Class flying boats to Singapore before the war with the Japanese started. When that route ceased to operate he flew on the very long-range flights from Perth to Koggala Lake in Ceylon on Catalina flying boats. I can remember him saying that the sector flying time was usually between 28 and 30 hours but that on one of his flights to Perth, it took 36 hours! By the time I arrived at Koggala during the war he had been transferred to fly on converted Liberator bombers or Lancastrians, the civil version of the Lancaster bomber, flying to Ratmalana close to Colombo. I am still in touch with him 40 years later and saw him in February 1999 when we were in Sydney on holiday. Sadly we will not see him again as my health at the time of writing this book will not allow me to fly long distances

Having been engaged in operations against the Japanese during the war, initially I had little regard for them in the light of the atrocities that were committed. I tried to learn something of their culture and their customs and discovered that they thought a great deal of their families. I met a retired Japanese Army Colonel and his wife, getting to know them quite well. I suppose inevitably one of the questions I asked was, 'Why did the Japanese attack the Americans when they knew that they could never win.' He did not directly answer the question but did say that unless I knew something about Japanese culture and religion, I would never be able to understand the Japanese race. He did explain that if a Japanese person performed a deed that was heroic in Japanese eyes, that person would become immortal. For example, the attack on Pearl Harbour was an act of treachery in the eyes of the world, but those who planned or took part in it, became heroes in the eyes of their people. That's not the whole story, but it is the closest I could get to an explanation.

I was told that the Japanese family's eldest male is revered, and other members are subservient to him at all times. However, I learned that the senior female controls the household in most other respects, including the finances. When my wife joined me in Tokyo, we would often have dinner with the Colonel and his wife, but I could not get used to having a lady opening doors, or holding my chair as I seated myself. My wife told me to enjoy it while I could, as it certainly would not be a custom we would take home with us!

The two months I spent alone in Tokyo before my wife and son joined me were rather tedious and I missed them a great deal. The other members of crew had their families with them and I was able to join in some of their activities. My wife and son flew out to Tokyo by BOAC Comet from London, flying First Class on some of the many sectors. It was a tiring flight for them and with the eight hours time change, they were quite exhausted on arrival. There was some doubt as to whether they would be able to come because a careless motorist opened his car door and knocked my son off his bicycle breaking his collarbone. BOAC required medical permission be obtained from the hospital before he was allowed to travel.

Once settled in, we took full advantage of everything to be seen. A weekend was spent in a Japanese hotel near to Mount Fuji, living in Japanese style for three nights, which we found to be enjoyable and quite amusing. Sleeping Japanese style was not as uncomfortable on the Tatami as I imagined it might be, but it was no substitute for a comfortable bed. Shoes were not worn in the room, these being left at the door where lightweight slippers were available. The food was entirely Japanese with green tea always available. I did not care for that and would always opt for a good English style tea.

We visited Kamakura and saw the huge Buddha Statue, the largest in the world, set in a most wonderful leisure area. We travelled by train to Nikko and sailed across the beautiful Lake Nikko nearby. Trains have to be mentioned because they were so clean and punctual. A train arrival was almost to a second of its schedule and when it stopped at the station, the doors were exactly opposite paint markings on the platform. It's a pity that we do not have the same efficiency with our train services.

There was plenty to be seen in Tokyo and Yokahama and it was no trouble finding things to do on the three clear days I had off. Tokyo tower was, I believe, the largest structure in the world at that time, giving views in all directions over the city. It looks similar to the Eiffel Tower but was much larger. Seeing such a structure it was easy to understand how the Japanese did become such a powerful industrial force. I visited a factory producing large electric generators and other large electrical products. Although it was a hive of activity no rubbish was allowed to accumulate on the factory floor with cleaners constantly clearing and cleaning up behind the lathe operators. The floors appeared clean enough to eat a meal from!

Japan being in an earthquake zone, experiences earth tremors several times a day. I was in a camera shop close to the hotel when without warning, all the windows and display cases started to rattle and the floor seemed to be rippling under my feet. I must have looked startled, but the assistant just laughed and told me that it was nothing to worry about. After a time I got used to what were considered to be only minor tremors.

The wildest experience was to take a taxi ride and I became convinced that all taxi drivers were training to become kamikazi pilots. Once in the taxi, they would accelerate away with no regard for other road users, using maximum power until they reached the destination. It was always a most hair-raising experience but surprisingly, accidents were quite rare. Taxi fares related to the size of the taxi, there being three different levels but regardless of the size of the taxi, the driving was always in the same reckless style. The most economical way to get around was on a tram, which like the trains, kept to its schedule and was spotlessly clean. Japanese are very conscious of health and cleanliness and wear white masks over their mouths in public if they have a cold to prevent it being spread to others. Again something that could be copied by less healthy countries!

Riots, mainly by university students, were frequent in Tokyo whilst I was there. They would block roads and cause the police to turn out in force to deal with them. Oddly enough, they never seemed to bother Europeans and would generally be quite friendly as we passed by. The Diet Building, the Parliament of Japan, was just a short distance away from my hotel and was an obvious place for the rioters to congregate.

Eating out could be a problem as small restaurants did not have menus printed in English and few waitresses spoke English. However, in the window of the restaurant were photographs of the various dishes available with an identifying number alongside. If you wanted to order steak and chips, you looked in the window to find its number and wrote it on the waitresses' pad when she came to take the order. The Japanese Kobe steaks were quite superb and I found most Japanese food attractive and appetising. Sushi was the only dish I did not particularly care for.

Tokyo in 1960 was not an expensive place. The rate of exchange was fixed at 1000 Yen to the English Pound and radio and electrical equipment could be purchased very cheaply, particularly at Aki Habara, a huge area selling just radio equipment and parts. The standard of equipment was not as good as the present day and consequently not very reliable. Noritake china was an excellent buy and most people bought 96 piece dinner and tea sets at ridiculous prices. We had the privilege of freighting home our purchases by BOAC and there were very few of the crew who did not take advantage of that 'perk'.

Early in August problems occurred with my eyes and it became necessary to see the BOAC appointed doctor who, unable to diagnose the problem, referred me to a Japanese specialist at a hospital. The consultation was quite weird because the specialist could not speak a word of English and the interpreter did not know the English words for the diagnosis given by the specialist. It transpired that I had contracted infectious conjunctivitis that was to be treated with eye drops. I had gone to the hospital alone by taxi and after the consultation I had planned to return to the hotel by the same means. Unfortunately the specialist had put drops in my eyes that did not seem to cause anything worse than blurred vision but when I got outside in the brilliant sunlight, I was virtually blind and could not see well enough to walk or find a taxi. Luckily the interpreter had followed me out of the hospital on her way home, and seeing my dilemma, took me back inside the hospital. After about an hour I could see well enough to leave and she put me in a taxi, directing it to my hotel. The treatment prescribed by the specialist soon brought my eyes back to normal.

One of the hazards of Japan is getting taxi drivers to understand where you want to go. At that time, and probably still is, the numbering of houses in a street was not done in numerical order. The Ginza, perhaps one of the longest streets in the world, may have had number 1 at one end and number 2 some miles away at the other end. I always carried a supply of the hotel business cards, which not only gave the address of the hotel, but also had a little map showing the location of the hotel in relation to a known landmark. All crew members based in Tokyo were provided with personal BOAC business cards with the BOAC office address printed in Japanese so that if everything else failed, a taxi could be taken to the office from where it was simple to find one's way back to the hotel.

In leisure time during the week it was normal to relax at the hotel pool that was in a most pleasant setting. My navigation colleague on my posting was Terry Playford and we used to go to a bathhouse on the Ginza once a week, which believe me, is quite an experience. First there would a spell in the hot box something like a Turkish bath, this being followed by squatting on a wooden stool and being soaped all over and scrubbed by a Japanese female attendant. After being rinsed off, there followed immersion in a bath filled with almost scalding water that was agony to get into, but sheer bliss as the body became accustomed to the heat of the water. Finally cool water was sloshed over the body before the masseuse got to work. This was a reputable establishment and no kinky things took place. All impurities were washed from the body but one was left with a raging thirst and all the good work was undone by quaffing two or three large glasses of beer on the way back to the hotel. Terry and I went through this bath ritual most Sunday mornings if we were not out sightseeing.

Towards the end of the posting, Terry and I received some new charts from the Fleet Navigation Officer in Heathrow. The instructions with them were of a grid navigation system that was going to be implemented on the Atlantic routes. Hitherto the company had used normal Rhumb Line procedures, but by changing to the grid system, the aircraft would fly less distance between reporting points giving the company some cost savings. Terry and I spent some time going through the instructions so that on return to UK, we would be completely conversant with the procedures. We were in agreement that errors could arise with the new system, and great care would have to be taken with it. Several years later with another company, I had problems with a navigator I was supervising who could not come to grips with the procedure.

During my posting, the aircraft operated on schedule for all except one flight that ran so late, it was terminated in Tokyo and returned to Honolulu. This meant that a Tokyo based crew had to operate the aircraft back to Honolulu due to the inbound crew running out of duty hours. I was scheduled to operate to Hong Kong and had been hanging about waiting for news of the aircraft's arrival, which effectively put my crew out of hours. Rex Tapley, the Captain in charge in Tokyo, nominated the crew to operate to Honolulu and this resulted in a little friction as Terry Playford thought that it should have been my task. In the event, he and his crew operated the flight, returning to Tokyo on Japan Airlines, travelling First Class.

As the postings came to an end, replacements travelled out from UK to replace each crew member. My turn came on 19th August when my wife and son checked in for the flight as passengers and I prepared to navigate the 12 hours sector to Honolulu. The aircraft was on the best time track to Honolulu, routing well north of Wake Island and as it was never possible to take off from Tokyo with sufficient fuel to satisfy the direct flight, fuel requirements had to be reviewed at a decision point along the aircraft's track. If the fuel remaining was adequate, the flight continued to Honolulu. If insufficient, it would be necessary to divert to Wake Island, a long distance away to the south east of the decision point and would add nearly two hours flying time. Fuel at the decision point was always very tight but most flights were able to continue direct to Honolulu. At the decision point, just as I expected the fuel required to continue was exactly matched by the fuel the flight engineer said we had on board and we continued on track to Honolulu where we arrived 11 hour 35 minute after leaving Tokyo. The landing was on the same day as the departure from Tokyo having again crossed the Date Line.

The weather experienced was very turbulent with many thunderstorms on the track, necessitating a great deal of weaving around storm cells. The Loran signals en route were poor and turbulence made astro navigation difficult, but not impossible. About eight hours into the flight my eyes started to give trouble making it almost impossible to see the plotting chart properly. Fortunately the First Officer was an ex navigator who had retrained as a pilot and he relieved me for a while until my sight came back to normal. That particular pilot, Terry Brand, became a Senior Captain on Boeing 747's before he retired from BOAC.

The family had not visited Honolulu before and we were lucky to have five days off before continuing on to San Francisco. During the stay, every opportunity was taken to show the family many of the attractions that were available. Naturally I took them to see Pearl Harbour where the masts of the battleship *Arizona* that was sunk in December 1941, could still be seen. Today the battleship is part of a permanent memorial to the hundreds of sailors who lost their lives when it sank on that day of infamy in December 1941.

I hired a car and drove completely around Ohahu Island, a particularly lovely drive through beautiful countryside with its mountains and huge fields of pineapple. A visit was made to the Dole Pineapple processing factory, where we learned that a pineapple, that takes two years to grow, is converted in minutes to canned fruit, canned juice, animal feed and fertiliser with absolutely nothing wasted. An amusing thing discovered at the factory was that what was thought to be a drinking water fountain, actually dispensed cooled pineapple juice.

The front of our hotel was only a few steps away from Waikiki beach and we particularly enjoyed relaxing there in the sun. My son Terry enjoyed surfing and proved to be far better at it than myself, often managing to stand up on the board, albeit for a short time. I became rather concerned when he paddled out to the larger rollers well away from the beach, but fortunately he came to no harm. The temperature of the air and the sea was shown daily on a board kept up to date by the lifeguards and mostly showed the sea to be about two degrees warmer than the air temperature, about 86 and 84 degrees respectively.

Those five glorious days soon went by and it was time to leave for San Francisco, departing Honolulu at 1p.m. on 25th August and arriving at 9.30p.m. after a perfect 7 hour 30 flight that I navigated. There was a scheduled night stop in San Francisco which was disappointingly short as there was so much there that I would like to have shown the family. We continued as passengers for a 7 hour 49 minute flight to New York, immediately followed by a particularly long 10 hour 27 minute flight to Heathrow. The Captain on the last sector was Ron Sledge who I had known from my early days in BOAC, and as he was going to drive through Southampton on his way home to Bournemouth, he offered to drive us to the Civic Centre in Southampton where we took a taxi home. Although very weary, we were happy to be home, Terry particularly so because he could then boast to his friends that he had flown completely around the world!

After two weeks off to sort things out following the three and a half months away in Tokyo, normal Atlantic route flying was resumed. The threat of navigator redundancy had re-emerged and training of pilots as navigators was in full swing. Nobody knew exactly when the axe would fall but it was known that the least senior would be the first out. That almost certainly meant that I would be amongst the first to leave but there would be another three years of uncertainty before redundancy did actually commence.

Considerable thought had been given to what I might possibly do, but no final decision could be made until redundancy actually occurred. I loved flying and it was going to be difficult to give it up. I had always said that if I could not fly for BOAC, then I would not fly for anyone else. BOAC were good employers and I had made many friends over the years. The worst thing about the redundancy that lay ahead was the uncertainty of when it would commence, and ironically of course, having to train pilots to take over my job.

The Britannia 312 Series was ever expanding on the Atlantic and Caribbean routes and most of the routes were multi-sector that allowed no margin for delays. Possibly the worst schedule was from Heathrow to New York with stops at Manchester, Prestwick, Gander and Boston. I departed from New York on the return flight of that particular schedule but on arrival at Boston an engineering delay occurred. Engineering delays are notoriously difficult to pin down due to the many and variable factors involved. A small replacement part may take only 5 minutes to fit but if the part is not readily available, it could take hours to get it! This particular delay crept from one hour up to three and still the aircraft was not serviceable. Flight time limitations for crew duty hours were always observed but these could be extended at the discretion of the Captain and he was already using his authority to do so on this occasion. After four hours I told him that as I did not have a comfortable rest seat or use of the bunk, I considered that my ability to navigate to the required standard could be impaired. He accepted this without question and asked operations to call out the standby navigator, knowing full well that the nearest one was in New York. With none available, he urged me to continue, putting the ball back in my court! However, due to lack of the necessary spare part, the engineering problem could not be fixed for another ten hours and the crew was stood down. That was only the second time I ever protested that my duty day was too long for me to remain efficient.

A similar multi-sector operation was rostered for the route from New York to Trinidad with stops at Bermuda, Antigua and Barbados. If the flight went completely to schedule, the crew duty day was 13 hours that again left no margin for delay. Departure and arrival delays at New York could be horrendous at peak times, with priority given to landing aircraft. It only needed bad weather in the form of low cloud and poor visibility for delays to build up. On one trip from New York to Trinidad the departure was delayed by fog. With little or no wind, aircraft were queuing at the threshold of almost every runway in the hope that the reported visibility would improve sufficiently to allow take-off. After over two hours of waiting with the engines running, the fuel was depleted to the point that there was insufficient to reach the first destination with the required reserve fuel and the crew had to stand down.

Flights over the Atlantic are normally without incident and can almost be boring for those who have little to do other than keep the aircraft on the correct compass heading given by the navigator. Over the Atlantic the emergency VHF frequency of 121.5 megacycles is always monitored in order to give assistance to anyone in trouble. I recall one incident when we gave assistance to a light aircraft heading for Narsarsuaq in Greenland. We were en route from New York to London, flying above cloud at 23,000 feet between Goose Bay and the southern tip of Greenland when a Pan American pilot was heard talking on the emergency frequency to the pilot of a single engine plane heading for Narsarsuaq in Greenland. The pilot of the light aircraft appeared to be totally confused having passed his arrival time for the coast of Greenland without seeing any sign of it. He was randomly changing his course in an attempt to sight land and we could detect signs of panic in his voice. The Pan American pilot patiently talked him into descending until he could see the water and then got him on a sensible heading for his destination. Initially we could not hear the light aircraft but told the Pan American pilot that we were listening on the frequency to give assistance if needed. Eventually the Pan American pilot started to lose contact with the light aircraft and we were asked to take over. By this time he was on the correct heading but reported that he was in and out of cloud at 500 feet. My captain told him that it was essential that he remain clear of cloud and should descend to be in the clear where he might be able to see land. After a few minutes he reported that he was at 100 feet just below cloud with rain and poor visibility but thought that he could see land ahead. His signals then started to break up but the pilot of a Scandinavian Airways plane behind us, took up the communication.

This was a lucky break because the Scandinavian pilot knew the difficult approach procedure to Narsarsuaq very well, having been there many times. The last we heard was that the light aircraft had entered the fjord and had been told which direction to take when he reached a wrecked ship where the fjord splits into two directions. We learned later that it landed safely, albeit it with very little fuel remaining.

Incidents like this are very few but any requests for assistance on the emergency VHF frequency are always taken seriously and on this particular occasion, the outcome was successful. The Canadian authorities had been advised what was happening by the Pan American aircraft when it first contacted the light aircraft.

As previously stated, very few engine failures occurred on the Britannia, most delays coming from electrical and other associated equipment. The Britannia's engines were started by a starting control panel, which I believe controlled a sequence of relays essential for ignition. At Trinidad about to depart for New York with stops in Barbados, Antigua and Bermuda, one of the relays failed and it was impossible to start the engines. As no spares were available to correct the fault, the ground engineer climbed into the forward cargo hold where the electrical panel was located, and manually operated the faulty relay to successfully test start an engine. The Captain was quite impressed and asked the engineer if he would travel with the aircraft to start the engines at each stop. He was quite unwilling to do this, but said that as a last resort, he would start all four engines which would allow the aircraft to depart, suggesting that we could then fly direct to New York where spares were available. It was not really safe for him to get out of the hold and close the door with the engines running, but he managed it and the aircraft then flew direct to New York.

There was an incident at Boston when after landing and the engines had been shut down, the engineer discovered some very fine gravel lying in the wing close to the control surfaces. Apparently, the runway used for landing had just been resurfaced but had not been fully swept, so that when reverse thrust was used, it caused the very fine gravel on the runway to be thrown up into the wing. Soon after take-off considerable vibration was experienced from the engines and when the Flight Engineer thought that he had determined which one it was, it was shut down and the propeller feathered. Vibration was still present but to a lesser degree, so it was ignored and the flight continued to New York. On landing it was discovered that all four propellers were quite badly pitted, presumably by the gravel at Boston. One propeller was changed immediately and over the next two or three sectors two engines and two more propellers were changed, all attributed to the gravel at Boston. I have no idea of the truth, but there was a rumour that BOAC sued the Boston Airport Authority for the damage caused to the aircraft, only to be threatened with being counter-sued by the FAA for flying an aircraft in an unsafe condition. A 'no win' situation for BOAC!

The last year with BOAC was quite soul destroying once I had been advised of a firm termination date of 31st October 1963. I had never experienced unemployment since leaving school and the prospect of this was quite unsettling, particularly in the light that I had no qualifications other than my flying licences. It was perhaps comforting to know that I was not alone as there were many other navigators who had been given the same termination date. However, with a year still to go there seemed ample time to reorganise my working life.

Most flights had me instructing or supervising pilots and sometimes giving other navigators a flight check if they were posted to my Fleet. One of these was an old friend from Number 4 Line days, Eric 'Timber' Woods. With his great experience I thought it farcical that I should be giving him a check, but as he had just joined the fleet there was a legal requirement to do so. In 1964 before he was made redundant, he resigned and joined the Ministry of Aviation, as an Operations Officer. Although he had to forgo his redundancy payment from BOAC, it was a wise move that gave him a second career in civil aviation. Ultimately he became the Head of Flight Crew Licensing (Examinations) with the Civil Aviation Authority and, I am happy to say, we still see each other from time to time.

In the last year with BOAC, my wife and I decided to take advantage of a combination of my long service concession and part of the redundancy package that was a free confirmed seat on a round the world flight. It had been our intention to go completely around the world in one direction, stopping off in India, but political problems there forced our plans to be altered. We had stopovers in New York, San Francisco, Honolulu, Tokyo and finally Hong Kong where we stayed a week with my radio amateur friend who came from Southampton. On the return journey we stopped over in Tokyo, Honolulu, San Francisco, New York and finally a week with another radio amateur in Bermuda before returning home to London. We were away exactly a month in January/February 1963 when UK experienced one of the worst spells of snow and cold weather for many years. On arrival at the BOAC staff car park on a bitterly cold morning I discovered that there was about a foot of frozen snow on the roof of my car. Luckily the battery was in good condition and the engine started at the first attempt.

In June 1963 I was quite unusually rostered to fly out to Singapore as a passenger on a BOAC 707 when, after a suitable rest period, I operated a Britannia 312 series to Hong Kong and back to Singapore. No details of the flight come to mind except that it was a scheduled service probably being operated in place of a 100 Series Britannia. It was a very comfortable schedule that gave a day off in Hong Kong and another in Singapore before returning to Heathrow. This return flight was as a passenger on a QANTAS Boeing 707–138B, an aircraft type that sometime in the future I would navigate for many thousands of hours on two that had been acquired by another company.

Inevitably I was rostered for my last flight with BOAC, which departed from Heathrow on 9th September 1963 flying to New York via Gander. I operated two separate round trips to Bermuda before returning to Heathrow via Prestwick arriving back on 16th September 1963. The round trip went exactly to schedule with no technical problems being experienced throughout. It was a sad moment when I left the aircraft at Heathrow knowing that it was the last time I would navigate an aircraft for BOAC.

Although my termination date was 31 October, I was given paid leave to that date, plus the agreed redundancy payment. It seemed a lot of money in those days but today, nearly 40 years later, it would be a very small amount. Having been with BOAC for nearly 17 years I would be eligible to receive a pension from BOAC when I reached age 51, and become eligible for staff travel anywhere on its route structure. Although this is a valuable concession, to date I have never taken advantage of it, mainly because it is on a space available basis.

In my seventeen years flying with BOAC I had seen many changes, the most significant being the emergence of propjet and jet aircraft. These had dramatically reduced flying times and perhaps more importantly, had brought about a higher level of safety. Civil Aviation Authorities had examined in detail the question of Flight Crew fatigue and introduced legislation that brought about more stringent restrictions so necessary to ensure safety. Doubtless in the future, more restrictions would be necessary until crew fatigue could be reduced to the absolute minimum. Obviously such measures increase the operating costs of airlines that have to be reflected in the fares

I counted myself fortunate to have survived flying during the war and then continue flying in Civil Aviation in an almost accident free career which at that time I thought was completely over.

Chapter 16

Air Traffic Control

At 42 years of age, I knew that it was going to be difficult to find a suitable job but it would not be for lack of trying. Every day I scanned the *Daily Telegraph* to see what jobs were on offer, eventually finding one in Air Traffic Control that appealed to me. Whilst still on my termination leave from BOAC, I wrote to International Aeradio (IAL) at Southall Middlesex, applying for the post of Trainee Air Traffic Controller that had been advertised. Almost immediately I was invited to attend for an interview and I drove to Southall where my potential ability as an Air Traffic Controller was assessed. Subsequent to the interview I was offered a place on a forthcoming course and after discussion with my wife, I accepted. There was to be a twelve-week course, at the end of which I would be required to take the ICAO and the UK Ministry of Aviation Air Traffic Control licence examinations. It was mandatory to pass the ICAO licence examination, but although the Ministry licence would eventually be needed, it was not immediately essential.

Without suffering the indignity of unemployment, I commenced the course early in November 1963 with a syllabus that covered the many subjects associated with Air Traffic Control. Navigation was included in the syllabus and some found that subject rather difficult. One person was Ron Parfitt who became a close friend. He had recently left the RAF where he served as a Corporal Air Traffic Control Assistant. He was on the verge of being failed until I was able to assist him in Navigation, a subject that I obviously knew very well. This was the start of a long friendship that still exists today. There was one other ex BOAC Navigator on the course I had not met before and as he and his wife lived close to Southall he asked if I would like to use their spare bedroom during the course. This was a godsend as it spared me the bother of finding bed and breakfast accommodation that was not too plentiful. He finished the course but later immigrated to Australia when QANTAS offered him employment as a navigator.

The course was well conducted by extremely good instructors who had worked as ATC controllers at Aeradio stations overseas, and they made it all seem so easy. It lasted into February 1964 when the ICAO and Ministry licence examinations were held. These examinations were quite straightforward and I passed both at the first attempt. The practical side of controlling was something quite new to me, having had no previous experience, but everything quickly fell into place.

At the commencement of the course, students had been told that when the licence(s) had been obtained, postings would be to Aeradio stations overseas to do practical controlling under supervision until ready to take the Aerodrome and Approach Rating examinations. IAL rules prevented trainee controllers being joined by their families until the required ratings had been obtained, a restriction that I found quite irritating. Although I did not agree with such a condition, it had to be accepted. When postings were notified, Ron Parfitt and I were told that we would be sent to Idris Airport near Tripoli in Libya. I had stayed there many times during my flying career and always found it to be a very pleasant place to stop over for a night or two. I very quickly learned that visiting with a night stop or a day off, is totally different from being resident.

There was no doubt in my mind that I would get my ratings so, before I left for Tripoli, my wife and I made plans to let our house when she joined me. Effectively it was necessary to make arrangements for everything that we would need in Tripoli to be packed and sent to a shipping agent. Personal possessions that would not be needed were carefully packed and stored in the loft of our house with the access being secured by a lock. I contacted an estate agent and placed the house on his books requesting him to vet prospective tenants with view to letting the house when my wife joined me. In the event, everything went well and a tenant took up residence immediately after my wife left UK to join me.

Preparing for departure was an anxious time, as we had to ensure that everything that would be needed in Tripoli was included in baggage taken on the flight, or sent as freight beforehand. Although I would not have staff travel facilities from my previous employment with BOAC until I reached age 51, since IAL was a subsidiary of BOAC, staff travel concessions were available through them.

On 16th March 1964, Ron and I left Heathrow for Tripoli and on arrival were met by the Senior Air Traffic Controller who took us into the town office to meet the General Manager, Libya. After the arrival formalities had been completed we were taken to an apartment close to the palace in the Garden City area of Tripoli, which was to be our accommodation for the next three months or so until our wives joined us. The apartment was reasonably large but somewhat sparsely furnished and lacked the 'lived in' look! It was a sobering thought that I now had to take care of myself completely in respect of cooking, cleaning and laundry. The thought of sharing the apartment with Ron did not appeal to me but I was given no alternative to that.

Transport was provided to and from the airport for duty but it was up to each individual to provide his own for leisure purposes. Ron admitted to having no domestic skills whatsoever, so it fell to me to do what cooking was necessary. My cooking expertise was quite basic, being mainly confined to stews and hot pots, which soon became rather boring. Fortunately there were plenty of good restaurants in town where one could eat fairly cheaply, so cooking never became a problem.

I was quite disappointed that so little information about Tripoli was available prior to departure from UK. Had the employer been BOAC, there would have been an information sheet giving full details of the place and emphasising everything that one needed to know. IAL provided absolutely nothing in advance and information had to be gleaned from other Controllers when we arrived. Not really the right way to start a new career. From the moment of arrival I could sense that it was not a happy place and it was blatantly obvious that there was friction between some controllers and the management.

My first personal priority was to apply for a Libyan Amateur Radio Licence, set up my amateur radio station and get it operational. This would enable me to make contact with close radio amateur friends in England and effectively keep in touch with my wife and keep up to date with news from home. There was no trouble getting a licence once the authorities had been given sight of my UK licence (G3HUA), and I was quickly issued with the call sign 5A3TH enabling me to operate almost immediately.

Having ascertained that the flat Ron and I were occupying would be mine when my wife arrived, preparations were made to put up antennas. The allocation of accommodation left a lot to be desired with the best villas with nice gardens going to those already established in Tripoli, or having seniority within the company. I suppose I could have asked for something better than the flat I was given but that would possibly have delayed me getting my amateur radio station operational, something I wished to avoid.

Soon after arrival, I made contact with the Tripoli Radio Amateurs Club based at Wheelus Field, a United States Air Force base. It was a most pleasant club with a friendly atmosphere, and there were many pieces of amateur equipment to be had at little or no cost. My flat was on the ground floor of a building that had a flat roof, making it very easy to erect antennas. Soon after joining the Radio Club I was given a surplus 30 feet lattice tower on which I could mount my beam antenna when it arrived. The IAL building contractor assisted me to erect the three-section tower on the flat roof and ensured that everything was securely fixed. A simple dipole was very quickly put up, after which the equipment was switched on and a call put out. The rarity of the call sign brought immediate results and contacts were made with the stations of my close friends in England who conveyed messages to my wife. Very early on I established contact with Roger G3LDI in Norwich and talked to him most mornings, except those after night duty. We were to have many contacts during my year in Libya and have remained firm friends ever since.

The personal possessions needed in Tripoli were sent by sea before leaving UK and these arrived not long after I got there. The exception to this was the beam antenna, which, although manifested to be off loaded from the ship in Tripoli Libya with the rest of my possessions, in error it went on to the Tripoli in Lebanon! It took three weeks to get it back to the correct Tripoli. When the beam arrived, I had to go personally to the docks and clear it through customs, quite an involved procedure. Once delivered to the flat, I wasted no time installing it on the tower and testing it. When the tests had been completed, I found that it worked extremely well, giving me a great deal of pleasure during my stay. It also enabled me to have contact with my wife in Southampton through a close amateur friend near Lymington, with whom my wife stayed from time to time. The Senior Air Traffic Controller at Idris was also a radio amateur, although not particularly active.

I soon got to know most of the amateurs living in the Tripoli area, one who was a Lieutenant Colonel in the American Air Force who commanded a Military Air Transport Squadron at Wheelus Field. He gave me a great deal of assistance setting up my station and made available many items of surplus equipment. Another amateur met was Gene Walsh N2AA who had the call sign 5A1TW. He was from New Jersey, working as a civilian radio technical advisor at the US base. I got to know him and his wife Mary Anne very well, often visiting them at their home in Edison New Jersey in later years. Gene offered to buy a television set for me from the American PX so that I could watch the television programmes broadcast from their base. That offer was gratefully accepted and when I left Tripoli, I sold it for more than it cost me.

One rather inactive amateur, also an American, was a member of the American Diplomatic Service in Tripoli. His inactivity was due to terrible interference that he caused to his neighbour's radios and audio equipment, including his own. I was able to help him overcome most of the problems, enabling him to operate more frequently. When I left Tripoli he purchased my two antennas for his own use and I gave him my tower.

Garden City was a pleasant residential area located very close to the palace occupied by King Idris. The palace was always heavily guarded and the gates closed. One of my neighbours, a Colonel in the Police Force, was a most charming and hospitable person. On the occasions I visited his house, he always offered a variety of refreshment, alcoholic and otherwise, but abstained from alcohol himself. I never saw his wife at any time, the custom apparently being that wives always kept in the background out of sight. I first met him when I asked if I could borrow his ladder to do something with my antennae. He not only allowed the use of the ladder but he sent his servant with instructions to do the job for me. The immediate next-door neighbour was a Captain in the Legal Department of the United States Air Force. Our wives became good friends and we often had meals with them and went to parties at the base.

I was immediately assigned to a watch at Idris Airport doing Aerodrome and Approach controlling under supervision. The duties were not particularly arduous, having only a rush of Oil Company DC3's to control from dawn onwards for about an hour. They queued up to depart but returned at different times during mid to late afternoon. The DC3 pilots were mostly retired Captains from Pan American, TWA and other US carriers with many thousands of flying hours to their credit. Their voices were so recognisable that controllers scarcely needed to know their aircraft call signs. There were scheduled airline arrivals and departures during the day and night shifts, but these were well separated and it was unusual to have any delays due to congested airspace.

The 4-day shift pattern was unchanging throughout my stay, Day 1 being a twelve-hour day shift from 8a.m. to 8p.m., Day 2 a night duty from 8p.m. to 8a.m. on Day 3, Day 4 off and thereafter repeating itself. In the hot season, the working shift of 12 hours was quite exhausting with temperatures at the airport well over 100 degrees and with air conditioning in the glass sided tower that was totally inadequate. The night shifts were usually quiet allowing plenty of time to observe the stars with the normally clear skies. Being very much further south than Southampton, many stars that could not be seen at home became visible, but watching them made me constantly wish to be back flying again.

Ron was sent to the Flight Information Service (FIS) at another location in Tripoli where he communicated with aircraft flying in the Flight Information Region, passing them to Tripoli approach as they approached Idris. He and other controllers manned the station operating mostly daytime shifts, starting at dawn and continuing to dusk, but with the inconvenience of having their duty periods extended if aircraft ran late. His shifts conflicted with mine and it was always a problem trying to sleep after a night duty.

The RAF had a base at the north end of Idris airfield and operated a squadron of Canberra aircraft that was stationed there. Hastings, Argosy, and Beverley aircraft were frequently sent out from UK to carry out training details in Tripoli where they were unlikely to be bothered by poor weather. The detachments were usually for about two weeks, but there always seemed to be some RAF aircraft doing training. The army had a small unit that operated Auster aircraft and it was not unusual for them to request to land on the taxiway at the north end of the airfield, saving them a long taxi in. Idris was not a busy airfield other than when the DC3 aircraft were departing and arriving, and those occasions when the RAF did night flying training. By midnight the airfield was dead with perhaps only an odd movement to deal with in the early hours of the morning.

Most people took a collapsible sun bed on night duty in the hope of getting some sleep. There were always two controllers on duty and each would take turns to rest. Some years before when only one controller was on duty, a certain controller who shall be nameless, was awakened in the early hours of the morning by an airline Captain who had landed without being able to contact either Tripoli Approach or Tripoli Tower by radio! In those days there was only one controller on duty at night, and he handled both the approach and tower frequencies.

The weather in Tripoli throughout the year is pretty good by any standard, with very few days when flying conditions are really bad. Rising sand and dust caused by strong winds gave the worst problems with visibility dramatically reduced to almost nil. It never seemed to bother the DC3 pilots who knew every landmark in the area. They flew Visual Flight Rules (VFR) except in bad weather when they were compelled to revert to Instrument Flight Rules (IFR) to enter the Control Zone. However, they seldom carried out a full instrument approach, cancelling their IFR clearance saying that they had the airfield in sight. There was little anyone could do except clear them to land. Ten minutes or so later they would appear out of the gloom and land – so much for having the field in sight!

They were very safe pilots and I only saw one aircraft have any problems, and that was nothing to do with the pilot. On landing, the port undercarriage leg folded up and the aircraft veered off the runway with very little damage or injuries to the crew. The aircraft was quickly jacked up, the wheel extended and then towed away for repairs, probably being back in service the next day!

From time to time, the American Air Force carried out evacuation exercises that involved getting *every* serviceable aircraft into the air. If the weather deteriorated during the recovery phase, things could become very hectic. Wheelus field had arrester wires at the end of their only runway and if a fighter overshot its landing and got caught up in the wires, it took some time to get it clear, during which time the runway had to be closed down. On such occasions the jet fighters would be diverted to Idris where they landed in a formation of three aircraft, all having to use their parachutes to slow the aircraft down on the longest, but nevertheless quite short, runway. Care had to be taken that the pilots did not release their parachutes on the runway, as that would then have closed Idris down until the runway was cleared. The procedures used to get the fighters safely down were military ones and were totally different to civil procedures.

A daily occurrence was two B52 bombers that flew eastbound down the Mediterranean in the morning, returning westbound in the afternoon. Being military aircraft on patrol, there was little if any advance notice of their movements, it being an advisory call as they passed through Tripoli Control Area. They would give their flight level but never any other information.

After two or three weeks of living with Ron in the flat, I was absolutely fed up and wanted my wife to join me. I went to see the General Manager to discuss this but he seemed totally indifferent, saying that I was fully aware that this was not possible until I had obtained my ratings. Without any unpleasantness, I pointed out that they could arrange for her to join me amicably, or I would bring her out at my own expense. After a lot of bluster and muttering I was told that they would arrange to bring her out, but I would have to reimburse them if I failed to get my ratings. With my successful negotiation, Ron made the same argument and both wives came out together. Ron admitted afterwards that he did not have sufficient funds to reimburse the company if he failed, but the General Manager did not know that or if he did, chose to ignore it. However, there was little chance of either of us failing to get the necessary ratings.

My wife came out on a BOAC VC10 and quickly made the flat's appearance more acceptable by unpacking personal possessions that I had not bothered with. Ron, whose wife and baby daughter came out on the same flight, had been allocated a smallish villa and had moved into it just before the wives arrived.

The flat had a very small garden much to the disappointment of my wife who was a keen gardener. The soil was sandy and quite dry so little could be grown other than Morning Glory that seemed to be about the only plant that would tolerate the dry conditions. My wife wished that we had been given a villa with a decent sized garden with citrus trees growing in them.

In spite of Idris being a fairly quiet airfield, there were some hectic moments! I was on aerodrome control and had given a Lufthansa Boeing 707 clearance for take-off. Half way down the runway an engine caught fire and exploded with the burning fragments setting fire to the very dry grass beside the runway. The 707 Captain abandoned the take-off and despite repeated calls from me to stop and allow the fire services to approach, he continued taxiing with the damaged engine still smoking, past parked RAF and civil aircraft until the parking area was reached. As if that was not enough, a Royal Air Force Hastings on three engines was requesting permission to land, as was a Royal Air Force Canberra with a bomb hang up. Both had to be diverted to Wheelus Field, as the grass fire became quite extensive with smoke reducing visibility to almost zero on the approach to the runway.

An IAL examiner came out to Tripoli and on 4th June 1964 I successfully sat the aerodrome and approach rating examinations. I was told that the next stage would be an area rating examination after which there would be a radar course back at Southall. However I knew that a radar course was unlikely to happen before the end of my spell of three years in Tripoli.

Soon after arrival I had managed to buy a much used Morris Minor from a controller who was leaving Tripoli. Considering its age it was in a remarkably good condition and gave me good service during my stay, providing me with transport for leisure purposes. It was necessary to obtain a Libyan driving licence that in addition to having to show my UK driving licence, required me to take the same eye test as Libyan drivers. With many Libyans unable to read or write, the eye test was to identify symbols shown at a distance and then point them out in a book. Quite farcical really! Everything to do with roads and traffic in Tripoli was farcical. Out driving one day, I was given a traffic ticket for failing to indicate that I was turning right. In fact, I was not making a turn, as there was NO right turn that I could take. It was simply that the main road along the sea front curved to the right around the harbour. The policeman told me that if the road is turning, I had to indicate likewise! I tried to get the ticket withdrawn at the driving centre without success.

In spite of its proximity to the Sahara desert, Libya had some very beautiful places, most created by the Italians who lived there in large numbers before the war. The olive groves were well tended and at Tarhuna, a grape growing area, some rather nice wines were produced. There were some rather spectacular Roman ruins at Sabratha on the coast to the east of Tripoli. Across the border into Tunis were the Roman ruins at Carthage that were well worth the long drive to see them.

Social life within IAL was not easy with those who had been there some time organising their parties but not including newcomers. IAL

Radar staff employed at Wheelus Field seemingly had little social contact with Idris staff and there were feelings of frustration that Wheelus Aerad staff could buy all of their needs very cheaply from the American PX on the base, whereas Idris staff could not enjoy the same privilege. It goes without saying of course, that the Idris management did.

Although an ex RAF Officer, I was prevented from being a member of the RAF Officers Mess at their base by the SATCO, himself an ex Naval Petty Officer. Having commanded a signals unit in the RAFVR, probably all I really had to do was introduce myself to the Chairman of the Mess Committee and doubtless would have been invited to be a member. People had done this in the past but in so doing, had incurred the wrath of the SATCO. It was hardly worth the trouble for the small advantage it gave.

It was always possible to take a flight on one of the many oil company DC3s to oil wells located in remote parts of the Sahara Desert. Having spent most of my life flying, and a lot of it over deserts, I could hardly consider it to be the best way to spend my day off and declined the opportunity. Ron Parfitt was quite enthusiastic about flying and did several flights including one well south of Tripoli where there were petrified trees, evidence of forests before the land became eroded into sand.

Prior to my joining IAL, my son Terry had joined the RAF as an Engineering Apprentice and was due to pass out in December of 1964. Initially he had hoped to join as aircrew but to his disappointment, was categorised as colour blind and could not be accepted. In actual fact, he had flown solo in a glider before joining the RAF and had passed the appropriate medical to do that. Shortly after my wife and I had settled down in Tripoli, he paid for a private pilot course and became a qualified private pilot. He used this licence to hire a plane and fly himself and one of his RAF colleagues to Germany where his colleague's parents lived. I heard later that the flight over was quite hectic and not without incident, but he flew the round trip safely.

When I joined IAL I told them that I would need to have home leave to attend Terry's passing out parade at Halton and this had been agreed. As December approached I requested UK leave, which was promptly rejected by the SATCO on the grounds that I had not been there long enough to qualify for leave. Another argument ensued but after putting my views very firmly, my wife and I flew home for the parade.

Whilst on leave I was asked to attend the IAL School at Southall to be given my Area Rating examination. This was a practical test that was passed with no trouble, adding a third rating to my ICAO licence. By this time, being totally disenchanted with life and conditions in general in Tripoli, I was absolutely determined to seek other employment. I knew that I had to serve a complete year in Tripoli to satisfy IAL contract requirements, but this suited me perfectly because I needed to be out of the country for a complete year for UK tax reasons. Whilst in England for Terry's passing out parade, I contacted the College of Air Training at Hamble who had advertised in the *Daily Telegraph*, inviting applications for Air Traffic Controller posts at Hamble. I was interviewed and accepted for a position that I arranged to take up in April of 1965. Accordingly I submitted my resignation to IAL, giving them the required three months notice and completing a full year at Tripoli.

Having resigned, the first priority was to take steps to ensure that my house in Southampton would be available to me on my return. Fortunately I had a very reliable estate agent looking after the property, which had been let furnished to a college professor at Southampton University. The professor was quite happy to relinquish the tenancy as he was in the process of buying a house and would have been giving me notice within the next month, so everything worked out very well.

The final departure from Tripoli was on 23rd March 1965, flying in a VC10 of BOAC that also carried Princess Margaret back to England after a tour of Africa. At the end of my contract with IAL, I was asked to go to Southall to see the Chief Air Traffic Control Officer of the company. When we met, he asked me to reconsider my resignation and more importantly, asked why I had resigned. I glossed over the many problems at Tripoli and just indicated that there were clashes of personality that were unacceptable to me. He indicated that another posting away from Tripoli could be arranged but I did not consider this to be a real option and declined. I felt that it was inevitable that my complaints about Tripoli would follow me around and give me trouble at other stations in the future.

The year in Tripoli was a good experience, being so totally different from my flying career, but I had no real regrets about leaving. I must emphasise that IAL was a very good company to work for and it was only the poor relationship that existed between staff and management at Tripoli that caused me to take the course that I did.

Ron has remained a friend over the years although we have not met up for well over 35 years. I think that the only ones who regretted that I had resigned were my wife and my son. My wife liked her very relaxed and leisurely life in Libya, but she did not have to endure the intense desert heat of Idris or the boredom that the job had for me. My son Terry did manage a two weeks leave with us during the summer and met my radio amateur friend Gene Walsh who, like himself, held a private pilot's licence. Gene and he flew together occasionally in a small aircraft belonging to the Wheelus Air Base Flying Club. Most of the friends made in

Tripoli did not survive the test of time, other than Ron and his wife Kate and Gene Walsh and Mary Anne.

The Morris Minor was sold to Ali, the Libyan Air Traffic Control Assistant who worked on my shift, the keys being handed over to him on the day before I left. I gathered from Ron that some months later it ran out of oil and the engine seized up! I must admit that it did burn quite a lot of oil, but as I meticulously kept it topped up, it never gave me the slightest problem.

The year that followed my return from Tripoli was perhaps the most settled existence that I had experienced since joining the RAF in 1940. The Air Traffic Controllers at Hamble were a splendid bunch of chaps and I enjoyed working with them. Dick Hunt, the SATCO, ran an efficient and friendly Air Traffic Control Unit and there was none of the rivalry and professional jealousy that went on at Tripoli.

The College of Air Training was used to provide British Airways with the pilots that it would need in the future, and I must say it did a fine job. I already knew the calibre of the ground instructors from my days at Hamble when I was studying for my Flight Navigators licence. Students commenced training for their Pilots licence with a ground course and when they had reached a certain stage, flying training commenced. The Chief Flying instructor (CFI) was Peter Duff-Mitchell who had Tony Farrell as his deputy. Both Peter and Tony, and indeed all of the instructors, were extremely experienced and superb at their job. Peter in similar fashion to Dick Hunt, ran an efficient and friendly flying training unit and it was a pleasure to work with them. Peter and Tony encouraged Air Traffic Controllers to fly whenever there was an opportunity to do so and I had quite a few flights that gave me an opportunity of practising my somewhat rusty take-off and landings.

Living on the outskirts of Southampton at Bitterne, it only took about 15 minutes to drive to the airfield 7 miles away. The hours of work were very civilised unless night flying took place, which could bring about a very late arrival home in the summer months.

The college used Chipmunk aircraft for basic training and twin engine Apache aircraft for advanced training. I cannot remember exactly how many aircraft the college had, but when the weather was good the sky around Hamble seemed to be full of aircraft. Given suitable weather conditions, flying took place every weekday, usually starting around 8.30a.m. The college did not fly at weekends but the RAF had a flying unit at Hamble and if they wanted to fly, the airfield was manned. The airfield was available for use by other aircraft with prior permission, so there was always a need for a controller to be available if and when required.

One weekend I had the pleasure of meeting the late Donald Campbell who flew his twin-engine aircraft into Hamble for a business meeting nearby. He was a charming person and sent me a personal letter of thanks for keeping the airfield open for him. Night flying was not scheduled too frequently, and the sessions were never very lengthy, generally finishing at a reasonable hour except in high summer. There was always an instructor detailed to be in charge during night flying and he had the authority to stop flying if at any time he considered weather conditions to be unfit.

There were four controllers, including SATCO Dick Hunt, all available for duty and a roster was produced weekly. Strangely enough, there was another controller also named Holloway, but not related to me. An Air Traffic control assistant named Ernie normally worked five days a week, but as he was responsible for laying out the flare path for night flying, his hours were not fixed. He was a remarkably efficient assistant and nothing ever seemed to worry him.

Students commenced flying on Chipmunk aircraft doing circuits and landing at Hamble and general handling. Once advanced from this stage, they could fly to Bembridge on the Isle of Wight to carry out circuits and landings there, with perhaps handling exercises en route. They also did cross country flights on fixed routes without landing away, followed by flights with landings at one or more airfields for fuel. All day flights were flown under Visual Flight Rules (VFR) with Hamble ATC providing advisory service and filing of flight plans. There were no runways, ATC simply giving the direction for take-off and landing according to the wind direction and speed. Except at nights, in emergency or poor weather, there was no positive control in the circuit, aircraft landing and taking off as they wished. If weather conditions deteriorated, the duty pilot would decide if the recall of aircraft was necessary. Students graduated to twin engine Apache aircraft, initially carrying out circuits and landings before progressing to cross-country flights by day and night, followed by their final flight checks at the end of the course. When an instructor considered his student competent enough to fly solo, he usually came to the tower to monitor his performance. One could almost sense his tension until the student had landed safely.

At night, training could be circuits and landing, cross-country or a mixture of both using Apache aircraft. Hamble was situated in a controlled zone and flight clearances had to be obtained from the zone controllers, with departures and re-entry into Hamble Approach area via pre-determined corridors. Very seldom did things go wrong but there were occasions when students became a little unsure of their position and would ask for a Magnetic Course to Steer (QDM), to reach Hamble.

On one occasion a student was really uncertain of his position and it could be sensed that he was starting to panic. The instructor and I talked to him and eventually by answers to questions we asked, it was possible to get him heading in the right direction back to Hamble.

Incidents did happen from time to time but only one fatal accident occurred whilst I was there. An Apache doing simulated single engine approaches with an engine throttled back, commenced the overshoot procedure but the throttled engine failed to produce power causing the aircraft to crash in the grounds of an estate near to the perimeter of the airfield. The instructor and one student got out safely but the other student got into difficulty and the instructor had to re-enter the aircraft to assist him. He managed to get the student out but the aircraft exploded and the instructor was burned so severely that he died in hospital. His very brave action certainly saved the life of the student.

One of the joys of being at Hamble was that there were many opportunities to fly in both Chipmunk and Apache aircraft. Instructors had to fly a required number of hours without a student to conform to college regulations and they were quite amenable to having a controller on board. I did many of these flights and was always given the opportunity of handling the aircraft, really enjoying the pleasure of taking-off and landing. Perhaps the most exciting were those when the instructor went through a whole series of aerobatics.

My son Terry who had obtained his private pilot's licence while I was in Tripoli, hired a Tiger Moth from Thruxton and flew it to Hamble enabling us to fly together. However, such opportunities were quite rare. On another occasion, a Saturday with no flying taking place, a helicopter that periodically inspected the Fuel Pipe between Fawley and Gatwick, dropped in for fuel. With no other traffic around and the pilot having plenty of time, he asked me if I would like a ride, which I gladly accepted. He demonstrated its performance and even gave me an opportunity of handling it for two or three minutes, a rare and most enjoyable experience.

Since returning from Tripoli I had been getting telephone calls from the Chief Navigator of British Caledonian Airways asking if I would like to join them as a navigator. Apparently they were greatly expanding their North Atlantic Operations and urgently needed navigators with North Atlantic experience. It was very tempting but I had always spurned the opportunity, my attitude still being that I would not fly unless it was with BOAC, by then renamed British Airways.

At home, my wife had been not been too happy since our return from Libya and she seemed to be making a life away from mine. I don't really think that she wanted to leave Tripoli where her life was so pleasant and settled. She had taken a job as a doctor's receptionist and seemed more interested in that than doing the normal things at home, and to a degree I was being neglected. This unsettled me greatly and it was then that I decided to go back flying. I had been invited to an interview by the Chief Navigator of British Caledonian Airways and was told that the job was there if I wanted it. At that time it just did not seem to be right for me and I declined, a decision I am sure was perfectly correct, as future events proved.

Chapter 17

Transglobe Airways

Late in October 1966 I saw an advertisement in *Flight Magazine* in which a Charter Company, Transglobe Airways Ltd, invited applications from North Atlantic experienced navigators. An application was made in writing and almost immediately I was asked to attend for an interview at their Gatwick office. At the interview, David Barbour, the Chief Navigator, offered me a job with the company to commence a month later. I was delighted to have been accepted without any need for a reference from BOAC, but my spirits were damped on my return home to learn that my father had died during that afternoon. I knew that he was seriously ill and not expected live and it was my intention to visit him at hospital in Northampton on the day after my interview. Sadly this was not to be. On reflection I was glad that we had settled our differences of many years ago.

I had not heard of Transglobe Airways before but learned that they flew Britannia 300 Series aircraft to many destinations throughout the world, mainly to the USA and Canada. It was three years since I had last flown and things were moving perhaps a little faster than I really wanted them to. As I had not navigated for over three years, I was aware that I would have do 20 hours of route navigation to renew my navigation licence, but this apparently was quite acceptable to Transglobe who saw no problem with the requirement. Fortunately, as the Transglobe Fleet was Britannia 300 series aircraft on which I had considerable experience flying with BOAC, this would help me to quickly get up to the required navigation standard.

Before leaving after the interview, Transglobe asked me to let them have my decision as soon as possible as there were several other applicants to be seen. My wife and I discussed the offer and as she gave me the impression that she had no feelings either way, I accepted Transglobe's offer of employment. I had to undergo a Ministry of Aviation medical examination to ensure that I could still satisfy the licence medical requirements, but that was passed without a problem.

Dick Hunt knew that I was considering a return to flying and it was no surprise to him when I informed him of my decision. Knowing how much flying meant to me, he accepted my resignation with good grace.

I gave the required month's notice and Dick very kindly re-arranged my roster so that I could attend my father's funeral in Northampton.

I reported to Transglobe at Gatwick on Thursday 1st December 1966 and after completing the normal joining forms, David Barbour gave me a training session to acquaint me with Company Procedures. I was introduced to Captain Ted Parker the Chief Pilot and was immediately struck by the lack of formality with everyone being addressed by his or her christian name. If anything I found that until other members of crew got to know me, they were more suspicious of me being ex BOAC than I was of them. The training session was completed in one day, and I was advised that David would supervise me on a flight departing on Monday 5th December 1966, for Las Palmas, Ascension Island, Barbados, Ascension Island, Las Palmas and back to Gatwick. This round trip would give more than the required navigation hours to satisfy the licence renewal. The schedule was very tight with only minimum rest at both Ascension Island and Barbados, something that was rarely rostered when I was with BOAC.

It soon became apparent to me that flying with a charter company was quite different from BOAC, it being far more demanding and with many extra duties to be carried out before flight. BOAC always provided everything needed for flight so that on reporting for service, the only task was to check the flight plan at operations and carry out pre-flight checks on the aircraft. Not quite so simple in Transglobe! The weather folder had to be collected from the Meteorological Office, and Notices to Airmen and other briefing material collected from the Aeronautical Information Service (AIS) office. After checking the weather, the flight plan needed to be prepared manually, extracting wind information from the appropriate weather charts. When the fuel requirements had been calculated, the Captain decided on the amount of fuel to be carried and the flight plan could then be completed. The Air Traffic Control flight plan had to be filed with AIS before proceeding to the aircraft. The simple task of completing and filing the ATC flight plan was something that I had seldom done before but it was most important and needed to be done correctly to ensure that no delay occurred.

Once on board the aircraft, a full pre-flight check has to be carried out to ensure all navigation equipment and instruments are serviceable, and the Sextant, Air Almanac and Star Tables are on board together with appropriate charts for the flight. In BOAC, this was all done for the navigator and one did not have to think about it!

On this first flight with Transglobe, I reported about two hours before the flight was due to leave and carried out the tasks for which I was responsible. Nothing particularly arduous about it but if it hasn't been done before, a routine has not been established and something can easily be overlooked. It was reassuring to have David on board but nevertheless, he made me do everything the navigator had to do without help from him. The real chore was carrying my own luggage and navigation necessities to the aircraft, something never necessary in BOAC. Once on board, pre-flight checks were carried out and the Loran equipment and the Kollsman sextant, one I had not seen or used before, checked as serviceable. It was a delightful sextant to use and I soon preferred it to the Hughes. There was an external battery case to provide illumination of the bubble and spare batteries and bulbs were always carried. The mechanism of the sextant was clockwork and had to be wound up before the sextant could be used. Winding removed a shutter that closed to block the view from the eyepiece at the end of the two minutes run.

The last liaison between the aircraft and the ground was when the handling agent gave the Captain the final load figures enabling him to complete the load sheet, which he then signed, giving the agent a copy. Some handling agents, depending on the contract, would provide the completed load sheet ready for the Captain's signature so that there was nothing for him to do other than check it for accuracy.

The sector to Las Palmas was not a navigation sector but David thought that as I was not in current practice, it would be in my own interest to take a couple of astro fixes. The take-off from Gatwick was at 6.30p.m. on a beautiful clear frosty night and as the aircraft tracked close to Hamble I could see the airfield and called Hamble Tower on R/T to tell them that I was off on my first flight. Dick was on duty and was delighted to hear me on the radio!

After passing Oporto, two practice astro fixes were made en route to Las Palmas and the results certainly boosted my confidence. David used a slightly different astro procedure to that with which I was conversant, but after the first fix I decided to revert to my own procedure that I had used so often in the past. The 5 hour 30 minute flight went without incident and a landing was made at Las Palmas for refuelling. An hour later the aircraft departed for Ascension Island taking 7 hours 40 minutes and landing on schedule at 8.47a.m. The flight was perfect and I had quickly got into the swing of things with everything falling into place nicely. It certainly did not seem like three years since I had last navigated and I was particularly pleased with the astro fixes made on that sector, astro being the primary navigation aid. Perhaps I was a little slower than I would have liked but with time, that would obviously improve.

The crew was accommodated in a rather shabby Nissen hut that had sufficient beds for the crew, plus toilet and shower facilities. I confess to being absolutely worn out by the time I got to bed, which was hardly surprising considering the length of the duty hours and the fact that it was almost totally a night flight. One of the Captains told me that the moment my head hit the pillow I started to snore and continued to do so for the next hour or so, disturbing everybody. He gave me the name 'Z Man' because of the number of ZZZZs that could be heard emanating from me!

The sectors to Barbados and back to Ascension were limiting sectors and the fuel margins were extremely tight. As the fuel management was the navigator's responsibility, these sectors certainly brought home to me the importance of that task. The Inter Tropical Convergence Zone (ITZ) was flown through in both directions with the usual large cumulo-nimbus thunderstorms being encountered, resulting in the inevitable 'bumping' from the Bristol Proteus engines. The remainder of schedule was flown without incident or difficulty and the aircraft arrived back in Gatwick exactly on time just over four days after leaving, having flown 47 hours 15 minutes on the round trip, and remaining serviceable throughout the whole schedule. With my considerable experience on Britannia aircraft I felt completely at ease and knew that I was back doing a job I had always enjoyed. It was particularly nice to have informality with other members of the crew but of course the flight deck discipline was always there.

Having completed the necessary number of hours of navigation to renew my navigation licence, the logs and charts were taken to The Ministry of Aviation for the navigation licence to be re-validated. This was shown to David and the Operations Manager and I was then cleared to navigate company aircraft on all but polar routes. During the trip I learned that David held a Master Mariner's Certificate but gave up the sea when he got married, presumably due to the length of some of the voyages.

At the time of joining Transglobe, the company had four Britannias, two being ex Canadian Pacific 314s, one ex Ghana Airways 309 and the other a rather oddball ex Air Mexico Britannia 304. The 314s and 309 were similar in most respects to the BOAC Britannia 312s, but the 304 had a much less fuel capacity giving it a restricted range. With the fuel available on that aircraft being less than the normal Britannia 300, the aircraft commenced flight much lighter in weight, but having the same engine power, it had the ability to initially cruise at higher flight levels. The limitation of that particular aircraft was that it could not cross the Atlantic from Gatwick without a fuel stop. Usually it would be a maritime airport but when strong headwinds were forecast, even this could be marginal requiring an extra stop in Shannon.

I learned that Transglobe started as Air Links in August 1958, commencing operations with a Dakota on 22nd July 1959 from Southend Airport. Various types of aircraft were operated over the next few years on charter routes until 1st August 1965 when Air Links officially changed its name to Transglobe Airways. Its first Britannia was acquired in mid July 1965 and it flew a 3 month programme to holiday destinations. The second Britannia was acquired on 12th December 1965, this being followed by a third early in 1966 and the fourth early in 1967. At the time I joined the airline, a new board of directors had been formed with Mr Stanley Wilson as Managing Director and Captain Ted Parker as Chief Pilot/Operations Manager. I never met Mr Wilson but understood that in addition to his airline activities, he owned a successful non-airline business in the north of England.

My next trip was to Kingston Jamaica via Gander, a duty day of over 20 hours of which 16 hours 50 minutes was flying time. After a short night stop in Kingston, I positioned to Toronto to operate back to Gatwick via Prestwick, flying nearly 27 hours in slightly under four days. In my first two weeks with Transglobe nearly 74 hours had been flown which was far more than I ever normally did on Britannias with BOAC. Despite feeling quite exhausted, I found it to be most enjoyable and that made it all worthwhile.

The roster gave Christmas and New Year completely off, the next departure being on 6th January 1967, flying to Toronto via Prestwick. I then flew on to Kingston and finally back to Gatwick via Gander, a total flying time of 34 hours 35 minutes in just over three days. In 33 days, three round trips had been operated, flying 108 hours 40 minutes, which was very close to the maximum permitted by the regulations.

Transglobe operated flights on the Polar route to destinations in Western Canada and David advised me that his intention was to give me a Polar Route check on the next polar flight to Calgary, via Sondestrom in Greenland, on 23 January 1967. The proposed schedule was that the crew would operate to Calgary, then without any rest, continue as passengers on the aircraft back to Gatwick via Kingston and Gander. I told David that this was quite out of the question as far as I was concerned and would not agree to do it. He explained that if I got off in Calgary, I would be compelled to stay for a week until the next flight arrived. As the company could not legally order me to do what they had proposed, the Operations Manager agreed that I could get off in Calgary whereupon David immediately opted to do the same.

Prior to departure, it was necessary for me to do a course to familiarise myself with company polar procedures. When flying in high latitudes, the true track can change significantly between two reporting points and furthermore, if the aircraft's track passes close to the North Magnetic Pole, the magnetic compasses can become unreliable or even unusable. Both of these circumstances required that compasses be operated in the Free Gyro Mode, navigating the aircraft using a GRID system. The grid system adopted by Transglobe was a well tried one used by Canadian Pacific Airways on their polar flights. They used their own specially produced navigation chart with a grid system that effectively gave Vancouver as Grid North and London as Grid South. In the margin of the chart was printed the divergence angle between True North and Grid North and overprinted were lines of GRIVATION, these being the value in degrees to be applied to Grid directions to convert to Magnetic. In my humble opinion it certainly was not the ideal chart to use because the Loran stations were printed on the *reverse* of the chart and in order to plot Loran position lines it needed under chart illumination that the Transglobe aircraft did not have. David got over this by providing a separate chart on which the Loran fix could be plotted and then transferred to the Canadian Pacific chart. A rather tedious and somewhat time consuming procedure but when adopting another company's system it's Hobson's choice!

At a predetermined point along the prescribed track while the magnetic compasses are still reliable, the aircraft's compasses are changed from the normal Slaved Magnetic mode to Free Gyro with the aircraft then flying Grid headings. The aircraft's heading in relation to the ground remains the same although the compass indications have been changed. The changeover procedure is to first set the Compass Gyro Latitude Corrector to the Latitude being flown, free the gyro from the magnetic flux and then align the compass card to read the grid heading calculated from the magnetic heading. Only one compass is changed at any time, it being checked against the other still magnetically slaved. When satisfied that the grid heading is correct, the same procedures are applied to the other gyro and its compass card aligned to agree with the now established Grid heading. Having changed to free gyro, heading checks using astro are made at frequent intervals to establish the compass deviation and allow for it on the aircraft's heading. The Astro Azimuths would be changed from true to grid by applying convergence at the assumed position. The more stable of the two gyros is used for navigation and it is usually possible for a trend of gyro drift to be established and taken into consideration when calculating the heading to maintain track. positive identification of the star used for the heading check is absolutely essential, but obviously no ambiguity can arise if the sun or moon is used.

On 23rd January David and I departed for Sondestrom on a 6 hour 25 minute flight during which normal compass and navigation procedures were used. The weather conditions en route and at Sondestrom was perfectly clear and it was a perfect flight in all respects. Sondestrom airport is not the easiest airport for landing, being situated at the eastern end of a fjord about 60 miles long, and surrounded by mountains. Britannia aircraft could only land to the east and take-off to the west. High performance aircraft can take-off to the east but the Britannia was not in that category. The main operating constraint of the airport is usually the strength of the wind as civil aircraft cannot normally take-off or land with tail winds in excess of the Flight Manual's maximum, which for the Britannia is 10 knots. In winter there is always a large accumulation of snow on the ground but strangely enough this results from light snowfalls, which does not seriously affect aircraft movements. The runway was always kept clear of snow during snowy weather and I was told that there were very few occasions when the airfield was closed due to weather. The American Air Force operated an extremely good GCA approach system, controllers descending the aircraft in a safe area over the fjord before turning it for landing towards the east. I must say that when I first saw the airport in daylight I was quite horrified by the surrounding terrain.

After the warm and cosy atmosphere of the aircraft it was quite a shock to leave the aircraft and find the temperature on the ground to be minus 40 degrees. This is the same in Centigrade or Fahrenheit and is *very* cold! So cold in fact that when the engines were about to be restarted, the propeller brakes had frozen in the locked position. It took a lot of engineering 'know how' (a large hammer) to get over that problem, but it was managed. Walking the short distance to the terminal building and back without any protection on my face against the extreme cold was unpleasant and I thought that my ears and nose were on the verge of freezing.

As we took-off, the aircraft was identified by radar on the runway and when airborne the controller then gave headings to keep the aircraft over the fjord away from high ground. Once the safe altitude was reached, the aircraft was cleared direct to Holsteinsborg radio beacon at the western end of the fjord. The onward flight went like clockwork, gyros behaving perfectly and with clear skies for astro fixing and heading checks.

The routing was almost direct from Holsteinsborg to Fort McMurray, passing close to Cape Dyer, Coral Harbour on Southampton Island, Chesterfield Inlet, and Rankin Inlet. Defence radar stations in the area were available to provide position fixes on request, if they were not otherwise engaged on defence duties. Approaching Fort McMurray, normal magnetic compass steering was resumed, having reached the area where magnetic compasses are normal. There was no significant deviation from track throughout and a landing was made at Calgary 6 hours 50 minutes later, well before dawn. The temperature on landing with clear skies was a 'warmer' minus 35 degrees Fahrenheit, which again is very cold. David, completely satisfied with my polar navigation, signed the polar route clearance certificate authorising me to operate all company routes.

Some of the places mentioned en route are very small airfields, usually with unpaved gravel surfaced runways that are used by Canadian 'Bush' pilots. Their runways would be unsuitable for a Britannia to land, but are designated as emergency airfields that could be used if it became absolutely necessary to land. Undoubtedly the aircraft might over-run the runway but that would be far preferable to making a landing away from a populated area. A landing in the tundra in the depths of winter could be disastrous and does not bear thinking about.

The seven days in Calgary were extremely pleasant despite the cold temperature, David and I spending quite a bit of time with a Canadian Radio Amateur, RCAFVR Group Captain George Sergenia VE6AO, with whom I had spoken many times from home. George and his wife were most hospitable and his wife drove us to Lake Louise and Banff. At Banff, with the temperature hovering around minus 30F, David and I swam in a thermal pool that was both inside and outside the hotel. When outside, it was not advisable to get more than one's shoulders above water due to risk of freezing, but the water was delightfully comfortable when immersed in up to the neck!

A rather unique experience was a 'Chinook' wind that occurs occasionally at points just to the east of the Rocky Mountains. At 2p.m. in the afternoon the temperature sign on a building in town was showing minus 25F, but by 5p.m. the same afternoon it rose to plus 35, a change 60 degrees brought about by a warm current coming over the mountains to the west. Three hours later it was back to minus 25!

George and David were talking about navigation and George asked David if he was teaching me. David explained the legal requirements of navigating and said that I had far more aeronautical experience than he had. David and I got on very well and he told me of plans afoot for expansion, asking me if I would like to become the training and check navigator of the company. Acceptance gave me a welcome increase in pay and relieved David of duties that he really had no time for, thus being of benefit to both of us.

The next aircraft came in a week later and its crew had the minimum rest before operating back to Gatwick. I navigated the aircraft on the return flight, David and the inbound navigator travelling as passengers on the empty aircraft. The flight had a few moments of anxiety for me when the sextant froze solidly in its mount as I tried to use it for the first heading check. It was fortunate that there was an identifiable star about twenty degrees to port that could be used for a heading check, the aircraft being turned in line with the star so that the check could be obtained. Eventually with the flight deck heating at maximum and hot dry towels put constantly around the electrically heated mount, it thawed sufficiently to enable the sextant to be retracted. After that it behaved itself and worked normally for the remainder of the flight. In winter when above cloud in polar latitudes, the air is absolutely crystal clear and the sight of the sky is absolutely breathtaking. With so many stars visible it almost becomes difficult to identify even the brightest of stars embedded in the mass of other stars.

With no passenger load on board the aircraft, the intention was to attempt to fly direct to Gatwick without a fuel stop at Sondestrom. This was stretching the 'elastic' to its full limit but it was accomplished in 13 hours 10 minutes, the aircraft getting up to 34,000 feet on the final part of the route. Quite high for a propeller driven civil aircraft, so much so that when the flight was handed over from Keflavik control to Prestwick, the Scottish controller seemed astonished when we reported 31,000 feet requesting 33,000 feet. He asked what aircraft type we were flying and when told, questioned if we meant 21,000 feet. He was quite taken aback when we repeated 31,000 feet! The aircraft landed with more reserve fuel than legally required, which conformed to the flying regulations.

Being winter, the flights scheduled were few and far between and I had almost a month off before departing on another Ascension Island – Barbados flight. The rest periods were much the same as the last one, but on this occasion I was instructing a new navigator who had just joined the company. He performed very well and was checked out by me on the last sector. Unfortunately, bad weather prevented a landing at Gatwick and the aircraft was diverted to Luton where on arrival the crew was taken by coach to Gatwick.

Some captains held navigation licences and if I flew with them, invariably I would be asked if they could navigate under my supervision. None were ever checked out by me to navigate unsupervised but it was beneficial to the company to have pilots who could navigate if required to do so.

On Atlantic flights, the navigator had to determine the best time track by assessment of the winds given by the Meteorological Charts. There was no procedure laid down by David for this assessment and I was most concerned that navigators with little North Atlantic experience would choose an incorrect route. From my BOAC days I remembered that their operations department used a Best Time Track Computer to analyse three different tracks between points on each side of the Atlantic to find the best one. Normally the three analysed were the Great Circle (shortest), the polar curve to the north of the Great Circle, and the Rhumb Line (longest) to the south of the Great Circle. I suggested to David that we could provide navigators with tables of tracks and distances for these three routes from gateway points in UK to gateway points on the Canadian coast and return. I also drew a picture of the BOAC Best Time Track Computer how I remembered it, suggesting that we could have some made for use by navigators. David agreed and very quickly computers were issued to each navigator together with instructions for its use. This made the navigator's task at flight planning easier and possibly saved the company money by flying a faster track.

There were many charter destinations and this made life more interesting for me. As I mentioned in the chapters covering flying with BOAC, it can be very boring flying the same route week after week. My flying log shows that I flew Gatwick to Helsinki and then on to Vancouver via Sondestrom. I was particularly pleased to operate into Helsinki with a two night stop over as it gave me the opportunity of meeting up with two radio amateurs (man and wife) who had visited me in Southampton. I was taken to their home at Elimaki, about 100 km north of Helsinki where I enjoyed Finnish hospitality, which involved drinking lots of Aquavit. Just to visit Axel and his wife Carolla took away the pain of the 'hangover!'

Another flight was from Gatwick to Berlin and on to Kingston via Gander. Another took me to Accra where I was joined by another new navigator whom I supervised on a flight from Accra to New York via Cape Verde Islands and Bermuda. On that particular flight, there was no passenger load and it had been hoped that the direct flight to New York from the Cape Verde Islands would be possible. Unfortunately the en route head winds were abnormally strong and after 11 hours 15 minutes, the attempt was abandoned and a landing made at Bermuda for fuel. After take-off from Bermuda, it became obvious that the decision to land at Bermuda was absolutely correct as the headwinds became even stronger, it taking another 3 hours and 10 minutes to get to New York.

The early summer months became extremely busy with little time off between flights, and on almost every trip I was training or checking new navigators. In June, when the sun is at its furthest declination north, although it may have set and is not visible, it does not really get dark at night in the areas in which we flew. The result of this twilight is that it is not always possible to see suitable identifiable stars for astro heading checks. On one flight to Sondestrom my crew night stopped with the aircraft continuing on to Calgary with another crew. The aircraft left Gatwick at 8p.m., flying toward Sondestrom for 6 hours 30 minutes with the sun only just disappearing below the horizon. Twilight conditions prevailed with the sea and ground being clearly visible and on landing at 11.30p.m. local time, the light conditions were as if the sun had only just set.

On the following night we operated another flight to Vancouver and experienced the same twilight conditions throughout the sector, making it difficult to see any but the brightest stars for a heading check. On that particular flight the Captain did not carry out the instructions I gave to him when the compasses were changed to free gyro and we finished up with both compasses having large errors. Fortunately an identifiable star was just visible and I was able to get the compasses set correctly. I think that incident convinced the Captain that the laid down procedures were important and a departure from them could cause serious errors! In later years with another company, a Kollsman sky compass was carried that enabled a sun heading check to be obtained with the sun just below the horizon in twilight conditions, a marvellous aid for the navigator.

In my first year with Transglobe, I did over 900 hours flying which isn't bad going for a Charter Company that does not fly as frequently in the winter months. In July, I did the maximum allowed of 100 hours flying in a period of 28 days; this followed by 85 hours in August.

On a flight from Toronto to Belfast, an elderly passenger died in flight. She was a lovely lady who had just achieved the wish of seeing her daughter and grandchildren who lived in Toronto. She had been chatting to the person sitting next to her, saying how lovely it was to see her grandchildren for the first time. She just fell asleep and did not wake up. The senior hostess called me when she could not awaken her for breakfast, asking my advice. Unfortunately there was nothing I could do, other than confirm that she had died and log the death in my navigation log. I instructed the hostesses to move her into a crew rest bunk out of sight of the other passengers for the remaining 1 hour and 30 minutes of flight. Happenings such as that in flight are quite rare but none the less, are quite upsetting for both passengers and crew.

In my days with Transglobe there was a Board of Trade Navigation Inspector named Wally Luther who flew with British Airline Companies from time to time to ensure that the required navigation standards were being maintained. He was a very pleasant fellow and had been a navigation inspector for many years. Inspectors have the authority to carry out inspections at any time, provided that they do not displace revenue passengers. With Transglobe's permission, he was allowed to navigate the aircraft for the purpose of keeping his own licence valid, but always under the supervision of the rostered navigator. Wally arrived at Gatwick hoping to navigate on the flight to Toronto, only to find that I was supervising a navigator on his annual route check. He decided to continue and navigate on the return trip if it was possible. The aircraft was only scheduled for a fuel stop in Toronto, and I was returning on it as a passenger. On arrival in Toronto I pointed out to Wally that if he navigated back to Gatwick he would exceed the flight time limitations in force at that time, but did not forbid him to do so. Very diplomatically he decided that he was too tired to navigate and took a passenger seat, sleeping throughout the flight back to Gatwick. Rather a wasted trip for him.

I spent most of the return flight chatting to an attractive young lady who had been an airhostess on a summer contract with Transglobe. After leaving the company at the end of her contract she had gone to Canada with thoughts of looking for work, but found the country far too cold and was returning to her home in Hove. The aircraft landed at Manchester where everyone disembarked to clear customs and that was the last I saw of her on that trip.

In mid November 1967 I was rostered on a trip to Hong Kong with the entire crew being sent as passengers on an Air India Boeing 707 to Bombay to await the arrival of the Transglobe aircraft. At check in, I met the same young lady who had travelled back from Toronto on my last trip, she having rejoined the company as an Air Hostess and was on the same crew as myself. After two days in Bombay, where the crew stayed at the Taj Mahal Hotel, the incoming Transglobe aircraft was flown to Hong Kong via Bangkok where we stayed for another two days before flying to Singapore and then on to Bombay. At Bombay, the schedule called for my crew to remain on the aircraft as passengers to Dubai where we disembarked for a stopover of 6 days.

The weather in the Arabian Gulf in late November is glorious with clear skies, warm temperatures and a sea temperature that is simply marvellous. It was on this stop over that I became friendly with Sue, the hostess whom I would eventually marry. At the end of the six days, we flew to Benina in Libya for refuelling stop before continuing on to Gatwick. When I filed the flight plan at the control tower in Benina I learned that the AERAD SATCO was a watch supervisor with whom I had worked when I was in Tripoli. I left a message for him but no reply was ever received. This did not surprise me.

December 1967 was extremely busy for me, flying a round trip to Karachi stopping at many places. On one of the sectors in daylight, I managed to get a Sun, Moon, and Venus fix, something that is rarely possible due to the constant changing position of the bodies in relation to each other. A round trip to Bermuda was flown followed by a trip to

Lagos finishing up in Palma at 5.15p.m. on Christmas day. The company could get no volunteers to be away for Christmas but as an incentive, they offered to fly my wife out to Palma on Christmas Eve to be there when I arrived. I believe that she enjoyed the trip but by this time we had really drifted apart and it was not the best of times.

On 10th January 1968 I was rostered to go to Buenos Aires taking a load of freight, returning via Georgetown where passengers were to be picked up. Due to flight time limitations, my crew were flown as passengers to Madrid and on to Las Palmas where we would await the aircraft's arrival on the following day. The flight to Madrid was on a BOAC Comet commanded by my old friend Dougie Hadley. The last time I had flown with him was on a York freighter to Singapore when a double engine failure was experienced soon after leaving Singapore. Happy days!

After a stopover of 24 hours in Las Palmas, the aircraft departed for Recife in Northern Brazil on a night flight taking nine hours. Astro navigation was the only aid available on that sector, the results of which were perfect until near to the equator where we crossed the very active ITCZ with many severe thunderstorms lying across the track. There was a great deal of weaving around storm centres and the engines were frequently 'bumping', much to the crew's discomfort. Eventually the worst of the weather was cleared and the flight continued to Recife where a stop was made for refuelling. It was the middle of the night and no one seemed to be aware that fuel was needed, it taking an hour and a half to turn round the aircraft before continuing to Buenos Aires. That sector took 8 hours and 5 minutes arriving at 10a.m. local time after a duty day of over 20 hours. The entire crew was completely exhausted and the thought of departing at 7a.m. the next morning was indescribable. I know that everybody slept during the day arranging to meet in the early evening for a meal at a local steak house. The steak served was simply enormous; seemingly only lacking the hoofs and horns at each end! I can remember eating some of that very succulent steak but the rest of the evening was a blur due to fatigue.

The return to Gatwick was scheduled to be a direct flight to Georgetown but when the flight plan was filed, Argentine Air Traffic Control would not accept it. We were told that it was mandatory to land in Brazil if over-flying that country, a requirement of which we had no knowledge. Looking at the charts, the Captain and I decided that the best airfield was Porto Allegre, this apparently satisfying the Argentine authorities who accepted the flight plan. In addition to increasing the company's operating costs for the flight, this extra landing also increased my workload considerably, since I had to prepare two more flight plans and re-plot the new track on my navigation chart. On arrival in Porto Allegre, the authorities asked why we had landed there, it transpiring that there was absolutely no reason why we could not have gone direct to Georgetown!

The flight to Georgetown took eight hours, flying over the Mato Grosso where the jungle was so dense it looked as though it was ocean rather than trees, making map reading impossible. The entire flight was in daylight and the sole navigation aid was the sun. There were some low power radio beacons at locations close to the route, but none were received well enough to assist in fixing the aircraft's position. Fortunately there was little wind to contend with and my dead reckoning navigation was sufficiently accurate to get the aircraft tracking correctly into Georgetown. On landing the crew were informed that as sufficient passenger seats were available, we were to continue to Gatwick as passengers. This was extremely irritating, as we had already been on duty for nearly sixteen hours and the aircraft had still to fly to Gatwick, with fuel stops at Barbados and Santa Maria. The arrival at Gatwick was about 32 hours after leaving Buenos Aires, and I felt absolutely worn out. How I longed for the good old BOAC days at that moment!

The company seemed to be doing very well and David Barbour told me that over the next few months, it was going to acquire eight CL44D–4 freighter aircraft from Seaboard World Airways, (formerly Seaboard and Western Airlines), to supplement or replace the four Britannias. This was good news but it meant an increase in my workload, as I had to learn about the new aircraft and then teach and check out other navigators. In the meantime I did round trips to Bombay, Trinidad, Georgetown, Baltimore, New Orleans and, oddly enough, Gibraltar.

The company had taken delivery of its first CL44 in early April and Ted Parker with David as his navigator had carried out a series of proving and training flights prior to it entering service. In mid April a Training Captain, First Officer, Flight Engineer and myself were detailed to go to Halifax to collect the second CL44 that was just completing its conversion to a Freight/Passenger configuration. On 20th April we flew on BOAC from Heathrow to Montreal, then transferred to an Air Canada flight for Halifax. Three days were then spent thoroughly checking the aircraft over for any faults before it was accepted. An air test was flown with all systems being tested by a Seaboard World Captain, Stan Lebedis, after which he supervised the Transglobe pilots on circuits and landings. I was not needed for those flights as all navigation equipment could be checked on the ground.

The CL44, built by Canadair under licence from Bristol Aviation, was based on the Britannia airframe but had a longer fuselage than the

Britannia. It had a maximum take-off weight of 210,000 lbs against the Britannia's 185,000 lbs. In a passenger configuration, it seated 180 passengers compared to the 125 of the Britannia, but it did not have the same level of comfort. The Rolls Royce Tyne engines fitted were more powerful and certainly more fuel-efficient than the Britannia's Bristol Proteus engines, giving extra range. More importantly, the Rolls Royce Tyne engines did not suffer the engine icing that affected the Britannia so badly in the tropics. Being designed as a freighter aircraft, it had a swing tail that could be opened to load bulky freight pallets into the passenger cabin. The galleys were mounted in the swing section of the tail where it was uncomfortably cold and thoroughly disliked by the cabin staff. The conversion from passenger to freight configuration was by simply removing the seats and carpet from the passenger cabin.

The aircraft, again commanded by Captain Stan Lebadis, took off from Halifax at 8.20p.m. on 24th April 1968 and I was quite impressed by its take-off and climb performance, it being far superior to that of the Britannia. Although the aircraft was carrying spares, it was well below its maximum take-off weight and I recall that the aircraft climbed straight up to about 24,000 feet where it was completely above cloud. Soon after take off, the two main compasses had a difference of 30 degrees between them, the ambiguity of which was easy to resolve by reference to the standby compass, but it did need an astro heading check to confirm it. When I came to open the sextant hatch on the sextant mount to carry out the heading check, I found that the mechanism on the mount was jammed, although it had been quite serviceable when pre-flight tested on the ground. Using spanners and screwdrivers from the engineer's tool kit, I removed the whole mount, covering up the small hole in the fuselage with a thick sheet of cardboard to stop the noise caused by the pressurisation leak. I found that the mechanism was frozen solid and needed thawing out before it could be thoroughly cleaned. Having done that, lubrication was needed but having no oil or grease, margarine spread was used as a substitute. When re-assembled and put back on the fuselage, it worked perfectly which was most gratifying. A heading check confirmed the faulty compass and the flight went without further incident, landing at Gatwick at 8a.m. after a 7 hours 40 minutes flight. On arrival, a note was put in the technical log stating that the sextant mount needed proper lubrication. I know that was never done because on my next flight with that same aircraft some weeks later, it was a hot day at Gatwick, and when checking the sextant and its mount, I got a suggestion of grease on my fingers that smelt of rancid fat! That particular aircraft and other CL44s were being fully utilised and the ground engineers obviously considered that my request was not urgent enough to require attention.

The company had secured a contract taking cargo to Lagos at the time of the civil war in Nigeria and no guesses were needed to know that the cargo was arms and ammunition. Without a day off after the previous trip, I was sent to Lagos on a Britannia stopping at Castel Benito airfield Tripoli for fuel. When that flight took place, King Idris had already been deposed by Colonel Gadaffi and the attitude of the Libyan authorities had changed dramatically for the worse, resulting in the transit time at Tripoli being much longer than normal. Having no return load from Lagos, Tripoli was over-flown en route direct to Gatwick with no difficulties being encountered.

Shortly after I did another freight trip, again carrying arms to Lagos with a landing at Tripoli en route. The return schedule was the normal direct flight to Gatwick but on entering Libyan airspace, the aircraft was ordered to land at Tripoli. No reason was given and after landing the aircraft was impounded and the crew put under armed guard at the airport. Following interrogation by a military officer, the crew was released and allowed to go to a hotel in the city.

The Captain attempted to telephone Gatwick from the hotel but was told that he would have to go to the Post Office to do so. Doubtless there his call was to be monitored. The company did its utmost to get the crew and the aircraft released, but with little success. The crew were allowed to leave the hotel but each time anyone went out for shopping or a walk, a policeman would follow not far behind. There was only one hostess on the crew; a very slim and attractive young lady named Carol, a particular friend of Sue. One morning she went out shopping with one of the pilots, dressed in very tight shorts. As they left the hotel a policeman stopped her and said that her appearance was unacceptable and ordered her to return to the hotel and dress herself properly. When she protested, she was told that she would be arrested if she did not comply. It was a tense situation and rather frightening for Carol as a crowd gathered around shouting at her. After four days of negotiations, the aircraft and crew was released without explanation and the aircraft flown back to Gatwick. I was never told why we were forced to land but could only assume that it was due to over-flying Libya carrying arms.

Freight flights using CL44 aircraft were frequently operated and, on one to Beirut that I was not operating, an incident occurred whilst off loading the freight pallets. To off load freight, the swing tail is opened and each pallet moved back along tracks to the rear of the aircraft where the tail is open and high lift equipment takes them off one at a time. It is important that only one pallet is moved towards the tail otherwise the balance of the aircraft would be disturbed. The ground handlers neglected to take this precaution, moving all pallets to the rear as soon as one was taken off. Inevitably the aircraft became tail heavy and tipped backwards on to its tail. It took a great deal of time to restore the aircraft to its normal attitude without causing further damage. Some damage was sustained at the bottom of the rear fuselage that hit the ground and the nose gear was subjected to a great deal of strain when it hit the ground heavily as the normal balance was restored.

My next CL44 trip was to Amsterdam where 180 passengers were embarked and flown direct to New York in 11 hours 10 minutes, arriving with more than ample fuel reserves available, clearly demonstrating its advantage over the Britannia. The aircraft was then ferried to Winnipeg where a full passenger load was very easily flown to Gatwick in 11 hours 30 minutes, again arriving with ample fuel reserves. During that flight I was checking out a navigator using polar grid procedures, but he got into such a mess applying grivation to his grid headings, I was compelled to take over and get the aircraft back on track. Needless to say, he failed his check but on arrival at Gatwick I was *ordered* by the Chief Pilot to clear him for polar grid flying. I would have none of that and refused, compelling him to have further training followed by another check flight.

The CL44 was certainly a very impressive aircraft but did have its problems. The engines needed to be started by a special air compressor and if one was not available on the ground, there was no way that the engines could be started. Seaboard World Airlines had a compressor fitted on board, but Transglobe had this removed for weight saving reasons. This resulted in some delays to Transglobe's CL44s in the months ahead at airfields where Air Start equipment was not readily available.

I was further impressed with the CL44 when ferrying one empty back to Gatwick from Lagos. Just after take-off, the oil contents on number 3 engine dropped to zero and the engine was shut down. The flight continued on three engines to Gatwick where it landed 11 hours 20 minutes later. Before take-off the incoming crew had told us that there was a bad leak from an oil seal and that the oil contents would be rapidly lost, necessitating that the engine be shut down. In anticipation of this I calculated the fuel requirement for flight with only three engines operating so that we would not have to make an en route landing. It was known that there was nothing seriously wrong with the engine, the fault simply being the faulty oil seal that could not be replaced at Lagos, as no spare was available. When the seal was replaced at Gatwick, the engine was completely serviceable.

With more aircraft arriving, I was checking navigators on almost every Atlantic sector I flew, sometimes taking-off with two on board, one to be checked westbound and the other eastbound. I became very friendly with one ex RAF navigator I checked out and some years later when my wife gave birth to our son James, he became one of the godfathers. Sadly I have lost touch with him.

Transglobe did a series of flights to Johannesburg operating via Malta and Luanda in each direction and I found myself doing several of these. It was nice to go back to South Africa again and be on a route where astro navigation was the primary navigation aid. The weather on that route is never without the severe thunderstorms in the area of the ITCZ close to the equator, often necessitating large deviations from track. It was unfortunate that Malta to Johannesburg was such a long duty day, making everyone too tired to do much shopping or sightseeing on arrival.

A technical fault encountered on a CL44 caused my crew a little more than normal concern. After a freight flight to Toronto, the aircraft was flown on to Bermuda with another load of freight. Whenever the swing tail has been opened, it is the duty of the flight engineer to close it and ensure that it is locked securely. Once the freight had been off loaded in Bermuda, the engineer attempted to close the tail, only to discover that the very large hydraulic jack that closes the tail had corroded and would not operate. In spite of everything done to rectify the fault, it became necessary to fly a replacement jack and actuator from London to Bermuda on a BOAC Boeing 707. The delivery and fitting took three days during which I spent most of my time with a radio amateur, Johnny Swainson VP9DL, whose hospitality I had enjoyed on my many trips to Bermuda with BOAC.

After the repairs had been completed and the tail closed, the aircraft got airborne for Gatwick and was about four hours into the flight when the tail unlock warning light came on! There is not a lot anyone can do at 24000 feet with a thousand miles between the aircraft and the nearest land. The Captain told the engineer to go back and see if anything was evident, but *NOT* to touch the swing tail controls! At the time the crew were too horrified to think about anything except getting down safely. The engineer, a very experienced chap, could see nothing out of the ordinary, saying that it was almost certainly a false warning caused by a micro-switch. None of us were quite sure about that statement but as the Captain said, there was not a lot we could do about it, except get on with the flight. A radio message was transmitted saying that the tail unlock warning light had illuminated so that if we disappeared, the authorities would have a good idea what had happened to the aircraft. After 9 hours

15 minutes of flight, much to everyone's relief, a safe landing was made at Gatwick. The cause of the problem was, as the flight engineer had diagnosed, a micro-switch that was slightly out of adjustment. Although simple, it nevertheless caused a lot of anxiety during the flight. The ground engineers assured us that if the swing tail latches are physically in place, and they were, there is no way that the tail would open! Try convincing a crew of that when they are at 24,000 feet and a long way from land!

Late in July of 1968, my (then) only son, an RAF Flying Officer stationed in Norfolk, married a Norfolk young lady at a double wedding ceremony with her elder sister marrying one of my son's fellow officers. It was a grand affair with a guard of honour of other officers providing an archway of swords for the newly weds to walk under. The reception was held at Little Massingham House, the home of Lady Joan Cator who was godmother to the two brides. Soon after the wedding, I left home to live in a flat at Southwick near Brighton. It was not a decision taken lightly, but it was final, I having hopes of making a new life for myself.

On 1st September 1968 two CL44 aircraft started a long-term lease to Trans Mediterranean Airways and they together with a third back up aircraft, were painted in Trans Mediterranean's colourful livery. These aircraft flew most of TMA's International scheduled freight flights, presumably providing a financial benefit to Transglobe.

August, September and October were quite busy, but after that I had nearly six weeks off between flights. Some of the time off was leave, but mainly it was because the summer charter season had finished and the company had too many navigators available. On 27th November 1968, I departed from Gatwick on a CL44 taking a load of freight to Khartoum. The flight was scheduled to have 19 hours on the ground after which it was to fly to Hamburg to pick up a large and quite valuable load of industrial silver. On arrival at Hamburg the Handling Agent came on board and his first question was, 'What are you going to do now that your company has ceased to operate?' We were absolutely astounded by his remark, scarcely believing it to be true. The Captain asked why we were still flying if the company had gone down and in reply was told that the fees for the flight from Hamburg had been guaranteed so that the aircraft could get back to Gatwick. The news was devastating and it was a miserable flight to Gatwick where after landing, the aircraft was parked in a remote area well away from the terminal. No company transport was available but two crew members awaiting the aircraft's arrival collected us in their own cars and took us to the office. There everything was in a shambles, looking as though vandals had gone through the building, which they probably had. There was little to do other than get into my car and drive back to the flat at Southwick to rest, having been on duty for well over 16 hours. Prior to departure for this flight, there had been no hint of any company problems and the future had looked pretty secure!

This was perhaps the most depressing time in my life and I knew that at my age, it was not going to be easy for me to continue flying, or even get another decent job. I immediately contacted David at his home and found him to be just as shocked. He had received no warning of the company's failure so could not enlighten me further.

Staff members were told to go to their local office of the Department of Social Security to register as unemployed and make a claim for a redundancy payment. This I did without delay and was placed on the Professional and Executive Register, for what it was worth. Being the off peak winter period, all charter operators were at minimum flying staff levels with no additional staff needed.

It looked as though it would be a very bleak Christmas, with divorce proceedings taking place and arrangements already made for Sue and I to be married. Sue and her parents were extremely supportive and were confident that the situation would change for the better. Ironically it did not for Sue and her family, as her brother was suddenly taken ill and died a week later.

During December I learned that the collapse was brought about by two of Transglobe's major shareholders, The Bolton Steamship Company and The Ocean Steamship Company, introducing winding-up proceedings. There seemed to be no logical explanation for this action, particularly as forward charter bookings were looking good. Transglobe also owned an engineering company, Air Couriers (Gatwick) Ltd that serviced Transglobe's aircraft and also carried out work for other airlines. I later learned that it was self-supporting and need not have been liquidated. The shipping companies gave all staff an ex gratia payment of a month's full salary, which although generous, was hardly adequate compensation for the loss of gainful employment. Eventually all staff who had been with the company for at least two years, received government redundancy payments, and over the next few years as the receiver realised company assets, payments were made to staff for a small percentage of what they were owed contractually.

Soon after Christmas, I learned that a new freight airline was in the process of being formed that would be known as Tradewinds. It would use the Transglobe CL44 aircraft and be crewed by some of the ex Transglobe crews, led operationally by Captain Ted Parker, the former Chief Pilot of Transglobe. Key ground staff positions apparently would be filled from senior ex Transglobe non-flying staff. Another airline, Donaldson International, was also just about to be formed and I immediately applied to both airlines for the position of Chief Navigator. Early in December I had applied to Laker Airways, but had been told that there were no vacancies at that time.

My applications for employment with both Donaldson and Tradewinds were acknowledged and late in December I was asked to meet the Managing Director of Donaldson concerning my application. The interview went well and I was told that he would be in contact with me when a final decision had been reached. On Friday 3rd January 1969, I was offered the Chief Navigator appointment with Donaldson and by a remarkable coincidence Ted Parker contacted me inviting me to be the Chief Navigator of Tradewinds. As if that was not enough, also on the same day, the Chief Navigator of Laker Airways, my old ex BOAC friend Dick Bradley, asked to see me very urgently to discuss joining Laker. What a dilemma! It was 3.30p.m. when Dick phoned but I immediately drove to Gatwick where he told me that Laker Airways had acquired two Boeing 707–138B aircraft and intended to operate them on Atlantic routes. Dick wanted me to assist him to get the aircraft on the Air Operating Certificate and then become the Check Navigator to check out navigators as they were recruited. When I asked him when he would want me to start, he looked at his watch and said that perhaps it was too late to start then, but asked me report at 9.30a.m. on Monday when we would discuss pay and conditions. David Barbour apparently had been offered this job but had decided to leave aviation for a more secure occupation and recommended that Dick approach me to fill his requirement.

On reflection, I was aware that two years with Transglobe had taught me far more about Civil Aviation generally than the nearly seventeen years with BOAC had done. Professionally I was the same as before but I now possessed a much greater depth of knowledge that over future years would serve me in good stead.

Chapter 18

Laker Airways

On Monday 6th January 1969, I arrived at the Laker Offices by 9.30a.m. and without any preliminary discussion of pay and conditions of service, Dick started to assign tasks to me. When told of the other offers that I had received over the weekend, he was thoughtful for a moment or two and then threw the ball completely into my court by asking me if I wanted to be a Chief Navigator or a Deputy Chief. My reply was that it was not quite as simple as that, this then leading to his next question: 'Is it money?' When I confirmed that was so, he went immediately to Freddie Laker and put him in the picture. Freddie, ever the pragmatist, told him that if I was the person he needed, he should go ahead and make an offer that would be mutually agreeable. Dick came back and told me what Freddie had said and what salary he had initially proposed to offer me, followed by a new offer. In the light of his discussion with Freddie and the revised offer, I commenced work immediately. My contract and salary was backdated to the 1st January 1969 but then Dick explained that as it would be some time before flying could commence, I would be expected to work normal office hours helping him produce operational manuals to the Civil Aviation Authority (CAA) requirements. The decision I made on that Monday morning certainly proved to be the correct one and I was to spend many happy years with Laker Airways and develop a great deal of respect for Freddie Laker.

I then had the somewhat unenviable task of informing Donaldson and Tradewinds of my decision, but doubtless both companies had other applicants to consider so I was not unduly concerned. Dick was not aware that I had already decided to join Laker when I reported on Monday morning and my mentioning other job offers was simply to arrive at the right salary and terms of reference. I felt sure that Laker Airways was there to stay whereas the other two airlines were somewhat speculative. The Chief Navigator post of Donaldson was taken by Doug Bishop and Tradewinds by Wally Philips, both ex BOAC navigators. My feelings about the future of Donaldson and Tradewinds certainly proved to be correct as both companies went out of business a few years later.

My first weeks with Laker were quite hectic with Freddie wanting to get the two Boeing 707–138B aircraft he had acquired into service without delay. Both aircraft had originally been owned by the Australian

Airline QANTAS and were part of the fleet of British Eagle who had gone into liquidation. I wondered at the time if either aircraft had been the one I had flown back from Singapore as a passenger with QANTAS in my latter days with BOAC.

This particular type of Boeing 707 had much less load capacity and range capability than the 707–200 series being flown by British Airways and other 707 operators, but it was Freddie's intention to operate them on both Atlantic and European routes. Ultimately they did this very successfully despite fears that its ability to reach New York non-stop might be marginal. Indeed, it always was with a full load of passengers.

I found Freddie Laker to be a very approachable and likeable person and he made a point of coming to the Navigation Office to meet me in person and welcome me to his airline. My respect for him strengthened over the years as I discovered that he knew almost every aspect of airline operations and was able to discuss everything at a sensible level. His office door was always open to staff who had personal problems and he gave as much advice and assistance as was possible, sometimes financial.

Dick's first task was to get the 707s on to the Laker Air Operating Certificate (AOC) and he asked the CAA if they would accept the British Eagle Operational Manuals as being those of Laker. They agreed to the content of the manuals provided that *every page* had British Eagle deleted and Laker substituted. A monstrous task which required everybody, including the newly employed 707 flying staff, to pitch in and help.

The company was fortunate to have recruited from the redundant British Eagle staff three very experienced pilots, Captains Sanders, Batchelor, and Herd, plus two Flight Engineers, a First Officer and a Navigator all whom, with the exception of the Navigator, could assist in the training of Laker Flight Crews. Although the amendment of the Operations Manuals was not entirely completed, flying training was able to commence with crews carrying out circuits and landings.

The Laker Chief Pilot was Captain Alan Hellary, a very experienced captain and a superb pilot with many thousands of flying hours to his credit. He had flown with all the companies that Freddie Laker had been associated with and I would fly as his navigator on many flights in the future. At the time I joined Laker, Alan had CAA authorisation to fly both the BAC 1–11 and the Boeing 707, something that CAA did not normally approve.

Laker had started with two ex BOAC 100 Series Britannias that later were supplemented by two new BAC 1–11s that Freddie had shown great foresight in ordering. At a later date, the 1–11 fleet was increased to five aircraft to satisfy Laker's ever-increasing share of the Inclusive

Tour market. When the Boeing 707s commenced operations, the Britannias were disposed of to an Indonesian airline, Indonesian Angkasa Civil Air Transport. Laker crews ferried both aircraft to Jakarta where they were utilised on Charter Operations, but by mid 1970 that airline became bankrupt and the Britannias were scrapped.

The Operations Manager was Wing Commander 'Attie' Atkinson, DSO, DFC, a very approachable and likeable person who ran the Laker Operations Department most efficiently. He was a pre war career RAF Officer until medically discharged from the Air Force after the war with chest problems that sadly, in 1980, became terminal cancer.

Dick Bradley possessed a brilliant mind, being able to unravel in seconds, performance problems that would take others hours. He was not a good instructor, being seemingly unaware that those he instructed were unable to keep up with him, his mind always being about three stages ahead of his trainees. He devised a method of utilising reduced take-off thrust on the BAC 1–11 aircraft, a procedure that was taken up by BAC and is now a standard performance procedure with most aircraft manufacturers. Reduced take-off thrust greatly increases the life of engines, as full thrust is not necessary for every take-off. I learned a great deal from him and when he was satisfied with my ability, most of the training was delegated to me.

The first stage of the Air Operating Certificate was to obtain approval to fly to holiday destinations in Europe and the Canary Islands. In February 1969 I did one round trip to Tenerife to get the feel of the aircraft and to check the Loran, Kollsman Sextant, and other navigation equipment. As a navigation exercise I did an air plot in both directions, taking Loran and Astro fixes to confirm that the navigation equipment was satisfactory. Another familiarisation trip was to Tel Aviv mainly to check fuel consumption and the compasses.

Although having a great deal of experience when I joined Laker Airways, I had not operated on pure jet aircraft and CAA required me to demonstrate my navigating ability to an approved examiner before I could train navigators that Laker would recruit. During the first week of March, Dick arranged for me to do two complete round trips from Las Palmas to Rio on a VC10 of British United Airways. By a remarkable coincidence I was supervised on both by Navigator Terry Playford, my old friend and ex BOAC colleague who was based in Tokyo with me. Terry said that supervising me was farcical and apart from the fuel control, which was not my responsibility, he sat back in a first class seat and relaxed. Doppler was fitted on the BUA VC10 and I found this to be of great assistance for track keeping. The supervisory flights cleared me on the 707 for navigation in all areas except the Atlantic. Although I had a great deal of experience on the North Atlantic, Wally Luther the CAA Navigation Inspector required me to operate at least one Atlantic sector under supervision on the 707 before Atlantic clearance would be given.

In the middle of March, six days after arriving back from the Rio flights, an Atlantic trip came up at very short notice, taking part of a ship's crew to Florida. Attie arranged for David Page, the Chief Navigator of BUA, to supervise me on my first Atlantic flight with Laker Airways. David held Captain rank, the only navigator I ever met with that rank, and was able to provide the necessary route clearance for Captain Hellary who commanded the aircraft. At the time of that flight, the company did not hold Navigation Approval for North Atlantic routes, so the flight was planned to transit Santa Maria en route to Fort Lauderdale. On the day of departure, 14th March 1969, abnormally strong winds were forecast between Santa Maria and Fort Lauderdale, making it impossible to fly direct to the destination from Santa Maria. Attie requested dispensation from CAA to fly across the Atlantic in Region H with a refuelling stop at Gander. With the very experienced BUA's David Page on board, the request was granted and the flight departed from Gatwick at 1.25p.m., arriving in Fort Lauderdale at 7.28p.m. local time after an uneventful 9 hours 40 minutes flight time for the two sectors.

On the return flight, although not able to get maximum fuel on board, a non-stop flight to Gatwick was achieved in 8 hours 40 minutes using the en route re-clearance procedure. David Page signed Atlantic Clearances for Captain Hellary and myself, giving Laker Airways a complete crew cleared on the Atlantic. The winds on that flight from Fort Lauderdale were extremely strong and variable in direction, taxing my navigation skills to the utmost. It would have been easier if the aircraft had the Doppler aid that BUA installed on their VC10s, but that would come in the not too distant future.

Laker Airways BAC 1–11 fuel flight planning for holiday flights within Europe was done by the pilots using pre-printed flight plans for each route. With the routings from UK being quite varied, the navigation folder held a multiplicity of flight plans for each destination, one of which would be selected and filed for the flight. Dick produced flight plans in a format that made it a simple task for the crew to calculate the fuel requirement using an average wind component for the sector assessed from the Meteorological Office wind flow charts. With the introduction of the Boeing 707, similar format flight plans were produced for that aircraft's holiday destinations within Europe. However, it was obvious that fuel and route flight planning on Atlantic sectors would be much more complex and would have to be done by the navigator. If the

707 flew long-range routes that did not require a navigator, pre-printed plans were produced in a similar format to those of the BAC 1–11. If the flight were in a navigation area on an established route, the navigator would produce a fuel flight plan to calculate the fuel required and a pre-printed flight plan would be used for position reporting.

Looking ahead to the North Atlantic, clearly it would be quite a headache for the navigator whose job it was to select the most suitable track and prepare the fuel flight plan. An organised track system was in force for flights over the Atlantic, the use of which was mandatory when flying in the Minimum Navigation Performance Airspace (MNPS). The MNPS is a large area of Atlantic airspace within defined latitudes and longitudes, and between flight levels 27,500 feet to 40,000 feet. Aircraft flying within the MNPS airspace needed to be capable of navigating to strict prescribed limits and if unable to do so, were compelled to fly below 27,500 feet or above 40,000feet.

To a certain degree, the published track system could give guidance on which track to use between points in UK and points in eastern USA and Canada. Tracks, valid for ten hours, changed twice daily with two hours of dead space between the end of each track period and the start of the next. Westbound flights had priority by day with tracks lettered by the start of the alphabet, A, B, C etc, and Eastbound flights by night with tracks lettered by the latter part of the alphabet, W, X, Y etc. There was always a track(s) available for flights operating against the general flow of traffic but this was not necessarily the best time track, so important for keeping fuel costs down.

I urged Dick to take up my idea of using the best time track computer that I had successfully used with Transglobe, but for some unaccountable reason he did not think it would be of great use. He asked me to teach navigators to assess the best time track visually using the appropriate meteorological wind chart. I considered this to be very much a hit or miss method and that became obvious to him later when he chose to use computer flight planning. As I still had my Transglobe computer, I continued to use it but had to give other navigators instruction and guidance on track selection by other means.

Dick realised the importance of flying the best time track and negotiated a contract with MEMRYKORD, a computer flight planning company who would provide flight plans to the format of his choice, thus relieving navigators of the responsibility of track selection. It was some time before Dick finalised that contract, only doing so when it became essential due to escalating fuel costs. At a later date the contract was awarded to Continental Computer Services who produced a more efficient and less costly flight plan. When DC10 aircraft were acquired, computer plans were used on all but fixed routes. It is interesting to note that on some occasions, the track I selected using the Transglobe computer was the same as the computer flight plans of other companies flying to the same destination. On one or two occasions using my Transglobe computer, I selected a track that was different to other aircraft flying the same route at the same time, but which proved to be shorter in time, proving that using the computer could be advantageous. Unfortunately Dick was not convinced.

Dick made application for Region H, (North Atlantic routes), to be included on the AOC, but as the granting of this was contingent on satisfying CAA that company crews were trained to operate on these routes, training commenced immediately. In addition to Graham Brett, an ex British Eagle navigator who had joined when Laker acquired the 707s, Dick recruited Robbie Robinson who I knew from Transglobe Airways, and I was contacted by George Andrews, also ex BOAC and Transglobe, asking if I could get him into the company. I was able to do this and after ground instructions I route checked both on the West African route then being operated for Nigerian Airways. This gave enough navigators to cover the flights being operated at that time, but their North Atlantic flight checks would need to be carried out by me at the appropriate time. The commercial department of Laker had been extremely efficient in securing the contract with Nigerian Airways to fly their scheduled services from Nigeria to Heathrow via various places in Europe. These flights took slightly more than the capacity of one of the Boeing 707s, leaving available capacity for other flights. Early in August, a charter was flown to Mauritius via Djibouti, returning via Jeddah. This was followed in September by a charter to Kuala Lumpur and another charter to Nairobi early in December. That flight was scheduled to transit Malta but after re-fuelling, number 3 engine refused to start and the flight was delayed until a Laker ground engineer and spare parts arrived from Gatwick. Once serviceable the rest of the charter went without incident with a scheduled night stop in Nairobi before returning to Gatwick via Malta again.

Dick Bradley's assistant when I joined the company was Brian Webb who had been employed soon after Laker Airways had been formed. Brian Webb was an experienced ex RAF Navigator, but had done very little Civil Aviation navigation. As a reward for his loyal and valuable service in the early days of Laker Airways, Dick asked me to train him as a line navigator. Brian was a very likeable chap, meticulous in his work and possessed a lively sense of humour. A multi-sector charter flight came up to take passengers from Zurich to Johannesburg, followed by a round trip from Johannesburg to Bangkok via Mauritius. It finally returned to Bangkok via Mauritius before continuing on to Gatwick via Bombay, Nicosia and Zurich. Brian needed twenty hours of navigation time to validate his licence and this seemed an ideal and pleasant way of achieving it.

The crew positioned to Zurich by scheduled airline, discovering on arrival that the nearest place that hotel accommodation was available was Basle, the handling agent having failed to book a hotel in Zurich as requested. Captain Batchelor was not amused, but by a remarkable coincidence he bumped into an old Captain friend flying for Tellair who was about to leave for Basle with an empty Britannia. 'Batch' scrounged a lift and the crew got to the hotel in Basle. Unfortunately, no scheduled flight was available to take the crew back to Zurich for the departure and it was necessary to travel by train for the 8.30p.m. departure from Zurich airport.

On May 9th 1969, the Laker Boeing 707–138B GAVZZ arrived in Zurich on time and a departure was made for Johannesburg with an en route refuelling stop at Luanda. The flight went without incident, apart from a very severe line of thunderstorms associated with an active line squall over Nigeria, causing the flight to deviate nearly 100 miles from track. The aircraft flew for 8 of the 9 days it was away from UK, during which time it remained fully serviceable throughout with no significant technical problems being encountered. Brian took a little time to settle down, after which he performed well, enabling me to check him out with the necessary number of hours to validate his licence.

In Bangkok I had the pleasure of meeting and lunching with Amara, a Thai lady who had been at college in Brighton with my soon to be bride Sue. She went around the shops with me and I was planning to buy Sue an attractive ring that had previously caught my eye. Price haggling is normal in the east and Amara was able to get the price down to half that the shopkeeper had wanted when I haggled the day before. The crew was accommodated in a super luxury hotel, so very different from the Trocadero Hotel of BOAC flying boat days!

During the flight back to UK, a problem arose flying over Lebanese air space en route from Bombay to Nicosia. Beirut Air Traffic Control informed the Captain that he did not have the necessary over flight clearance and instructed him to land at Beirut airport. Had a landing been made as instructed, doubtless the aircraft would have been unable to continue due to crew duty hours and the obvious political problems. Batch simply ignored the instructions, telling Air Traffic Control that their transmissions were garbled and unreadable. It was a little tense until the aircraft had left Lebanese air space and reached Nicosia, where a landing was made to refuel. In fact, we did have a copy of the over flight clearance on board, but there was no doubt in anyone's mind that the captain had made the right decision! Nothing further was heard from the Lebanese Authorities.

The round trip over nine days took 60 hours 24 minutes flying time and the aircraft remained on schedule throughout. The captain was very familiar with the aircraft, but other members of crew including myself, lacked experience on the type. 'Batch' was a fine pilot but possessed little sense of humour and was quite bad tempered if things did not go exactly how he thought they should. Both First Officers became Laker Captains on the 707 some time later, and Brian Webb retrained as a pilot, ultimately reaching Captain rank on Laker 1–11 aircraft. He was to lose his life in a house fire when living and working for an airline in Saudi Arabia.

I did no flying after the Bangkok flights, working mainly in the office assisting Dick until the 12th July when Sue and I got married. It was a glorious hot sunny day with the temperature well over 80 degrees and we honeymooned for two weeks in Majorca where the temperatures were no higher than those in England.

Three days after returning from honeymoon, I flew a round trip to Tel Aviv to check that the compasses and Loran were operating correctly, and carried out fuel checks as we suspected that the fuel consumption was much higher than it should have been. At a later date more exhaustive checks were carried out in a attempt to improve the high fuel consumption.

At the end of August, Donaldson Airways were short of a navigator for one of their flights and asked Attie if Laker would allow me to navigate one of their Britannias on an Atlantic flight. Wally Luther of CAA was contacted and he authorised me to operate the Donaldson flight to Toronto and return. It made a nice change to fly on the Britannia again but I certainly missed the altitude capability of the 707 that cleared most of the cloud en route.

The remainder of the year was taken up with a mixture of West African flights and working in the office with Dick on North Atlantic procedures. In 1969, my first year with Laker, I only flew about 400 hours but as my duties included training and very frequent sessions in the office, my time was fully utilised.

The year 1970 saw the West African Airways flights continuing, but with the AOC extended to cover the North Atlantic, as only I was the only navigator cleared to fly on the Atlantic, it would always fall to me if a flight came up. A flight to New York came up in March 1970 and as Dick Bradley needed to keep his navigation licence current, I took the opportunity to give him a North Atlantic flight check. I supervised him outbound to New York and flight checked him on the return sector. He was a skilled navigator lacking only practice, which resulted in him being a little slow, particularly with astro. When I commented on this, he could only agree with me but said that as his office work was so demanding, it was doubtful if he could annually do more than the hours necessary for his licence renewal. It was fortuitous that this was an Atlantic flight as clearance for the Atlantic Region H automatically gave him clearance for other Regions on the AOC and Navigation approval.

Late in April 1970 on the day immediately following my return from a Lagos flight, I had gone to the office for routine work when an urgent request for a sub charter to New York came from British United Airways. With Dick not available for flying, I was the only navigator qualified and had to hurriedly drive back home, get into uniform and return to Gatwick with my baggage ready for a 5.30p.m. departure. Attie used the flight to train another captain by rostering Alan Hellary to supervise him. The weather at New York was extremely poor with very low cloud and poor visibility giving unacceptable landing delays, and a diversion to Boston had to be made. My choice of diversion was Baltimore where the weather was fine after the frontal system had moved through, but the pilots made the decision to go to Boston where the weather was just on our landing limits with cloud at 300 feet and only just adequate visibility. Other than the diversion, the flight was completed satisfactorily; giving the company another captain qualified for Atlantic flights.

Freddie Laker's real plan was to break into the lucrative North Atlantic charter market and in fact, some flights commenced in May 1970. These flights were affinity group charters operating under special charter rules that were easily broken and could result in fines being imposed on the companies concerned.

The CAA requirements of Region H of the AOC had been progressively implemented, but with the navigation rules on the Atlantic becoming even more stringent, CAA together with other Aviation Authorities ruled that aircraft should be capable of maintaining track more accurately than previously required. Following discussions with CAA, Laker installed Doppler on both 707 aircraft and commenced a period of evaluation.

The Doppler installation provided ground speed and drift indications that allowed the pilots to use the drift to maintain track. It also had a computer on which the required track and distance could be set for the leg being flown and the next one after that. This computer gave a cross track error indication if the track was not being correctly maintained allowing pilots to adjust the heading of the aircraft as and when required to maintain a zero cross track error indication. The navigator's task was to cross check that the correct tracks and distances were set on the computer by the pilots and check the aircraft's actual position during flight using any navigation aids available. The freedom to alter heading without being told by the navigator had its drawbacks, particularly if an alteration was made while the navigator was shooting a star, resulting in the shot being useless. The navigator always told the pilots when he was starting an astro fix, but quite often they forgot and altered heading.

There was seldom any trouble with the Doppler equipment and the operating procedures worked well at all times. For Doppler to operate efficiently, the aircraft must be flying over surfaces that will reflect transmitted signals back to the aircraft. With flat calm seas the signal sometimes is not reflected and the computer will continue to work using its 'memory' until signals are received again. That would mean that the last drift calculated by Doppler would continue to be used until signals were received again. If that happened over a long period of time, track errors would obviously occur if the wind direction and speed changed. Fortunately, sustained calm seas over the Atlantic are rare.

The accuracy of the Doppler system is dependent on the accuracy of the compass that is coupled to the Doppler. The Doppler tracks set on the computer were offset by any deviation being experienced and for this reason it was necessary for the navigator to check the compasses with an astro heading check just prior to entering a navigation area, repeating these as often as necessary. Either of two compasses could be switched to the Doppler with the most reliable always being used for navigation.

Notwithstanding the accuracy and reliability of the Doppler, it was essential that navigators fixed at very frequent intervals to ensure the track keeping was in accordance with CAA requirements. At the end of each flight when Doppler had been used, the System Tracking Error (STE), was calculated and logged, thus enabling the logged STE to be immediately used on the next sector prior to establishing the compass deviation from an astro heading check.

The Doppler system was thoroughly tested on European and African routes with the first flight using the system in anger being on 4th March 1970. I navigated that flight to West Africa with Alan Hellary in command and the system worked perfectly. The data from that flight, together with many other flights, was submitted to CAA for their evaluation, and Wally Luther then issued an approval for the use of Doppler on the Atlantic.

As stated earlier in this book, the West African route is ideal for navigation training, and I was asked to supervise two Laker captains who held navigation licences. Training Captain Steve James was a licensed navigator having navigated with BOAC when he first joined them. I supervised him on several West African flights, eventually flight checking him so that he could be rostered if necessary. Captain Chris Radford was an ex RAF navigator who retrained as a pilot before joining Laker. I also checked him out but to my knowledge, neither Captain was ever called upon to navigate.

Since the 707s had been operating, I noticed that the actual aircraft performance in respect of fuel consumption was very much degraded from the book figures and as most of the Atlantic flights carried the maximum passenger load, the direct flight across the Atlantic was always marginal. The aircraft's optimum cruise speed was Mach . 83 this being indicated on a small Mach Meter that I suspected was not accurate enough. The actual speed of the aircraft in knots for a given Mach number varies with temperature and altitude and as there was a very accurate True Air Speed indicator fitted on board, I decided that perhaps it would better to use that instead of the seemingly inaccurate Mach meter.

The Chief Flight Engineer and I flew a round trip together to New York with him adjusting the power to cruise the aircraft at the required true airspeed calculated by me for Mach .83 against the ambient temperature and altitude. Although flying at the correct true airspeed for Mach .83 and the ambient conditions, both Mach Meters indicated much less than .83. However, on each sector of the round trip the fuel consumed was very close to the book, proving to me that we had flown at the correct speed. Obviously the Mach Meters were reading low! It was concluded that the Mach Meters were not sufficiently accurate and Jock Stewart, the Chief Flight Engineer instructed Flight Engineers to use the True Air Speed Meter. Flight Engineers needed to carefully keep the speed correct because if the speed was allowed to bleed off, it needed a great deal of extra power with its associated high fuel consumption to restore the correct speed.

Amongst the many other problems confronting Dick and I was which navigation chart we would choose from the many available for Atlantic routes. The US government produced navigation chart 3071G and 3097G both having Loran and Grids overprinted on them. We considered the 3071G to be perfectly adequate for North Atlantic, but it did not completely cover the route to Barbados. The 3097G covered Northern Canada and West Coast Canadian and USA destinations, also having Loran and Grid overprinted, but with the disadvantage of having the grid based on 54 degrees west rather than the more conventional Greenwich Meridian. Swissair printed their own charts, the APC 660 for North Atlantic, APC 500 for West Indies and APC 770 for west coast USA and Canada, all having Loran and Grids overprinted with the grids based on Greenwich. The APC series of charts were certainly the most desirable, but were quite expensive. A navigator doing conventional navigation can use any chart available to him but if using free gyro and grid navigation, he needs to know the details of his chart. Dependent on the charts in stock, initially the 3071G was used on the North Atlantic, the APC 500 or 3071G on Barbados and the 3097G or APC 770 on North Canadian routes.

After consultation with Dick it was decided that navigators would use Grid Navigation on all routes in order to fly the shortest possible distances between each reporting point. The shortest distance between any two points is the Great Circle and a grid track would more or less equate to that. Therefore, by applying the average grivation between any two points, a shorter distance than the Rhumb line could be flown. If the compasses were unslaved and stable, the shortest distance **would** be flown. I believe that Swissair did use free gyro on all their navigation sectors with significant fuel savings over a whole year.

Dick and I decided that Laker's navigation policy would be to use slaved magnetic compasses on all routes except those where magnetic compasses could be unreliable, when free gyro would be used with tracks measured from Grid North. In my opinion, when using grid navigation and unslaved compasses, the APC 770 was a superior chart, having its grid aligned with the Greenwich meridian and having all divergence angles east. With the 3097G grid aligned with 54 degrees west, the divergence angles could be east or west, which is not ideal. Dick's decision to use the 3097G was presumably dictated by the price of the chart.

In early May 1970, the North Atlantic flights started in earnest and I had to do three round trips in rapid succession, checking navigators on each of them to ensure that the company had sufficient navigators cleared to satisfy the roster. The frequency of flights increased dramatically in July and August when I flew twelve round trips across the Atlantic in those two months, sometimes only getting 24 hours off between flights.

In early September, just after that hectic period, I tripped on the stairs at Laker Operations, breaking the big toe on my left foot. Being in considerable pain, the standby navigator George Andrews was called out, but as he lived in Christchurch some two hours plus away, I was asked if I was well enough to do the flight. In the light that the flight would be delayed by nearly four hours, causing a rolling delay to subsequent flights, I agreed to operate. The senior hostess on board was a trained nurse and she filled a bucket with cold water and ice so that I could sit at the navigation table with my foot in it. Not the most comfortable way of travelling, and one that did not allow me to use astro easily. During the flight the foot became black with bruising and so swollen, that on arrival at New York I could not get my shoe on. I was put in a wheel chair and wheeled to the crew bus taking us to the hotel, where on arrival, I stayed in bed for the entire stop over, dosing myself with aspirin. I navigated the return flight to Gatwick hoping on arrival to be able to see my doctor, but this was not to be! Attie met me personally and asked if after a night rest period I could fly to Toronto, adding that the flight would have to be cancelled if I could not do it. With the pain mostly gone, I agreed to fly to keep the aircraft going.

When eventually I did get to see my doctor, after an X-ray he confirmed that the toe was broken and strapped the foot up. When I asked if it would be permissible to continue flying, he said there was no medical reason why I should not and commented that as I had kept flying through the worst of it, there seemed to be no reason to stop. As I was no longer in pain and was reasonably mobile, I carried on flying. Resultant from my accident, standby navigators were expected to be on call not more than 45 minutes journey time away from the airport, a decision that did not please those living further away.

As the summer season drew to its close, the frequency of Atlantic flights progressively decreased until early October when they almost came to a standstill. In the winter the company operated one flight a week to New York, which with the schedule operated, meant that crews spent a full week in New York awaiting the next flight. I do not think anyone liked to be away that long and I suggested to the commercial department that if they scheduled the aircraft to have 12 to 14 hours on the ground, the crew could have minimum rest and then operate the aircraft back to Gatwick. Obviously this could not be done if the aircraft was required for other flying but, as with most charter operators, the winter was pretty slack and the amended schedule was implemented, saving the airline money on accommodation and allowances.

Freddie Laker always seeking new ventures was instrumental, with others, in setting up International Caribbean Airways, the Barbados Flag Carrier, to operate scheduled services to Europe. This airline used Laker aircraft to fly passengers and freight from Barbados to Luxembourg and return. Having no traffic rights with UK, the aircraft had to fly empty between Gatwick and Luxembourg, then operate to Barbados and return with fuel stops in Santa Maria. The departures from Gatwick and Barbados were both mid evening, resulting in almost the whole schedule being flown at night. The same crew operated out and back, having only the mandatory minimum rest period during the day in Barbados, a most exhausting schedule that was not popular with crews. The only joy of the Caribbean Airways flights were the very attractive Barbadian air hostesses who, once on board, took off their jackets and skirts, revealing themselves wearing halter top and hot pants! I had not seen this uniform before and was quite startled when a feminine vision appeared and asked me what I would like. She was, of course, asking if I wanted tea or coffee, but there was a strong temptation to be facetious.

The flights were intended to be non-stop between Luxembourg and Barbados, but with the short range of the Boeing 707–138B aircraft, this could only be achieved if the load allowed full fuel tanks, and even then it was tight. When the Barbados route was started, on December 28th 1970 I flew to Luxembourg with no passengers and then on the following day with only a small load of passengers and full tanks, we flew direct to Barbados, taking 9 hours 15 minutes. This flight was in daylight and we had a night stop in Barbados. On the following day, again with a light passenger load and full tanks the direct flight to Luxembourg was achieved. International Caribbean Airways had no traffic rights between Gatwick and Luxembourg so these sectors were non-revenue flights. Several different schedules were tried, but in the light of crew and aircraft utilisation it was decided to have night departures with the same crew operating the round trip. The arrival in Barbados at 4.30a.m. local time and a departure at 9.30p.m., allowed about seven hours sleep and a short session swimming or sunbathing on the lovely sandy beach at the hotel.

Often there were VIPs on board the Caribbean Airways flights, the most notable being 'Mrs Jones', Royalty travelling incognito who flew on two of the flights I operated. Sir Douglas Bader was a passenger on two occasions I was navigating, but for reasons known only to him, he only spoke to the Captain, never the others on the flight deck! Mr Edwards, one of the founders of Caribbean Airways flew on one of my flights, taking with him his friend Amie Macdonald, the TV actress with the squeaky voice. He invited the crew to his luxury villa for lunch and swimming which was most enjoyable, the only drawback being that none of the crew could drink alcohol, being within 8 hours of commencing duty. Miss Macdonald was a very charming lady.

The year of 1971 started slowly with me flying one charter to Mauritius, but by March the North Atlantic programme was again in full swing. On April 25th 1971, Attie asked at very short notice if I would agree carry out a flight check on Tony Willson-Pepper who had just joined the company. Since Transglobe, Tony had been working for East African Airways, but with redundancy looming there, he had asked if I could get him into Laker, which fortunately I was able to do. Sue was expecting our first child and as the arrival was quite imminent, Attie did not pressure me to do the flight, leaving the decision entirely to me. Sue told me to go, as she felt sure that the birth would not happen in the 29 hours that I would be away, and she did have her aunt staying with her. I left home at 6.30a.m. on a very sunny Sunday morning with Sue getting up to give me breakfast and see me off. It was quite a normal flight with an arrival in New York at just before midday local time. There was no way I could know that about the time I was landing in New York Sue was in labour, having been taken to the hospital by our neighbour.

Shortly after 10p.m. in New York, I was telephoned with my scheduled wake up call for the return flight but as soon as I put the phone down, it rang again with the New York Handling Agent telling me that my son James had been born. My first thought was that he was joking until I realised that only Sue and I knew the name we were going to call our child. He was born shortly after 2a.m. UK time that was 9p.m. in New York, so the news had reached me very quickly indeed. On arrival at the airport there was a telex from Laker operations giving the news of James' arrival. A gynaecologist doctor friend, also a radio amateur, sat in on the birth and gave Laker Operations the details of the birth.

Having checked out Tony on the outbound flight, my good friend Captain Gordon Steer told me to relax back in the cabin and celebrate the arrival in style. The arrival at Gatwick was with freezing temperatures and snow, Tony driving me to the hospital in a blinding snowstorm where I was able to meet my son James for the first time. Tony became one of James' godfathers but we have lost touch over the years. When I got back to the house, I found Sue's elderly aunt shivering in the cold, having forgotten how to switch the central heating on!

Laker had been, and still was, taking bookings for charters across the Atlantic. These were mostly affinity groups, all being members of the same club or organisation. As already mentioned, the rules were quite complex and I believe that most charter carriers were in breach of the rules from time to time. Freddie Laker made reference to the problem in a letter to staff in which he said that the commercial department was doing all it could to ease the situation. Those responsible for authorising fare levels seemed unable to make decisions causing affinity group travel to drop to almost nil. Freddie also said that fuel costs had risen by about 30% and urged crews to ensure that the most economical cruise procedure was always used.

Soon after James was born, the flying programme became busy again and life became very hectic with very little time off. New navigators had been recruited, all requiring company ground training followed by a check flight with me. Additionally of course, the recurring annual checks became due for those navigators already employed.

I was not involved in the recruitment of navigators, Dick preferring to do it himself and one navigator he employed, who shall be unnamed, got the company into quite a bit of bother. Dick interviewed and employed this navigator who had just finished a short contract flying with Aer Lingus. Apparently Dick inspected his flying logbook, but *not* his licence. I gave him his company training followed by a check flight, finding him to be a very competent navigator and had no problem checking him out. Some months later, Wally Luther was doing one of his routine navigation checks on the aircraft with the navigator in question doing the navigation. As they had not met before, Wally asked to see his CAA navigation licence and was quite staggered to see that he only held an Irish one. Wally was obviously quite concerned about this, but as the aircraft was en route to Gatwick and the navigator was obviously competent, he allowed him to continue navigating. However, on arrival at Gatwick he contacted the operations manager and insisted the navigator be suspended until he had obtained a CAA licence. Attie was very cross that this had happened and asked me if I had inspected his licence during his flight check. I had not, assuming that as Dick employed him, he would have done so. Happily no blame was attached to me but as a safeguard against future problems of this nature, Attie insisted that any crew member being flight checked must have his licence checked for validity by the supervising crewmember. That navigator's employment was terminated without notice and I have no idea where he went after the incident.

Both aircraft were flying very hard but they stood up to the task very well considering how much they were utilised. On one flight I operated, in mid Atlantic the number 1 compass failed and fairly soon after, number 2 developed very high deviation which fortunately I was able to deal with. Then an hour out of New York the hydraulic system failed and the undercarriage had to be lowered using the emergency procedures. Even those problems only delayed the aircraft by three or four hours!

A rather stupid incident occurred at Toronto. The aircraft took off quite normally but when the undercarriage was selected up, nothing happened and the wheels remained down in the locked position. It soon became obviously that a landing would have to be made back at Toronto, but as the aircraft was well above maximum landing weight, a large amount of fuel had to be jettisoned. Once on the ground, it was discovered that the ground engineer had omitted to remove the locking pins from the undercarriage. This should have spotted by the Flight Engineer whose job it was to ensure that the locking pins were on board. Nearly three hours later, the flight continued to Gatwick. A very expensive mistake!

On one take-off at Gatwick for New York with the engines only just reaching maximum thrust, there was a loud bang from number three engine and the take-off was abandoned. The aircraft was taxied back to the runway threshold where the engine was taken up to full thrust without a repeat of the problem. Cleared again for take-off, the aircraft had reached 60 knots when the engine gave another loud bang and the take-off was again abandoned. Unfortunately one of the compressor stages had failed and the engine had to be changed.

On another occasion, the aircraft had been fuelled for a departure to Mauritius and passengers were boarding. The ground engineer standing by the front of the aircraft heard the sound of metal breaking and felt the aircraft lurch. The boarding was stopped and several engineers inspected the nose bay where they thought that the noise came from. It turned out that a large bracket holding the nose gear had fractured and needed major repairs. Fortunately the other 707 was available and the flight was not badly delayed. The repair took several days under the supervision of a Boeing Company engineer.

Mauritius flights had a scheduled fuel stop at Djibouti southbound but at Jeddah northbound. The sector length from Djibouti to Gatwick into head winds was outside the range of the aircraft with a full passenger load, hence the stop at Jeddah. The airport at Mauritius was one of those difficult airfields where, due to high ground to the north, the take-off weight in that direction was severely restricted. Landings could be made to the south, provided that the approach was clear of cloud, which in the season we were flying, seldom was. On one flight, the runway was completely visible as the aircraft passed to the south, but on the downwind leg on two separate attempts, low cloud forced the approach to be abandoned. With the fuel state and crew duty hours getting close to limits, the captain elected to land with a tailwind slightly in excess of the maximum allowed. With plenty of runway available, this presented no problem, but it was 'Murphy's' law that by the next evening, the wind had completely swung around committing the aircraft to a down wind take-off, and making the fuel very tight for the flight to Jeddah. Mauritius is a beautiful island and the 36 hour turn round there gave ample opportunity for sightseeing despite us being very tired from the outbound night flight.

Scheduled services for International Caribbean Airways continued throughout the year, together with a very full charter flight programme to New York, Toronto, Ottawa and Montreal in the period from Easter to the end of September 1971. Early in October, I operated a flight commanded by Barry Rawlins, the Chief Training Captain, to Winnipeg using Free Gyro Grid navigation. As this was the first time that the Free Gyro procedures had been used, only one compass was un-slaved. The procedures worked perfectly and there was little or no deviation from track. The aircraft returned to Gatwick via Toronto giving no opportunity for a further check.

In mid October, one of the Boeings approaching Barbados had a fire warning that could not be cancelled despite the appropriate fire drills being carried out. On landing it was discovered that electrical wiring in the engine pylon that had been on fire, was still smouldering and had to be extinguished by the airport fire department. The aircraft was ferried to Trinidad where the pylon wiring was replaced together with burnt and overheated panels. I was sent to Trinidad with a Training Captain and a Flight Engineer to fly it back empty to Dublin where Aer Lingus were to complete the repairs. The senior ground Engineer of British West Indian Airways at Trinidad informed the Captain that one of the bolts holding the engine on to the pylon had become slightly 'Blue' from the heat of the fire. He was apparently unwilling to certify that it was safe to use but there was no spare available and the nearest was at the Boeing plant in Seattle. He telephoned Boeing to get an opinion from one of their engineers but was told that they could not possibly make a decision without seeing the bolt in question. It was left for him to decide and he, perhaps reluctantly, signed the aircraft as fit to fly and we flew to Dublin without incident. Later I learned that had severe turbulence been encountered, the bolt **could** have sheared; leaving no doubt that it should have been changed!

Late 1971/early1972, Freddie Laker negotiated with McDonnell Douglas for the purchase of two DC10–10 aircraft to be delivered late in 1972. Freddie envisaged that he would introduce a low cost scheduled service between Gatwick and New York in the not too distant future and the purchase of the DC 10s was to ensure that there would be sufficient capacity when the licence was granted. The scheduled service would become known as SKYTRAIN but would take much longer to implement than Freddie ever anticipated. Dick Bradley had been deeply involved with the planning and operational performance of the new aircraft, and never a man to shirk responsibility or spare himself, almost worked himself into the ground getting the aircraft on to the British Register.

Buying an aircraft is not like going into a showroom to buy a car. Before an aircraft is acquired, it is essential to know how well it can perform at those airfields from which it will operate. It must also be capable of flying the sector lengths of the airline's route structure plus a host of other things. The most important task was to get the aircraft on to the

British Register and that is easier said than done, particularly if a British operator has never operated that aircraft type.

It was quite usual for British Charter Operators to buy or lease second hand aircraft from scheduled airlines through aircraft brokers, but if they bought a new aircraft it usually would have been a type already in service with another British operator. If the aircraft was originally owned or leased by BOAC (British Airways), or another British operator, it would have a CAA approved Flight Manual from which it would be a relatively easy task to produce company manuals, establish company procedures and obtain CAA approval to operate the aircraft. If the aircraft type has NOT been on the British register, the whole procedure starts from scratch.

The 'Bible' of an aircraft is its Flight Manual and the manufacturer of the aircraft produces this. An American aircraft operated by a British company must have a Flight Manual that conforms to the Federal Aviation Authority (FAA) regulations, *and* the Regulations of the British Civil Aviation Authority (CAA). Therefore, there had to be a great deal consultation between McDonald Douglas, Laker and the CAA before the Flight Manual could be approved. The onus is on the airline to ensure that CAA's requirements are met, but there is liaison with CAA who will provide assistance and guidance as necessary.

Another requirement is that the CAA Flight Inspector assigned to an airline is usually qualified to fly the aircraft in addition to co-operating with the airline to approve the Operations Manuals and operating procedures. If the aircraft type is already on the British register, a Flight Inspector may already be qualified on the type and need not have to be specially trained by the airline. No Flight Inspector was qualified on the DC10–10 and the one nominated had to do his training with the Laker crews in Los Angeles. Dick Bradley, as expected undertook the Flight Manual and Operations Manual task virtually by himself.

The aircraft manufacturer will obviously do everything in its power to sell the aircraft by providing as much information as is needed. McDonnell Douglas were no exception in this respect, assigning Larry Raymond, a very experienced Performance Engineer to work solely with Dick and be based at Gatwick. He liaised almost daily with McDonnell Douglas as he and Dick worked their way through the Flight Manual and the operations manuals. The easy option with Operations Manuals is to use the manufacturer's manuals with suitable amendments reflecting company procedures. However, if this easier option is taken, there will still be the requirement to conform to CAA rules and furthermore, that option is not popular with crews who would be responsible for carrying a large manual and keeping it amended. Dick preferred to produce his own into which he wrote the normal and emergency company procedures for each and every mode of operation. He also produced simplified graphs or tables for fuel flight planning, take-off thrust, take-off speeds, tracks and distances, etc.

The engines fitted as standard on the DC10–10 were General Electric CF6–6D but Dick soon found that the thrust from these was insufficient at a given specified take-off temperature to give the take-off weight required at Gatwick for a direct flight to New York with a full load of passengers. After discussion with General Electric, MDC and CAA, a higher thrust rating called CF6–6D1 was agreed and this gave the required take-off weight. This change necessitated extra work being done to the performance section of the Flight Manual and Operations Manuals.

For aircraft fitted with three engines, CAA requirements are that if TWO engines fail, the aircraft can maintain the minimum safe height for the route to be flown. This could entail dumping fuel to get the aircraft down to a satisfactory weight to comply with this, but it must have sufficient fuel to fly from the point where the second engine fails to an airfield where it could land with a specified amount of reserve fuel. This was an extremely time consuming task but eventually Dick and Larry produced tables and graphs which satisfied CAA.

The DC10 did not have provision for a navigator on board, his place being taken by three Inertial Navigation Systems (INS) produced by the American Company, Litton. The magic 'Black Boxes' can navigate the aircraft virtually anywhere in the world far more easily, and certainly more accurately, than a human navigator can. My task was to learn how the equipment worked so that I could assist Dick to produce a chapter of the Operations Manual giving instructions on the use of the INS. I also had to produce a training course for pilots and flight engineers that I would conduct. On completion of the course there was a compulsory examination paper that crews had to pass before they could be cleared to use the equipment on the aircraft. British Caledonian Airways, who already had INS equipment installed on their 707 aircraft, gave me a course of instruction so that I could then instruct Laker crews. All at a fee, of course!

Before flight, the INS has to be set up very carefully and this procedure *must* be completed before the aircraft can be moved. The set up procedure requires entering the exact latitude and longitude in degrees, minutes and seconds, seconds being entered as decimals of a minute. The system mode switch is then set to the Alignment Mode to start the alignment procedure. Alignment takes between 15 and 20 minutes after which the green 'Ready Nav' light illuminates and the mode switch can be set to the Navigation position. Once the Mode switch has been set to 'Navigation' on ALL THREE systems, the aircraft can be moved. If the aircraft is moved whilst still in the Alignment Mode, or the systems have not been switched to 'Navigation', the alignment is destroyed and the whole procedure has to be repeated. The INS will accept very small errors of the latitude being entered, but internal circuitry will detect larger errors, flashing a warning light. However, it will accept ANY longitude entered since there is no means of detecting an error. This obviously makes the correct insertion of 'Present Position' on the ground of paramount importance. The requirements above have been described in a few lines but it took several months to produce everything to CAA's satisfaction. While all this was going on, I still had to fly three or more Atlantic round trips a month, which kept me very busy. The procedures detailed are for the INS equipment in use at that time and clearly could be quite different to today's more modern installations.

I returned to Gatwick from New York on 30th September 1972 and was asked to go immediately to see Attie in operations. Attie told me that Dick was seriously ill after inadvertently overdosing on pills that had been prescribed for him. Laker had several complete crews at Long Beach in California who were attending an MDC DC10 training course and would need to have company training whilst carrying out their flying training at Yuma Arizona on Laker's first delivered DC10. As it was most unlikely that Dick would be fit for some considerable time, Attie expected me to take up the reins and continue Dick's task that included company crew ground training in Yuma. I was quite taken aback by this and wondered if Attie really knew what he was asking of me. Attie said that he would take me off the navigator's roster and I could sit down with Larry Raymond and learn enough to teach the crews company procedures and get the aircraft back on time. Quite an undertaking!

Rather than go into the office every day, I collected the necessary manuals and took them home. Larry came down from time to time and together we went through the many and complex subjects that I needed to know. Fortunately, Dick had completed the writing of the operations manuals before he fell ill and CAA had approved most of the contents. I had 40 days to get up to speed with the aircraft, but with some help from Dick towards the end, I felt that I was ready for the task. I later told Dick that he should have had me working with him to bring the DC10 into service, which would have avoided the panic when he became ill. He could only agree but said that at the time he thought that I had more than enough to do without increasing my workload. I don't think that he ever realised how much my workload was increased by his illness!

On 2nd November 1972, Larry and I flew to Los Angeles where we were to board the Laker DC10 that was going to Yuma for flight training. In error we were misdirected to the wrong area at Los Angeles airport and by the time the boarding point was reached, the aircraft was already taxiing away to the runway for take-off. Unfortunately none of the crew saw us waving frantically trying to attract their attention and it was necessary to stay the night in Los Angeles. On the following day, MDC arranged for us to fly on a Lockheed Electra charter flight to Yuma where we met up with Alan Hellary and the crews.

Leaving Heathrow, I had almost 100kgs of excess baggage that included bags of manuals, crew briefings, navigation charts and other material needed by the crews on the course in Yuma, and the flight back to Gatwick. I was sure that something would be missing at Yuma but despite my misgivings, it all got there safely. Customs at Los Angeles were curious about the large number of bags that I had, but after opening one bag and being assured that they only contained manuals, they let them through.

I spent eight days in Yuma instructing crews during the morning and afternoon on most days, as and when they were free from flying duties. The aircraft was carrying out flying training round the clock with circuits and landings and airborne handling, only stopping long enough to refuel before the next detail. The aircraft was supposed to be delivered to Gatwick on 11th November and before I left Gatwick, Freddie Laker told me that he wanted the aircraft to do a low fly past over the runway at EXACTLY 11 o'clock on the morning of arrival. I was quite taken aback by his request and did say that flying the Atlantic cannot be that precise. His flippant reply was that as I had flown over the Atlantic so many times, I must surely know every wave and wind there! Freddie, ever the optimist!

The aircraft ran into trouble on training when it had several tyres burst and catch fire after a particularly heavy landing. It was thought initially that the undercarriage leg might have to be changed, but fortunately that was not necessary. However, the repairs disrupted the programme sufficient to cause the delivery flight to be put back 24 hours to 12th November. Once the ground training of crews on company procedures was completed, I issued them their own manuals and briefing sheets and was able to relax.

One afternoon with no crews to train, Larry and I drove over the border into Mexico at San Luis but found it to be such a frightfully dirty and smelly place, we just had a cool beer and headed back to Yuma! There was quite a contrast between the clean conditions of Yuma and the almost squalid condition of that Mexican border town. In fairness Larry told me that the tourist areas of Mexico are quite clean and tidy and very different to the town we visited.

There was plenty to see in the Yuma area, most notably the beautiful rugged scenery seen so often in Hollywood Western movies. The old prison in Yuma has been preserved as a museum and it was obvious that prisoners had to endure terrible and harsh conditions during their incarceration there. The cells were extremely small and had only bars at the windows with no glass to give protection from the weather elements.

At that time I was a member of the 'Lions' and a Convention was being held in Yuma. I was invited to take part and went to a breakfast meeting that started at 7a.m.! I was invited out to dinner on several evenings with Lions and their wives making my stay more enjoyable.

Attie's plan for the delivery flights was that four sectors would be flown in two days. On each day a complete crew would fly two sectors, so that when the aircraft arrived at Gatwick, the company would have two crews checked out. CAA required the sectors to be of reasonable length so that the INS navigation equipment and en-route navigation procedures were used. The sectors I chose were Yuma to New Orleans and New Orleans to Toronto for the first two sectors, followed on the next day by Toronto to Gander and on to Gatwick for the final two. The departure from Yuma was delayed by technical problems and the aircraft did not leave until early evening for New Orleans where, after a two hour transit, continued to Toronto arriving at just after 7a.m. There was to be a night stop in Toronto where the Laker station manager had laid on a publicity shot, capitalising on the fact that this was the first DC10 to be delivered to UK. The publicity shot went ahead but those crews operating the next two sectors had to rest during the stop over. For the delivery flights, the Commanders of the aircraft were MDC DC10 Training Captains Jack Allavie and Stan Freiburg. Although running late, the sectors went according to plan but en route to Toronto the Captain was told that there was a security alert at Toronto and all aircraft movements had been stopped. Fortunately the situation was resolved before the aircraft reached the approach area and no material delay arose.

The aircraft would normally have 345 seats fitted, but for the delivery flight there were only enough seats for the returning crews. The immense size of the aircraft was quite astonishing and I wish that I could have taken a picture of it. Walking across the widest part of the aircraft in flight without seats to hold on to was quite strange. The view from the flight deck was also quite different from other aircraft I had flown, being so much higher off the ground.

Apart from the training of crews on company procedures, I was also there to assist and supervise the operation of the Inertial Navigation Systems fitted on board, and navigate if it became necessary. Rather farcical really as I had no plotting charts or navigation aids that could be used over the Atlantic. Had all systems broken down, doubtless I could have got the aircraft safely across the ocean, but not with the degree of accuracy needed on the Atlantic. The CAA flying inspector had done the same course and flying training as the rest of the crews and was on board to observe and report on the operation. For some reason not known by me, Wally Luther the navigation inspector, was not on board.

Before I departed from UK, Attie told me which Captains he wanted to command the aircraft on the four sectors home and it was a great disappointment for Alan that he could not command the flight into Gatwick. The reason for this was that the two Training Captains were required to be cleared first so that they could then immediately start to check out others crews on training flights out of Gatwick. I was quite cross that Attie had made me the messenger for that instruction, feeling that it would have been more tactful of him to have contacted Alan direct by telephone and spoken to him about it.

By reducing the time on the ground at Toronto, the flight was back on schedule and remained so to Gatwick. The Captain on the sector Gander to Gatwick was the Laker Airways Chief Training Captain, and when told of Freddie's request he said that he wanted nothing to do with it. He told me to fully brief myself on the winds and when satisfied with the flight time, tell him when to get the aircraft airborne. With the best will in the world and the greatest expertise available, it is a matter of luck to fly for four and a half-hours across the Atlantic and get to Gatwick exactly when required, which is pretty well what did happen. About 11a.m., Gatwick ATC cleared the aircraft to carry out a low pass over the runway, followed by a wonderfully smooth landing. After the Customs Officer had given his permission, Freddie was the first person on board and was over the moon, shaking hands with everybody he saw. He threw his arm round my shoulders and said, 'I knew you would do it, you old bugger!' He is a year younger than me, hence 'the old.'

History was made that day as Laker became the first operator in Europe to bring the DC10 into its fleet! I am sure that Freddie knows that without the exceptional skill and expertise of Dick Bradley, it would not have happened as smoothly as it did. Freddie told me that there was a reception in the boardroom to celebrate the occasion and I was invited together with Sue, who was waiting with James in the car to drive me home. It was amusing to see James sitting on Freddie's desk playing with telephones and I seem to remember that it was Freddie who sat James on his desk. When I said that he would probably break a telephone, Freddie in his euphoric state said, 'That's OK, we will buy another!'

With two crews trained and two MDC Captains available, Freddie laid on demonstration flights to/from many airports in UK to publicise the aircraft, but also to clear more crews by getting their sectors flown. One Captain needing to be cleared was my old friend, Gordon Steer and he was put on the second DC10 delivery flight. Eight days after the first aircraft had been delivered to Gatwick, Gordon, First Officer Don Thomas, a Flight Engineer (cannot remember his name) and I went back to Los Angeles on TWA to collect the second aircraft. Inevitably the aircraft was not ready and the crew had a day to relax in Los Angeles before going to Los Angeles airport to prepare for departure. Even then there was a delay of four hours due to last minute engineering faults.

Prior to start up, the First Office inserted the actual aircraft's position into the INS to commence the alignment procedure. Doubtless due to operating in longitudes less than 100 degrees, he entered the Los Angeles longitude of 118 degrees 24.0 minutes west as 18 degrees 24.0 minutes west. Needless to say, it was quickly spotted by both Gordon and myself, and corrected. In the early days of crews using the INS, quite a few mistakes were made, crews entering east instead of west or south instead of north, easy errors to make and some the INS will accept.

Gordon flew the two sectors needed for him to be cleared, landing at Toronto where the aircraft night stopped before continuing to Gatwick, landing at 10p.m. on 23rd November 1972. Unfortunately for Gordon, the radio altimeter was not working for the landing at Gatwick and his landing was quite heavy causing a piece of ceiling trim to fall down close to where Cliff Wenzel, the Toronto Station manager, and his wife Grace were sitting. There was no was damage or injury to Cliff or Grace.

MDC Training Captain Dan Colburn who held a radio amateur licence commanded that delivery flight. Whilst en route, we spoke to hams at many places around the world using Dan's American call sign. One English amateur actually recognised my voice and called me by name and my personal radio amateur call sign.

During October 1972, CAA informed the company of changes in the renewal procedures of Navigation Licences. The normal system was that after the Authority had issued a licence, annually the holder had to submit logs and charts to the Authority in order to renew The Certificate of Competency. The changes allowed an approved company navigator to annually inspect logs and charts of each navigator employed by the company and issue Certificates of Competency. The only proviso was that the FIRST Certificate of Competency had to be issued by the Authority. As Deputy Chief Navigator of Laker Airways I was authorised to do this by the Head of Flight Crew Licencing (Examinations) CAA, my old friend Eric (Timber) Woods. This authority enabled Laker navigators to readily renew their licences through me without the need of going to CAA. I was not permitted to sign my own certificate and arrangements were put into place for it to be done by an authorised navigator of British Caledonian Airways. The navigation licence was invalid without a current medical certificate from an approved medical officer.

After the eight or so weeks of intensive work, Attie kept me off the 707 navigator's roster until mid January 1973. With Dick still not fit, there was a lot to catch up with in the office and additionally, I had two navigators who were due for their annual Flight Check. To ease the pressure, Attie had me check George Andrews going south to Barbados, where I left the crew and stayed for three days until the next flight arrived in Barbados. I then checked Brian Webb northbound back to Luxembourg, having had three very pleasant days in the sunshine of Barbados, which many others and I consider to be the most beautiful island in the Caribbean. It would have been much nicer if I could have had Sue with me for that mini break but she was not able to travel due to the flights being fully booked.

Late in January 1973, I was authorised by CAA to conduct flight tests for the issue of a Flight Navigator's Licence, subject to rules laid down by the authority. The only proviso was that I could NOT Flight Test candidates from my own company. I was never asked to exercise that authority.

International Caribbean Airways flights proved to be very popular and the passenger and freight loads continued at high levels. Apart from carrying out the annual checks on navigators as they became due, I found myself doing much more ground training of crews. Dick was back in harness again and had been told to take things much easier but being a workaholic, continued at much the same pace as before. I took over all navigation and performance training of crews for DC10, 707 and 1–11 aircraft, and the INS courses. These duties kept me off the flying roster until April 1973 when the 707 charter flights began their seasonal increase.

Wally Luther was a frequent visitor to the office, regularly inspecting navigation logs and charts of each flight. I also had to do the same thing, sometimes finding flights where the navigation procedures and/or fuel management had not been done correctly. If this occurred it was my responsibility to take the appropriate action with the navigator concerned. In the whole time that Wally was the company flight inspector, only on one occasion did he discover that a navigator had not performed his duties to Company and CAA requirements. On that occasion he insisted that I suspend the navigator in question until he was Flight Checked. Wally did frequent navigation inspection flights on all Laker aircraft, having right of access to the flight deck unless an emergency was taking place. This right of access was never abused and the

Captain's permission to enter the flight deck was always requested. Wally was not permitted to make any direct comments to crews during a flight, his brief being to observe and report in writing to the airline, who were then expected to take the necessary action.

A vacancy arose for a company Meteorological Minima Officer arose and Attie invited me to take up the appointment, which carried an increase in salary. Previously this task had been done by a pilot and required him spending time in the office to keep the company's operating minima up to date. It was ideal for me since I spent a great deal of time in the office between flights and could easily dove tail it in with my other office work. The salary increase was sufficient incentive for me to accept an appointment that did not materially increase my workload.

When time permitted, I flew supernumerary on the flight deck of BAC 1–11s to some difficult airfields such as Funchal, Corfu and Berlin Tegel to see the sort of problems with which crews would be confronted during approaches in difficult weather conditions. I particularly remember an approach into Funchal flown by Alan Hellary with wind and weather conditions at their worst. Alan seemed unconcerned and landed the aircraft safely in his usual highly professional manner.

On 11th September 1973, I flew from New York to Dublin where the aircraft was due to have a maintenance check, going on to Heathrow as passenger on Aer Lingus and then returning home. On the following day, 12th September, our daughter Melanie was born. The builders had just finished work, having been with us for 8 weeks extending the house to give more space for when Melanie arrived. Just after lunch with James sleeping and Sue having an afternoon rest, I decided to go to Lewes to buy furniture for the newly completed breakfast room. I arrived back home by 3.45p.m. to be greeted by Sue who was having sharp pains at regular intervals. She was quite sure these were not significant, but when I spoke to the Sister at the Maternity Unit, I was told to get her to the hospital immediately. I had to telephone Sue's mother who had agreed to stay with us to look after James during the birth, and then took Sue and James to the hospital. James and I got home just as Mother in law arrived and as I was going to be present at the birth, we waited for the telephone call to summon me when Sue was in labour. At 9.30 having heard nothing, I telephoned to learn that the birth was imminent. The sister said that it had all started so quickly that they had forgotten to telephone me, but asked me to get there as soon as possible. I was there within 15 minutes and had the pleasure seeing our daughter arrive into the world. Within a few minutes she was put into my arms and rewarded all my efforts by wetting me! Sue's mother was waiting for me when I got back at 11p.m. when very happily we 'Wetted the baby's head!'

In 1973 I flew about 400 hours, which was becoming my average per year, but with frequent ground training and many other duties to carry out, I was kept very busy. I quite enjoyed training and often received complimentary remarks from those I instructed. The Chief Medical Officer of CAA, Doctor Geoffrey Bennett, a qualified civil aviation pilot, was checked out to fly on Laker 707 aircraft as a First Officer and I had to give him his navigation and performance training. He enjoyed flying with the company and performed his duties well. Unfortunately, it was always necessary to have another First Officer on board, not to check him but more to ensure that he was not depriving a pilot of a job. Rather pointless I thought, as he did not fly that often.

Early in 1974 a Laker 707 was chartered to fly pilgrims from Nigeria to Jeddah for the Hadj at Mecca. It is amusing to look back on some of those flights and recall what went on. On one occasion the Senior Hostess discovered a pilgrim attempting to light a primus stove and cook food in the aisle of the aircraft, rather than eat what was provided. He could not understand why he was prevented from doing that! The state and smell of the aircraft during and after a Hadj flight was indescribable, particularly on the second phase when pilgrims were returning home, having been possibly living in extremely primitive conditions with little or no washing facilities. I went out to Jeddah with two navigators as Attie thought that navigators might be required to satisfy the crew duty hours on the flights to/from Lagos. An extra duty hour was allowed if a navigator was carried. It turned out to be unnecessary and after a week we navigators all travelled to Kano on the Laker 707 where we transferred to a scheduled British Caledonian service for London.

Getting into Jeddah was often quite difficult with Immigration and Customs formalities taking a long time and all baggage being closely inspected. It was not unusual to have books confiscated as unfit material to enter Saudi Arabia if there were pictures of women on the cover. Books with plain printed covers seldom caused problems regardless of their story content. Leaving Jeddah was also time consuming, as crew's visas had to be inspected and passports stamped to allow them to return to Jeddah. Despite an alcohol ban in Saudi Arabia, it seemed that there was a party going on somewhere every night, often hosted by wealthy Arabs. Plenty of 'liquid refreshment' was always available at those parties regardless of the alcohol ban!

Having flown all over the world, I had never visited Australia or New Zealand but a chance to do a trip to Australia came up late in January 1974. Laker had been chartered to provide two 707 flights to Sydney carrying members of a ship's crew. I was heavily engaged on training duties at the time of the first flight, but at my request, I flew on the second charter, operating the sectors from Singapore to Darwin and on to Sydney with a 30 hour stop before the return to Singapore. The crew flew as passengers on a Pan American Airways Boeing 747 to Bangkok, transferring to a Thai International DC8 for the last sector to Singapore, the journey taking 24 hours. It was a greatly changed Singapore from my first landing there in 1945 and subsequent visits with BOAC and Transglobe, so much so that I could scarcely recognise the place.

Two days later the 707 arrived and we flew it to Darwin for a fuel stop, and then on to Sydney. About two hours out of Singapore, the weather radar failed and it then became necessary to divert visually around the many very large thunderstorms en route, particularly between Darwin and Sydney. On the sector to Darwin, astro fixing was used, taking sights of stars I would not normally see in the Northern Hemisphere. Apart from the Southern Cross, that is not visible in UK, I think that the sky seen at home in winter is a great deal more interesting than in the Australian summer. It was quite amusing in the Southern Hemisphere to see the sky 'upside down' from the normal sight of it in England. The sector to Sydney was in daylight and only sun shots were possible and then only when clear of the large number of storm cloud en route.

On arrival in Sydney, it was hoped that QANTAS would have spares to fix the weather radar, as they previously owned the aircraft. Their engineers worked on it and it seemed to be serviceable when tested on the ground but as they no longer held spares for that particular type of radar, there was little more that could be done.

The 30 hours stay in Sydney gave me an opportunity to contact an old BOAC colleague, Johnny Harrop, who was then working for QANTAS, navigating a Sandringham flying boat to and from Lord Howe Island. I also spent some time with Bob Mann (and his wife Joy), the son of an American radio amateur K2CJN who I previously visited at his home in New York. Bob had gone work in Australia where he met and married Joy and was so taken with Australia that he made it his permanent home and became an Australian citizen. He and Joy took me on a long drive showing me most places of interest around Sydney, including Bondi and Manley beaches. Unfortunately I was so tired that I was unable to appreciate those sights. They did visit us in England and we have met up with them each time that we have visited Australia on holiday.

The following day, the aircraft took off about midday for a four hours flight to Darwin carrying the returning members of the ship's crew as passengers. Unfortunately the weather radar stopped working soon after departure and in consequence, the flight was very bumpy despite the pilots' efforts to avoid the many thunderstorms en route. The passengers, all male, were a hard drinking bunch and soon many became quite affected by their over indulgence of alcohol. On the final approach for landing at Darwin, a piece of the wing flap became detached and fell off. Unfortunately an aggressively drunken man saw this happen and after landing, tried to force his way onto the flight deck demanding to see the Captain. The police were called and he was forcibly removed from the aircraft and put in a police cell to be charged later with drunken and violent behaviour on the aircraft.

Meanwhile, the Flight Engineer inspected the aircraft flaps and confirmed that a section was missing. The airport authorities then searched the landing path and recovered the piece that had fallen off, bringing it back to the aircraft. The piece in question was a honeycombed strip that appeared to be just a fairing and had little to do with the aircraft's performance. The first action was to telephone Laker Engineering at Gatwick who in turn contacted CAA. After a long delay and many telephone calls, permission was given to continue the flight back to Gatwick.

Before departure the policeman asked the Captain if he wanted to charge the passenger who was in jail. He pointed out that if he was allowed back on board and more trouble arose, he could be taken off in Singapore where he would get a much stiffer prison sentence. The Captain withdrew the charges and the policeman, a giant of a man, escorted the passenger back to his seat and advised him to behave sensibly. The time in jail had certainly sobered him up and not a word was heard from him during the flight to Singapore or indeed, on the entire journey back to UK.

Notwithstanding that CAA had cleared the aircraft to fly, the Captain was concerned that the handling characteristics at the heavy take-off weight might be different from normal and as I was the company performance instructor, my opinion was sought. I knew Boeing 707 performance very well when all of the aircraft's surfaces are in place, but could not presume to make any judgement for the condition of the flap. I simply suggested that as CAA had approved the flight to proceed without any provisos, the take-off would be safe, but cautiously suggested that it might be prudent to increase the minimum speeds by a few knots. The Captain agreed with me, and the take-off was normal with the flight proceeding without incident to Singapore where another crew took over.

My crew left the aircraft at Singapore, returning to UK as passengers again on Thai International and Pan American Airways on another 24-hour marathon. The ambition to visit Australia had been achieved but I still had not visited New Zealand and it would be many years before I would manage to do that. After the flight, the Australian Aviation Authority complained to the CAA that the aircraft had been flown in Australian airspace whilst not being fully airworthy. There was talk of legal action being taken against Laker but nothing came of it.

The company's Air Operator's Certificate had been extended to permit flights to be operated in an area between 66 degrees 33 minutes north and 75 degrees north covering the Northern Canada routes. This was done to accommodate the Charter bookings that were being taken for flights to Western Canada including Vancouver, Calgary, Edmonton, Saskatoon and Winnipeg.

Dick and I discussed how these flights would be operated, the equipment to be carried and training required. Dick deferred to my knowledge of the route procedures but I decided not to operate the same system used by Transglobe Airways, primarily because the Canadian Pacific charts were no longer available, but really because I was not convinced that it was the ideal system. As far as the plotting charts were concerned, the Swissair Chart 770 with its grid lattice based on the Greenwich Meridian was my choice, but it was very large in size and perhaps more importantly, was much more expensive. Wally Luther insisted that a Kollsman Sky Compass should be carried for heading checks when the sun would be below the horizon in twilight conditions and no stars visible. This proved to be a wonderful aid for navigators.

All flight deck crew members were given a polar navigation course conducted by me, and inevitably there were some who were not very happy as we worked through the examples. I could appreciate their misgivings when seeing the large difference that could arise between magnetic and grid headings, but could only emphasise that by learning the procedures correctly and trusting the navigator, all would be well.

The Chief Medical Officer of CAA gave a very interesting talk to Flight Deck and Cabin Crew on arctic survival. The emphasis was on what to do in the event of a crash landing in the frozen wasteland of northern Canada in winter. He emphasised that in order to survive in the intense cold, body heat must be retained. To assist this, a very large roll of thick plastic material was to be carried in the hold, and according to Doctor Bennet, maximum heat would be retained by a group of people huddling together in the plastic, (saying tongue in cheek) preferably without clothes that could have become soaked by melted snow. The mind boggled at that! A great deal of survival equipment normally has to be carried by aircraft flying very close the North Pole, but as the Laker flights would not be that close, dispensation was given for lesser amounts to be carried.

Navigation using free gyro is not very different from navigating with conventional magnetic compasses, but as I pointed out in the last chapter, great care must be taken when the compasses are changed from magnetic to grid and converting astro true azimuths to grid. If the magnetic compass deviation is known, and it always should be, the difference between a magnetic heading and a grid heading is the algebraic sum of deviation and the amount of GRIVATION at the point on track where the change is to be made. Grivation is the angular difference between grid north and magnetic north at any point, and is the correction to be applied to grid tracks and headings to obtain magnetic. Easterly grivation is MINUS and westerly PLUS. Lines of grivation are overprinted on charts with a grid lattice and can be extracted to an accuracy of half a degree, or less.

The change over procedure is quite simple, first setting the Latitude Controller on the compass control panel to the latitude the aircraft is flying. With the aircraft heading unchanging, at a predetermined point on the track where the grivation is known, the compass is switched from its magnetic slaved mode to free gyro, and the compass card rotated to read the required grid heading. From the previous paragraph, it can be seen that the sign is reversed when going from magnetic to grid. When the compasses have been cross checked against each other, the second compass can be un-slaved using exactly the same procedure, at the end of which, both compasses should read the same. As soon as possible after the compasses are changed to Grid, an astro heading check is taken, repeating at 15-minute intervals until the compasses become stabilised. Thereafter, an astro check every 30 minutes is quite adequate. No two gyros behave exactly the same and it is normal to find them drifting slightly apart. The more accurate compass would be used with the Doppler System, the computer track adjusted for any deviation known and an allowance for the gyro drift trend when it has been established.

After agreement with Wally Luther, I started giving navigators polar flight checks on the North Atlantic, George Andrews being the first checked to be out. Only one compass was unslaved in order to ensure that the required level of track keeping was maintained, but navigators carried out polar procedures as though they were in the North Canada area. The first polar flight was in May 1974 when I flight checked Graham Brett on a direct flight (with no passenger load) of ten hours from Gatwick to Vancouver. The procedures worked well and no problems were encountered on either the outbound or the return flight. With my previous experience on the route, I was able to sign the area competency check forms for the crew who needed it.

In northern Canada today there are Fixed Tracks connected by lateral tracks, the structure being known as The Northern Track System. The selection of tracks and laterals is at the discretion of the operator, but it was mandatory to use the track system when flying over the prescribed area, random tracking not being permitted. During the time Laker was flying in that area, there were less tracks and laterals and their use was only mandatory at peak traffic times. The Company opted to use them at all times to avoid possible re-routing if the aircraft was in the area at the times they came into operation.

The Canadian Authorities rules were very rigid for flights within the Northern Track System, and no deviation from the cleared track was allowed until a re-clearance had been obtained from ATC. On one occasion whilst attempting to fly direct to Vancouver, it became obvious that there was insufficient fuel to continue and a request was made for re-clearance via a Lateral to Edmonton. The Captain was told to standby for re-clearance, but the First Officer who was flying the sector, without consulting anyone, turned on to the Lateral for Edmonton. This became apparent to ATC when the next position report was sent and they ordered the Captain to report to ATC on landing. They took a very serious view of the unauthorised deviation from track and a report was sent to the CAA in UK. The Company was officially warned that further infringements would result in losing approval to fly over Canadian Airspace. Had that happened, it would have severely penalised future flights. That particular First Officer was not very popular with the Captain, the Authorities, or the Company! I was flight checking Graham Brett on that flight and remember him being quite upset with the First Officer for changing course and not telling him that the alteration had been made.

Laker were approached by Marconi and asked if they would consent to have a navigation system called Omega fitted on the 707 aircraft for evaluation purposes. The equipment would not actually be used for the navigation of the aircraft but would enable Marconi and CAA to evaluate its in-flight performance. Each time the navigator fixed his position, the Omega position would be recorded on an evaluation form that was sent to Marconi and CAA. On the ground check before flight, the navigator had to set the correct time on the Omega System's clock and enter the aircraft's actual position, both settings being essential for the equipment to operate correctly.

Very briefly, the aircraft Omega equipment receives low frequency radio signals from transmitters sited throughout the area, these being fed into the aircraft Omega computer which computes the aircraft's latitude and longitude and displays it on a screen that constantly changes with the movement of the aircraft in flight. Ron Plater, another Navigation Inspector, was assigned to Laker to evaluate Omega results on the routes flown. Ron had been specially trained for the evaluation task by Marconi and was extremely competent and knowledgeable, ultimately replacing Wally Luther as Laker's CAA **N**avigation Inspector.

It was very early days for the equipment and many modifications were necessary before it was of any significant use as a navigation aid. Furthermore, although the intention was to have world coverage, at the time of the trials not all ground stations were operational and certainly not sufficient to provide first class fixing. If reception became intermittent the system would go on to 'Memory', using the track and ground speed last computed. If it remained on Memory for long periods of time, ambiguity of position could result due to something called 'Lane Slip'. On the Barbados route, the results were not impressive due to lack of coverage by the ground transmitters, but the North Atlantic results were much better.

When first used on polar routes, massive fixing errors occurred and needed to be investigated. Fairly quickly it was determined that the errors were due to the compasses being operated in free gyro mode, this giving incorrect headings to the Omega computer. The computer must know fairly accurately what the aircraft heading is and compare it to the computed track between two points. This necessitated that we had to decide which plotting chart would be used, and of the APC770 that I preferred and the 3097G, doubtless for reasons of cost Dick selected the 3097G. Marconi then had to write a separate computer programme for the area where free gyro grid navigation techniques using the 3097 chart would be used. A compass change over switch was then fitted to the Omega Controller labelled Magnetic/Grid, it being switched to Grid at the same time that the compasses were changed to the grid reference. The massive position errors that had been experienced due to the difference between grid and magnetic headings immediately disappeared. However, if the gyro deviation reached too high a value, the system would still be unable to resolve the ambiguity between the correct position in the correct lane and another position in an adjacent lane. The trials went on for a very long time before being accepted as an accurate navigation aid.

A comparison of Omega operating with **perfect** reception of the required signals against the Inertial Navigation System on an eight hours sector showed Omega to be superior. With no Lane Slip occurring, Omega would **always** give the aircraft's correct position, whereas the Inertial Systems in use at that time would suffer from some real gyro wander, three miles per hour being the maximum allowed. Typically in 1980, Inertial Navigation Wander averaged about one mile per hour giving an error of about 8 miles at the end of an eight hours sector. Omega operating perfectly would have no error. However, in all fairness today's latest State of the Art Inertial Navigation systems have Laser gyros that have effectively eliminated real gyro wander, so there is little to choose between them. I suppose most of the Omega 'bugs' must have been eliminated as some years later in January 1977 I did a flight from Barbados and was able to report that the Omega fixing was perfect.

Throughout May, June and July 1974, I was kept busy giving polar flight checks to navigators on flights to/from Vancouver. I gave Dick his check in June, finding him woefully slow but he navigated exceptionally well considering how little practice he had. He found the 10 hours 15 minutes sector very exhausting and spent most of the day off in Vancouver in bed. On the return flight he was much more confident, carrying out the polar procedures with greater speed and ease.

Polar flying gave me personally a greater sense of achievement than any other form of navigation. It was hard work and with little or no Loran coverage, the fixing aids en route were short range and very limited, necessitating regular astro fixing. Map reading was always a back up and for that reason, Topographical charts were always immediately to hand for use by the pilots when cloud conditions allowed sight of the ground. This was never easy in any season, the landscape being completely snow covered in winter, often obscuring land features, whilst in summer the snow melted and the area became flooded which changed the shape of lakes and landmarks. It was possible to map read using the weather radar when the ground was obscured by cloud, and if a *positive* feature could be seen as a relative bearing and distance on the radar, it was always more accurate than looking out of the flight deck windows.

A curious thing about map reading by radar in winter is that ground indications become reversed. Frozen lakes give hard returns looking like land on the radar screen. Land also frozen, but covered by several feet of snow give a soft return looking like water on the radar. One can only admire the Canadian Bush pilots who flew regularly in all weather conditions into the many small airfields, relying largely on map reading and their knowledge of the terrain en route. Baron Holstein my wartime Sunderland pilot was a Bush pilot during his career.

Only on one occasion did I fail a navigator on his polar route check. Although a very experienced navigator, he always became extremely nervous when being given his annual check. On a direct flight to Vancouver he became so flustered with me on the flight deck that I had to take over to get the aircraft back on track and flying in the correct direction. He was a heavy smoker and at one time when trying to map read through broken cloud, he had a lighted cigarette in each hand and one alight in the ashtray on the navigation table. To the discomfort of

Alan Hellary who was the Captain, he leaned across him trying to see the ground and burned a hole in Alan's shirt. Alan, a non-smoker, was not amused! He failed that check and on the ground we went through what he had done wrong, trying to find some way of restoring his confidence. I discussed the problem with Alan and we agreed that I would stay away from the flight deck, only going there if called upon. He navigated the return flight perfectly using the correct procedures and passed his flight check. Some may think that the navigator in question might have gone to pieces in an emergency, but this was far from the truth as he was on board one of the 707s when a 'Jet Upset' occurred and his actions in that emergency were highly commended by the Captain.

I did a flight to Saskatoon that gave me the opportunity of meeting and having dinner with a cousin and his wife. They were sheep farmers who lived about 100 miles north of Saskatoon and drove the 200 mile round trip just to meet for the first time. This was a very infrequent destination for Laker and that was the only opportunity I ever had to meet them.

The take-off on the return flight from Saskatoon was quite frightening with the aircraft only just reaching flying speed at the end of the runway. Had an engine failed on take-off, there would have been little chance of getting airborne. Back at Gatwick when I analysed the take-off, I found that it was due to a combination of high temperatures, low atmospheric pressure, variable wind and the aircraft heavier than thought to be. The flight was perfectly legal having observed all the requirements of the regulations. I was able to determine that the temperature given by ATC in the control tower was about five degrees cooler than the actual temperature at engine level on the black tarmac runway. (One Canadian company did not use the reported temperature, but lowered a thermometer from the flight deck window to engine level and used that to determine the regulated take-off weight.) In Laker performance was calculated using geographical elevation rather than pressure altitude, an option taken up by Dick and allowed by the regulations. However the engines produce **less** thrust at higher pressure altitudes and this doubtless affects the take-off run. Combine that with a variable wind speed and direction plus the extra weight of hand baggage carried on by passengers, it is quite clear why it was so marginal! Frankly, I could never understand why Dick Bradley used geographical elevation instead of the safer pressure altitude, but as it was legal to do so and gave an increased take-off weight, I suppose that he thought that he was doing what was best for the company.

With full passenger loads, most polar flights were planned to route via Keflavik for a fuel stop. Unfortunately the weather there can often be poor with very strong winds, low clouds and heavy rain. The price of fuel at Keflavik was very expensive and it was cheaper to carry fuel up to the maximum landing weight of the aircraft on arrival, giving very adequate fuel reserves. If bad weather prevented landing, the preferred alternate airfield was Prestwick in Scotland, but a diversion there would almost certainly put the crew out of duty hours. I well remember one diversion en route to Keflavik from Gatwick when I was flight checking a good friend, Dennis Dinneen an ex BOAC colleague, who was also a neighbour when I lived in Southampton and whose daughter is my god-daughter. With each weather report, the conditions got progressively worse and were well below limits for landing. George Newby, the Captain, was on the point of returning to Prestwick but after a short discussion. I managed to persuade him to continue on track to Sondestrom. He was quite uncertain about this, but when I told him that I had been there many times and the weather was seldom bad, he decided to divert there having first obtained from Keflavik ATC a weather report for Sondestrom that gave good landing conditions. On arrival, it was a beautiful day with scarcely any cloud to be seen and the aircraft landed with no trouble whatsoever. George, suitably impressed, passed the word on to the Chief Pilot with a recommendation that Sondestrom should be used on westbound flights when Keflavik weather was marginal. Sondestrom certainly was the most suitable alternate for westbound flights as it kept the aircraft going in the same direction as the ultimate destination airfield. Eastbound flights continued to use Prestwick as it also kept the aircraft going in the right direction. Some months before, a Laker Boeing 707 I was navigating, landed at Sondestrom on a flight from Vancouver to Gatwick with a planned fuel stop at Keflavik. On that occasion the load was very heavy and with abnormal headwinds instead of tailwinds, the fuel on board was marginal. When the head winds became much stronger we were committed to landing at Sondestrom, there being insufficient fuel available to continue to Keflavik and have Prestwick as the alternate airfield.

When flying over or near to Greenland, the views from the aircraft are magnificent with visibility often much greater than theoretically possible. On one occasion I was seeing mountains 400 miles away quite clearly, being able to identify them on a topographical chart. I remember reading Ernest Gann's book *Fate is the Hunter* in which he referred to the incredible visibility he experienced in the same area, explaining it as some sort of light refraction. During the war, quite a few aircraft being ferried to UK were lost over Greenland and in recent years some have been recovered from the glaciers. Those found, all things considered, were in good condition, having been preserved by the ice and after overhaul it was even possible to run the engines. Some aircraft were sound enough to fly again!

The American Air Force had bases in Greenland at Sondestrom and Thule together with radar stations dotted over Greenland, all of which could provide aircraft with fixes on request. In typical American style, the radar stations had strange names for these stations such as 'Big Gun', 'Sob Story' and 'Sea Bass'. The aircraft usually tracked directly from Big Gun to Sondestrom, the track passing fairly close to 'Sob Story'. On one occasion in extremely clear conditions, I could easily see the sun being reflected by the very large radar dome of the installation at 'Sob Story'. As I was talking on VHF to 'Sob Story' at the time, I told them that I could see their radar dome, whereupon the radar operator went outside and said that he could see our contrail. Usually when in contact with these very isolated outposts, a stewardess was allowed to talk to them on the radio giving their operators a morale boost.

Further deliveries of DC10 aircraft were received and eventually, by March 1979 Laker would have 6 Series 10 aircraft in operation. The DC10–10 had taken over the Barbados route from the 707s, operating up to twice weekly in addition to operating very frequent charter flights to New York, Montreal, Toronto and eventually to Florida and Los Angeles. The DC10–10 could not possible to fly direct to Florida or Los Angeles with a full load and a stop was usually made in each direction at Bangor in Maine. The DC10 charter flights were very popular with passengers as it's wide body and large cabins allowed them the freedom to walk around during flight. Two years after the start of DC10 operations, the flights had been so successful that the first DC10 was completely paid for. Freddie Laker, travelling to New York on a 707 that I was navigating, came on the flight deck for a chat and gave me that piece of good news!

The period from 1974 to 1977 is very hazy in my mind and my Flying Logbook does very little to assist. However, it is sufficient to say that in the period in question, considerable expansion did take place. The additional DC10s were actively engaged on Atlantic charter routes, inclusive tour holiday destinations and International Caribbean Airways scheduled services. Charter flights were operated by DC10s to destinations in Western Canada to supplement those flown by the Boeing 707s. As the DC10 used inertial navigation and true headings were available from that system, the free gyro operation used by 707s was not necessary. CAA insisted that emergency procedures be put into place against the possibility of ALL three inertial systems becoming unserviceable, a most unlikely occurrence. The procedure adopted was not difficult but it did require amendment of the operations manual to cover the procedures and crews had to be instructed in its use. It was a grid navigation system using a Polar Stereographic chart based on the North Pole and with its grid based on the Greenwich meridian. Initial Great Circle tracks had to be converted to grid, this being achieved by ADDING the longitude at the reporting point to the true track on the flight plan. If one inertial system failed, one of the slaved gyrocompasses would be unslaved and the heading set to the true heading indicated by a serviceable INS PLUS the longitude in whole degrees of the aircraft position. As no gyro correction device is fitted, the compass card would need to be adjusted by one third of the 15 degrees real wander per hour. Corrections would be applied at the rate of 5 degrees every 20 minutes until the area of magnetic certainty is reached when the compass could be re-slaved. At that point the compass would be reset to the grid heading PLUS the grivation at the same point. The procedure worked extremely well and crews who practised on the route, found that the calculated magnetic heading was seldom more that a degree or two in error.

In the period from the acquisition of the first DC10 up to 1977, the battle to start SKYTRAIN scheduled services was waged with most scheduled carriers objecting to it. Eventually permission was obtained and on 26th September 1977, in a blaze of publicity a DC10–10 SKYTRAIN took off from Gatwick for New York with a full load of passengers. Many prospective passengers were unable to get on board, some continuing to queue all night for the following day's flight. At the incredibly low fare, the response from the public was tremendous and day after day the aircraft was completely full in both directions with many unable to buy a ticket for the flight. People could take their own food on board or they could purchase it from the cabin staff. I flew back from New York on Skytrain and seated beside me was a Jewish gentleman who had brought a small hamper full of kosher food and drink. As time went by, Freddie found that most people did not want the bother of providing their own food and normal in-flight catering was resumed.

The success of the DC10 Series 10 on the Atlantic charters and subsequently on Skytrain was quite outstanding and it was not long before scheduled Skytrain services to Los Angeles replaced charter flights. With the DC10–10 unable fly to/from Los Angeles non stop with a full load, Freddie Laker became interested in acquiring DC10–30 aircraft which, with its greater range, could fly direct to Florida and Los Angeles. Dick Bradley commenced evaluation of the DC10–30 with Pratt & Whitney and General Electric engines.

Another task was dropped into my lap at fairly short notice when Freddie negotiated with Cathay Pacific to acquire two Boeing 707–351B aircraft to replace the two ex QANTAS 707–138Bs. My task was to work with CAA to get the aircraft on the British Register. At first sight it did not appear to be a difficult task, particularly as 707–200 series aircraft were on the British register. It suddenly became very difficult when I learned that the Cathay aircraft had different engines from those in the approved CAA Flight Manual for British Airways and British Caledonian 707 aircraft. To complicate matters further, the entire fuel system was in pounds instead of kilograms! Although a Crown colony, the Hong Kong Civil Aviation Authority allowed Cathay Pacific to use a flight manual unique to their authority and certainly not acceptable to CAA. This required careful thought and a whole series of discussions took place between Laker, CAA and Boeing before matters could be resolved. Boeing did have a Flight Manual in pounds for a 707 fitted with the engines of the Cathay aircraft, but that was not CAA approved. Boeing quoted an extremely high price to produce this in a CAA Approved Flight Manual format, but this was not acceptable to Freddie Laker. His view was that it would have been impossible to recoup the high cost within the short period of time that he intended to operate the aircraft. (They were only scheduled to operate until the end of 1979). Boeing offered a CAA approved manual at a cost of about £1000 but it was in kilograms, not pounds and the engines were slightly different in thrust rating. After discussions with a CAA Flight Manual Inspector, Laker was eventually allowed to use that Flight Manual provided that a Laker produced amendment to the Flight Manual accurately converted kilograms to pounds, and gave a performance weight reduction in respect of the lesser thrust of the engines. It was also necessary to produce a supplement containing take-off graphs for each runway at every airfield the aircraft was scheduled to use. Quite a monstrous task, but the CAA was eventually satisfied and the amended Flight Manual was approved. The CAA inspector Bill Horsley told me that this would be the last time that CAA would allow a Flight Manual with a mixture of pounds and kilograms.

On 22nd November 1977 I flew to Hong Kong by British Airways to spend a week looking over the first aircraft before acceptance. It had conventional navigation equipment fitted, including a Kollsman sextant. To give the necessary Atlantic MNPS requirement, a dual Inertial Navigation System was being installed. Whilst assisting in the acceptance of the aircraft, I was also there to provide navigation cover should it be needed on the flight back to Gatwick.

Seven days after my arrival in Hong Kong, an acceptance air test was flown and the aircraft departed for Gatwick. It almost did not depart due to the suspected failure of both Inertial Navigation Systems. On the pre-flight check no display could be seen on either display unit and it took some time to discover that some idiot had turned the brilliance of the displays down to nil. Two Laker Captains, both 707 training Captains, were on board and they each flew two sectors back to Gatwick landing at Bangkok, Bahrain and Istanbul. These sectors qualified them to train and progressively check out other pilots on the new type. The aircraft night-stopped in Bahrain and I was able to have dinner at the home of AERAD controller Ron Parfitt and his wife Kate who had moved from Tripoli to Bahrain.

On arrival at Gatwick, the aircraft was soon inspected and put into use training crews. The INS equipment was located in the forward freight hold and there was great concern that the cooling to it might be inadequate. It also had to be protected against loose baggage that would be bulk loaded into the forward hold. A dual installation of INS is not realistically adequate for flights over the Atlantic, as there is no margin against one becoming unserviceable prior to entry into MNPS airspace, the point at which it is mandatory for two to be serviceable. The second Boeing 707–351B rapidly followed and this effectively sounded the death knell for a navigator with the Boeing 707–138Bs then scheduled to be withdrawn from service. My flying career lasting 37 years was virtually at an end and I only flew two more Atlantic round trips before taking up a pre-arranged desk job as Dick's deputy. The remainder of the navigators were made redundant and soon left the company to seek other employment

I suppose after 37 years of flying, I should have been quite happy to 'hang up my wings' and settle down. Not a bit of it! I loathed being grounded and had I been able to carry on flying, doubtless I would have done so. However, in the last two years of flying, my medical examinations had shown slight irregularities with my heart which had made me undergo medical checks more rigorous than normal, perhaps indicating that a change of pace was required.

Looking back over the years, I remember the nice things that happened, but seldom the bad ones. That wonderful feeling of climbing through cloud and breaking out into brilliant sunshine, seeing the aircraft's shadow chasing along on the clouds below. The joy of seeing just before dawn, the sheer brilliance of the planets Venus and Jupiter with their light fading as the sun appeared. The wonder at night of looking to the sky and seeing the magical canopy of stars in their millions that have been there since time on earth began. The feeling of exhilaration as the aircraft flies seemingly effortlessly through the sky leaving one with the thought, 'How on earth did this metal monster ever get into the air?' I am digressing!

Freddie Laker had become seriously interested in acquiring DC10–30 aircraft, which with its greater range, could fly direct to Florida and Los

Angeles. In September 1978 a Cargo Airline based in New York had a DC10–30 Combi aircraft surplus to its requirements, a type that could be used in a passenger or freight configuration. Freddie told me to go to New York to look through the records of that particular aircraft to see if was capable of operating non-stop to Los Angeles with 377 passengers and their baggage. I spent a day there and it became quite obvious to me that the aircraft was basically much too heavy and could not perform the required task. Having reported this to Freddie by telephone, he then told me to go on to Los Angeles and get further information from McDonald Douglas for the newer Series 30 aircraft. I had to go via Tulsa to see people at the American Airlines Maintenance Facility and eventually on to Los Angeles and Long Beach where I spent several days gathering information for Dick Bradley and the company. In Tulsa it was the tornado season and local radio stations constantly warned of tornados. I never saw one but what I have seen on TV makes me glad that I did not! Whilst I was in Los Angeles, the DC10–10s were grounded following the fatal crash of an American Airlines DC10 just after take-off, when an engine dropped off the wing. There was a lot of speculation as to what precisely caused the accident, but after about a week, the grounding was lifted and I flew direct back to Gatwick in an empty Series 10. The remedial action was to replace the bolts holding the wing engines to the wing pylon, but subsequently it was discovered that faulty engine change procedure used by American Airlines was probably responsible.

I considered the DC10 to be a superb aircraft and was quite happy at the prospect of the company acquiring the longer range Series 30. However the Laker technical director was not quite so keen, feeling that the acquisition of more aircraft simply to fly direct to Florida and Los Angeles was not justified and he asked me to indicate this in my report. In some ways he was right because a comparison of the cost of the Series 10 aircraft operating via Bangor in each direction for both destinations showed it to be more economical than the Series 30 on non-stop flights. However, passengers obviously preferred to fly non-stop to their destination and Freddie intended to satisfy that preference. Furthermore, there was always the possibility of flying charters to destinations outside the range of the Series 10 that could extend the utilisation of the Series 30 aircraft. The DC10's reputation had suffered badly and passenger confidence was seriously eroded due to the two fatal crashes that had occurred. When the cause of the crashes had been established, Freddie's confidence in the aircraft was fully justified.

Dick Bradley thoroughly evaluated the Series 30, finding that with General Electric CF6–50C2 engines it was just a little short of take-off weight to give the range capability required. Other DC10 operators were operating Series 30 aircraft fitted with General Electric 50C1 or C2 engines and others had orders being processed with similar engines. It came as a surprise at a McDonnell Douglas conference I attended when reference was made to Laker taking up the option of the up-rated CF6–50C2B engine that would give an extra 8000 pounds of take-off weight. Freddie, Dick and MDC had been discussing this option for some weeks and I believe that Laker was probably the first customer to be offered the up-rated engine. There was some comment amongst those attending the conference who thought that they should have been among the first to be given information about the new rating.

It is perhaps appropriate here to say that when buying a new aircraft such as a DC10, the choice of the engines can often be an option given to the buyer by the aircraft manufacturer. It was usually Pratt & Whitney, General Electric or Rolls Royce engines that the manufacturers offered, but the thrust levels would not necessarily be the same for each engine type. Freddie Laker and Dick certainly did evaluate all engine types on offer before the General Electric engine was chosen. Of course, some aircraft are designed for a specific engine. For instance, Korean Airlines and (I believe) North West Airlines operated Pratt & Whitney powered DC10s that were known as the DC10–40.

Freddie, being a very shrewd person, negotiated a performance guarantee drafted by Dick for both Series 10 and 30 aircraft. This was in the form that with specified en-route upper winds, the aircraft would be able to carry out the task for which it was intended. For the Series 10 aircraft it was 345 passengers and their baggage non-stop to New York JFK, and for the Series 30, 378 passengers and their baggage non-stop to Los Angeles. The return sectors, normally with tailwinds, presented no difficulties. The guarantee also covered the take-off weight at Gatwick under given temperature and wind conditions. With the Series 30 performance guarantees in place, orders for five Series 30 aircraft went ahead. The appearance of both DC10 series 10 and series 30 was very similar with the only obvious visual difference being an additional undercarriage leg positioned between the two main legs of the series 30. Curiously, although the series 30 max take-off weight was considerably greater than the series 10, if the additional undercarriage leg was not operational, its max take-off weight reverted to the series 10 weight.

Dick Bradley had been immersed for some time with the task of getting the DC10–30 on the British Register, working again with Larry Raymond, but as there were many performance differences between the Series 10 and 30, Dick had to start things from scratch. Needless to say, once again he almost worked himself into the ground achieving it. However, this time I was kept informed about what was going on and was able to help. In November 1979, Gordon Steer and other crew members attended a McDonald Douglas DC10–30 conversion course in preparation for the new aircraft after which Gordon operated his first commercial flight to New York JFK on 21st December 1979. He followed this by operating a direct flight to Los Angeles with a full passenger load on 1st January 1980. There was considerable publicity when Freddie accepted the first DC10–30, the entire aircraft being gift wrapped and tied with a large ribbon bow.

I cannot remember the exact date, but it was about this time that Freddie Laker was made a knight, an honour that was well and truly earned by his long and continuous battle to establish the British Charter industry. I can remember seeing him on TV when he said that he was quite surprised, but nevertheless very happy, when Prime Minister James Callaghan honoured him. To his credit, the knighthood did not change Sir Freddie in the slightest and he remained the same likeable and approachable person.

Sir Freddie had been interested for some time in the new twin engine Airbus A300 with a view of it operating his European Inclusive Tour holiday flights. There were many meetings between Airbus and Dick who evaluated its performance and made his own recommendations. The aircraft used performances procedures that were not in general use but which proved to be most beneficial. It had an extremely good range with a full passenger load and flights to the Canary Islands would no longer be marginal and subject to possible en-route fuel stops. Laker duly ordered three aircraft, the first to be delivered in December 1980, with options for several more. This time Dick kept me completely in the picture and I was sent to the Airbus School at Toulouse in February 1979 to attend a two weeks performance course. I left home on a Sunday on a BCAL flight to Paris Charles de Gaulle airport where I took a taxi to Paris Orly airport for the flight to Toulouse. I almost missed the flight having completely forgotten the one-hour time difference between London and Paris. Passengers were boarding the flight when I realised the correct time and I was lucky to get on board as they were filling up the aircraft with stand by passengers. I seem to recall that the passenger announcements for French domestic flights were only given in French.

Toulouse is a very attractive city and I found much to do and see in my leisure time. Others on the course included a CAA inspector who was attached to Malaysian Airways for the purpose of getting the A300 on the Malaysian Register. Four of us on the course, travelled around together in the leisure time available, making a point of having dinner at a different small café each evening. Some small cafés were really just private houses with seating for about twenty people, but the food was really superb. We always had a drink before dinner at any bar that took our fancy, sampling some very nice French wines.

I must say that Airbus Industries looked after us extremely well, providing transport to/from the hotel each day of the course. At the Airbus school there was a large restaurant for the use of people on courses, catering for the tastes of the many different nationals attending. Due to the very large number of students, each course was allocated a time to eat which had to be strictly adhered to. I found it to be a superbly conducted course and much more comprehensive than the DC10 performance course that I attended in Long Beach with McDonald Douglas. The performance back up given by Airbus was also extremely good and they wrote a Take-off Weight computer programme specifically designed for Laker operations that included everything that Dick required of it. On the last day of the course, transport was laid on to the airport for the flight home and once again I had to change airports in Paris. I arrived at Charles de Gaulle airport well in time for my flight to Gatwick only to find that the BCAL flight had been cancelled, necessitating a four-hour wait for the next one.

Unfortunately Dick's health had been deteriorating for some time, and it was no surprise when he suffered a severe stroke. I cannot remember the exact date when this happened but have an idea that it was mid/late 1979. Laker operations telephoned me on a Saturday morning to tell me that Dick had been taken into Crawley hospital but had no news of his condition. I immediately drove to the hospital where I was informed that he was in a stable condition and was allowed to see him. The stroke had affected the right side of his body and the right side of his face making speech almost unintelligible. Nevertheless he attempted to converse with me trying to give me instructions of what I should do during the following week. I could only tell him to rest and recover as quickly as possible. He was in a small ward but later on Freddie Laker's instructions, was moved to a private room.

I returned home where Sue told me that Freddie Laker had telephoned three times and wanted me to call him urgently. Once in contact I was able to give what information the doctors had given me and to advise him that it was unlikely Dick could return to work for some considerable time, if at all. Freddie's reply was that I was now in charge and had better start making decisions for the future. On the following Monday morning, Freddie stepped out of his Rolls Royce just as I was parking alongside. My first words to him were that I would need to employ someone to help in the office to cope with day-to-day matters. His answer was short and to the point, 'You are in charge and you make you own decisions'. Fair enough, but easier said than done!

Losing Dick effectively lost two people from the Navigation Department, as he must have worked at least 70 hours a week. I looked for someone suitable to take on and was most fortunate to talk to a Laker 707 Training Captain who asked me if I needed any one to assist me. Apparently one of his neighbours, an ex BOAC and British Caledonian navigator named Harry Cowsill, had become redundant from BCAL some time before and was looking for suitable work in aviation. As Freddie had given me the authority to hire whoever I deemed necessary, I interviewed Harry on the following day and offered him employment provided that he could start work immediately. We had never met during our BOAC days but he turned out to be a thoroughly reliable and conscientious person who could perform most tasks allocated to him. We became, and still are, close friends

The DC10–30 operated very well but it was soon noticed that its fuel consumption was greater than it should have been, giving doubts about its performance guarantee. Degradation in the en route performance of an aircraft as it ages is quite normal. Engines become dirty and lose power needing more fuel to compensate for this, but by far the most important item affecting performance is the progressive weight increase. After manufacture and before delivery, the aircraft is weighed in its pristine clean and dry state. From then on it starts to accumulate dirt and moisture, the amounts accumulated being quite significant, particularly in the early years of its life. For this reason, the aircraft has to be weighed at intervals laid down by CAA. Moisture accounts for a lot of the increase in weight, something that cannot be avoided. The sound proofing in the aircraft absorbs moisture from the humidity of the air and as the aircraft flies a large number of hours each day, there is very little 'drying out' time. It would not be unusual to find that a wide-bodied aircraft weighed two years after its delivery would have considerably increased its weight. This weight 'growth' causes more fuel to be consumed at an approximate rate of 3.5% of the extra weight per hour. For example: If the aircraft's weight has increased by 1000 pounds, on a flight of 11 hours to Los Angeles, it will need 11 x . 035 x 1000 = 375 pounds (about 59 US gallons) of extra fuel. If the regulated take-off weight would not permit this, the payload would have to be reduced by 375 pounds or 2 passengers! Clearly it can be seen how important it is to keep the aircraft as clean and dry as possible. The aircraft performance is constantly monitored and an appropriate adjustment made when calculating the fuel required. Normally this would be shown as a percentage increase of the fuel required from the manufacturers fuel data.

The DC10–30 had an improved Thrust Rating Computer fitted which was intended to assist crews to set the correct take-off thrust for either full or reduced thrust. Dick had his own method of calculating reduced take-off thrust which crews were completely at home with and really did not need to refer to the computer fitted, other than to cross check for a gross error. A DC10–30 about to depart from Prestwick for Los Angeles had been given the take-off conditions by the Control Tower which *seemingly* allowed a take-off towards the north west AND allowed a small reduction of take-off thrust. On the take-off run, the aircraft accelerated quite slowly, so slowly in fact that half way down the runway the Captain realised that something was wrong and immediately applied the maximum possible thrust. The aircraft lifted off the runway so late that the undercarriage lightly touched an approach light causing damage to it. The Captain, unaware that anything was wrong, retracted the undercarriage and turned on course for his first reporting point. The Controller advised him that the aircraft had damaged an approach light but the Captain decided that the aircraft was undamaged and continued to Los Angeles, a decision which the CAA questioned and resulted in an enquiry being set up by the Accident and Investigations Branch of CAA.

As the Company Performance Instructor I was told to look into it and discover what had caused the incident. On inspection of the flight documentation, I saw that the take-off had been to the north-west and a small thrust reduction had been calculated. In fact, the First Officer incorrectly evaluated the wind speed and direction given by the control tower and the take-off should have been to the south-east with FULL take-off thrust used. The First Officer then correctly read the percentage N1 to be set from the N1 graph but inadvertently transposed the figures so that a very low thrust was used, far lower than minimum thrust allowed. Neither the First Officer or the Captain crosschecked the figure from the graph nor did the Flight Engineer check it against the Thrust Rating Computer for the assumed temperature being used. Fortunately, the aircraft was undamaged but the reputation of all three members of the crew suffered considerably with disciplinary action being taken by the company.

After quite a long period of time off, Dick recovered sufficient strength to attempt a return to work. This was done very much against medical advice but he was probably far better off with something to occupy his mind than sitting around doing nothing. On his return to the office, his speech was slurred; he could not use his right hand properly, and walked with a pronounced limp. While he was seriously ill, Wally Luther said that as I was in charge, Dick's name should be removed from the AOC document and mine substituted. I was opposed to this, my view being that such a measure should only be taken if and when it proved impossible for Dick to resume working. The whole purpose of my appointment as the Deputy Chief Navigator was to take over from Dick when he was temporarily unable to carry out his duties.

During his convalescence, Dick had learned to write quite legibly with his left hand and soon demonstrated that he had not lost any of his mental skills. Initially he came into the office for about an hour each afternoon, gradually increasing this over several months to almost a full afternoon. He did not come to the office during the mornings as the doctor had told him that it was essential that he got plenty of rest. Freddie provided him with a company car that had an automatic transmission, which with his disability was the only gearbox he could manage. Although I was theoretically in charge, there was never any intention by me of usurping his authority whilst he was unwell. To his credit, he left things very much to me and only took on tasks that were within his capability. Often I would go to his house to discuss things that were going on rather than have him come to the office.

Although the passenger loads continued at very high levels, political problems involving Middle East oil producing countries caused fuel prices to escalate dramatically, putting severe financial pressure on charter operators and scheduled carriers alike. Laker Airways aircrew had a contract that included a cost of living clause whereby a 5% salary increase was automatically given when the official retail price index rose by 5%. As inflation rose very steeply at that time, it became obvious that the automatic salary increases could not continue and it came as no surprise when Sir Freddie imposed a freeze on all salary increases within the company. Not a popular decision to make but a very necessary one that had to be accepted by all staff if the company was to survive.

Freddie Laker had to deal with vicious competition from Scheduled Airlines who were offering fares that undercut SKYTRAIN in an attempt to force him out of business. There was a great deal of public support for Freddie that obviously gave him a great deal of encouragement and he did his utmost not to be defeated by the opposition. The last three DC10 Series 30 aircraft were delivered and in service by summer 1980, this giving sufficient capacity to fly SKYTRAIN to Los Angeles twice a day with good loads. However, late in the season the passenger demand dropped off dramatically and the second service became really too uneconomic to run. The first flight would be full but the second often had less than 25% load, a situation that could not continue for very long. In the short Islamic Hadj seasons, DC10 series 10 and 30 were chartered to fly pilgrims to Jeddah and back from places as far away as Malaya.

Although this took up some of the spare capacity, it only utilised a small amount of what was available.

It was in 1980 that 'Attie' succumbed to the cancer from which he had been suffering for some time. He had been a tower of strength to the company and was sorely missed. He was one of the original team who joined Freddie Laker when Laker Airways was formed. I spoke to him a short time before his death to ask how he was but all he wanted to know was how Sue and my children were. The Assistant Operations Manager, 'Pidge' Palmer was appointed as the Operations Superintendent, carrying much of the responsibility held by 'Attie.' Pidge had joined the company as a duty officer in October 1970, becoming a senior duty officer in February 1972 and progressing to Assistant Operations manager in April 1977 when Attie's health really deteriorated.

Late in 1980 the first Airbus arrived and after considerable crew training it went into service early in 1981. The aircraft proved to be very popular with passengers and crews and was ideally suited to fly to Laker holiday destinations. The second Airbus was delivered and with the summer bookings looking good, it seemed that the company was recovering from its setbacks. Unfortunately there were many irritating things happening such as Fuel Company staff going on strike causing delays to refuelling and subsequently to flights. Laker had contracts with several fuel suppliers that theoretically should have helped but in fact, did not. I believe the contracts were worded in such a way that each fuel supplier knew which Laker flights they were to supply. When a strike occurred, the fuel companies not on strike refused to refuel those flights allocated to the company whose employees were on strike, as it would effectively mean crossing theoretical picket lines! This caused many very expensive delays to Laker that rolled on from day to day.

From time to time, Canadian and American Air Traffic Controllers went on strike, which closed down large areas of Atlantic airspace necessitating dramatic re-routing of aircraft. This in turn caused massive and expensive delays to all flights. The company had to take all of these things in its stride when they happened and it needed total dedication and co-operation from the crews and ground staff. At times the flow of traffic was so slow that if an allocated departure slot could not met, the next available slot might well be several hours later. Crews often sat on an aircraft for four or five hours without getting a slot and another crew would have to take over from them.

When American Air Traffic controllers went on strike, President Reagan fired them all and allowed military controllers to take over. This initially resulted in massive delays but these lessened as more controllers were trained and commenced working on a 'no strike' agreement.

Towards the end of 1981 it was obvious to everybody that the company was under intense financial pressure and in December 1981, Freddie wrote to all staff telling them a little of what was happening and asked for everyone to be patient. The future looked quite bleak for the company but on December 24th 1981 Freddie Laker announced that agreement had been reached in principle to re-structure the Company's financial affairs with a view to securing its long-term viability. The sigh of relief could be almost heard and Christmas was not such a depressing time as had first been envisaged. The worries started up again in the New Year with Freddie Laker doing his utmost to reach an acceptable agreement and indeed, on Monday 1st February 1982, he thought that the stringent conditions demanded had been met. Unfortunately this proved to be not so and late on Friday 5th February 1982, Freddie dictated a letter to all staff announcing that he and the directors had been compelled with utmost regret, to request the bank to appoint a receiver and manager. I knew nothing of this until I got to work about 8.30 on Monday morning to find that the receiver was already in attendance. He called a mass meeting of staff at which he addressed them and spoke about what would happen. Managers of each section were told if they or their staff's services were required, but in general, most staff were released. The Receiver set up an office where staff could meet with Department of Employment officials to get advice. Laker aircrew and cabin staff actively campaigned with many of them going to Parliament to demonstrate their support for Laker Airways, urging the Government to take action to assist the airline. Sadly it all came to nothing. Dick and I were kept on at our contractual salary to assist the Receiver until the aircraft were disposed of. We both remained employed until 27th May 1982 when the offices were taken over by British Caledonian Airways. At just over 60 years of age I thought that my career had finally ended since it was most unlikely that I would find other work in aviation.

My years with Laker had perhaps been the happiest of my long flying career and even in 1978 when I ceased active flying, I still enjoyed my work. In ten years of flying with Laker I had flown just over 5000 hours which, at an average of 500 hours per year plus ground duties and crew training, was quite hard work. In the thirteen years employment, my salary had increased through annual increments and cost of living indexing by a massive 510%!

On 27th May 1982, British Caledonian Airways took over the Laker offices and hangar, and both Dick and I were declared unemployed by the receiver with a somewhat uncertain future ahead. At least my Laker Airways pension had been given the benefit of another three months contributions, and I had been paid my salary since February, when most other staff had been made redundant. I was lucky but what lay ahead?

Chapter 19

Virgin Atlantic Airways

It seemed very strange not to go off to work in the mornings but nevertheless; there was plenty to be done. I had to apply for any redundancy payments that I was entitled to, register as unemployed, plus the continuing search for suitable work. I certainly found it a very difficult time but with Sue and her parents being most supportive, I felt that it was only a matter of time before work would be found.

Soon after the collapse of Laker whilst still retained by the receiver, I was approached by an ex Laker Captain who had become a salesman for an aircraft broker. He asked if, on a consultancy basis, I would provide performance studies for a Cessna Citation aircraft operating into and out of a particularly small airfield in UK. I knew little about that particular aircraft and had to study the Flight Manual very carefully before producing what was required. The work done was charged at what I thought to be a reasonable rate for the job but later learned that I could have easily doubled or even trebled my fee.

After the receiver had dispensed with my services, other consultancies followed, one of which was to provide a Weight and Balance schedule for a BAC 1–11 that had been converted into an executive jet. That was a most interesting task and I did get to see the aircraft before it went off to its customer. The transformation was quite remarkable, having a luxury interior with large comfortable leather seats and a very attractive shower room/toilet. Quite a change from the standard BAC 1–11 with economy seating!

Freddie Laker's lawyer in Washington DC USA was working with the Laker Receiver with a view to bringing a lawsuit against McDonnell Douglas alleging that Laker's DC10–30 aircraft failed to meet the mission guarantee. He telephoned me to ask if I would do some consultancy work, which involved meeting a lawyer who would fly to London to discuss the performance shortfall in support of a proposed legal action. The task was quite complex, involving performance analysis of Laker's DC10–30 aircraft from flight records to prove that there had been a performance deficiency. It took a great deal of time intensive work and turned out to be a fairly lengthy consultancy. When the task was completed, I was asked if I would be prepared to give evidence in Washington if and when the case was brought to court. In the event, it was settled out of court and no further service was required from me. When I submitted my account to the receiver, he told me that I had grossly undercharged and that they would have been prepared to pay considerably more than the amount I actually billed. I did suggest submitting another invoice but quite obviously that could not be agreed.

In the middle of June 1982, I received a telephone call from Randolph Fields, an American lawyer whose ambition was to own an airline. Knowing nothing about airlines or aircraft, he needed a team of experts to assist with the venture and had contacted Robbie Robinson, the former Chief Accountant of Laker Airways. Robbie had given him my name and those of Alan Hellary, Dick Bradley and Jock Stewart, all Laker senior flight deck crew. Randolph Fields was a qualified Barrister and an American Attorney at Law who had been educated in England and, I believe, held dual American and British citizenship. He certainly was a highly intelligent man who apparently had a very successful legal practice in the United States. I was somewhat bemused that he wished to have part of anything to do with running an airline with the attendant worry, both operational and financial, that such a venture would involve.

We all met at the Gatwick Hilton Hotel where he had taken a suite with lunch and a bar laid on. His opening remarks were that with the failure of Laker Airways, he thought that there was an opportunity to set up an airline to take its place. Not an impressive proposal in consideration that with all the expertise that Freddie Laker possessed, his airline failed. I was a little apprehensive about this, particularly because the people he had asked to come to the meeting were all aircrew, and there was no one there with commercial, engineering or financial experience. His first proposal was that with the Falklands war over, the airline could serve the Falklands, a somewhat ludicrous idea! His rather optimistic view was that with so many Laker pilots and crews out of work, it would be easy to recruit them for 'peanut' salaries. He also thought that the DC10 aircraft previously operated by Laker would be lying idle and could be leased or leased-purchased at very favourable rates. How very wrong those assumptions turned out to be!

His next proposal was even more ridiculous in that he wanted to offer an all Business Class service on the aircraft in an attempt to attract a Ministry of Defence contract to carry Senior Officers to/from the Falklands. Apart from this being totally unrealistic and economically unsound, it was quite impossible as the Falklands only had a small airfield at Port Stanley with an extremely short runway that was not capable of taking large aircraft. More importantly, the Islands were still under military administration, and that itself would almost certainly prevent a civil licence being granted. He told us that he had been informed that a larger airport was planned but nevertheless had to agree that it was only in the planning stage and it would be some time before it would become available.

I pointed out to Randolph that our expertise was operating aircraft and asked what provisions he had in mind for finance, marketing, servicing etc. He seemed quite unconcerned with what he considered to be 'minor details' and proceeded to ask me to find out what was the largest aircraft that had sufficient range for the sectors to/from Ascension Island and Port Stanley, and could use Port Stanley airport. The meeting lasted from 10a.m. until 7p.m. by which time we had agreed in principal to start things moving towards what seemed to be a quite impossible task of creating an airline. During that meeting he countered every objection we raised by saying **'Think positive.'** It was blatantly obvious to me that the team of experts he had assembled was eminently qualified to advise on aircraft operations, but he would have to quickly bring in others with commercial, financial and engineering experience.

Starting up a scheduled service is not just a matter of obtaining a licence to operate a route, an airline has to be formed and an Air Operators Certificate, (AOC) granted. This is very much a chicken and egg situation in that it would be uneconomic to set up the airline without being certain that a licence would be forthcoming. Conversely, a licence is useless without an airline with an AOC. This was explained in some detail to Randolph whose reply yet again was **'Think positive'** and that he intended to set wheels in motion for both the Licence *and* an AOC, potentially a very expensive exercise.

The embryonic airline would be started as Ritter plc trading as British Atlantic Airways, Ritter being a company name he had bought off the Company Register in November 1981. Ritter plc was itself controlled by Fields Investments Ltd of which he was the chairman. When asked about finance, he said he would personally arrange for this, provided that we agreed to 'help' with our services. It was pointed out that everyone except him was unemployed and none of us could afford to get into debt trying to get things moving. In the light of that, he offered each of us a cheque for £200 towards expenses, promising further amounts when that had been used. Not a particularly good arrangement but at least it gave a glimmer of hope. After the meeting broke up, Dick Bradley expressed the view that Randolph was living in 'cloud cuckoo land' and the venture would never get off the ground. His advice was to bank the cheque and run! This perhaps made sense, but if there was a chance of getting an airline started, my view was that we should give it our best effort. Dick was not a well man and obviously it was unwise for him to be subjected to the strain that the project would bring. Nevertheless, in the interim period he did agree to carry on, but soon became disillusioned and dropped out. I kept in touch with him but sadly he developed cancer and died within two years. It was constantly pointed out to Randolph that the ex Laker group he had assembled was one with all the necessary operational expertise, but had no one with experience in sales, marketing or engineering, so important to the venture. Randolph considered this argument as something that would be addressed at a later date, in my view a glaring error!

Randolph decided that if 'The Airline' was to be taken seriously, a base needed to be set up and asked Alan to look into it. A small office was rented in The Beehive at Gatwick and a full time receptionist employed to answer the telephone and take care of the secretarial side. The receptionist/secretary was the wife of ex Laker First Officer Tim Hutton who hoped to be employed if the airline commenced operation. As time went by, Randolph formed a Board of Directors with each of us on the Board together with accountant Richard Holman and Simon Wakefield, a close legal associate. Eventually others joined the Board and Randolph allocated shares to each director.

A licence application was submitted for flights to the Falklands, but one question on the application form specifically asked if it had been ascertained that the airfield(s) intended for use was suitable for our use. Obviously Port Stanley airfield was not and therefore, the application was unlikely to be treated seriously by the CAA Licensing Authority. Randolph continued with his legal work in the USA, which kept him out of the country for long periods, but he remained in contact by telephone. Of the four members of the operations team, only Alan and I actively worked on the project, both using our aviation contacts to obtain as much information as possible for the forthcoming licence application. Jock Stewart took the view that until the airline was formed and flying was about to commence, he could contribute very little.

Using contacts in Boeing, I learned that it *might* be possible for a modified executive style Boeing 727 to use the short PSP runway at Port Stanley, but as the islands were then still under military law, it was extremely doubtful if permission would be forthcoming. Even if it was, given the 3000+ nautical mile sector from Ascension Island to Stanley and a very long diversion clear of Argentine airspace to Uruguay, the payload would be extremely limited making seat costs quite astronomical. After considering these arguments Randolph agreed that perhaps the application to serve the Falklands should be put on hold and that we should look at other routes.

He then came up with the idea of applying for a licence to fly from Gatwick to New York JFK using DC10 or Boeing 747 aircraft, again with an all Business Class configuration that theoretically would attract frequent flyer businessmen. The number of business seats that he proposed to have fitted was not practical and in my opinion, would make the operation quite uneconomic. He also proposed that instead of providing a conventional meal service, a buffet and bar would be laid out at each end of the aircraft to allow passengers to eat and drink when it pleased them to do so. This idea we immediately rejected on the grounds that with the aircraft's extremely low humidity, food would rapidly be rendered unattractive and inedible. Only Randolph thought that this seating and catering was likely to succeed, the rest of us expressing grave doubts on a prime route to the USA. Randolph in his **'Think positive'** mood was not in the least deterred by our arguments and went ahead with his plans. When he asked what type of aircraft would be best, given the large number of ex Laker DC10 aircrew being unemployed, it seemed logical for Alan and I to elect for the DC10. Alan's intention was to continue flying himself for as long as it was legally possible and in theory, that could make the training of aircrew much easier and possibly less expensive.

At that stage the intention was to employ as many ex Laker aircrew as possible, with Alan as Director of Flight Operations, Captain Barry Rawlins as Chief Pilot and Jock Stewart as Chief Flight Engineer. If a DC10 were to be operated these appointments made a great deal of sense, but would not necessarily be so if a Boeing 747 were to be chosen. However, there was a long way to go before any appointments could be considered. Barry Rawlins was then employed flying DC10s for a foreign operator, but agreed to join if the airline appeared likely to get off the ground. It had become obvious to Alan and me that Randolph knew nothing about airline operations or marketing and simply had an ambition to own an airline. Furthermore he admitted to being totally scared of flying which did not make him the ideal person to be running an airline! On the credit side, he was an extremely intelligent and ambitious man, qualities I was sure would help in the struggles that undoubtedly lay ahead.

I took on the task of the operational evaluation of each aircraft type likely to be used and additionally agreed to provide basic estimates of operating costs. I had never done costing work before and had to spend a great deal of time finding out the details of the many and variable costs that would arise. I knew nothing of the commercial/marketing side of an airline and despite Randolph's repeated attempts to involve me, I would have nothing to do with it.

In preparation for the licence hearing, Alan and I used our own expertise to gather information in support of the application, albeit it with a great deal of misgiving about the success of the application. With the Commercial and Marketing problem unresolved, Randolph brought in Americans Robert Booth and Eli Timoner to use their considerable expertise in the USA market. Randolph emphasised that although he had complete faith in the operational team, he now knew (at last!) that he needed to have people with sound marketing experience who could accurately provide revenue forecasts in support of the application. This still left the UK marketing unresolved and although Randolph indicated that the Americans involved could take care of that, neither Alan nor I were convinced that his assumption was correct.

I told Randolph that it was essential that an Engineering Director be nominated to give guidance on technical matters, including the selection of the aircraft to be operated. That person would ultimately have to take over the responsibility for all matters pertaining to the technical operation and maintenance of the aircraft. Randolph was under the misguided impression that the operations team could take care of Engineering and it took some time to convince him that a Specialist Engineer was needed.

Alan and I discussed this in depth and he suggested that Peter Yeoman, the former Laker Chief Engineer should be approached and offered the appointment. Whilst conceding that Peter was eminently suitable, my own choice was Roy Gardener, a former RAF apprentice who had risen to the rank of Chief Technician before leaving the Service to take up a career in Civil Aviation as a ground engineer. He had been employed by Laker working in Laker's Quality Control department under Peter Yeoman and I had met him when Peter Yeoman had asked him to provide me with technical information connected with a navigation task that I was working on. Although I knew him to be an efficient and likeable person, Alan was bitterly opposed to him joining, claiming that he did not have sufficient experience for the job. Perhaps he was right in that respect, but in order to prevent it becoming an argument, I left it to Alan to try to contact and recruit Peter Yeoman who was then employed by American Airlines. Alan had no success and eventually Randolph asked me to arrange a meeting with himself and Roy. At that meeting Roy agreed to join the company provided that he retained his anonymity in order to protect his job with British Caledonian Airways. He was concerned that British Caledonian would dispense with his services if they became aware that he was part of a potential new airline that could be in competition with them … Alan did his utmost to prevent the Roy's appointment, but with no other candidate available, the appointment was made.

Many meetings took place on both sides of the Atlantic prior to the hearing with everyone preparing to give evidence in support of the application. I had three good friends employed by major aviation fuel companies and arranged with them to provide me with monthly updated fuel prices for supplies at Gatwick and JFK. This enabled me to give reasonably accurate forecast of fuel costs together with the other operational costs that I had agreed to provide to Richard Holman. At that time, with the aircraft type still undecided, I had to provide forecasts for DC10 and Boeing 747 aircraft.

Randolph arranged for financial backing from an investment company, and Bob Booth hired an American to produce and present our marketing and commercial plans when the hearing took place. Meetings were held with members of The Airline Users Committee whose function is to protect the interests of the flying public. That committee examines in detail the type of service to be offered by an airline applying for a licence to ensure that it would acceptable by passengers. They officially attend public hearings and can question witnesses, but do not take sides with any party.

As a matter of some urgency, Randolph called a meeting on Good Friday 1983 to meet Ron Davies, a prospective Commercial Director who was then employed by Air Florida. He had finally accepted our view that despite the marketing expertise of the American team, there was no one on the board to control and co-ordinate commercial sales within the company. Ron was in a similar situation to Roy Gardner whereby he had to retain his anonymity in order to safeguard his job, but agreed to join subject to the airline obtaining its licence.

Only days before the CAA hearing commenced, no firm decision had been taken on the aircraft that would be operated. I had evaluated many different aircraft types and to Alan's disappointment, the economics always favoured the Boeing 747. Through a contact in Miami, Randolph had secured a lease option on a fairly old ex Air Canada Boeing 747–100. However, with the engines fitted its performance out of Gatwick would be marginal giving concern that with abnormally strong headwinds over the Atlantic, a direct flight would not be possible with a full passenger load. It was important that the aircraft's performance was adequate as it was Randolph's intention to set up a freight company that would channel all its freight to/from New York to the airline.

The hearing was held in late May 1983, but just prior to this Randolph assembled everyone who would give evidence to meet with Robert Webb, the Barrister representing British Atlantic. I cannot clearly remember the details of that first hearing, but believe that a financial hearing was held in camera prior to the public hearing, during which the details of the financial support was discussed. I was wary about giving evidence because I thought that the cross-examination might become aggressive. Robert Webb assured me that it was not a court hearing and told me just to answer any questions carefully and not volunteer information. In actual fact, I was only questioned on operational aspects and was asked very little other than what action would be taken if the aircraft we proposed to operate became unserviceable. Lacking a decision on the aircraft that would be operated, I could only say the company would sub charter if it became necessary. The arguments presented by British Airways and British Caledonian opposing the application was very convincing and gave little comfort to me. The turning point of the hearing came when Chairman Ray Colegate asked both Randolph and Bob Booth to explain a particular marketing formula that had been used to produce the revenue figures. Unfortunately, the American expert responsible for producing the figures was unavoidably detained in the USA, and it was left to Randolph and Bob to explain them. Although having some knowledge of the formula, neither knew it sufficiently well to convince the Chairman that they knew what they were talking about. When the Chairman commented, *'Neither of you appear to know how the formula works, but fortunately I do'*, the moment of truth had arrived, and I knew that the application would fail. It did!

Ever the optimist, Randolph immediately appealed against the decision and was told that the evidence already given, together with any further evidence produced in support, would be considered at a future date when the final decision would be given. Doubtless the application had foundered on the marketing formula and lack of commercial and marketing expertise and unless something more convincing could be produced, the appeal would also fail. I felt that there was a great deal more that should have been done on the commercial and marketing side before we applied for a licence. I also thought the lack of communication between the directors who were involved in setting up the airline, contributed to the failure. Randolph did not agree and ever the optimist **(Think positive!)** asked each of us to contact our Members of Parliament to urge them to support the licence appeal. He also asked us to contact as many ex Laker aircrew as possible and urge the to write to their MP's. I went to Westminster to discuss the matter with Tim Renton MP and later, Alan and I met Lord Orr-Ewing in the Lords with MPs Tim Renton and Nicholas Soames present. They listened patiently to what we had to say, and I would like to think that they were sympathetic to our venture. Realistically it was the task of our team to present a far better case than had been done at the hearing. I remember thinking that although the expertise of the operational and engineering team presumably was probably quite adequate, there were still grave doubts in my mind as to the ability of those responsible for marketing matters, but how could I get Randolph to see that!

Randolph invited me to dine with him at the Savoy Hotel where I was introduced to Hugh Welburn, an experienced marketing consultant who it seemed, had commenced working with Randolph. He certainly put commercial and marketing ideas forward that Randolph acted upon, and some years later Hugh was still a Virgin Atlantic consultant. Randolph arranged press conferences to give publicity and information about British Atlantic Airways, and although Alan and I attended, we were seldom asked to speak. I did have an off the record conversation with Christopher Wain, the BBC's aviation correspondent, who told me that his stepfather, like me had flown Wellington bombers during the war. This was a time of great expense for Randolph but he seemingly took it all in his stride as though it were nothing. The operations/engineering team of course, was still only being paid expenses!

Late in November 1983, Alan and I were invited to the offices of The Board of Trade to meet an official who voiced an opinion (unofficial of course) that the appeal was unlikely to succeed. He asked if we were aware that there was an unused licence formerly held by British Airtours to serve Newark (New Jersey) from Gatwick. He went on to say that as British Airtours had given up the licence, there was little likelihood of any objection from British Airways if British Atlantic applied for it. I personally had grave doubts about this destination, particularly as British Airtours had apparently been unable to make the route pay its way. With their marketing expertise, if they could not make a success of it, how on earth could we? How wrong that assumption proved to be. I can recall a friend telling me that he was booked to fly to Newark with British Airtours but both outbound and return flights were sub-chartered to an obscure American Company and operated well off its schedule. Doubtless there was a good reason for this such as technical problems with the Airtours aircraft, but this should not have occurred on both the outbound and homeward flights separated by 14 days.

Some years before, I had passed through Newark airport and found it to be a quite magnificent airport. It was then under-utilised and seemed like a ghost airport with apparently no great activity. Its location was considered by some to be on the wrong side of New York City and lacked interline connections to other parts of USA. Over the years this has changed quite dramatically and today is a very busy airport.

After the disappointment of the application for the New York JFK licence, and the uncertainty of the appeal, Randolph agreed to take a chance and apply for the vacant Newark licence. However, this time he listened to our advice and opted for conventional economy seating. A licence application to serve Newark from Gatwick carrying passengers and freight was duly submitted with, I might say, a greater degree of confidence than the previous application. The Commercial and Marketing expertise was still flawed and there was a great deal to be done to improve it before the licence hearing. If this application was successful, and we cautiously thought it could, larger premises would be needed to accommodate the increased numbers of staff that would be needed to start up the airline.

Late in October 1983, the office in the Beehive was shut down and a lease taken on offices at Lowfield Heath which ultimately became the airlines first Gatwick HQ. By this time only Alan and I remained of those who had attended the initial meeting in 1982 and we both had become quite concerned that Randolph had brought in a number of consultants who were being paid large fees for their services while we were only getting our expenses. This was discussed somewhat amicably, but nevertheless forcibly, with Randolph whose argument was that expenses must be kept to the minimum. However he did agree to commence paying a small salary of £6000 plus £1200 expenses from 1st December 1983, assuring us that this would be increased to the budgeted level if and when the airline was started. The size of the payment was disappointing considering the large amount of time and work that we had put into the project, compared to those who were picking up very large consultancy fees!

I had continued to take on whatever consultancies had come up since Laker had folded and it was only these that enabled me to keep some semblance of financial stability. After the failure of the JFK licence application, it became apparent to me that with the new application having no firm chance of success, I should try to find employment that would be more secure. Earlier in 1983, a group of ex Laker BAC 1–11 Captains headed by Training Captain Dave Bowen had become involved in starting up a new Welsh airline, which was to be called Airways International Cymru Ltd. The Managing Director of this new airline, a Cardiff businessman, owned a well established travel agency and thought that it would be more profitable for him to sell package tours direct to his own airline. I had done quite a lot of work for Dave and his team in their earlier days, including writing the BAC 1–11 Operations Manual (Navigation) for an agreed sum of £1000, payable only if and when they became operational. As the time was fast approaching when that airline would start, Dave asked if I would be interested in becoming the Chief Navigator. The salary on offer was pitiful but I was assured that it would become more realistic once the airline became profitably established.

In December 1983 I agreed to join them, but reminded the MD that I was owed £1000 for the Operations Manual I had produced earlier. We had met some weeks earlier at Gatwick when I told him of my involvement with British Atlantic and he was fully aware that if British Atlantic became licenced, I would continue with them. Furthermore, I had told him that I would not commit myself to working in Cardiff during the build up period as all my technical information was at my home in Lindfield, Sussex. He agreed to those conditions and I was put on the payroll as The Superintendent of Planning and Performance. It was fortunate that the CAA inspector assigned to the airline was co-operative and in principle, accepted the operations manuals in the format I had written them, thus greatly reducing the amount of work that remained.

The two BAC 1–11 aircraft that the airline intended to operate were owned by a Canadian Airline based in Quebec and would have to be ferried from Canada to UK. The range of the particular series BAC 1–11 was about 1500 nautical miles with a full load, but if empty, a significant increase could be achieved. There was no possibility of being able to cross the Atlantic non-stop, so I planned both aircraft to fly to Cardiff with fuel stops at Goose Bay and Keflavik. Ultimately both aircraft were successfully ferried on that route.

In effect I was working simultaneously for British Atlantic and Airways International Cymru Ltd and eventually would have to decide which one I would join permanently. Randolph had paid expenses since we had first met and had just started to pay a small salary, so clearly my loyalty was to him. I was also still doing a small amount of other consultancy work as and when it came up. In fact, one came at very short notice in December 1983 through an ex Laker Captain who was flying Boeing 707s for Libyan Arab Airlines based in Tripoli, Libya. He told me that one of their Boeing 707s had a serious trim problem and asked if I would to agree look into it. The only trouble was that I would have to go to Tripoli to do what was necessary and that could be very time consuming.

I needed to get Libyan entry and exit visas from the Libyan Embassy before I could leave UK but the ex Laker Captain told me that he would arrange for Libyan Arab Airlines to obtain the necessary visa's and return airline tickets, and arrange accommodation in Tripoli. The outward journey showed a reservation but the return date was left open, as I was not sure how many nights I would need to stay. I departed from Heathrow under the impression that hotel accommodation in Tripoli had been arranged and that transport would be provided. On arrival another ex Laker Captain met me and told me that Libyan Arab Airlines had not made any arrangements for my stay, leaving me apparently stranded with no Libyan money. Luckily, yet another ex Laker Captain was on leave and I was allowed to use his hotel room whilst I was in Tripoli. As I was without Libyan funds for expenses, the chap who met me went out and got chicken and chips from a take away in town that solved the immediate problem of food.

On the following morning, a Libyan Arab transport took me to the airport to meet the Chief Pilot of the Boeing 707 fleet. He, a Libyan, seemed most friendly and appreciated my coming to solve the problem. In reality it was all quite simple. When I went through the Weight and Balance documents I discovered a simple mathematical error that should have been found by anyone conversant with Weight and Balance. I had been told that if I could correct the problem, I should make a written report when I got back home and post it and my account to Tripoli. I informed the Chief Pilot that I had discovered what had caused the trim error and asked if I should address my account to him for payment. That went down like a lead balloon and he refused to accept any responsibility whatsoever, saying that I would have to write to the Managing Director for it to be paid. I realised that I was going to get nowhere with him so simply asked him to instruct his staff to book me on the next day's flight. I was astounded when he told me that all flights to London were full until after Christmas, which was only 5 days away. Apparently I was expected to go to the airport and standby in the *hope* that a seat would be free at the time of departure. I asked if I could travel on the flight deck if no seat was available but even that was refused.

On checking out of the hotel, I was presented with a huge bill that had been run up by the Captain who supposedly occupied the room and it took some time to explain that it was not my responsibility. I learned later that the occupant of the room had severed his connection with the airline and had left the country with no intention of paying his hotel bill. I did not know that at the time and fortunately, neither did the hotel. I arrived at the airport well before the flight was due to leave and found that although there was a seat available, I would have to pay a departure tax in Libyan pounds before they would check me in. After queuing for an hour at the currency exchange counter, I paid the tax and was checked in for the flight. It was a great relief when the aircraft got airborne and had passed the point of no return. Had it returned to Tripoli I was convinced that I would be stranded which would have created serious problems at home. My wife Sue was due to be admitted to hospital on 29th December for surgery on her knees and I needed to be home to take care of our children. Fortunately for all concerned, I got home safely.

On the following day I wrote to the Libyan Chief pilot giving instructions that corrected the trim of the aircraft and enclosed a copy of my account. In another letter addressed to the Managing Director, I enclosed my original account and a copy of the report. despite repeated letters to Libyan Arab Airlines in London and Tripoli, no acknowledgement was ever received, or indeed any payment.

Weeks later the Captain who asked me to do the work came to see me. I was rather cross that he had not ensured that my accommodation and food had been taken care of and that the account had been paid. He said that the aircraft trim was now perfect and gave me his personal cheque to cover my out of pocket expenses but said that he could not settle the balance of the account as he had no way of recovering it from Libyan Arab. A rather shabby excuse for a thoroughly nasty experience!

Although I wished to remain working with Randolph, if the Newark licence did not succeed I knew that I might be compelled to go to work at Cardiff. Ironically, it was Airways Cymru who did emerge first. Their licences and engineering approval had been granted, operations manuals approved, leaving only the AOC to be issued after a Proving Flight. This was planned to take place immediately after crew ground training had been completed and everything seemed to be on course for the first commercial flights. Late in January 1984 I travelled down to Cardiff to attend meetings and give navigation training to the pilots, mostly ex Laker, prior to operations commencing. Everything went well and I travelled home feeling quite satisfied with the progress that had been made.

Very soon after this in early February, Randolph phoned to ask me to go to London to meet Mr Richard Branson, the Managing Director of Virgin Music. I had no knowledge whatsoever of Virgin Music or Richard Branson. He may have been well known by the younger generation, but certainly not by me. Randolph arranged to meet me at Richard's office in Ladbroke Grove, but had not given me the slightest indication what the meeting was about, other than it was very important. Richard Branson has changed very little from that first meeting early in 1984 when I found him a pleasant, but very down to earth businessman. His informal appearance of slacks and sweater certainly has been quite consistent over the years! The first real question he asked me was 'Why don't you like DC10s?' This was quite an extraordinary question because we had never spoken before and he could not possibly know my preferences and in any case, it was not correct. I realised later that it was Randolph who did not like DC10s and had possibly indicated incorrectly to Richard, that I felt the same way. After a fairly brisk question and answer session, Richard said 'What aircraft shall 'WE' get'. The 'WE' put everything in context, I then realised that the sole purpose of the meeting was for Randolph to secure a financial agreement with Richard. The answer I gave to Richard's question was that we had not reached any decision on a specific aircraft, but would tell him when the right one was found. This seemed to satisfy him and he immediately went into financial discussions with Randolph. As we left the building, I asked Randolph why he had not told me in advance the purpose of the meeting. His casual reply was, 'I thought that you knew!'

Randolph's biggest failing was that he did **not** keep his associates in the airline fully informed of what was going on. I later learned that there had been several meetings between Richard Branson, Richard Holman and Randolph to discuss Branson's involvement with the airline, but I was not told of them, neither was Alan! Certainly I had no idea that he would finance and ultimately take over the whole company. I discovered that Branson has a wonderful memory, but to supplement it he always made longhand notes in a rough notebook that he carried with him at meetings. If an argument ever arose about what was said at a particular meeting, it was not unusual for him to produce his notebook and quote almost verbatim, things that had been said.

During the next week two things happened. I learned that the CAA Inspector assigned to Airways Cymru would not agree with me working from Lindfield and that I would have to be in Cardiff during the working week. I had no intention of acceding to that but the next thing that happened took it out of my hands. Alan telephoned to say that Randolph was quite confident that the licence would be granted and wanted to immediately start working towards getting an AOC. I must admit to being quite surprised by Randolph's optimism, knowing that if the licence application failed again, an even larger amount of money would have been wasted. Randolph obviously saw things quite differently. The immediate (and most acceptable) effect of that decision put Alan and myself on the realistic salary that had been budgeted. I telephoned the Managing Director of Airways Cymru to inform him that I would be unable to assist him further and asked for payment of the fee agreed for the production of the operations manual. He, quite rightly I suppose, demanded that I give him one months notice AND arrange for a suitable replacement acceptable to CAA to take my place. Although I could agree that I had to give a month's notice, there was no obligation for me to provide a replacement. Fortunately Harry Cowsill, who had worked for me in Laker Airways, was between jobs and agreed to meet the MD with view to taking over from me. Subsequent to their discussions, Harry accepted the position with Cymru. I worked out the required month notice from Lindfield, working closely with Harry and passing all my BAC 1–11 files over to him.

No payment was ever received for the operations manual that I had produced, despite repeated requests to the MD and Dave Bowen. The

MD said that it was a personal matter for Dave and me to resolve, but Dave did not agree! Ironically, Airways International Cymru only lasted for a small number of years but in that time their fleet did increase to include Boeing 737–200 aircraft. Virgin Atlantic of course is still operating as an established International Scheduled Carrier serving many destinations throughout the world.

No firm decision had been taken about the specific aircraft that British Atlantic would operate, other than it would be a Boeing 747. It was important to have this settled as there were many things related to the performance of the aircraft that needed to be worked on prior to the impending licence hearing set for 1st and 2nd of March 1984. Just before the hearing, Richard Branson stated that he required the airline to be called British Virgin Atlantic Airways, this of course being no surprise to anyone once it was known that he was financing the venture. It was subsequently learned that the word 'British' could not be used by the airline, as permission had not been obtained for its use. Accordingly the airline would be known as Virgin Atlantic Airways. At the licence hearing, the seating space allocated to us was shown as 'Ritter plc trading as Virgin Atlantic Airways.

The licence application, opposed by British Caledonian, had financial hearings in camera on 16th and 27th of February, followed by the public hearing on 1st and 2nd of March 1984 at the Civil Aviation Authority in Kingsway. The hearing progressed quite slowly and appeared to be running over the allocated time prompting comment from the Chairman. Once again, Alan and I were only questioned on operational matters without any problems being encountered. Inevitably, we were again asked about the risks of operating a single aircraft and what provision had been made for back up equipment. The Boeing 747 aircraft to be operated was still in the negotiating stage with Randolph having talks with potential suppliers, albeit without much success.

The hearing was dominated by commercial and financial arguments on the first day with Randolph being questioned at length. Robert Webb was occupied elsewhere on legal business and Randolph was given permission by the Chairman to perform Robert's duties until he arrived. My own interpretation of BCAL's objection was that they did not want Virgin, or anyone else for that matter, to commence operations to Newark despite the fact that they had no intention of operating that route themselves. Prior to our application, it had seemed most unlikely that they would utilise the licence they already held for New York JFK. However, on the second day of the hearing they announced that they intended to do so and asked for their rather complicated and ambitious plans to be heard in camera.

The entire hearing was lengthy and drawn out, necessitating continuance on the second day until well after 6p.m. in the evening. Just before the break for lunch on the first day, Mr Grobel, Counsel representing Travel Trust Ltd, dramatically interrupted the proceedings. Apparently they were seeking a restraining order in the High Court that afternoon against British Atlantic's licence application. Travel Trust were the company with whom Randolph had arranged finance for the unsuccessful application. The afternoon's proceedings began without any reference being made to Travel Trust Ltd but it was learned later that the injunction had failed with costs awarded to Virgin Atlantic. As Robert Webb our Counsel put it, our first trading profit had been made.

Perhaps the most significant statement made by Richard Branson, unusually dressed in a light beige coloured suit with pink open necked shirt, was: *'We believe that we can make it work. If it runs into two or three months where it is tough, we will do everything we can to make it work. We do not venture into a business unless we are convinced that we can make it work.'* This together with other statements he made whilst giving his evidence at the hearing and the financial hearings, undoubtedly influenced the final decision. Richard Branson in his book refers to opposition from his own Virgin Music directors when he announced his intention to invest in the airline, but as with most of his ventures, it became successful.

There was a private financial meeting held on Friday 16th March 1984 when the final details were discussed, but Alan and I were not asked to attend. During that meeting the Chairman, Mr Colegate, stated that they had not reached a conclusion on the application and were still agonising over it. Randolph however, was very positive and had started the wheels turning towards Virgin's first commercial flight late in June. During the hearing he had emphasised to the Chairman the need for an early decision on the application to ensure start up in the peak season.

The selection of the aircraft became reality in mid March when Boeing approached the airline offering Virgin a Boeing 747–200 aircraft formerly owned or leased by Aerolineas Argentina. This aircraft was a magnificent machine that had undergone a complete overhaul by Boeing and had flown a relatively small number of hours. Boeing gave Virgin a film presentation of the aircraft at a hotel in London when it soon became obvious that this aircraft was just what was needed. There followed many meetings to discuss the financial arrangements and very quickly agreement was reached and the lease purchase of the aircraft signed in May 1984. Roy liaised constantly with Boeing, working out maintenance schedules and technical support. The aircraft was fitted with Pratt & Whitney JTD9–7FW (wet) engines that were not currently approved by CAA. The performance advantage of these engines was most desirable but in order to get CAA approval for the Flight Manual, a great deal of work would have been necessary at great expense, and there was insufficient time to do so. At a more economical price, Boeing could provide a Flight Manual for Pratt & Whitney JT9D–7A engines and after discussions with CAA, it was agreed that the aircraft could be operated with the 7F-wet engines operated at 7A thrust. Roy obtained the necessary technical clearances and additionally, negotiated a maintenance contract with British Caledonian Airways to provide full technical support for the turn round of the aircraft at Gatwick and its scheduled maintenance.

We were at that time occupying an office at Lowfield Heath near Gatwick and this was becoming quite overcrowded and there was a need for larger premises. Advertisements were placed in Flight Magazine for Boeing 747 Captains, First Officers, and Flight Engineers with another advertisement for cabin staff and ground staff. We certainly did not anticipate the quite staggering response to the advertisements. Pilot and Flight Engineer applicants without Boeing 747 experience were immediately rejected and this reduced the applications to a reasonably short list.

One thing that quickly emerged was that there were many applications from retired, or soon to be retired, British Airways pilots and Flight Engineers, amongst them qualified training staff. Most British Airways aircrew normally retired at age 55 but could still legally fly until age 60. (Pilots can now legally fly up to age 65 except that at that after age 60, they cannot command passenger aircraft over a specified size.) Alan took on the responsibility of interviewing and selecting the flight deck crews and initially asked me to sit in on the interviews. It soon became too time consuming for me and I had to leave it entirely to him. I received two applications from Cathay Pacific Captains sent direct to my home address and subsequently both were recruited, although initially only one as a Captain.

Alan wanted as many ex Laker staff as possible and as soon as it was possible to offer employment, he stated that he would have Barry Rawlins as the Chief Pilot, Jock Stewart as the Chief Flight Engineer and Doug Smith as a First Officer. As the aircraft would be a Boeing 747, I was not convinced that recruitment of ex Laker pilots and engineers was economically sound despite Alan's obvious ideas to the contrary, but I did not oppose him. Subsequently my doubts proved correct.

An even greater number of applications for cabin crew jobs piled up and although Alan and I had no intention of interviewing these, we did need to appoint a Cabin Staff Manager who would select and employ those suitable. In my opinion there were two applications that stood out above all others as potential Cabin Staff Managers. The two in question were ex BA purser Gordon McKenzie and ex Saudi Airlines Senior

Hostess Jane Harrison. To say that Alan was not amused at my suggestion would be a total understatement!

Randolph had been interviewing people for commercial sales and reservations and had reached agreement with Air Florida to use some of the reservations computers and part of their offices just off Oxford Street. This arrangement was only just adequate as a short-term measure but eventually Virgin reservations would need to be set up separately. He had also employed David Tait in USA, (ex Laker and ex Air Florida), who was very experienced in sales. David took on the responsibility of settings up sales and reservations in New York City and negotiated ground handling at Newark by United Airlines. It appeared that we had three groups of people wishing to get involved with Virgin Atlantic, these being ex British Airways flying staff, ex Laker flying staff and Air Florida sales, computer and reservations staff. On every occasion Randolph and I met, it seemed that he had brought someone new into the company without informing us in operations and engineering. It was most disconcerting to be almost totally in the dark concerning financial arrangements and commercial progress. Randolph may have been a brilliant lawyer but he appeared to be completely out of his depth with sales and marketing and I wondered how long this situation would be allowed to continue.

Apart from producing the company's operations manuals, I took on the responsibility for obtaining departure and arrival slots at Gatwick and liaised with David Tait for the Newark slots. The latter presented no problems whatsoever but those at Gatwick required a great deal of negotiating with the scheduling committee. With only a single runway at Gatwick, arrivals and departures are slotted together at intervals that vary with size of the aircraft. Thus at peak periods the runway can become saturated with all aircraft movement slots taken up. The two passenger terminals each have a limit on the number of passengers that can be handled and with the large numbers of passengers on wide-bodied aircraft, terminal constraints can be exceeded which in turn can limit runway movements.

I had recommended that Gatwick Handling should be appointed as the Handling Agent responsible for checking in and boarding passengers, loading freight and other associated handling duties and a contract was duly signed with them late in May 1984. As they handled many airlines at Gatwick, it was normal for them to represent those they handled at the scheduling committee meetings when slots were allocated. I soon learned that it was desirable for a Virgin representative to be present at those meetings to ensure that the Virgin slots allocated were of, or near to our choosing.

As a newly emerging airline, we had no previous operating rights (Usually referred to as Grandfather Rights) and had to accept whatever slots were on offer. A somewhat ridiculous situation did arise where the allocated landing slot was only two or three hours after the allocated departure slot, and would not allow the aircraft to fly to Newark and back. Being new to the slot negotiation business, I was not aware that the initial allocation was only provisional and a system of swapping slots took place at subsequent meetings in an attempt to satisfy everyone's requirement. Peter O'Boyle, the then General Manager of Gatwick Handling, patiently explained the system to me and told me that by the time the airline was operational, almost certainly slots acceptable to Virgin would have been put into place. Oddly enough, Peter O'Boyle had employed Dawn Turner, who had worked for me in Laker. Together with her supervisor, Gary Greenwood, she negotiated slots with the scheduling committee for airlines they handled. It was comforting to know that we would eventually get acceptable slots, but as an emerging operator, we had to publish a commercial timetable well in advance of operations commencing and would actually need to hold slots for those published departure and arrival times. Ideally we were looking to depart from Gatwick late morning in the prime departure time that would give a prime arrival time at Newark. This proved to be quite impossible and a compromise had to be accepted, departing Gatwick around 4.30p.m. and returning at about 9a.m. the following morning, both times outside the peak period.

Richard and Randolph were not happy with the allocated slots and urged me to continue negotiating for prime times. Personally I was quite pleased with the slots as they would not get the aircraft into the New York area when traffic congestion was at its worst, often with horrendous arrival delays that could cause expensive diversions and lead to disruption of the schedule. A further complication was that initially we could not get the same slot time for each day of the weeks operation, ending up with a very odd inbound slot on one day. When I told the scheduling committee that it would not be possible to operate to the slot of that day and would always run late, I was informed that this was not acceptable to them and the company would have to publish a schedule that reflected the actual slots allocated. However, before Virgin Atlantic services commenced, with Peter O'Boyles's help we got the same slot each day.

Amongst the flight crew applications were two ex British Airways 747 training Captains who were working with Alia, the Jordanian airline. These two, Captains Eric Davies and Dickie Doddwell, were immediately contacted and invited to join the airline as Training Captains subject to the licence being granted. By a remarkable co-incidence I had supervised First Officer Eric Davies when he was navigating a BOAC Britannia flight from Heathrow to Gander in mid June 1963, three months before I left BOAC. His navigation performance must have been satisfactory, as I made no comment in my logbook.

Alan discussed with CAA the training requirements needed to validate flight deck crew and negotiated a contract with British Airways for the use of their Boeing 747 Flight Simulator at Cranebank, Heathrow. Eric Davies and Dickie Doddwell were particularly valuable as they personally knew many of the ex British Airways pilot and engineer applicants and could recommend those who should be recruited. They also negotiated with CAA how much simulator time would be needed for each crew member, and the requirement for actual flying time on the aircraft. Eric and Dickie were not opposed to recruiting ex Laker pilots and engineers, but both did express concern as to the wisdom of doing so due to the extra training that could be needed. Alan was quite unmoved by their opinion and his policy to use as many as possible remained the same! His loyalty to former colleagues in Laker was praiseworthy but not necessarily of benefit to Virgin. Alan was approached by ex Laker Flight Engineer Ted Burns who was employed by British Caledonian Airways as a Boeing 747 Conversion Course instructor. Alan immediately employed him to do the same work with Virgin Atlantic with the promise that he would become a Flight Engineer when flying commenced.

Frequent board meetings took place, some on Richard's houseboat at Little Venice in London and others at a club owned by Richard in Kensington. Immediately prior to the first meeting, Randolph called the Ritter plc directors together to inform us that Richard would not agree to have shareholders in the airline other than himself and Randolph. This came as quite a shock and put doubt into our minds as to our future when the airline became operational. Another director, a legal colleague of Randolph, thought that the move was not in the best interest of Ritter Directors and that a firm commitment should be obtained before signing away our shares. In reply to this, Randolph explained that we would be adequately compensated for the shares and our future with the airline would be assured. The timing of this announcement gave only minutes for a decision to be reached as Richard was on his houseboat at Little Venice waiting to start the first Virgin Atlantic board meeting. Randolph said that without our agreement Richard would not finance the airline and it would not go ahead. There was little that we could do other than accept. The Virgin board became Richard Branson as President with Nick Alexander and Terry Bourne from Virgin and from Ritter/British Atlantic, Randolph (Chairman) and Richard Holman.

The licence application was successful and was issued as Number 1B/35 effective from 18th April 1984 allowing not more than one flight in any one direction in any one-day, and only Boeing 747 or DC10 aircraft to be used. With the licence granted and the airline's first flight scheduled less than two months away, work on the AOC had to be dramatically speeded up. A CAA Flight Operations inspector, Captain Bernie Mitchell was assigned to the airline to inspect and approve Operations Manuals as they were being produced. He was a tremendous help, giving advice on the production of the Operations Manuals and Training Procedures.

Roy Gardener resigned from British Caledonian to take up his position as the Technical Director and quickly appointed another ex Laker engineer, Dick Plowes, to be his deputy with the title Chief Engineer. Alan was confirmed as the Director of Flight Operations/Operations Manager and myself as Director of Planning and Performance. Life became very hectic for everyone involved and I personally was working more than 12 hours a day.

We had not employed a secretary and were using typists from an agency to do work that was required. With everyone virtually queuing up to use this typist, it became obvious that more help was needed. Roy learned that the secretary of his former boss in British Caledonian was looking for a new job and asked me if I was interested in employing her. This was a golden opportunity and I interviewed her on the following day, immediately offering her the job, which she accepted. In order to produce the operations manuals, a photocopier was urgently required but by a remarkable co-incidence, on the day the requirement was discussed, a photocopier salesman called into the office to see if he could sell or lease one to us. That was quickly organised and it started churning out pages for the manuals.

My old friend Captain Gordon Steer was taken on as a self employed Crew Planning Manager and Gordon McKenzie employed as the Cabin Staff manager. Alan's main task was to draw up the training schedule and allocate simulator time for each of the flight deck crews that had been recruited. Both Eric Davies and Dickie Doddwell, having negotiated a suitable salary with Randolph, were confirmed as training Captains. Similarly, Flight Engineer Peter Greig was appointed as the Training Flight Engineer and these appointments provided the company with Flight Training personnel who would train the other flight deck crews.

Looking back to those early days working up to the granting of an AOC, although the tasks of the operations department were very demanding, equally important were those associated with sales and reservations, with which Randolph as the Managing Director spent most of his time. Richard Branson exercised his right to protect his interests and brought in several people from the Virgin Group, including Bill Sutton as the financial head. Nigel Primrose, who eventually became Financial Director, ultimately replaced Bill Sutton although Bill remained with the airline. Richard, wanting to give passengers a little more than the average in respect of service and food, brought in the head of one of his smaller Virgin companies called 'Top Nosh' to work with the airline. This was not successful and the catering contract went to an established Gatwick company.

Richard also had contact with Freddie Laker who gave him and Randolph a great deal of advice on the pitfalls that undoubtedly lay ahead. Richard wanted to name the aircraft 'Spirit of Laker' but Freddie said that that probably was not a good choice in the light of what happened to him in 1982. However, a Virgin aircraft would later be named after Freddie in recognition of the help and advice he gave Richard.

From my Laker days I remembered that Laker had some personalised aircraft registrations and made enquiries with CAA to see if this option would be available for Virgin. I learned that for a small additional fee, the company could have the aircraft put on to the British Register with registration letters of its choice, provided that these had not already been allocated. Further enquiries revealed that my choice of registration GVIRG was available and could be reserved by payment of a small reservation fee until the aircraft was ready to be put on to the British Register. Thus the company's first aircraft registration became fully indicative of the parent company and was named 'Maiden Voyager'

Meanwhile, Gordon McKenzie was selecting his cabin staff crews from the mountain of applications with his deputy, Jane Harrison who had drawn the short straw when the cabin staff manager was appointed. Amongst the first batch of cabin staff applicants was one from Jane who not only very attractive, was also eminently qualified for the Cabin Staff Manager post. Her application had been on my study desk at home for some weeks whilst Alan and I were deciding who should be offered the job. My wife Sue, seeing Jane's photograph pinned to the application form every day, jokingly said that I should either employ her or get rid of the photograph.

Alan and I were in total disagreement about the appointment of the Cabin Staff Manager, he wanting it to be an ex Laker Senior Hostess as he disliked male cabin staff. My view was that as long as it was a qualified person, it could be male or female and not necessarily ex Laker. Alan had gone to a great deal of trouble to contact as many ex Laker senior hostesses but all were either employed elsewhere or were not interested. With time creeping on it was essential that a decision was made and I proposed that it should be either Gordon or Jane. Alan was bitterly opposed to Gordon, his personal view being that stewards were either 'queer' or on the 'fiddle'. In my view, an incorrect assumption. Gordon McKenzie was a very normal family man and certainly proved to be very honest and loyal. With no agreement from Alan looking likely, at my request Randolph interviewed both Gordon and Jane. He found them equally acceptable and allowed them to decide who would be in charge. Once decided, Gordon was appointed and it was left to him, with Jane as his deputy, to recruit and train cabin staff.

In the hectic period of cabin crew selection, Gordon took on Keith Barlow, also ex British Airways, to assist him. Keith's wife Jane joined with him and in later years held a very senior post with the airline. Keith was appointed as the Flight Safety Officer whose responsibility was the production of the Flight Safety and Emergency Manual and training the crews on Emergency and Safety procedures. That particular task led to legal action being taken by British Caledonian against Virgin for using their manual reprinted with a Virgin Atlantic logo. Keith had copied their manual word for word without getting permission to do so. Virgin settled the action amicably and somewhat fortuitously, for had Keith started from scratch, it is unlikely that he could have completed the task on time. Keith then arranged an agreement with BCAL to use the BCAL Emergency Training facilities set up in their hangar to train Virgin crews.

As for me, I was writing operations manuals chapter by chapter and getting them typed up ready for inspection and approval by the CAA Flight Inspector, Bernie Mitchell. This arrangement worked well, because having discussed each chapter with him before going into print, little correction was needed. As Bernie read each page of the manual, any corrections needed were immediately changed on the master copy and photocopies made for each of the many manuals needed. This method saved an enormous amount of time and effort to produce the manuals for which I was responsible.

The Weight & Balance manual needed to be produced and although I was quite competent to do so, there just was not enough time available to me. In the light of this, I took on Brian Payne of British Caledonian as a Weight and Balance Consultant to produce what was necessary to satisfy CAA. Many years on, Brian was still the Weight and Balance Consultant for Virgin.

Alan was responsible for Flight Crew training and only consulted me if another opinion was needed. He had discovered that apart from the basic ground training and ARB examinations, Barry Rawlins and his ex Laker Crew would need more simulator time than those already current on the aircraft. Unfortunately he had booked insufficient slots on the British Airways Flight Simulator and furthermore, had allocated the first of those to Barry and his crew. It was quite obvious that the first simulator slots needed to be given to Eric Davies and Dickie Doddwell so that they could then train and check out the rest of the crews, including Barry's. The outcome was that Barry's crew was taken off the simulator roster and their slots allocated to the qualified Boeing 747 crews. The only requirement remaining was a ground course on Company Navigation procedures, Inertial Navigation System, and Aircraft Performance, followed by flying training on the aircraft. Alan, with considerable difficulty, had to re-negotiate with British Airways the urgently needed additional simulator slots for Barry's crew.

By this time, although totally overloaded with work, I was needed to conduct the ground course instructing crews on Company Flight Planning, Operational Procedures, 747 Performance and the Inertial Navigation System. I gave the first course on 25th May followed by a second on 6th June but was so exhausted that I could only just manage to complete the second one satisfactorily. The first of the crews were due to fly to Seattle at the weekend and with less than three weeks before the maiden flight, there did not seem to be enough hours in the day to do what still had to be done. I was feeling desperately tired and far from well!

With the aircraft in Seattle being prepared by Boeing for hand over to Virgin, I contacted Boeing to establish which airfield could be used for flying training. Their suggestion was that the aircraft could fly daily from Seattle to Moses Lake and return, giving the crews their required sectors and allowing for circuits and landings at Moses Lake. This was an excellent arrangement as it meant that the aircraft would spend each night at Boeing Field where any technical problems that might arise during the day could be rectified. Eric Davies and Dickie Doddwell were in total agreement with this and it was arranged for all crews, excluding Barry's, be sent to Seattle once their ground training and simulator flying had been completed. This was subject to Boeing providing a firm date when the aircraft would be ready for flying. Boeing normally used Moses Lake when they trained crews of companies who had bought Boeing aircraft and needed help with flying training.

The only remaining task was to ensure that fuel could be supplied at Boeing Field and Moses Lake by Chevron, my contract USA fuel supplier. The last Captain to join Virgin was ex BA Training Captain Jim Smillie. I seem to recall that he left BA one day, joined Virgin on the next to do his simulator training, then flew to Seattle on the following day to fly the last detail on the aircraft at Moses Lake, returning home on the delivery flight. Had Alan booked sufficient simulator time when he initially negotiated with BA, Barry's crew could have done something very similar, except they may have needed more handling time on the aircraft.

Roy had strengthened his team by employing a very experienced senior British Caledonian ground engineer named Paul Chappell. Paul, an exceptionally capable engineer, was sent to Seattle with Dick Plowes to work with Boeing while the modifications for Virgin were being carried out. When flying training commenced, Dick returned to UK leaving Paul to oversee the servicing between training sessions, and to take delivery of the aircraft prior to its departure for Gatwick. I was told that Virgin nearly lost its aircraft whilst training at Moses Lake. Apparently Air Traffic Control was using two runways and cleared two aircraft to land simultaneously on separate runways that actually crossed each other. I gather that it was only the extraordinary skill of Dickie Doddwell that avoided a calamity.

Another task delegated to Alan was the production of the Minimum Equipment List (MEL). This very important document lays down the absolute minimum equipment that must be serviceable on an aircraft before it can fly. With all that was happening, Alan completely overlooked this task and eventually had to delegate it to Gordon Steer who really had no responsibility for it. Needless to say, Gordon performed the extra task in his usual efficient and cheerful manner.

With everything seemingly working smoothly towards the AOC, Randolph telephoned me and asked if I would go to a telephone where I would not be overheard. It seemed to be rather secretive and quite naturally I was very concerned that something might have gone wrong. Alan and I went to a telephone in another room and called Randolph only to be totally astounded when he told me that CAA had informed him that Alan was not acceptable as the Director of Flight Operations. Randolph's opinion was that Alan must leave the company. I strongly protested and argued that Alan was one of the most experienced pilots in the country and had held a similar position in Laker Airways. Randolph's reply was that the AOC was unlikely to be granted unless Alan was replaced, and I was told to inform Alan immediately. Very firmly I told him that he should be talking to Alan about it and not me. His rather feeble excuse for not doing so was that as we were good friends and directors of equal standing, it would be better coming from me rather than himself. He added that success of the airline was more important than any one individual's pride! I told Randolph that if he forced Alan out of the company, I would immediately resign and have nothing more to do with Virgin. His reaction to that was that I would simply destroy everything that we had worked for over the past two years and would put many jobs at risk.

I was absolutely furious with what was happening and felt quite helpless. It seemed to me that the reasons were political and had nothing to do with Alan's qualifications. I was in a most difficult position and felt that I was being almost blackmailed into something that I did not agree with. When I told Alan and Bernie what had been said, they found it as unbelievable as myself. We were all completely stunned, and had no idea what to do about it. Although extremely upset, Alan would not hear of me resigning. Bernie said he knew nothing of any objection in the CAA Flight Operations Department and in his opinion; Alan with his vast aviation experience was suitable in every respect. I did wonder at the time if the fact that neither Alan or Barry Rawlins, who would hold the most senior appointments in Virgin Flight Operations were not Boeing 747 qualified, may have been the reason behind the objection. I asked Bernie if he would make enquiries and attempt to find out who was objecting, but no information was ever forthcoming.

I contacted Randolph again and asked for the name of the person who had made the ruling and if he was in CAA Flight Operations. Randolph either could not, or would not divulge any further information, insisting that Alan be replaced. To me it was outrageous that anyone could be so malicious. I felt quite helpless! I thought at the time, (much as I do now), that there may NOT have been any official objection to Alan, but someone wanted to remove him from the key position. My suggestion to Alan was that he took up the matter himself but he was unwilling to get into an argument with whoever had started the action!

Another Director of Flight Operations had to be appointed and obviously Alan wanted no part of arranging that, although I did discuss with him who should be invited. That evening I telephoned Barry and asked him if he would accept the appointment, only to be told that Alan had contacted him earlier with a similar offer and in loyalty to him had refused it. The only alternative open to me was to ask Eric Davies if he would take on the task. When invited, he said that before making a decision, he would like a meeting with Barry, Randolph and myself to discuss the terms of the appointment.

Prior to that meeting I suggested to Alan that he could remain as the Operations Manager by just dropping the Director of Flight Operations title, having told Randolph that if he accepted Alan as the Operations Manager at his same salary, I would not resign. Although not entirely in agreement, Randolph accepted the compromise that was offered. With little option available to him, Alan decided to remain as Operations Manager but hardly surprising, was thoroughly demoralised by what had happened.

The meeting to decide the appointment of The Director of Flight

Operations was held at the Air Florida office we were using in London. I travelled up on the train with Barry and in conversation with me he was quite frank, saying that he had no intention of taking Alan's place. In fact, all he wanted do was enjoy his last few years of flying without having to accept a great deal of responsibility. The last remark was curious because when checked out on the 747, as the Chief Pilot he would have great deal of responsibility! The meeting was quite brief with Barry refusing the appointment and Eric being offered it. Eric immediately asked what the difference was between the Chief Pilot's salary and a line Captain, and when told, said that he would accept the appointment provided he had the same differential applied to his training Captain's salary. Randolph had no alternative but to confirm his appointment.

Inevitably this led to other changes, Eric insisting that as Jock Stewart was not qualified on 747s, another Chief Flight Engineer should be appointed until Jock was qualified. Furthermore, he required another Flight Engineer to be nominated as a Training Engineer. Accordingly Peter Greig became Chief Flight Engineer and Bill Lindsay a Training Engineer, both immediately having their salaries increased in line with their extra responsibilities. Randolph's theory that unemployed air crew would work for 'peanuts' had long since been disproved and although Virgin's flight crew pay scales were not equal to BA's, they were certainly much higher than had been budgeted!

I needed to have computerised flight plans produced for the use of the crews and negotiated a Flight Planning contract with Continental Computer services in Los Angeles to provide flight plans for all sectors to be flown. The ex British Airways crews were most aggrieved that I had not used the services of British Airways Flight Planning, but my decision was based on the costs involved. Some time later I arranged a meeting with David Hayward-Cole of BA's Flight Planning Department, (who I knew from my Flying Boat days with BOAC), and discussed Virgin's requirements in depth. This resulted in a contract with them at a price and terms mutually acceptable to both parties. It was some time after the commencement of scheduled services that this contract was implemented, but it effectively silenced the complaints from ex BA crews.

Before Virgin commenced flying the aircraft, I met my old friend Bob Ollerenshaw of British Airways AERAD and negotiated a contract with him to supply Virgin with complete world coverage of Radio Navigation Charts, together with Aerodrome Approach and Landing Charts for airfields capable of taking Boeing 747 aircraft. Always a co-operative person, Bob produced a tailored set of charts for use in the Simulator and another set for the training in USA and the delivery flight, covering everything needed without being too bulky.

It was about this time that Richard brought in Terry Bourne from the Virgin Group to use his considerable managerial experience to assist in the general running of the airline. It had become obvious to me that the relationship between Richard and Randolph had deteriorated to the point where Richard's confidence in Randolph's ability to carry out the reservations and marketing tasks had been completely eroded and ultimately this brought about dramatic changes.

Randolph told me that he was concerned that the aircraft would only carry out 14 hours 20 minutes block time a day and in order to utilise the aircraft more fully, wanted to serve a destination on the continent on a daily basis. Aircraft block time is counted from the time the aircraft moves under its own power until it has stopped moving at the end of the flight and the engines are shut down. Flight time is the elapsed time between take-off and landing. I advised him that the 747 would be flying daily apart from every 21st day when scheduled maintenance would be carried out, plus a period of 20 or so days a year allocated for a 'C' check. The utilisation figure would therefore, be at a respectable level and it would be unwise to attempt to increase this by the addition of short sectors. I pointed out that the 747 was essentially a long-range aircraft and was not cost efficient on short sectors. In any event, of the nine and half-hours remaining in any 24-hour period, after turn round and servicing, only about 4 hours would be available to carry out a round trip. He still persisted with the idea and of the airfields within the required range, I chose Maastricht. It was chosen because it was remote enough to ensure that delays would not occur due to congestion or passenger handling. I had no idea if it had any commercial potential but it was unlikely that any short sector in continuance of the Atlantic sector would attract many ongoing passengers. Nevertheless, I did work out the costs for it and in fact, Maastricht was used for the proving flight. Eventually Virgin was licensed to operate daily flights there, but if my memory is correct, the 747 was only used on one round trip. When Virgin was granted a licence to serve Maastricht, British Air Ferries was contracted to operate the flights using a Viscount aircraft painted in Virgin livery.

With crew training in Seattle completed, the delivery flight departed on time for Gatwick on the scheduled departure day. I drove to Gatwick on a very misty morning to meet the aircraft on its first arrival, seeing it emerge from the mist to touch down very smoothly. I confess to feeling quite elated at sight of the aircraft looking splendid in its Virgin livery. There was also a deep feeling of self-satisfaction that I had been one of the five people who had started the whole airline from nothing nearly two years before. Needless to say there was still a lot to be done before the aircraft would take off on its maiden flight! With all crews except Barry's checked out, he and his crew were allocated simulator time on the British Airways simulator at Heathrow but unfortunately did not get particularly good slot times or continuity of slots.

When Roy and his team had supervised the remaining work to be done on the aircraft, the aircraft was readied for its proving flight to Maastricht and back. The aircraft was fitted with nearly 480 seats of which 12 on the upper deck were first class fully reclining seats. Whilst working towards the start-up of the airline, Richard and Randolph realised that it would be difficult to install economy seats on the upper deck and decided to leave the upper deck in its first class seat configuration. Ultimately this was marketed as 'Upper Class' with a business class fare. This was an attempt to attract frequent traveller businessmen by offering a very high level of comfort, good food and wines, plus other incentives. This idea became remarkably successful although it took some time to establish itself.

The proving flight was a non-commercial flight for the purpose of demonstrating Virgin's operational capability, so only staff could be carried. All available Virgin staff, including flight crew, were detailed for the flight as passengers but even so, the aircraft was less than half full. I sat next to Randolph on the upper deck and after take-off, as the aircraft became airborne there was a very loud bang as the nose wheel retracted. Randolph with his fear of flying was quite startled and asked what had happened. Tongue in cheek I explained that it was just the nose wheel retracting. He remained unconvinced saying that he had never heard a noise like that when flying on other 747s. I knew that the noise had not come from the nose wheel and suspected an engine fault, but when I put my head into the flight deck; all engines appeared to be operating normally. However, Captain Magnus Magnussen was having an in depth discussion with his First Officer and Flight Engineer and I had no wish to disturb them. After landing everyone was taken to a press conference where Richard, Randolph, Eric Davies, and I were available for questions. Before going to the press conference, I did notice that engineers had taken the cowling off one engine and were inspecting it. After the press conference, passengers were re-boarded and the aircraft returned without incident to Gatwick.

Roy, who had been on the ground at Gatwick watching the take off, told me that as the aircraft left the ground, there was a loud bang and a sheet of flame came out of an engine. The aircraft climbed away normally but Roy immediately contacted engineers at Maastricht requesting them to do an inspection on arrival, but nothing amiss was found. Once back at Gatwick, he had the engine inspected internally with a Boroscope when it was discovered that one of the compressor stages had failed. With no spare engine available, Roy contacted Boeing to obtain a replacement engine and Richard had to make rapid financial arrangements with Boeing to guarantee its delivery. With the maiden flight so close, the last thing needed was a technical delay that might postpone the maiden flight. Fortunately an engine was supplied and fitted in place of the failed one.

The aircraft commander for the proving flight, Captain Magnussen, told me later that after the bang was heard, there were no abnormal indications on any instrument associated with that engine other than an insignificant rise in temperature. The damaged part of the engine stood against a wall in Roy's office for months after the event, perhaps as a reminder of what can happen to engines! It was a tribute to the rugged design of the Pratt & Whitney engine that it did not completely cease working.

The timing of the completion of the AOC and other formalities was very tight, including filing of the Operations Specification with the United States Federal Aviation Authority. This latter looked as though it could not be done on time until I discovered that the American FAA official who had the responsibility of signing it was on holiday on the continent and would pass through London on the same day as the maiden flight to Newark. Through his USA office I suggested that he travelled as our guest on the maiden flight and I would meet him at Gatwick prior to departure when we could both sign the prescribed forms. This was agreed and yet another deadline was met without complication.

On the morning of the maiden flight, June 24th 1984, the signed Air Operators Certificate was brought to Gatwick by The Head of CAA Flight Operations Inspectorate, which together with the Navigation specification already issued, cleared the airline for operations. Randolph invited Sue and myself to be on the inaugural flight but I was absolutely exhausted and had to decline. I thought it to be rather strange that Roy had been invited by Richard to go on the inaugural flight, whereas I was not. I thought it might just have been an oversight and thought nothing more about it

In quite a sensational blaze of publicity, GVIRG 'Maiden Voyager' commanded by Eric Davies, took off for Newark where Dicky Doddwell was waiting to bring it back. From the amount of champagne consumed on both sectors, I suspect that there were many people suffering from hangovers! Gordon Steer and I stood at the airport boundary fence close to the office to watch the take off. Quite strangely, I had a feeling of anti climax now that the airline had started operations and the pressure was off! I had been feeling quite unwell for several days, but had simply put it down to the stress of overwork. However, it was the start of a heart condition that would give me much more trouble in the future and lead to open heart surgery.

One appointment made before the inaugural flight was Colin Rance as the airline's Chief Executive with Terry Baughn then returning to the Virgin Group. Colin had considerable experience in Civil Aviation having held a senior post in British Airways but nevertheless his appointment came out of the blue without any notice whatsoever. His experience was more on the commercial side of aviation than operations and in consequence he spent a great deal of time meeting with sales and reservations staff where much improvement was needed. Most operational matters, excluding engineering, Colin seemed to delegate to me and I seemed to be his (unofficial) deputy.

With the airline up and running, the complete reservations system was reviewed and dramatically updated to ensure that it was capable of efficiently handling passenger bookings. With so much invested in the airline, Richard was at pains to ensure its success and frequent board meetings were held at the Virgin London office in Woodstock Street, or on Richard's houseboat at Little Venice in London. Marketing and reservations took priority over most other items on the agenda at those meetings. The communication ability of Virgin's reservations department was initially extremely poor and it was not unusual for Richard to time how long it took reservations staff to answer a telephone call and the time it took to complete a reservation. It was blatantly obvious that there were insufficient telephone lines and reservations staff to deal with the massive numbers of calls and this was quickly remedied. Frankly I was quite amazed how Richard with all his other Virgin businesses, could find the time that the airline demanded of him! The reservations department was constantly reviewed and enlarged, becoming an efficient part of the airline. Obviously David Tait in New York had to deal with similar problems on his side of the Atlantic.

The operations department ran smoothly with very few problems and the aircraft kept fairly closely to schedule. With about five hours turn round time at Gatwick, there were many occasions when due to congestion, the aircraft had to be taken off the Terminal Gate and towed to a remote parking area, causing inconvenience for engineering, cleaning, and re-fuelling of the aircraft. If the aircraft tug used to take the aircraft back to the Gate arrived late, departure delays inevitably would occur. Despite the smoothness of the operations, I think everyone knew that sometime in the future there would be technical problems that would cause serious disruption to the schedule.

On arrival at Newark the procedure was for the aircraft to shut down its engines short of the gate and then be towed to the gate for offloading passengers and freight. It then had to be towed away to another terminal for departure. Needless to say, towing was at extra cost to Virgin!

Although Richard initially knew little about the operation of an airline, he rapidly learned what it was all about and was soon able talk to most people at their own level. Possibly he was the airline's greatest asset, using expertise gained from his other Virgin Companies to develop ideas that strengthened the airline, increased its revenue, and ultimately brought about its success.

Roy added to his engineering staff, taking on Les McKinty (ex Laker) who had just completed an overseas tour of duty with Saudi Arabian Airlines and wished to settle back in England. This appointment was really necessary to ensure that a Virgin engineer would always be available to deal with any problems that arose during the turn round of the aircraft. Prior to this appointment, Dick or Paul had to work every day if the other was on duty elsewhere, or on leave.

The aircraft's schedule had it flying a round trip to Newark each day for twenty days, with day 21 taken up by scheduled maintenance. Annually the aircraft needed a 'C' check that would take it out of service for about 21 days, during which period a sub charter would be needed. Roy had negotiated a contract with British Caledonian, to provide turn round servicing between flights at Gatwick, scheduled maintenance on each twenty first day, and the annual 'C' checks. He also had a contract with United Airlines in Newark for their engineers to carry out turn round checks plus rectification of faults that may have arisen during flight. He also had to consider that engine changes might become necessary at Newark and negotiated to use an engine pool in the USA. A spare engine owned by Virgin was available at Gatwick, but as soon as it was used, the unserviceable engine had to be shipped off immediately for overhaul.

Although Roy had everything into place to ensure that the aircraft could be serviced efficiently, one major worry was that the aircraft could be delayed by a small but nevertheless essential spare part that possibly could only be supplied by Boeing in Seattle, or another company operating the same type of aircraft. Problems of that nature did arise in the future but by then good relationships had been developed between other airlines and spares could be 'Borrowed'. A box of spare parts was carried on the aircraft containing items that were most likely to go wrong, but Murphy's Law says that the item that becomes unserviceable is NOT one carried in the pack!

Without incurring disruption of its schedule, the aircraft would annually have approximately 40 maintenance days and would fly 13 hours 40 minutes on the remaining 325 days of the year totalling 4,442 flight hours per year. Assuming that the aircraft flew all of its scheduled services, its average daily utilisation would be 12 hours 10 minutes. The utilisation could only be exceeded if short flights to onward destinations were flown.

Inevitably the aircraft became delayed by a serious technical fault at Newark and I arrived in the office at 9a.m. one morning to learn that the aircraft was still on the ground in America. Something had to be done immediately or there would be a rolling delay that would put the aircraft off schedule for days and involve the airline in considerable expense. One is totally reliant on the engineers being able to provide information on the progress being made with the rectification of a fault, together with a firm time the aircraft can depart. If such information cannot be given, action must be taken *immediately* to sub-charter another aircraft to carry out the delayed flight. Colin appeared to be in two minds about cancelling the flight and invited my opinion. It was obvious to me that the aircraft could not reach Gatwick in time for its next scheduled departure, or depart during night hours due to curfew restrictions. My suggestion was that having a full load of passengers out of both Gatwick and Newark, it would be impossible to get the passengers on to other airlines, and therefore, we could not cancel the departure, but should take immediate action to get a sub-charter set up. This would ensure that the passengers due to depart that afternoon would not be unduly delayed. Having accepted this, the search for an aircraft began. Sub-charters have to be approved by CAA and cannot be operated by foreign carriers if a British Carrier is available at the same cost. This involved contacting almost every British Carrier to see if spare capacity was available, which in the peak season was extremely unlikely.

Eventually an American carrier was located that had a Boeing 747 available, but the aircraft was in Florida and had to be ferried to Newark. By the time it arrived there, it operated about 22 hours late to Gatwick where it turned round quickly and departed for Newark about 19 hours late. The expense of the sub charter was probably more than double Virgin operating its own aircraft, plus the expense of nearly 480 passengers being put into hotels at Newark and the same number at or around Gatwick. The costs of the sub-charter included ferrying the aircraft from Florida to Newark and its return to Florida on completion of the Virgin sub-charter. This was a very costly operation, but fortunately for us, did not happen very often. Nevertheless, if a delay did occur, it became the duty of the Senior Operations Officer to immediately determine what capacity was available and arrange for it to be put on stand-by to operate for Virgin

The early days of Virgin were very hectic with everything being done to ensure the success of the airline. The passenger loads were very high and in addition, cargo loads were good. On some occasions with strong headwinds over the Atlantic, cargo had to be offloaded to ensure the flight could be made direct without a re-fuelling stop. Alan Chambers, the Managing Director of Virgin Cargo that was founded in October 1984, complained that his company would be financially penalised if this occurred frequently. More importantly it would create a backlog of cargo that would become difficult to move. On one flight, a person, who shall be nameless, ordered the Captain to take the full passenger and cargo load and make a re-fuelling stop en route. This caused great inconvenience to passengers holding onward bookings, prompting Senior Vice President USA David Tait, to point out that passengers were always the first priority on board the aircraft. In his opinion, under no circumstances should a fuel stop be made on account of cargo, a point of view that I endorsed, to the chagrin of Alan Chambers. I could sympathise with him but one had to get the priorities right.

Richard somehow got the idea that the length of the runway at Gatwick was responsible for the shortfall in the aircraft's take-off weight and wanted representation made to the airport authority with view to extending the runway. This assumption, of course, was totally wrong as obstacles located within the take-off flight path in each take-off direction restricted the take-off weight. I proved this by asking Boeing to calculate the take-off weight assuming a much longer runway at Gatwick. Needless to say, the weight remained the same despite the assumed increase in runway length. Had Virgin been allowed to use the higher take-off thrust of the 7F Wet engines, or fitted more powerful engines, a greater weight could have been achieved.

One afternoon just prior to departure for Newark, Captain Dickie Doddwell called on the radio to say that some of his flight documentation was missing, and asked for replacements. Alan drove me to the aircraft and I rushed up the stairs only to collapse as I was handing the papers to Dickie. The next I knew was that I was lying on a reclined seat on the upper deck with an oxygen mask on, and with a member of the fire service standing by. An ambulance arrived to take me to hospital but having partially recovered and beginning to feel better I refused to go. This was much against the wishes of the paramedic who required me to sign a release that would absolve him from responsibility if I suddenly deteriorated. Alan was sitting in the company transport totally unaware of what was going on until I was taken down from the aircraft. He insisted that I should go home immediately and drove directly to Lindfield from the airport. This collapse was the second that had happened to me and led to open heart surgery after I had retired from Virgin.

I had been unwell for two or three days so had little news from the office until Randolph telephoned me at home to tell me that on the following day he was going to Gatwick specifically to talk to Alan Hellary. When I asked what it was about, he told me that he was going to terminate Alan's employment with Virgin. Since the demotion to Operations Manager he had appeared to be totally demoralised and spent a great deal of time discussing with friends outside Virgin what had happened to him. Certainly to some extent his work had suffered and on occasions it was necessary for Gordon Steer or myself do tasks that were his responsibility. Neither of us was too concerned about that as it was our duty to cover for each other. However, the problem was discussed at a board meeting that I did not attend, the outcome of which was that Richard told Randolph to terminate Alan's employment. I could appreciate how Alan felt after his demotion but could not understand why he had not put it all behind him. Alan's salary had not been reduced when he lost the Director of Flight Operations post, so Randolph had kept good faith with me in respect of what we had agreed at that time. I urged Randolph to re-consider but was told that it was a board decision and there was nothing more he could do.

Alan telephoned me during the evening of the day Randolph had seen him and told me that he had been *asked* to resign from the company. When Alan asked Randolph why he should resign, he was told that his work was not up to the required standard and if he did not resign, his employment would be terminated. He was told that he would be given a payment of three months salary in lieu of notice and was asked to clear his desk and leave immediately. Randolph returned to London with the impression that Alan had accepted his dismissal. That was far from being so and for several days he continued to go into the office.

The next stage was when Randolph asked me to arrange for an Operations Manager to be appointed. My first choice was to ask Gordon Steer to cease being a consultant and accept full time employment as the Operations Manager. Being a close friend of Alan he quite naturally was reticent to accept the appointment unless it was definite that Alan was no longer a Virgin employee. When that was confirmed, he took up the appointment and from then until his retirement in January 1989, did a quite magnificent job for Virgin. Alan expressed dismay that Gordon had accepted the appointment, feeling that it was disloyal of him to do so. I greatly respected Alan but felt that his inability to accept the demotion was the cause of the dismissal. Alan continued to telephone me frequently until he told me that he was going to sue Virgin for wrongful dismissal. With that action in view, I said that perhaps he should not to be telling me what he was proposing to do as it might affect the outcome. In the end, he took no action and eventually found himself another job flying small freight aircraft.

On reflection I know that Alan really wanted to continue flying and had indicated this to Randolph. Originally it had been promised that he would be trained to fly on the 747 but with the airline taking much longer to be formed than had been foreseen, he passed the limiting age of 60 when it was no longer permissible to fly large commercial aircraft. Some years later he died suddenly after suffering a massive heart attack.

This was not the only bad news to hit me, the next being when Colin told me that Barry Rawlins and his crew were unlikely to be checked out on the 747. When I asked the reason, he said that the reports from the training staff were unsatisfactory, and additionally, with the aircraft flying every day, there was little chance of it being available for them to do the mandatory amount of flying training on the aircraft. I was aware that the availability of the aircraft could be a problem, but it was not insurmountable as occasionally training flights did take place between the aircraft's arrival at Gatwick and its same day departure to Newark. I knew nothing of unsatisfactory training reports and furthermore, could scarcely believe that to be so. Colin told me that it was in the company's best interests to terminate Barry, Doug and Jock, and wrote to each of them advising them of his decision.

Barry came storming into my office asking me if I knew what had been done. He was furious that an unsatisfactory training report was the reason given and asked if I had seen the training reports. Obviously I had not as it was not my responsibility but he angrily threw the training reports on to my desk and asked me if I could see an unsatisfactory report amongst them. When I repeated that the matter was not in my area of responsibility and was outside my control, he stormed out of the office and that was the last time I ever saw him. Jock Stewart later told me that in his opinion the three of them should never have been employed when the decision to operate a Boeing 747 was made. I could only sympathise with him and tell him that Alan took that decision without consulting anyone else. Had Barry accepted the appointment as The Director of Flight Operations when it was offered to him, the termination of he and his crew may not have happened.

Not long after that unfortunate affair, staff based at Lowfield Heath moved into more spacious offices in Crawley, engineering continuing to use Lowfield Heath for stores and warehousing. The new offices made a pleasant change from the very cramped conditions we had endured during the time that the airline was being set up, but even the new offices had problems. Parking was extremely difficult with only a small part of the public car park, not clearly defined, allocated to Virgin. It was not unusual to find company spaces used by unauthorised vehicles or the area being totally blocked by poor parking. Virgin leased two complete floors in order to house other departments of the airline but these soon became overcrowded.

Late summer 1984 the relationship between Branson and Randolph worsened and Randolph resigned as Chairman. I knew little about this at the time but was quite sad when it was announced. Undoubtedly there was disagreement over the reservations and marketing policy but on reflection, going back to 1982 when I first met Randolph, he told me that he wanted to own and run his own airline. Obviously he was not doing that as a partner with Branson. Later I learned that he resigned as a Director of Virgin Atlantic in May 1985, which was about the time he was planning to start another airline that would be named 'Highland Express'!

In November 1984, Colin told me that he had some bad news and hoped that I would not be upset by it. It seemed that Richard wanted Roy to be appointed as the Deputy Chief Executive, the appointment to take effect immediately. Colin said that this had been discussed at a meeting he attended in London with Richard and Roy when the appointment had been decided. Having been Colin's (theoretical and unofficial) deputy from the start of operations, I was disappointed that no one had seen fit to consult me before it happened. Colin also told me that in addition to being The Director of Planning and Performance, I would become The Corporate Planning Director. When I asked what that would involve, Colin could not give me a direct answer, saying that it would become obvious later. In actual fact nothing came of it. Early in December I learned that Colin would be taking medical leave of absence in January 1985 to have a double hip replacement operation performed, leaving Roy as the acting Chief Executive.

Shortly before Christmas Richard came down to Gatwick on one of his routine visits and dropped into my office for a chat. He was very friendly and said that he hoped that I was not upset by Roy's appointment. I was a little bemused by this and asked why it had been done? Was he was trying to get rid of me? Richard assured me that there was no intention of asking me to leave, explaining that at my age, (I was then 64) I should not be taking on additional responsibilities and he wanted to reduce my workload rather than to have it increase. Possibly he thought that pressures of work had brought on my collapse on the aircraft, and in some respects that might well have been so! Roy was Richard's choice and that was how it went. It was somewhat ironic that had I not introduced Roy to Randolph as a potential Technical Director in the early days of British Atlantic, he would never have joined the company unless it was as a ground engineer.

At Christmas 1984 Richard sent a large Harrods hamper to each director as a token of his appreciation for all that had been achieved since the airline had commenced operations. This generous gesture was repeated each Christmas whilst I was with Virgin.

Late in November 1984, I was invited to attend a luncheon meeting of the American Chamber of Commerce at the Dorchester Hotel, the guest speaker being the President of Pan American Airways. It was a most interesting talk, describing Pan American's role during the post war years of commercial aviation. He made a comment that Pan American, together with other major International Carriers, had done much towards improving the carriage of passengers throughout the world, complaining that some of the emerging 'Small Tiddler' airlines (His description) wanted to swim in the same ocean and enjoy the same privileges that the major airlines had fought so hard to establish. He went on to say that these should be prevented from doing so by the authorities. I spoke to him before leaving the hotel, introducing myself as one of the 'Tiddlers' flying over the large ocean, assuring him that Virgin were there to stay and were only interested in fair play. It is ironic that today Virgin has become a respected airline whilst Pan American went out of business several years ago!

Early in the New Year, Roy told me that Colin would not be coming back after his operation, and the way it was phrased clearly indicated to me that there had never been any intention of him doing so. The company had obviously negotiated a severance agreement with Colin, and Roy was confirmed as the Chief Executive.

At different times and at very short notice Virgin were approached by two other British carriers to operate sub-charters to European holiday destinations, one to Heraklion and the other to Munich. Captain Magnus Goodmundsson operated the sub-charter to Heraklion and advised me that the turning circle at the end of one runway was only just adequate to allow a 747 to turn through 180 degrees and indicated that he could not recommend further operations at that airfield. He alarmed me by saying that there was a slope on the turning pan he used and as it was raining at the time, the aircraft tended to slide slightly sideways on the wet surface.

Although not happy to have the aircraft utilised between its scheduled services or between maintenance periods, I was over ruled and two flights did take place. On both occasions the aircraft returned to Gatwick with insufficient time to enable the scheduled departure time to Newark to be met. Although sub-charter flights give an extra source of revenue, late departures on a scheduled service are to be avoided as passenger confidence can be so easily be eroded. I was perhaps more worried that the aircraft might become unserviceable at an airfield where there was no technical support and would cause a lengthy delay to our scheduled service.

Usually requests for sub-charters came up at very short notice and if it were during a weekend, as was a Munich charter, I would have to go to the office to attend to the operational details. The Munich flight took place on a Sunday and I was phoned by Roy before breakfast to cost the flight and to oversee the operation. I left home at 8a.m. and did not get back until late afternoon.

A hidden problem with sub-charters was that the stand by crew had to be used giving Gordon Steer an awful problem if someone reported sick for the scheduled service to Newark on the same day. In order to keep the operating costs to a minimum, only the bare minimum of crews had been employed and it was a serious problem for him to lose crew members through sickness, without losing them on sub-charters. Sometimes sub-charter requests from other operators were refused because Gordon simply had no crews readily available to operate. He explained that with virtually no reserve of crews, he had to rely on the loyalty of those he asked to crew any extra flights. Without their co-operation, none would have been possible.

Perhaps the most time consuming task during the first year or so was to obtain approval from CAA to operate the aircraft down to Category 2 landing limits. Approval for Category 2 permits the aircraft to approach and land with lower cloud base and visibility than that of Category 1, thus reducing the risk of a diversion in marginal weather conditions. It was necessary for Eric Davies, Dicky Doddwell and myself to attend many discussions with the All Weather Operations Branch of CAA, the first of which was held at CAA Kingsway London on Thursday 18th October 1984. During this first meeting Virgin was informed of the technical and crew training requirements for Category 2 operations and told the procedure to be followed to enable these lower operating limits to be approved. The requirements were very stringent, necessitating a new chapter being written into the Training Manual followed by a long evaluation of practice approaches before approval was given. Even when CAA approval was given, Category 2 landing was not permissible unless both pilots *and* the flight engineer on any crew had been previously cleared, and the prescribed aircraft equipment was serviceable throughout the approach and landing procedure. With a single aircraft operating, allowing only two approaches each day, it proved to be extremely difficult to keep pilots and flight engineers current even after approval was obtained. Often unserviceable aircraft equipment resulted in occasions when crew members could not carry out the practice approaches needed to clear or keep them current to Category 2 limits. Practice approaches were usually performed whenever the weather conditions permitted. The ultimate goal was to operate to Category 3b Autoland, but that did not happen until well after my retirement.

The first months of the airline saw flights operating with very high load factors and if these could be maintained, the success of the airline would be assured. However, caution was needed as these months were in the high season and a great deal of marketing expertise would be needed to sustain the good load factors in the low season that lay ahead. I was somewhat concerned that 'Special Fare' offers would dilute the revenue enough to make the operation unprofitable, but learned that the limit placed on the number of cut price seats made this unlikely. However it was good publicity and kept the Virgin name prominently in the market place.

Despite Richard Branson's statement that he would not seek other routes, it was not long before licence applications were filed for many other destinations. With a single Boeing 747 aircraft it was quite obvious that no additional routes could be operated unless another aircraft could be acquired. Although the applications were filed in good faith, some were really quite speculative.

The accumulated list of licence applications became so large that CAA eventually asked Virgin to 'prune' it down to a sensible level. However, one licence application that was of prime importance was for Miami, the lucrative holiday destination. I had carefully evaluated that route and found that even with the restricted take-off weight at Gatwick, the outbound flight time of 9 hours would just allow a direct flight with a full load of passengers, but virtually no freight. This was bad news for Virgin Cargo who considered that there was a good freight market between London and Miami. The good news for them was that with little or no take-off weight restrictions at Miami, the shorter 8 hours flight time to Gatwick would allow a decent amount of cargo to be carried. With flights to holiday destinations within Florida becoming likely, Richard formed Virgin Holidays to provide package tours to that area.

Late 1984 (or was it early 1985?) Richard announced that he was going to attempt to win back from the Americans, The Blue Riband for crossing the Atlantic in the fastest time. I recall that Hugh Band was Virgin's press officer and he was determined to get as much publicity as possible for the attempt, which in turn would give publicity to the airline. There was little for me to do in connection with this challenge but Esso, Virgin's Gatwick fuel supplier, did supply the boat with fuel, but I had nothing to do with that.

When 'Virgin Challenger's' journey commenced, most people in the airline followed its progress followed very closely and progress reports were put up in the Airline Headquarters. As 'Challenger', seemingly on course for success was rapidly approaching Lands End, I was talking to Hugh Band who was feeling absolutely delighted by the public interest in the project and the publicity that the airline had got from it. He casually said, 'You know we would get more publicity out of this if the boat were to sink!' I thought nothing more of that remark until about 30 minutes later when I heard that 'Challenger' had sent out a distress message and was sinking. It was just a remarkable coincidence that Hugh made that rather jocular remark when he did. Of course Richard took everything in his stride and immediately made plans for his next (and successful) attempt. Quite naturally however, the Americans would not give up the trophy!

As stated earlier in this chapter, in May 1985 the relationship between Randolph and Richard had deteriorated to the point where it was inevitable that their partnership could not continue and it came as no surprise when Richard bought Randolph's shares and the partnership was dissolved. Randolph left Virgin with a good financial package and an unlimited travel agreement that allowed he and his family plus two friends, firm seats on any Virgin flights in Upper Class for the rest of his life. These travel facilities and the associated lost revenue caused Richard sufficient concern to later take legal action, albeit unsuccessfully, in an attempt to nullify the agreement. With Randolph out of the airline I was the only person left of the original group of five that had started the airline's 'wheels' turning in 1982 and wondered how much longer I would be allowed to continue. It was also about this time that Randolph applied to CAA for licences to operate schedule services between Prestwick – Toronto, and Prestwick – New York (Newark). Richard saw these applications as competition and ordered an objection to be filed.

In November 1985, Virgin's licence to operate passenger and freight scheduled services to Miami was granted and plans were made to commence operations in April 1986. The inaugural flight to Miami was operated by GVIRG on 19th April 1986 with Jim Smillie in command, and of course, with the inevitable Virgin blaze of publicity. I can recall Jim saying (jokingly) that the passengers consumed almost as much Champagne on the flight as the engines did fuel. Chevron was awarded the contract to supply fuel in Miami as they could supply the cheaper duty free fuel that some competitors could not. Initially only three flights were flown each week to Miami and the number of flights to Newark was reduced to four a week.

The company had already turned its attention towards the acquisition of a second aircraft and negotiations were started with Boeing for a 747–200 aircraft previously operated by Alitalia, the Italian airline. The aircraft in question had accumulated far more flying hours than Virgin's first aircraft and fairly soon after its introduction into service, major engineering work known as the Section 41 Modification would be required. This involved the complete rebuilding of the nose section of the aircraft from frame section 41 forward, work that would take the aircraft out of service for several weeks. Although this major mandatory work could be deferred for a reasonably short period of time, other modifications were required before the aircraft could be brought into service. Boeing carried out those at their plant in Seattle and was contracted to supply the Flight Manual and amended Operations Manuals to conform to CAA regulations. Fortunately the engines fitted were Pratt and Whitney JT9D–7A and the performance level was identical to the aircraft already being operated. Before amendment of the Operations Manuals started, Boeing warned that if the aircraft were to be eventually disposed of, the manuals would have to be restored to their original state at Virgin's expense. The aircraft registration GVGIN was selected by Roy on this occasion and used when it was put on the British Register in June 1986.

Boeing carried out the necessary work on the aircraft and prior to completion, Captain Jim Smillie and a crew were sent to Seattle on 8th June 1986 to carry out the acceptance flight and ferry it back to England. CAA pilot Jock Reid flew the C of A test flight accompanied by Jim Smillie and two Boeing test pilots. Richard wanted some publicity for the second aircraft's delivery and it was arranged that a private Learjet aircraft with a professional photographer on board would take air-to-air photographs of GVGIN as it departed from Seattle. On 18th June, the day of the delivery flight, Jim Smillie took off and the photographing aircraft formated with him as he lifted off the runway. For the next hour they flew in formation over Puget Sound taking video pictures and still photographs, the result being a very interesting video. When the task was completed, GVGIN set course for Gatwick where it landed 10 hours later. There was still a great deal of work to be done at Gatwick before the aircraft was able to commence operations, but once this was accomplished the aircraft operated its first flight to Newark.

With two aircraft in service, the daily Newark service was resumed and the Miami frequency increased to four a week. Shell had been awarded the contract to supply fuel at Gatwick for Miami flights, their first contract with Virgin, and this undoubtedly gave a glow of satisfaction to my old friend Chris Fear of Shell who had been hoping to obtain a contract with Virgin since the airline started.

The second aircraft increased my workload still further and I started looking for a suitably qualified person to assist me with some of my duties. I was most fortunate to receive a letter from Peter Stanton, formerly a navigator with Laker, asking me if I had any vacancies. Peter had rejoined Laker as a navigation assistant about a year after he had been made redundant as a navigator, so I was fully aware of his capabilities. I had no hesitation in offering him employment and he proved to be well up to the task, becoming a useful employee and eventually taking over the ground training of crews from me.

Additional pilots, flight engineers, and cabin staff were recruited for the second aircraft through advertisements placed in 'Flight' magazine, and once again the response was quite outstanding. Gordon Steer and I had received constant enquiries concerning possible employment from ex Laker Captains and First Officers but these could not be seriously considered unless they were Boeing 747 qualified. One particular Captain contacted me several times and although he was Boeing 747 qualified and I could recommend him to the Flight Operations Director, he insisted that he would only join as a Captain and would not consider being a First Officer. Virgin was a small company and its policy was to promote from within its ranks, therefore the only pilot vacancies that arose were for First Officers.

George Newby an old friend from Laker days was flying Boeing 747s as a Captain for Kuwait Airways and he contacted Gordon to see if there were any vacancies for pilots as he was hoping to return to UK. George was quite happy to join as a First Officer and Gordon was able to get him accepted by Eric Davis. As Virgin expanded he was promoted to Captain rank fairly soon after joining and over the years reached senior management level. Ultimately several ex-Laker captains joined Virgin as First Officers and quickly advanced to Captain rank which undoubtedly would have brought a glow of satisfaction to Alan Hellary! Eric Davies brought in Captain John Hayward as a First Officer, an old friend from his British Airways days, and he was promoted to Captain rank prior to the second aircraft being delivered. Eventually he became the Director of Flight Operations but sadly died of cancer some years later.

From time to time I would be invited to an executive lunch hosted by Shell Aviation at Shell Mex House in the Strand attended by senior executives of various companies and airlines. Virgin had taken delivery of its second Boeing 747 and in those early days it was not being fully utilised. I was seated next to a gentleman from The Ministry of Defence and in conversation he asked me what we would be doing about the spare capacity that we had at that time. I said that plans for the long term were being put into place but in the short term, (tongue in cheek), hoped that we might be able to do some MOD work. I gave him my business card on which I hand wrote my direct telephone line that bypassed my secretary.

Some weeks later I received a call from the MOD on my direct line inviting Virgin to bid for a contract to fly three round trips from Brize Norton to the Falklands in July 1986. I discussed this with Roy and it was decided that we would bid for the contract. While working out the details of the operation prior to submitting Virgin's bid, it occurred to me that the original enquiry from the MOD had to come through on my direct private telephone line. Being curious how this could have happened, I telephoned the contact at MOD to ask how they had got my private number. It transpired that my seating companion at the Shell lunch was a very senior person in MOD who, with a requirement of Falklands flights coming up, had instructed his staff to contact me. The Virgin Commercial Director, Jonathon Wilson who had replaced Ron Davies some weeks before, was not particularly enthusiastic about bidding against British Airways but with both Roy and myself in favour, he went along with it. Once I had worked out the details and costs, it was left it to Jonathon to submit Virgin's bid to MOD and await their reply. Quite amazingly Virgin were awarded the contract for the three round trips to be operated in July 1986. British Airways had held the monopoly on Falkland's flights using Mount Pleasant, the new Falklands airport, since it had been opened. They were less than pleased when Virgin secured the contract.

Someone in British Airways, who shall be nameless, ordered that no assistance should be given to Virgin whilst operating these flights but this had no effect whatsoever. I had a Flight Plan contract with British Airways but that department's only action was to inform me that I must tell them precisely what route I wished the aircraft to take. I was told by the RAF Wing Commander co-ordinating the flights that a full briefing would be given to selected senior Virgin staff, which would include details of the route, arrival and departure procedures in the Falklands and en route procedures. Ascension Island, where fuel would be taken on in both directions, was a Category C airfield that required a Self Briefing Information Sheet from which the crews could brief themselves on what they needed to know about the airfield. Although contracted to supply such Information, British Airways refused to do so on the grounds that it had taken British Airways a great deal of time and expense to set up the route, and could see no reason why they should pass this on to a competitor. This again did not present too much of a problem as I had been to Ascension Island several times and was able to write my own information sheet.

Prior to the operation commencing, Gordon Steer and I went to RAF Station Brize Norton to attend a very comprehensive briefing given by a senior officer covering all the procedures to be observed. The information given was restricted and could only be used to brief crews who would be involved. Gordon needed to set into place arrangements to position crews to Ascension Island and Mount Pleasant in the Falklands, but this presented no problem other than the crews had to fly on RAF transport aircraft that did not afford the same level of comfort as civil aircraft. I needed to have a Virgin Operations Officer at both Ascension Island and Mount Pleasant who would liase with the RAF, provide loading instructions and prepare the load sheet. I chose Operations Officer Paul Hooper to be based in Ascension Island and asked Peter Stanton to go to the Falklands where his greater experience would be of paramount importance. There was a problem concerning the crew allowances in consideration that they would be effectively operating in a war zone. This was settled by paying them double allowances for the sectors to/from the Falklands and the stopovers. Peter Stanton asked for similar allowances but I could not agree to this as he was not flying staff and theoretically was only allowed out of pocket expenses. Since the RAF provided accommodation and food, there would be no expenses during his stay there. However, as a gesture of good will I told him that he would receive normal crew allowances for his time away from UK that would more than compensate him for the poor conditions under which he had to live in the Falklands. Initially he refused to go and I accepted this and said that I would go myself, knowing that with my disability it would have been very difficult for me in the icy conditions. Peter immediately retracted his refusal and accepted the assignment. Afterwards he told me that with the amount of slush, snow and ice around, I would have found it quite impossible to get around. In the event both Paul and Peter performed their duties in a thoroughly efficient and professional manner.

Two flights went exactly to schedule but the third suffered technical problems incurring a lengthy delay at Ascension Island as it was about to depart on the final sector back to Brize Norton, necessitating Virgin charter a Boeing 707 to fly out the spare part that was needed. The resultant delay caused major disruption to the scheduled Miami flight that was to be operated after the Falklands flight. The delay certainly eroded the profit margin but at the end of the day, the RAF was satisfied with Virgin's performance. None of the flights operated with heavy loads and on the final return flight there was sufficient space available to allow the slip crews to position home.

Gordon and I drove to Brize Norton to meet the last arrival and I flew back to Gatwick on the aircraft. The Captain on the last sector from Ascension Island was Dickie Doddwell and he was most unhappy with arrangements made for the crews, particularly in Ascension Island where the accommodation was sub standard ... He was opposed to doing any further flights to Ascension on the grounds that the airfield facilities were not really good enough. His real concern was that as the landing was always to the east just after sunrise, it was extremely difficult to avoid being blinded by the sun so low in the sky. I pointed out that I had operated there myself and furthermore, no other Captain had complained about its use. On further reflection I realised that on the occasions I had been to Ascension Island, the arrival was not at dawn so he did have a point. As Virgin's entire future capacity was to be taken up by scheduled services, it was unlikely that we would be able to bid for further flights. At that time I felt that it was a pity that Randolph was no longer with Virgin as his original idea was to operate to the Falklands, although not precisely in the manner we did operate.

MOD must have been satisfied with the Virgin operation because subsequently the company was invited to bid for MOD flights to Cyprus and other destinations. These invitations had to be declined as the capacity of both aircraft was being fully utilised. I have a rather nice photograph on the wall of my study showing the Virgin 747 on an ice covered parking area of Mount Pleasant airfield in the Falklands with an RAF fighter in the foreground, given to me by the RAF Wing Commander at MOD who liaised with Virgin.

Sometime in mid 1986, Eric Davies resigned as the Director of Flight Operations following a disagreement with Roy Gardner and it became necessary to appoint a replacement. Several Captains were considered, including one outside the company, but the appointment was offered to Jim Smillie who accepted it effective from 1st September 1986. Bernie Mitchell, somewhat dissatisfied with his job with the CAA, had been in discussion with Virgin for some time with a view of joining the airline. When an agreement had been reached, he resigned from the CAA Inspectorate and joined Virgin as a Captain. With Virgin's policy of promoting from within the company, those First Officers next in line for a command were quite naturally upset by Bernie's appointment. All the pilots saw this as creating a precedent that was unacceptable to them, and it did cause a great deal of dissent. Bernie's training was carried out and he flew the required number of sectors under supervision. When his final line check was rostered, both Training Captains refused to carry it out. It was left to Jim Smillie to check him out on a round trip sub-charter from Gatwick to Heraklion on 28th October 1986. Jim described the round trip to be 'Quite interesting.' The take-off from Gatwick was on the emergency runway 26R and the arrival and landing at Heraklion was in rain with very poor visibility that was just on company limits. The landing back at Gatwick was again on the emergency runway 26R and he remembers Gordon Steer, who was watching the landing, saying that the wheels looked very close to the terminal building! Regardless of that comment, I have no doubt that the required safe clearance was present.

The replacement CAA inspector was Captain Ralph Kohn, a very experienced and long serving member of the Inspectorate. Ralph had been responsible for organising the changes in format of Airlines CAA approved manuals and initially wanted me to change to the new system he had devised. Given the vast amount of work needed for this, I was most reluctant, but was relieved to learn that only those airlines that had not yet obtained their AOC had to comply.

Always looking for sources of extra revenue, Richard considered feeding passengers from Northern Ireland to connect with the 747 operating from Gatwick. Londonderry Eglinton was chosen as the airfield from which a feeder service could possibly operate and Roy asked me to go there to meet the airfield manager. It was arranged that I would fly to Belfast where I would be met and flown on to Londonderry in a light aircraft piloted by the airfield manager, who would then show me around the airfield. Prior to departure I was asked if I would have lunch with MP John Hulme and the Mayor of Londonderry before returning to Gatwick. DANAIR gave me a complimentary return flight to Belfast where on arrival I transferred to the light aircraft and proceeded to Eglinton. We circled the airport several times so that I could see the airfield and its approach paths.

The airfield facilities were very basic and certainly left a lot to be desired if it was to be used for scheduled services. The only approach and landing aid was a Non Directional Radio Beacon with a cloud break procedure that was barely adequate for regular operations. The runway, previously used many years ago by the Royal Navy, was short, its surface not particularly well maintained, had only low intensity runway lighting and no approach lighting. The improvements required were likely to be very costly and time consuming. I also had the impression that the Fire Service was staffed by part time firemen who carried out other duties at the airfield when fire services were not required. Boeing 737 aircraft did use the airfield for occasional charter flights from/to Kerry in Eire but the distance of these flights was very short compared to Gatwick and gave no guidance to me. Furthermore, the terminal was extremely small and had virtually no security arrangements in force, a very essential requirement if the airport was to be used regularly by Virgin, and again, a most expensive one to set up.

At lunch, both John Hulme and the Mayor said that the City Council were prepared to drastically improve the airfield against the guarantee that Virgin would commence regular flights. However, as my brief was simply to evaluate the airfield and report back, I had no authority to discuss what Virgin's plans were likely to be. After lunch I was driven back to Belfast in the Mayoral Limousine to catch the late afternoon flight back to Gatwick. Before writing my report, I established that a Boeing 737–200 could marginally operate from Londonderry to Gatwick with a full load but there could be occasions on high temperature days when this might not be possible. My own thoughts were that it seemed unlikely that passengers would opt to fly from Londonderry to Gatwick and transfer to Virgin for New York when the cheaper and quicker option of going via Dublin was available to them. That may well have been Richard's view because nothing came of it.

In 1987 Virgin flew several ad hoc flights to various airports in UK, amongst them East Midlands and Leeds/Bradford. Jim Smillie and Magnus Goodmundsson operated what they called 'The Shopping Trip' to Leeds Bradford where the arrival of a Boeing 747 created quite a stir, the advance publicity having caused hundreds of sightseers to travel to the airport. Jim was asked to do something 'unusual' after take-off for the benefit of the photographers and sightseers. With the aircraft weight being so low, with Air Traffic Controls permission he did a 45 degree banked turn immediately after becoming airborne. Apparently this was quite spectacular, but needless to say, perfectly safe!

I can recall that on two occasions at Christmas, Richard invited a full plane load of children to a Christmas party in the sky where they were served traditional Christmas dinner and plum pudding, and each was given a present. On one occasion Richard laid on the 747 to take large numbers of staff from other Virgin companies for a day flight to Palma and back as a reward for their loyalty. Flights such as these were not easy to fit in to the very full programme of scheduled services but by juggling maintenance slots it was achieved.

I was quite surprised when Randolph telephoned me early in 1987 to say that he had been granted licences to operate Atlantic flights and was in the process of setting up his new airline, Highland Express, and invited me to join his team. It appeared that he was looking to operate a very old Boeing 747–100 (based in Scotland) to Newark USA from points in UK. Although the routes to be operated were not directly in competition with Virgin, the emergence of another airline serving

Newark was bound to have some effect if it became successful. I certainly did not feel well enough to undertake the task of setting up another airline and declined his invitation to join. I must confess that apart from my physical limitations, I had little faith in his new airline succeeding. My old friend, ex BOAC navigator Ken Armstrong, took on the task and obviously did what was necessary.

Randolph's next request was that I supply him with copies of Virgin's CAA approved Boeing 747 operations manuals at a small cost to be agreed. Without authorisation from Roy, I could not agree to this request. Roy did in fact agree to him using Virgin's copyright but the extremely high price he put on the manuals, precluded agreement being reached. Furthermore, Roy ordered me not to assist Highland Express in any way whatsoever, which at the time I thought rather hard. I do remember asking Randolph why on earth he wanted to put his savings at risk by starting an airline that had little chance of success. I pointed out that there was little money to be made operating out of airfields in UK outside Gatwick, but he was quite unmoved and went ahead with his plans. The ambition to own his own airline was clearly still there and I could sense the elation that he would be the Chairman and Managing Director! The Boeing 747–100 registered GHILO, was limited in its operational performance and certainly would not be as reliable as the newer aircraft Virgin operated. However, an AOC was issued and Highland Express commenced operations on 30th June 1987 when its 747 carried out its proving flight from Brussels to Stansted and immediately operated Stansted – Prestwick – Newark. We in Virgin followed the airline's progress but it was not long before repeated technical problems caused severe delays and it came as no surprise when it went into liquidation on 11th December 1988. It was a disappointment to Randolph when it failed but at least he could say that he did own and operate an airline.

One of the first Highland Express Captains, Peter Ford was an ex BA Captain who joined Virgin as a First Officer, leaving only when Randolph offered him a command with Highland Express. After Highland's collapse, Peter rejoined Virgin as a First Officer and ultimately became a Captain until his retirement. Ironically, Virgin Atlantic acquired the Highland Express Boeing 747–100 GHILO, and changed its registration to GVMIA. It was operated successfully for many years until it was 'retired'.

Always ready to take up a new challenge, early in 1987 Richard decided to attempt to fly a hot air balloon across the Atlantic. For this venture he teamed up and trained with Per Lindstrand whose company produced hot air balloons. This was to be no ordinary balloon, but an absolute monstrous sized one that was capable of reaching very high altitudes. During the training period Richard nearly lost his life during a parachute jump when his parachute failed to operate correctly and he became entangled in the shroud lines. Fortunately he survived without any injury being sustained.

Roy and I went to Per's factory during the construction of the balloon to meet with Per and Richard to discuss the attempted flight and see the capsule that was only partially built. Roy was concerned with the safety aspects and asked how much oxygen would be carried since it was intended to fly at a high altitude in order to get into a jet stream. It was explained that an engine powered compressor would be mounted above the capsule to provide pressurisation and that the Boeing pressurisation system would be used. Roy asked what they would do if the engine stopped during flight, explaining that with the Boeing system, the pressure relief valve would OPEN if the pressurisation failed causing the altitude inside the capsule to rapidly climb to that at which the balloon was flying. Back to the drawing board!!

I was mainly concerned that the balloon would penetrate the airspace used by virtually hundreds of jet aircraft crossing the Atlantic and had many conversations with the authorities controlling the North Atlantic Airspace. It seemed that the balloon would not be authorised to climb above 27,500 feet, the highest level available to aircraft not able to conform to the navigation requirements of MNPS airspace. A balloon is simply carried along by the wind and apart from changing to an altitude where a different wind might be present; it has no ability to navigate. Notwithstanding all of these difficulties the plans went ahead for the attempt.

At 0810 GMT on 2nd July 1987 the balloon lifted off from Sugarloaf, Maine, USA and despite losing some fuel cylinders on lift-off, the Atlantic crossing was successful. The crossing took 31 hours and 41 minutes to cover 3075 statute miles at an average speed of 84 knots. Captain John Hayward was in command of a Virgin Atlantic 747 whose track over the Atlantic to USA took it very close to the balloon. With the aircraft and balloon both well above cloud and in brilliantly clear visibility, John sighted the balloon and obtained permission from Air Traffic Control to descend to the balloon's level and circle around it. He was able to talk to Richard and Per by radio and relayed their conversation through the aircraft public address system. I must confess to being rather envious of that experience and would have given anything to have been on the flight deck with John and his crew.

The arrival at Limavady in Northern Ireland was not quite as planned. Once the balloon was over the land, they descended too rapidly and were unable to prevent the capsule hitting the ground very hard. So hard in fact that some empty fuel cylinders were torn off which lightened the load and caused the balloon to soar back into the sky and drift out over the Irish Sea. Rather than attempt another touch down on land in Scotland, it was decided to ditch in the sea. The drama continued when, with balloon close to the sea, Per Lindstrand jumped into the water before Richard was ready and with that weight loss, the balloon once again soared into the air. Fortunately Richard was able to descend the balloon and jump into the sea when it reached a low enough level. The rescue helicopter that had been following the balloon immediately picked up Richard who then discovered that Per Lindstrand, who had jumped first, had not been picked up and was still swimming. All ended safely with no injuries being sustained. At later dates Richard and Per would successfully cross the Pacific, but would fail in their first attempt to go around the world by hot air balloon.

In August 1987 British Caledonian announced that they had agreed terms with British Airways who would take them over. Caledonian had been in trouble financially for several months so it came as no great shock when the deal was done, although I know that Richard was not too happy at the time. The maintenance agreement that Virgin had with British Caledonian was taken over by British Airways and this did cause problems for Roy. The annual heavy maintenance 'C' checks had to be done at Heathrow instead of Gatwick and that involved ferrying the aircraft to/from Heathrow and required Virgin's engineering representatives to be there the whole time the aircraft was there. The timing of the 'C' Check programme had to be very carefully arranged as the Virgin scheduled services would have to be sub-chartered. With the best will in the world it is impossible to guarantee that an aircraft will emerge from a 'C' check exactly on time, but it should not be very materially different. Virgin had a very long delay that turned out to be due to British Airways stopping work on the Virgin 747 in favour of work on their own aircraft. Roy thoroughly investigated the circumstances and Virgin subsequently sued BA for the loss of revenue and the cost of what were unnecessary extra sub-charters. Roy was very astute in such matters and Virgin won the legal action. I have no doubt that Roy had considerable unease knowing that he was totally reliant on BA honouring their maintenance agreement with Virgin.

With the holiday route to Miami established with four flights a week being operated, the next licence Virgin applied for was Orlando, the Florida holiday destination. In a comparatively short period of time, what had been an ordinary US town had become a large city and an extremely popular holiday destination. I imagine that this was largely due to the Walt Disney organisation that saw its potential and built Walt

Disney World. This, together with Epcott and the many other tourist attractions at Orlando is said to attract over 28 million visitors a year from all parts of Europe, Canada, and other parts of the United States.

Normally holiday visitors look for warm sunshine and beaches, but although Orlando has plenty of sunshine, it is some distance away from the nearest beach at Cocoa Beach, close to Cape Canaveral, which is a two-hour drive from Orlando. The John F Kennedy Space Centre at Cape Canaveral is also a major attraction and many thousands visit each year, particularly when a Space Shuttle is about to be launched! With beaches so far away, most Orlando hotels have at least one large swimming pool available for guests. I believe that Orlando airfield was built for the National Guard with runways long enough to satisfy the requirements of B52 aircraft. In fact, at the entrance to the airport there is a B52 set on a concrete stand dwarfing everything around it.

Prior to the licence application, I provided route studies and made calculations of the loads that could be carried. The Sector flight time to Orlando was about the same as Miami and the take-off weight constraints at Gatwick caused the same concern to Virgin Cargo who again intended to fully exploit its potential. Obviously again there would be some days when the direct flight would not be possible, and even if it were, the cargo carried would be almost nil. The licence was granted with little or no opposition, mainly, I imagine, due to the quite enormous growth in holiday passengers from UK. Shell was given the contract for fuel at Gatwick and Chevron in Orlando.

Implementation of this route in May 1988 took up all the capacity of both aircraft and in so doing, caused Gordon Steer problems to crew it. Initially I had thought that a crew could operate to Miami or Orlando and then immediately position by road or internal airline to Orlando or Miami to operate the next flight back to Gatwick. Gordon saw too many problems with this and arranged to have slip crews available at both destinations with the result that more crews were needed. David Tait negotiated with two Aircraft Handling Companies in Orlando and with both costing about the same, gave me the choice. I chose Page Avjet Corporation as they could handle Boeing 747's and had servicing and repair facilities that Roy might find useful. However they were not conversant with the Weight & Balance of the aircraft and asked for training to be given to their staff that would prepare the load sheet.

I decided that I would go out to Miami to have discussions with the Virgin Station Manager and then go on to Orlando to meet the first flight in and see it dispatched back to Gatwick. It seemed an ideal opportunity to take Sue with me to give her a break, so travel arrangements were put in place. Leaving our children with their grandparents, we departed from Gatwick on 22nd May 1988 on a Virgin Atlantic flight to Miami that was being operated by a DC10 of Martinair, Dutch Charter Company. This was due to Virgin's 747 GVIRG being out of service for two weeks having its annual heavy maintenance check.

It was a pleasant enough flight but did not have Upper Class so we were committed to fly economy. On arrival we were met and taken to the hotel where we would spend two nights before driving to Orlando. On the following day I attended meetings at the Virgin Office with Charlene Cooke, Virgin's Southern USA representative and afterwards was taken to pick up a rental car for the drive to Orlando on the next day. The drive was very pleasant with very little traffic on the Florida Turnpike, the journey taking about six hours with a stop for lunch en route. The only problem encountered was finding International Drive where the hotel was located.

On the following day I left Sue to relax in the sun and went to meet Joe Bagosy of Page Avjet Corporation who introduced me to the Page staff who would be handling the aircraft on arrival. I issued Page with all the manuals that were needed by them and then gave instruction to the persons who would be responsible for the loading of the aircraft and the preparation of the Load Sheet. Joe and a Page Vice President took me to lunch at a restaurant in the airport before returning to finish the instruction. This took up most of the day and it was late afternoon before I got back to the hotel to join Sue at the pool. By this time the temperature was in the nineties with very high humidity and all I needed was to get into the pool. The Virgin flight crew and one cabin attendant had arrived that afternoon to operate the flight out on the next day and we met them very briefly.

Mid afternoon on the following day I went to the airport to meet the flight that arrived on schedule with a full load of passengers. Charlene Cooke laid on a reception to mark Virgin's first flight and had invited many VIP's from the Orlando area. My job was to see that the return flight was dispatched on time and ensure that the loading of the aircraft and the Load Sheet was correct. Being the first flight out of Orlando, there were no passengers to return to Gatwick but Virgin Cargo had produced about 16 tons of freight, so the sector did have some revenue. Page staff performed well and the aircraft was turned round and departed on time for Gatwick leaving me clear to join the reception party. The next flight was not due for three days that allowed me further time to instruct other Page staff as well as enjoying the local sights. On the evening of the second day, Joe Bagosy and his wife Jeannie took Sue and myself into the city for a meal at a very nice restaurant decorated in an earlier period style with old time entertainment. There we ran into Captain John

Hayward and his crew who would be flying the aircraft that we would travel back on.

The following day being Sunday, Joe and Jeannie invited us to their house for the day where we lazed in and around his pool with a cold beer always at hand. After a late barbecued (enormous steak) lunch, Joe and Jeannie took us to Epcott to see some of the incredibly good attractions, including some of the national pavilions. The climax of the evening was a spectacular firework display that takes place nightly at Disney World and is clearly visible at Epcott.

On the day of departure, soon after breakfast I was told that the aircraft would be arriving on schedule about 4p.m. and arranged to be at the airport before it arrived. I drove the rental car to the drop off point and then proceeded to the Page dispatch office to supervise the departure. Sue and I were the only passengers travelling but Virgin Cargo had produced another 16 tons of freight. I learned later that the freight was mainly fruit, some of which had come all the way from California. The yield from this type of freight was not particularly high but at least it gave some revenue to the company. It occurred to me that if a delay occurred, fruit might not survive the journey but Virgin Cargo doubtless had the answers to that problem. I was not impressed with the loading instructions given or the Load Sheet produced by the person I had instructed and told Joe that he did not seem to have any confidence in what he was doing. In the event that person asked to be relieved of the task and the other person who had been instructed took over the responsibilities. Exactly on schedule the aircraft departed for Gatwick and Sue and I had a most enjoyable flight home. During the flight home, we had the entire Upper Class section to ourselves with an Airhostess and a Steward to look after us. I was on the flight deck for the take-off, then had dinner immediately afterwards followed by about 6 hours sleep before being awakened for breakfast 45 minutes before arrival at Gatwick. Subsequent flights to/from Orlando usually had full passenger loads and whatever freight that could be carried.

After returning from Orlando, Roy said that he was concerned about me being away from the office so long, and questioned my expenses. I pointed out that I had told him how long I would be away and had been in touch with the office daily. I also made it quite clear that I had paid my wife's expenses out of my own pocket and had not included them in my claim.

My health was not too good and I felt that if it deteriorated further it would not be long before I would feel compelled to retire but nevertheless, was determined to hold on as long as possible. Roy seemed concerned about this and gave me the impression that he would like me to retire, so much so that I asked directly if that was his intention. Whatever was in his mind, he was at pains to say that he wanted me to employ someone capable of taking over my duties before a date could be finalised

With flights to three destinations operating successfully, Richard's marketing consultant Hugh Welburn indicated that applications for licences to operate to Tokyo and Hong Kong should be considered. These were discussed in depth at Board meetings before a decision was taken to apply for a licence to operate to Tokyo. If I remember correctly, there were two Japanese airlines flying to London from Tokyo, but only British Airways serving Tokyo from London, so there was room for another British operator. It was obvious that there would be vigorous opposition from British Airways who held a monopoly on the route, and most likely some opposition from Japan Airlines and All Nippon Airways. Opposition always seemed to encourage Richard to take on rivals and the 'battle', so to speak, was joined.

Both 747 aircraft operated by Virgin were certified by CAA to operate up to a take-off weight of 351,000 kgs, against the maximum allowable structural weight of 362,873 kgs. The lower certified weight had been selected to reduce the cost of Landing and Parking charges at Gatwick, which are charged on the certified weight of the aircraft published in the Flight Manual. I had selected the lower weight in consideration of the restrictions imposed by the obstacles in the take-off flight path in both take-off directions at Gatwick. If Tokyo were to be operated from Gatwick, it would be impossible fly non- stop with a full load and a fuel stop would have to be made en route, making it less attractive to passengers. Gatwick's restricted take-off weight compelled Richard to take the view that the airline should be permitted to operate out of London Heathrow where the aircraft would be able to operate more effectively, particularly if they were re-certified to 362,873 kgs. Enquiries as to the feasibility of this were made, but the Heathrow Scheduling Committee told Virgin that no slots would be available even if Virgin's licences were to be amended to include Heathrow. This was like a red rag to a bull and made Richard even more determined. He ordered that an application should be filed immediately for operation to/from Heathrow. I drew attention to the fact that with certain take-off temperatures at Heathrow, the 7A-powered aircraft would not be capable of operating to the higher re-certified weight. Roy then told me that as it would be necessary to acquire more aircraft to operate the Tokyo route, the company would only consider those with an adequate performance level.

The route flown to Tokyo would be mainly over Russian Territory and diplomatic clearance would be needed before over-flight permission could be granted. Virgin's Ed Hullah had many contacts in the Department of Trade and Industry and used these to start things rolling with the Russian and Japanese authorities. It would take him a very long time to reach agreement with either authority.

My immediate task was to provide route studies to determine exactly what load could be carried on this route, knowing that with the present 7A-powered aircraft, the limitations would almost certainly prove to be unacceptable. The route via Anchorage was examined but it was quite apparent that this was not commercially viable. Roy asked me to evaluate Boeing 747's fitted with the more powerful Pratt & Whitney JT9D–7Q engines, Boeing having advised him that Singapore Airlines would have at least two of their 7Q powered aircraft available in the near future. Having no manuals covering 7Q performance I asked Boeing to produce RTOW's for Gatwick, Moscow, and Tokyo (Narita). Moscow was evaluated as Ed Hullah had learned that if the licence were to be granted, the Russian Authorities would require at least one flight per week to land at Moscow in each direction. Virgin Cargo also needed to know the minimum amount of freight that could be carried as they considered that the freight yields could be very high to/from Tokyo.

In November 1988 John Hayward and I went to Moscow to have discussions with the Russian Moscow Airport Authorities about Virgin's proposed operations over Russia. Before leaving for Moscow, Ed Hullah obtained, albeit with some difficulty, our arrival and exit visas for Moscow. By this time John had taken over as Joint Operations Manager of Virgin as Gordon Steer had decided to retire in January 1989. John needed to know about hotel accommodation, communications facilities and exactly what assistance Aeroflot would provide for our crews. We travelled to Moscow on a British Airways 747 whose Captain was a close friend of John, and he was able to take us through customs and immigration with his crew more expeditiously than if we had gone with the other passengers. It was dark by the time we left the airport for the city, in temperature well below freezing and with a considerable amount of snow lying on the ground. The roads were fairly clear of snow and ice but were uneven with many unfilled holes that made the journey uncomfortable. The hotel was extremely large and had an enormous lobby that reminded me somewhat of Grand Central Station in New York. There were large queues of people trying to check in but again we went with the crew and were speedily checked in and allocated rooms. In a whispered voice, the rather attractive receptionist asked if we wanted to change dollars or pounds into roubles and offered an extremely high rate of exchange that was obviously the black market rate. At first it was thought that she was also offering 'special favours' in our rooms because when John reached for his wallet, she said something to the effect that she would come to the room. John did exchange US$20 and got over 160 roubles, nearly ten times the official rate. The snag was that roubles were not accepted in any of the hotel's bars and only one of the restaurants. Even when we tried to pay our taxi with roubles, the taxi driver was unwilling to accept them. Dollars and pounds seemed to be in great demand wherever we went.

Breakfast was included in the room rate but to say that it was a moveable feast would be an under-statement. Buffet breakfast was in a huge room was that had large queues of people for every item on the menu. There were separate queues for fruit juice, bread or toast, cheese, cold meats and eggs. Hard-boiled eggs were the only eggs on offer and there was a huge vat containing literally hundreds from which you could have as many as you wished. Tea or coffee was extra and had to be paid for on the spot, again with a large queue. The most comfortable meal was dinner in a quiet restaurant with very few diners. Naturally it had to be paid for in 'Hard' currency and could not be added on to the room bill. Frequent visitors to Moscow such as British Airways crews obviously knew restaurants outside the hotel where roubles would be accepted.

My room was very uncomfortable with broken bathroom fittings and although the towels and bed linen was clean, it was quite old and worn. To get to the rooms it was necessary to surrender one's passport in exchange for the room key to the Floor Security Lady who was seated by the lifts. On leaving the room the key had to be handed in and the passport taken back.

The morning after our arrival, we went to a meeting at the airport with the Airport Commandant, the Chief Navigator of Aeroflot, a political representative and a female interpreter. Some of the time they spoke to us directly in English, but there were many things discussed in Russian with the interpreter telling us what was said. It was quite tedious trying to keep track of what was going on. When John asked questions about dispatch procedures the Aeroflot man said 'Do not worry, that will be taken care of.' I was mainly concerned with slots that would fit in with those of Tokyo and a great deal of time was spent discussing these. Every slot time we required seemed to be not available and we finished the discussion with two inbound slots and two outbound slots that were completely useless. However the Commandant said 'Do not worry, all will be all right on the day'. Now where have I heard that before?

The political chap, smartly dressed in a suit, only spoke in Russian during the meeting and did not address a single remark to us. However, as we were going out of the airport exit carrying our overcoats, he said in perfect English; 'I say chaps, I should put your coats on, it's very cold outside!' The drive back to the hotel was quite hair-raising in a taxi that was very old and so dilapidated that it broke down twice with an overheating engine before it got us to the hotel. We could have used that excess heat inside the taxi, as its heating system was not functioning at all.

On the morning of our departure, we hired a taxi and had a long tour around the city seeing as many of the sights as possible, including the Olympic Stadium area and Red Square. The taxi driver spoke reasonable English but of course, demanded a high fare in dollars or pounds. He was at least a good guide and took us to many places of interest. On reaching Red Square, he took photographs of us and pointed out where the political leaders usually stood to review the show of force that used to take place on 1st May every year. He also pointed out Lenin's Tomb, but at that time it was not open to the public. The buildings in Red Square are magnificent but contrasted sharply with the poorly maintained roads and seemingly unpainted buildings in adjacent areas.

When we checked out of the hotel we found it rather difficult to get a taxi from the hotel to the airport due to a huge queue of people waiting for them. We were told that easiest way was to go outside the hotel to a garage underneath the hotel where taxi drivers relaxed. This we did and quickly found one to take us to the airport provided that payment was in hard currency. We had quite a lot of roubles but regardless of how much we offered to pay, no one would take us without the assurance of pounds or dollars. On arrival at the airport there were no check-in desks to be seen in the large airport hall where hundreds of people were milling around. Eventually we discovered that passengers first have to go through Customs and Immigration before reaching the area where the check-in desks are located. Once checked in, we proceeded to a departure lounge that was full of 'so called' Duty Free shops that apparently were run by the Irish Company Aer Rianta of Eire who had very attractive Irish girls serving. The price of everything was more expensive than England and the small beer that we each had in the bar cost over £3 a bottle. Needless to say, again only dollars or pounds was accepted by the shops and bars. We were quite pleased to get on to the Japan Airlines 747 for the four-hour flight back to London. I felt that the visit had achieved very little but in fact, as the Airport Commandant had said, 'It turned out alright on the day', when that day did come in May 1989! This was my first and only visit to Russia and I am afraid that I saw little that would attract me back to that country. In all fairness it was wintertime and a long time ago; perhaps things have changed for the better now. Certainly many holiday companies advertise tours embracing St Petersburg and Moscow so there must be plenty to see as long as it is not during wintertime.

My last overseas trip with the company was to attend an IATA Conference in Montreal to discuss Virgin's slot requirements. I was particularly keen to attend this meeting, as it would possibly be my last opportunity to visit my former wartime Sunderland pilot Emil 'Baron' Holstein Rathlou. I travelled to Newark on the Saturday Virgin flight and on arrival took a taxi to La Guardia airport to connect with a late evening flight for Montreal. I had telephoned Emil before leaving Gatwick and he arranged to pick me up at my hotel on Sunday morning and take me back to his home to spend the day with his family. I spent a most enjoyable time with Emil and his wife Cecille and in the afternoon their daughter Christine joined us. The day went all too quickly and Emil took me back to the hotel about 9p.m. Little did I know that it would be the last time I would see him as he developed cancer and died some years later.

I attended the IATA Conference with a Virgin colleague on Monday and did what I needed to do during the day. With no further business for me, I left my colleague to stay for the remainder of the Conference, checked out of the hotel and proceeded to Montreal Mirabel Airport where I boarded a Wardair Airbus flight for Gatwick. This was my first flight on a twin-engine aircraft across the Atlantic, but it was a very smooth and uneventful flight. Well, that is until the Captain came on the public address system as we approached Gatwick to tell us that almost all of UK was blanketed by fog and we were diverting to Prestwick! We stayed at Prestwick for three hours before the fog cleared sufficiently to allow a landing at Gatwick

The year 1989 started with a great deal of work for me, evaluating the performance of Boeing 747 aircraft fitted with Pratt & Whitney JT9D–7Q engines formerly operated by Singapore Airlines. Boeing gave me a great deal of assistance with the evaluation but nevertheless, a great deal more had to be done. John Hayward had been a Captain with Singapore Airlines and was able to put me in touch with people in Singapore who knew the answers to most of the questions I wished to have. Even with 7Q power, the operation out of Gatwick was not going to be easy, as there would be many days when the necessary take-off weight could not be achieved. Perhaps it was Virgin Cargo who were most concerned as there existed a highly lucrative cargo market between UK and Japan and they obviously wanted as much space on the aircraft as we could offer. Unfortunately, if high passenger loads were carried, and this appeared highly likely, there would be little weight to spare for freight. The limited freight loads that I could offer were totally inadequate and this resulted in re-opening the negotiations for operating out of Heathrow with Richard Branson virtually demanding that Virgin be allocated Heathrow Slots. This argument would last for a long time and it certainly did not happen before I retired from Virgin.

Roy again brought up the subject of my retirement. Previously he had indicated that that I should retire in April 1989, but as the Tokyo service was due to start in May, the date was deferred until 30th June when the Tokyo service would be up and running.

I had been looking around for a suitable person to take over from me when I retired and over a period of eighteen months had been considering someone employed by British Airways who had formerly been with British Caledonian before they were absorbed into British Airways. In the light of my imminent retirement, Roy had asked me to finalise my choice and after due consideration, I told him that I would recommend that he take on Geoff Clark effective from 1st April 1989. This would allow three months in which I could instruct him in those duties for which he would assume responsibility. Peter Stanton was most aggrieved that having been my (unofficial) deputy since joining the company, he was not offered the appointment. In fact he was considered, but being almost the same age as myself, he was thought to be too old for what was expected to be a long-term appointment. Furthermore Virgin had implemented a policy that required employees to retire at age 65. Oddly enough, Roy was quite prepared to allow Peter to stay on in his job provided that he accepted Geoff Clark as his superior. Peter however, insisted that he would only report to me and certainly not to anyone as junior in years as Geoff Clark. The outcome was that Peter was compelled to retire on the same day as myself but was given the opportunity of working part time while someone was trained to take over from him. This suited Peter very well and he continued on that basis for several months. Some months later he told me that he was financially better off as a consultant than when working full time. Roy had decided that whoever took over from me would be a manager and not a Director. Although Geoff Clark would replace me, I informed Roy that he would not take over fully and that some of my work would have to be done by others.

The few months up to my retirement date were quite busy with constant re-evaluation of the loads that could be carried to Tokyo from either Gatwick or Heathrow. In the light of the commercial arguments, it was quite obvious that the Tokyo service should be operated out of Heathrow but by this time, Richard was saying that the whole of the Virgin operations should be moved to Heathrow. This made sense of course, but it would prove impossible in consideration of the large number of slots that would be required. Even as I write this early in 2005, Virgin still operates out of both Gatwick and Heathrow with presumably, little hope of consolidating everything at Heathrow, even if that was the intention.

In spring 1989, my major task was to invite tenders for fuel supplies in Tokyo and those alternate airfields that might be needed. Most Japanese fuel companies in Japan had links with major fuel suppliers in UK so that when Virgin invited bids for their Japanese fuel requirements, approaches were invariably made directly by companies both in Japan and UK. I had the impression that each year in late spring, Japanese fuel companies competed with each other to secure large amounts of crude oil for delivery later on in the year when the demand would be at its highest. This had the effect of exercising some form of artificial shortage on the Far East markets making advantageous price contracts somewhat difficult to obtain by new operators on the Tokyo route. I was also told that during the period when bids were being prepared, there would be constant visits from representatives of the various bidding companies to ensure that they were not being overlooked.

It was not unusual to have a whole team from an oil company visit Virgin to ensure that they were not being forgotten. Each person would ceremoniously present his business card that would have pencilled on it the holder's 'Nickname' that could be used instead of the often difficult to pronounce Japanese name. Not all the team would necessarily speak English fluently and in such cases an interpreter would be used. This I found rather tedious and thought that it slowed the proceedings down too much. One company's very senior executive flew from Tokyo especially to host a lunch for me before returning to Tokyo on the same evening. He had 6 members of his staff with him but only two spoke English. I must say that it was perhaps the most magnificent lunch I have ever had, albeit the longest. The number of courses served seemed endless, each accompanied by a different wine. The senior executive was an elderly man who did not understand a word of English but had a constant smile on his face as the interpreter translated for him. Sad to say, his fuel company was not awarded the contract.

One fuel company gave a presentation of their product and services to senior directors of Virgin and followed it by a magnificent lunch at which the traditional exchange of gifts took place. It was a time of great social activity with invitations to restaurants and occasionally to the homes of those Japanese executives in UK. No expense was spared and it was nice that on some occasions, Virgin Directors' wives were included

Each bid would differ in some way from others, some giving contract signing incentives, others different method of payment and/or levels of credit. However, taking any of the contracts separately, it could be calculated that over a year the price paid would not differ significantly from one major supplier to another. Once a Japanese supplier had been nominated, it would be difficult to change to another because in Japan it was considered that if a contract had been honourably obtained, other suppliers would be unwilling to bid against it. For that reason it was up to an airline to ensure that when awarding a contract, it retained the right to seek other suppliers if the frequency of their flights increased or other Japanese destinations were used. As with all other fuel contracts I negotiated, the Financial Director and the Managing Director were consulted before a decision was made. Fuel costs account for a large percentage of the airline's operating expenses and a change of 1 US cent per US gallon can make a significant change in annual fuel costs. For instance, on the 14 hours 10 minutes round trip to Newark New Jersey that used about 39,400 US Gallons, the annual total would be in the order of 11,817,000 US gallons. A one-cent change in price would add or decrease the annual cost by $118,170. The larger airlines employ people in a department whose sole purpose is to monitor fuel prices and negotiate the lowest possible price by some very hard bargaining. Fuel prices in most countries are normally quoted in US dollars per US gallon.

In May 1988 Virgin operated its first round trip to Tokyo using Boeing 747 GVGIN but I cannot remember if the flight operated via Moscow or flew direct to/from Tokyo. I have an album of photographs presented to me by Mitsubishi Oil Company who was awarded the fuel contract in Tokyo. The 36 photographs show the aircraft landing and taking-off in beautiful weather conditions with some showing refuelling taking place.

As my retirement date approached I had a mixture of relief and disappointment. Relief that once I had retired, the pressures on me would be removed and perhaps my health would improve. Unfortunately that did not happen. The disappointment was that having worked for no pay for the two years it had taken to set up the airline, I was being deprived of the chance of sitting back and enjoying what I had worked so hard helping to produce. It's now all in the past and perhaps things have happened for the best.

On 30th June 1989, the day of my retirement, Roy Gardner laid on a party to jointly celebrate Peter and me leaving the airline. As a surprise for me, Sue had invited Joe Bagosy to come over from Orlando and also there was John Salter and Mike Vickars from Chevron, Chris Fear from Shell and many other business associates who came to say goodbye. Roy, on behalf of Richard and the Directors, presented me with a charming engraved silver salver in recognition of all I had done for Virgin. A limousine was provided to take Sue, Joe Bagosy, who was staying with us, and myself back home to Lindfield.

This was not the end of my aviation career as Page Avjet Corporation, for whom Joe Bagosy worked, commenced discussions with me to be their UK Representative. The proposed contract would be for one year and this would be confirmed following a meeting with Page Directors after my retirement.

I did one final consultancy in 1990, and that was at Roy's request. With the Financial Director on leave, fuel prices escalated wildly and he asked me to negotiate with all the fuel companies concerned in an attempt to ease the situation. This I was able to do quite successfully and fully justified the fee that I charged.

After I had left, Virgin took delivery of two ex Singapore Airlines Boeing 747 aircraft fitted with the more powerful Pratt & Whitney JT9D–7Q engines that would allow far greater take-off weights out of Gatwick and up to the certificated maximum allowable weight out of Heathrow.

Jim Smillie flew the first 7Q-powered aircraft registered as GTKYO from Singapore attempting a direct flight to Gatwick. With fuel reserves looking marginal on arrival at Gatwick and with ferocious headwinds being experienced, the aircraft arrived at the Bahrain/Egyptian airspace border only to be told that over-flight clearance had not been given. Jim had no alternative but to return to Bahrain and wait overnight until clearance had been obtained. This was a somewhat inauspicious start to GTKYO's spell with Virgin, but least I was not to blame – but somebody was!

It was my ambition to complete 50 years in aviation and my virtually enforced retirement could have been thwarted that. However, as I was going to Orlando immediately after my retirement date, as previously arranged I met Joe Bagosy and two directors of Page Avjet Corporation. At the meeting I was offered the position as Page Avjet Corporation's UK Representative with a one year contract that gave me my 50 years total in aviation. I finally retired from Aviation in September 1990 having completed 50 years service with the RAF and many Civil Airlines. It was a happy ending and if I had my life over again, there would not be many changes that I could make for the better.

Postscript

During the course of writing this book I decided to attempt to trace my Wellington crew members. I had no idea if it was possible, but saw an advertisement for a computer program called UK-INFO DISK, which gave details of the Electoral Roll for the year 2001. I purchased this in February 2003 and discovered that there was only one male Verguson listed and his name was Robert. There was a telephone number given and I immediately dialled it and a lady answered the telephone. I explained that I was trying to trace Robert (Bob) Verguson who flew with me on Wellington bombers and I was quite astounded when she said 'You must be Eric?' I was quickly put on to Bob and we had a long chat about events of 60 years ago. I mentioned that I hoped to find Johnny and was told that he had taken up a political career and lived in Nottingham. My DISK gave 165 with the surname Peck, many of whom were John. I remembered that he was John H Peck and of those listed; only one had a Nottingham address. I telephoned and asked if he was Johnny who flew Wellington bombers. There was a pause before he said that I must one of his first crew because only that crew called him Johnny! We chatted for quite a long time and I learned that he was not particularly well as he was suffering from Parkinsons Disease. It was obvious that with age and our disabilities, it would be impossible to meet but did promise to keep in touch.

In the summer of 2003 Bob wrote to tell me that he and his wife Jean would be going to Eastbourne on holiday and wondered if we could meet there. Arrangements were made and Sue and I went to their hotel and spent the day with them. It was a wonderful re-union with the hope of many more to come. Sadly, it was not to be. Bob was suddenly taken ill in late autumn and after only two or three days in hospital, he passed away.

Meanwhile I had corresponded with Johnny and he sent me his autobiography that was mainly about his political career as a communist. I thought that I had lost touch with him when I could not get an answer to my telephone calls, but through a friend in Nottingham, I learned that he had fallen down and had broken his hip. Several weeks later I re-established contact with him, but he was in a hurry as he was being picked up by his daughter who was taking him home for lunch and there was little time to exchange news. That was the last contact I had with him as shortly after I received a letter from his son Joe telling me that his father had died on 21st March 2004.

I did try to trace Ray Wilson, but with no success and can only assume that he has passed away leaving me as the only survivor of the crew formed at Harwell in 1942. Efforts to trace members of my Sunderland crew also proved unsuccessful and I can only be thankful that I met up with George Hodgeson in 1966 and did get to visit 'Baron' in Montreal many times during my aviation career.

Reginald 'Eric' Holloway March 2005.

The author's Wellington Bomber crew about to leave Portreath for Gibraltar November 1942. Author second from right.

The author's Sunderland Flying boat crew Alness May 1944. Author rear row far right.

Attack on Japanese ship iin the Gulf of Siam

Author with Tony Ellwood

The war over, reunion of author and first wife. Easter 1946

The author at Khartoum en route to Johannesburg with BOAC

BOAC Stratocruiser at Idlewild (now JFK) New York

Damaged engine on BOAC Stratocruiser

Meeting with Emil (Baron) Holstein, the author's wartime Sunderland pilot. Montreal 1961

Author with son RAF Apprentice Terry (Later Group Captain). Southampton 1963.

Author at Darwin en route from Singapore to Sydney with Laker Airways. January 1974

Laker Airways first DC10 at Long Beach Arizona

Boeing 747-200 GVIRG arriving at Gatwick from Boeing Seattle June 1984

The author (with second wife Sue), being presented with Silver Salver from Richard Branson, Directors and colleagues at the retirement party June 1989. The Salver was in recognition of assistance given as a Founder Director of Virgin Atlantic Airways